Jungle Heart of the Khmer Rouge

NIAS – Nordic Institute of Asian Studies
New and Recent Monographs

NIAS Press is the autonomous publishing arm of the Nordic Institute of Asian Studies (NIAS), a research institute located at the University of Copenhagen. NIAS is partially funded by the governments of Denmark, Finland, Iceland, Norway and Sweden via the Nordic Council of Ministers, and works to encourage and support Asian studies in the Nordic countries. In so doing, NIAS has been publishing books since 1969, with more than two hundred titles produced in the past few years.

UNIVERSITY OF COPENHAGEN

norden

Nordic Council of Ministers

Jungle Heart of the Khmer Rouge

The memoirs of Phi Phuon, Pol Pot's Jarai
aide-de-camp, and the role of Ratanakiri and its
tribal minorities in the Cambodian revolution

Henri Locard

Jungle Heart of the Khmer Rouge:
The memoirs of Phi Phuon, Pol Pot's Jarai aide-de-camp, and the role of
Ratanakiri and its tribal minorities in the Cambodian revolution
Henri Locard

Nordic Institute of Asian Studies
NIAS Monographs, no. 157

First published in 2023 by NIAS Press
NIAS – Nordic Institute of Asian Studies
Øster Farimagsgade 5, 1353 Copenhagen K, Denmark
Tel: +45 3532 9503 • Fax: +45 3532 9549
E-mail: books@nias.ku.dk • Online: www. niaspress. dk

ISBN 978-87-7694-324-0 Hbk
ISBN 978-87-7694-325-7 Pbk
ISBN 978-87-7694-738-5 Ebk

Typeset in Arno Pro by Don Wagner
Printed and bound in the United Kingdom by Printforce
Cover design: NIAS Press
Cover image: Phi Phuon in Khmer Rouge uniform, Phnom Penh, 1976

Contents

Part III: Background Analysis

Figures

Maps

Table

Acknowledgements

I express my gratitude for the French Ministry of Education that granted me a sabbatical year in the academic year 1993–1994 for my re-orientation to Cambodian studies. I am also grateful for the contribution of my two interpreters Ung Rotha and Hing Nonn who, in 1994, not just made translations but also helped me find witnesses willing to describe the fateful ten years of Khmer Rouge sway over their province.

I am grateful to Martin Rathie for having spent much time to read my proofs and make a number of sensible suggestions.

I shall always be most indebted to the NIAS Press staff, copy editor David Stuligross and editor in chief Gerald Jackson for their tireless work and vital suggestions to make the book most readable – even to the general public.

My thanks also go to Rochœm Tveng whom I first met at the funeral ceremony of his younger brother Phi Phuon in Phnom Malay in 2015. He gave me a collection of family photographs of Phi Phuon and his relatives to enliven this book.

Almost all our interviews took place at Phnom Malay in So Hong's comfortable villa. Pol Pot's nephew was a most generous host and his wife provided us with the most delicious Cambodian traditional food.

Last, but not least, this book would never have come into existence without Suong Sikœun's interpretation from French into Khmer for my questions to Phi Phuon, and his answers from Khmer into French. Later, from the recorded tapes, he composed the oral answers into a written French version. That Suong Sikœun could be a writer in his own right is shown by the publication of his own autobiography in French: *Autobiographie d'un intellectual khmer rouge*, CERF Politique, Paris 1993.

Henri Locard
12 May 2023

Abbreviations

CGDK	Coalition Government of Democratic Kampuchea
CNRP	Cambodian National Rescue Party
CPK	Communist Party of Kampuchea
CPP	Cambodian People's Party
Dc-CAM	Documentation Center of Cambodia
DK	Democratic Kampuchea
DRV	Democratic Republic of Vietnam (North Vietnam)
ECCC	Extraordinary Chambers in the Courts of Cambodia
FARK	*Forces Armées Royales Khmères*
FUNCINPEC	United National Front for an Independent, Neutral, Pacific and Cooperative Cambodia
FUNK	*Front Uni National Khmer*
GRUNK	*Gouvernement Royal d'Union Nationale Khmer*
ICP	Indochinese Communist Party
KL	*Khmer Lœu* (highlanders)
KPNLF	Khmer People's National Liberation Front
KPRP	Khmer People's Revolutionary Party
KR	Khmer Rouge
MNDU	Movement of the National Democratic Union
NADK	National Army of Democratic Kampuchea
PAVN	People's Army of Vietnam
PRK	People's Republic of Kampuchea
RAK	Revolutionary Army of Kampuchea
RGC	Royal Government of Cambodia
UNTAC	United Nations Transitional Authority in Cambodia
VC	Viet Cong
WPK	Workers Party of Kampuchea

Chronology

1965   Increasing numbers of Vietnamese fighters establish themselves in Ratanakiri

US bombing intensifies

Saloth Sâr begins lengthy period in the DRV and then China, where he is converted to Maoism at the dawn of the Cultural Revolution

1966   WPK becomes the Communist Party of Kampuchea (CPK)

Sangkum repression worsens; decision made to relocate HQ of CPK to Ratanakiri

1967   Ieng Sary, and then Saloth Sâr, arrive in Ratanakiri; establish Offices 102 and 100

Saloth Sâr adopts the alias Ta Pouk

Limited attacks on FARK troops by a few disgruntled KL (later also by Phi Phuon)

1968   (January) Nuon Chea launches KR uprising in Battambang

(February) Sihanouk tours Ratanakiri; punishes unrest by executing KL hostages

(April) Ta Pouk, Ieng Sary and Son Sen launch KR uprising in Ratanakiri

First groups of KL flee to Laos and Vietnam

1969   US bombing heightens, no longer secret

1970   (March) Sihanouk deposed; Khmer Republic established

Sihanouk is persuaded to ally with the KR; FUNK and GRUNK established

Republic abandons NE, which is 'liberated' by KR and Vietnamese forces

Civil war shifts to lowland Cambodia

Ta Pouk becomes Pol Pot in 'Long March'; KR top leadership departs from Ratanakiri

Return from Hanoi of many Cambodian revolutionaries trained by the Vietnamese

1971   KR meetings plan future of war and economy, foreshadow future purges

Peace negotiations between US, DRV and Lao begin

1972   KR introduce collectivization in Ratanakiri; more KL flee to Laos and Vietnam

Pol Pot refuses to join Paris peace negotiations; tensions with Vietnamese

1973   Paris Peace Accords signed; US agrees to withdraw but escalates bombing

Sihanouk secretly visits northern Cambodia, now in KR hands

Pol Pot demands Vietnamese withdraw from Cambodia; some forces remain

Purges begin of people deemed too close to Vietnamese, especially Hanoi returnees

Fierce battle for Kompong Cham city

People's communes established; forced population transfer of KL begins; more flee

1974   Battle for Oudong, just north of Phnom Penh

Evacuation of urban populace by KR in Oudong and other captured provincial centres

1975   (17 April) Phnom Penh falls to KR; forced evacuation of city

Democratic Kampuchea is proclaimed with Sihanouk as head of state

Saigon falls to PAVN and VC forces; end of Second Indochinese War

DK and Vietnam briefly struggle over their maritime territory

1976   Sihanouk tours the provinces; resigns as President on his return; under house arrest

Ney Sarann, chief of NE region arrested and executed; purging of cadres in NE

1977   Ta Mok leads bloody purges across many DK regions

DK forces briefly strike deep into Vietnam

Pol Pot publicly reveals that *Angkar* is the CPK and it is led by him

Vietnam carries out a retaliatory invasion of DK

1978   Bloody purges continue, especially in Eastern region; DK defences thus weakened

Phi Phuon accompanies Sihanouk in trip to Kompong Som/ Sihanoukville

(25 December) Vietnamese forces begin invasion of DK

1979   KR leadership and Sihanouk depart Phnom Penh, which soon falls to Vietnamese

Vietnamese denounce 'Pol Pot–Ieng Sary clique', sentence them to death in absentia

Declaration of the PRK (aka Héng Samrin regime) by invaders to replace DK

Hun Sèn appointed PRK Minister of Foreign Affairs

DK forces (some led by Phi Phuon) carry out fighting retreat; regroup at Thai border

Huge numbers of refugees cross into Thailand, soon followed by most DK fighters

1980   Strengthening of DK guerrilla resistance, aided by Chinese and often operating from Thai sanctuaries

KL escapees begin trickling back to Ratanakiri from Laos and Vietnam

1981   PRK ruling party reverts to KPRP name

1982   DK allies with FUNCINPEC and KPNLF; CGDK is formed headed by Sihanouk and wins wide international recognition, preventing PRK from taking Cambodia's UN seat

1985   Hun Sèn becomes PRK Prime Minister

Vietnamese forces drive most DK fighters back into Thailand, also many refugees

1987   Vietnamese construct 'Bamboo Wall' along Thai border

1989   With a new constitution, PRK becomes the State of Cambodia and private property is re-established

Phi Phuon part of DK forces destroying 'Bamboo Wall'; Phnom Malay finally liberated

Under Soviet pressure following Gorbachev policy change, most Vietnamese troops withdrawn

1990   Refugees begin returning from their camps in Thailand

1991   KPRP renamed the CPP with Hun Sèn as its vice-president

(23 October) Paris Peace Agreements signed; China ceases to provide DK with military and financial support

1992   UNTAC established as a transitional authority to restore peace and civil government in Cambodia

1993   Ta Mok forces a DK boycott of UNTAC-supervised 1993 general election

FUNCINPEC wins election; two-headed government formed after CPP coup threat

Kingdom of Cambodia replaces UNTAC-administered State of Cambodia; Sihanouk reassumes kingship

FUNCINPEC and KPNLF part of RGC attack on NADK

1994 Henri Locard conducts interviews among surviving inhabitants in Ratanakiri

1996 Internal strife leads to DK split; Ieng Sary forms MNDU, later rallies to RGC

1997 (June) Son Sen and his family killed on Pot Pot's orders

(July) Ta Mok organizes a mock trial of Pol Pol and places him under house arrest; Nuon Chea and Khieu Samphân flee to Thailand

(July) Hun Sèn launches a coup, becoming sole Prime Minister; Norodom Ranariddh flees abroad

1998 Death of Pol Pot

Nuon Chea and Khieu Samphân rally to the RGC, the last major DK leaders to do so

1999 Ta Mok arrested by RGC authorities

2001 Henri Locard begins interviews with Phi Phuon

2006 ECCC convened

Death of Ta Mok before he can be tried by ECCC

2007 Nuon Chea, Ieng Sary and Khieu Samphân are arrested and brought before the ECCC

2012 Phi Phuon testifies at ECCC

2013 Ieng Sary dies while still being tried by the ECCC

2015 Henri Locard completes interviews with Phi Phuon

Death of Phi Phuon

2018 ECCC finds Nuon Chea and Khieu Samphân guilty, among other charges, of crimes against humanity and genocide against the Vietnamese and Chams

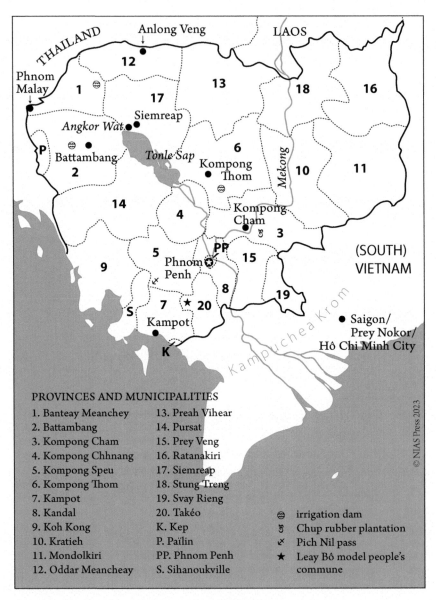

Map 1: Cambodia – general overview and key places

PROVINCES AND MUNICIPALITIES

1. Banteay Meanchey
2. Battambang
3. Kompong Cham
4. Kompong Chhnang
5. Kompong Speu
6. Kompong Thom
7. Kampot
8. Kandal
9. Koh Kong
10. Kratieh
11. Mondolkiri
12. Oddar Meancheay

13. Preah Vihear
14. Pursat
15. Prey Veng
16. Ratanakiri
17. Siemreap
18. Stung Treng
19. Svay Rieng
20. Takéo
K. Kep
P. Païlin
PP. Phnom Penh
S. Sihanoukville

⊕ irrigation dam
ಜ Chup rubber plantation
⤫ Pich Nil pass
★ Leay Bô model people's commune

Part I

Introduction

Figure 1: Phi Phuon in Khmer Rouge uniform, Phnom Penh, 1976

Penetrating the worldview of ex-Khmer Rouge apparatchiks
Introducing Phi Phuon

*I*n early 2001, I was seeking to meet Suong Sikœun, a former Khmer Rouge (KR) member then living in Phnom Malay, one of many villages on the Thai border established by and for ex-KR people. I arrived after nightfall and the place was poorly lit. I sought assistance, but the people I encountered were not familiar with the name Suong Sikœun. However, when I described the individual in Khmer, people exclaimed: 'Ah! You mean Ta Kuon!', which was his revolutionary name. He soon appeared, dressed as he might have been when the KR had been in power, in black clothes and a black Mao cap, flanked by a couple of black-clad guards. He burst with joy at my appearance, as if he was meeting an old friend at a Parisian café! His French was impeccable, as he had lived thirteen years in the heart of the Quartier Latin. Later, in our discussions, he had frequent slips of the tongue, saying 'Paris' instead of 'Phnom Penh'. Thus began a collaboration that continues to this day.

Sikœun was most interested in writing his own memoir, which was to be published in 2013. A significant passage from the text reads as follows:

> From the age of sixteen, he was committed to the anticolonial struggle under the flag of the Democratic Party, … and in January 1957, the author joined the clandestine revolutionary movement. August 1996: with his comrades from the Movement of National Democratic Union (MNDU), led by Ieng Sary, he then rallied the royal government formed after the parliamentary elections organized by the United Nations. Since 1957, more than half a century has gone by. For a man, an entire life has vanished into thin air. Today, at more than seventy years of age, the author finds himself empty-handed and with a broken heart. He has seen his dream of social and human fraternity liberation crumble like a house of cards. He has sacrificed the best years of his life and his personal happiness for a cause he believed was just and noble, but in the end proved most infamous and

criminal. In his twilight years, he bitterly regrets that his name has been associated with a regime whose cruelty and bestiality have been unique in contemporary history. How much to the point and truth is the aphorism "the road to hell is paved with good intentions"?[1]

The aphorism nicely captures Sikœun's ambiguous relationship with his past: the KR caused hell on earth, and the KR had good intentions. The memoir makes clear that the latter by no means excused the former.

Beyond his memoir, Sikœun introduced me to life in Phnom Malay in general and, in particular, he introduced me to Phi Phuon, a remarkable Jaraï tribesman who met Pol Pot in 1967, soon became one of his aides-de-camp, entered Phnom Penh with the revolutionaries in 1975, served as a mid-level functionary in the Ministry of Foreign Affairs, and became a military commander in 1979. Like Sikœun, but unlike most people associated with the KR, Phi Phuon wished to tell his story.

The book in your hands is the fulfilment of his wish. The first half is a memoir cast in Phi Phuon's narrative voice, drawn overwhelmingly from more than 50 hours of interviews, but also from short interviews with Philip Short[2] and Dany Long,[3] and from his testimony at the Khmer Rouge Tribunal.[4]

The second half adds context and analytical precision to the ideas presented directly by Phi Phuon. It is informed primarily by a collection of interviews I conducted in 1994, plus testimony from the Khmer Rouge Tribunal and an array of secondary sources.

Several themes percolate through the book. First and foremost, Ratanakiri, the far-northeastern province where Phi Phuon was born, and the highland tribespeople who live there had a multitude of relationships with the KR. On the one hand, Ratanakiri can be described as the birthplace of KR ideology as taught by the Vietminh, while also being regarded as original incubater for revolutionary idealism as locals and lowland Khmer radicals lived together in semi-autonomous villages producing locally almost all that was needed to be consumed for everyday life. As we shall see, Pol Pot's flawed understanding

---

1   *Itinéraire d'un intellectuel khmer rouge*, Avant-propos, Suong Sikœun, CERF politique, Paris, 2013, pp. 19–20 (my translation).

2   Philip Short, *Pol Pot: the History of a Nightmare*, London: John Murray, 2004.

3   Long Dany's interview with Phi Phuon on 19 December 2010 was published by the Documentation Center of Cambodia (DC-Cam).

4   The Tribunal was officially called the Extraordinary Chambers in the Courts of Cambodia, or the ECCC.

of the people's 'primitive collectivization' – neither word accurately describes highland lifestyles – led him to imagine that they were the models on which new men and women could be moulded. In the 1960s, a fair few tribespeople were inspired to join the revolutionary movement. This was no accident. They had close interaction with Vietminh soldiers and ideologues who so frequently sought refuge in Cambodia that their settlements were permanent from the time of the First Indochinese War, 1946–1954. With the persuasion of the KR's seniormost leaders via personal contact, the KR vision became 'real' in a sense that was not possible in the rest of the country, as those leaders saw the way of life of indigenous people as Marx's primitive communism.

Secondly, the book engages directly and indirectly with proceedings at the Extraordinary Chambers in the Courts of Cambodia (ECCC), the Tribunal that tried and convicted the seniormost KR war criminals. More importantly, the Tribunal's archives will become the primary source of information regarding atrocities committed between 1975 and 1979.

Along the way, narratives in both halves shed light on the leading KR cadres (who referred to themselves as *Angkar* – the Organization – to signify they were indeed a collective leadership, unlike all other communist regimes) and Nuon Chea's hidden role as Pol Pot's partner at the pinnacle of KR power. They also offer insights on life in the KR *maquis*; the fundamental reason Phnom Penh and other cities were 'evacuated' (the one-word answer is security); the influence of China on DK ideology, administration and methods; the importance of secrecy about, for, and by DK leaders; the power and relevance of extended DK political training seminars; conditions in people's communes and prisons; and finally the absolute devotion and obedience to the leaders demanded to all for fear of arrest, torture and death. All of this is presented in Phi Phuon's own words.

Genocide or politicide?

Despite the findings of the ECCC, this volume contends that the KR did not engage in genocide – defined as 'acts committed with intent to destroy, in whole or in part, a national, ethnic, racial or religious group'.[5] Rather, it practised 'politicide' – killing individuals because of actions or suspicions

---

5   Convention on the Prevention and Punishment of the Crime of Genocide art. 2, 78 U.N.T.S. 277, 9 December 1948.

Table 1: Kampuchea's class structure as viewed by
the Communist Party of Kampuchea

Class	Sub-Division	Membership Criteria	% Total Pop.
Feudal	Aristocrats	Members of the Royal Family	5
	'Feudalists'	Former ministers, provincial governors, high-ranking Lon Nol military officers	
Capitalist	Compradore	Businessmen with foreign trading connections; defeated during the war	
	Patriotic	Businessmen supplying NUFK during the war; eliminated by 1975 abolition of private trading	
Petty Capitalist	Upper level	High civil servants; individuals in possession of a license, a bac, or other forms of 'intellectual' capital	5
	Middle level	Teachers, hairdressers, tailors, craftsmen and other self-employed small businessmen	
	Lower level	Low-ranking civil servants, employees, clergymen (monks, priests, etc.)	
Workers	Independent labourers	Builders, joiners, bicycle cab drivers, plumbers	5
	Industrial workers	Rubber plantation workers, dock workers, factory workers	
	Party workers	Workers in mobile youth brigades and cadres employed in the revolutionary government and army	

Peasantry	**Rich peasants**	Landowners who employ hired labourers and modern equipment for all work	
	Middle peasants		10
	• Upper level	Landowners who employ hired labourers to work 60% or more of their land	
	• Middle level	Landowners who employ hired labourers to work 20¬60% of their land	5
	• Lower level	Smallholders who produce enough from their own land to eat throughout the year	
	Poor peasants		
	• Upper level	Peasants lacking one or more of the means of production, obliged to work the land of others or lacking in food to eat for various lengths of time each year. Material criteria varies from region to region.	70
	• Middle level		
	• Lower level		
Special Class (or 'Class Apart')	Revolutionary intellectuals (overseas NUFK supporters)	The special class was comprised of individuals outside of Kampuchea as of 17 April 1975, the date of liberation, and who returned to Kampuchea between 1975–1978	
	Reactionary intellectuals (overseas NUFK supporters)		
	Military men, policemen and high-ranking officials of the old regime		
	Buddhist monks (treated in practice as petty capitalists)		

Sources: Adapted from the *Journal of Communist Studies*, Vol 3, no. 1, March 1987, pp. 14–15 and based on Pol Pot, *Les grandioses victoires de la révolution du Kampuchea sous la direction just et clairvoyante du parti communiste du Kampuchea*, Phnom Penh: Ministry of Foreign Affairs of Democratic Kampuchea, 1978, pp, 44, 84, 87, 91, 94, 98; Francois Ponchaud, 'Vietnam-Cambodge: Une Solidarité Militante Fragile', *Echange-Asie*, no. 43, 1979, pp. 11–12, and refugee reports.

regarding them as individual political enemies who could grab power from them. This was on a scale never seen before or since. The horror is that otherworldly, paranoia-driven suspicions led millions to run afoul of the regime.

Unlike the Nazis, the revolutionary leaders did not have a racialist vision of the society. In reality, as in all communist regimes, society was divided into clearly identified classes, with intricate sub-divisions, and not according to their ethnic origins. Table 1 presents Democratic Kampuchea's elaborate class structure in which the most proletarian of proletarians are Party apparatchiks with no proletarian background at all. Like Lenin, they are proletarians in essence. This is purely ideological, and this is what really matters most.

It is therefore totally improper to speak of the KR 'genocide', as it obfuscates the relations of the KR leadership with Stalinism, and mainly Maoism, and puts the killings in the same category as those in Rwanda or Yugoslavia – to which they do not belong at all. The concept of a KR genocide was introduced by the People's Republic of Kampuchea (PRK) in the 1980s. Assigning Nazi-like attributes to DK not only undermined the continued Western recognition (motivated by Cold War considerations) of DK despite its overthrow in 1979 but also helped hide that the PRK regime was essentially a Vietnamese protectorate supported by the Soviet Union. Nonetheless, though not at all democratic, the PRK was vastly more humane than its DK predecessor.

The second interest of the table is the mention of 'revolutionary intellectuals' in a special category, as if they were more 'proletarian' than the proletarians themselves, that is, than poor peasants and the workers. Those people were to be led by so-called 'intellectuals' from overseas or inside the country. This a totally spurious category largely filled by people (including Pol Pot, Ieng Sary, Son Sen, and more) with no higher education diploma or even a baccalaureate. Pol Pot only had a primary school certificate and failed the 'diploma' at the end of grade nine. The only two persons among those leaders who could be called 'intellectuals' were Khieu Samphân and Thiounn Mumm, the Polytechnicien, although the latter had only had a marginal role in the regime and never took part in any major decision, and certainly not in the killings. They were 'intellectuals' in the Anglo-American sense: their vision of the future was far-removed from reality. The word has pejorative connotations for a culture that privileges practicality and relations with the real world – a world unknown to the KR intellectual apparatchiks.

As to the well-documented repression of Vietnamese residents in Cambodia, most had been expelled in early 1975 and, if the few who remained were hunted down at the end of the regime, it was only because – through the Communist Party of Vietnam – they were believed to be capable of wrenching totalitarian power from the Khmer Rouge leadership. The widespread slogan 'A Vietnamese head in a Khmer body' (*Kbal Yuon, khluon Khmer*),[6] demonstrates strikingly that to be Vietnamese was essentially a political category and not a racial one, since the vast majority of 'Vietnamese' victims were in actual fact Khmers who had been accused of spying for Vietnam. Besides, many Vietnamese had fled the country in the uncertain years after Sihanouk's fall and the bulk of those who remained were expelled at the beginning of the regime – a fate everyone, after the evacuation of all the cities, would have been grateful for. Many non-Vietnamese escaped with the Vietnamese and were let through the border if anyone in their group could speak a few words of Vietnamese. So, the Vietnamese were indeed spared by the regime and a tiny percentage was executed – far fewer than the Chams not to mention the Khmer themselves.

As to the Chams, I never found a single slogan targeting them,[7] and I interpret this absence as proof that the KR never intended to eliminate this ethnic group as a 'race'.[8] Rather, individuals in the thousands came to be specifically targeted as they refused to abandon their religious rituals and even rebelled against the revolution. Similarly, at the beginning of the regime, the few Buddhist monks who refused to be disrobed were brutally put to death. Persecution under DK was on political grounds, as is typical as in communist regimes. This is why the best term to describe their crimes – apart from the perfectly valid 'crimes against humanity' – would be 'politicide' and not 'genocide'.[9]

Besides, the tribal people did not rebel against Sihanouk in 1968 because of rubber plantations, but because Pol Pot and Ieng Sary had settled in the province and linked with tribal minorities representatives who had, in the recent past, been converted to a Soviet type of Marxism-Leninism and Maoism during the first Indochinese War (1946–1954). During 1967–1968, the region had only one large rubber plantation at Labansiek and only very small

---

6   This slogan can be found in my *Pol Pot's Little Red Book: The Sayings of Angkar*, Chiang Mai: Silkworm Books, Chiang Mai, 2004, p. 179, slogan 202.

7   Ibid., passim.

8   Mélanie Vianney-Liaud, *Controversy on the Characterization of the Cambodia Genocide at the ECCC*, International Crime Database, October 2014.

9   Barbara Huff and Ted Robert Gurr, 'Toward Empirical Theory of Genocides and Politicides: Identification and Measurement of Cases Since 1945', *International Studies Quarterly*, 32:3 (Sept. 1988) pp. 359–371.

ones elsewhere. There were no major land problems until the late 1990s and early 2000s. Today, it is a disaster, as the tribal people have been stripped of much of their land, and still they do not rebel against land deprivation, while they would have had plenty of reasons to do so.

This book focuses on the place of indigenous tribal minorities from Ratanakiri inside the Khmer Rouge revolution. It will show that the KR leadership was not at all racist against the minority groups of the periphery. Traditionally, indigenous upland tribes had been the most reviled ethnic groups of the pre-revolutionary society, regarded as 'savages' in the French Indochinese countries, Vietnam, Cambodia and Laos. The very name of one tribe had been, until recently, an ordinary-language term of abuse: 'Phnong!' On the contrary, the DK incorporated the indigenous tribes of the north-eastern periphery into its vision of a Kampuchean nation and, after the leaders themselves experienced a kind of epiphany in Ratanakiri Province from 1967 to 1970, celebrated elements of indigenous lifestyles as national ideals.[10]

The Jaraï, Tampuon, Krœung, Brao, Krâchok and others became the preferred disciples and role models for the KR leadership; they were the most basic of 'base people' – *mulethan* in Khmer – a condition that, in the upside-down ideology of the Khmer Rouge, placed them in a high caste as many of them had joined the revolution before the 17 April 1975 takeover. By contrast, those who lived or had taken refuge in towns became the low caste, especially if they had rejected the revolution. These were categorized as 'New People'[11] or '17 April People'. In fact, Democratic Kampuchea was the only regime in Cambodia since independence that placed those indigenous people at the apex of the social ladder. Party officials in all communist regimes have divided the population into social classes with intricate sub-divisions, but not according to their ethnic origins. The Khmer Rouge were no different. In the people's communes of Ratanakiri, all social and ethnic groups were to cohabit: no separate development and no form of apartheid, unlike conditions before the revolution. Thus, by design, the people's communes in Ratanakiri included not only various tribal groups, but also some Lao, Chinese and lowland Khmers. 'Old people' and 'new people', 'base people' or '17th April people', all were to work, eat and survive together.

---

10 Read for instance Chapter 6, 'The sudden death of reason' in Philip Short's *Pol Pot: The History of a Nightmare,* John Murray, 2004.

11 From 17 April 1975, the Khmer Rouge classified the entire population into two clearly defined 'castes': those who had joined the revolution before 17 April – the Old People – and the townsfolk and refugees – the New People – who had not.

I have no evidence that the tribal minorities from Ratanakiri, and the northeast in general, were in the least involved in arresting, imprisoning, torturing, interrogating or executing identified 'enemies'. In my investigation of the Khmer Rouge prison system over more than a decade, I have never come across or heard testimonies signalling the presence of those minorities in or around those dens of horror. If indeed, as in other Asian communist countries, repression was the job of the revolutionary army – unlike in the Soviet Union where it was the secret police – I have found no evidence at all that any representative of those groups were among torturers, interrogators and executioners. And this for the simple reason that only good Khmer speakers could perform those 'revolutionary duties' of interrogations and confessions under torture. The identification of enemies was done in two ways: analysis of confessions during daily public meetings in people's communes, and analysis of autobiographies. Both of these required a nuanced understanding of Khmer, and most tribal people did not know any Khmer when they first joined – or were tricked into – the revolution.

Their roles have been well identified. First, as Phi Phuon's memoir demonstrates, originally and from 1967, highlanders formed the core of the Khmer Rouge army in Ratanakiri, while lowland Khmers were the political commissars. If, among mainly the Jaraïs and Tampuons, those young men – and it seems never young women, contrary to the rest of the country – enthusiastically joined the revolution, many were more reticent when collectivization set in from 1968, while entire villages (in particular the Krœung or Brao) just ran away over the border to Laos and Vietnam, especially after 1973. It looks as if those battle-worthy, disciplined and faithful guerrilla warriors, who knew perfectly the forested terrain, were at first in the forefront of the fighting. As at least one testimony shows, an entire battalion constituted of ethnic minorities from Ratanakiri took part in the capture of Phnom Penh on 17 April 1975. These soldiers of course were totally ignorant of the Phnom Penh streets and even of all urban centres. If they were the masters of the forest, this utterly new environment was unknown and threatening to them. They could not control a city of more than two million, even for a single night. This was also true of the majority of the young soldiers who came from the periphery of the country. Thus, it was for purely practical and security reasons that all townsfolk throughout the territory were thrown onto the roads – ideological reasons or the romanticization of country life played a much smaller role in this decision. And there had been precedents for this during the civil war, with the evacuations of Kratieh, Angtasom and mainly Oudong. Only then, when thrown along the roads, could the revolutionaries control the citizens.

Once the population had been relocated and forcefully settled in the people's communes, highlanders certainly did not police the people's communes as the rest of the army. Instead, the task of the tribal people was mainly to be the foot soldiers of the leadership. In the course of the regime, they would become the most trusted revolutionaries in the eyes of *Angkar*. They continued to be the bodyguards, messengers and the drivers of those 'excellencies'. They even guarded the Royal Palace where Sihanouk and part of his family were detained. They would also be the truck drivers who were trusted with criss-crossing the entire territory and transporting all goods – rice and weapons in particular. They would come to great use again for the KR after the fall of the regime on 7 January 1979. They contributed significantly to hindering the invading Vietnamese, also battle-worthy troops, who sought to control the vast forested western areas along the length of the Thai border. With the Khmers, they spearheaded the KR troops that sapped the Vietnamese regulars from 1985 to 1989, along the Bamboo Wall,[12] killing some 50,000 invading soldiers during the 1980s – almost as many as the toll of American victims of the Second Indochinese War – some 58,000.

But, the main role of the tribal revolutionaries from Ratanakiri was to serve as bodyguards for the leadership, as they were regarded as more trustworthy than their Khmer compatriots. In an interview with Philip Short, Ieng Sary confessed that 'tribesmen would give their lives for you without a thought ... With a Khmer soldier you never knew how he would react. But a Jaraï would make sure I was safe no matter what the cost.'[13] Similarly, after returning to his country in 1991, Norodom Sihanouk trusted only the North Korean bodyguards given by his friend Kim Il-Sung and, from 1994, his son Kim Jong-Il. From 1994, Sihanouk felt safe and comfortable only in his palace in China, where he died in 2012, as if, he too, distrusted his own compatriots. Many indeed had not forgiven him having allied himself with the Khmer Rouge – his erstwhile political enemies – in 1970, in an attempt to take his revenge on those who unseated him and get back power ... or at least a symbolic fraction of it.

Phi Phuon had perhaps the highest job ever given to an indigenous representative from Ratanakiri: logistics and supplies at the Ministry of Foreign

---

12 Also called 'The Bamboo Curtain' or 'K5 Belt'. See Esmeralda Luciolli, *Le mur de Bambou ou le Cambodge après Pol Pot*, Paris : Régine Desforges, 1988.

13 Short, *Pol Pot*, p. 173.

Affairs, the largest Ministry under DK. He was also entrusted with checking on the morale of the staff, at least as far as his very novel knowledge of the Khmer language permitted. Pol Pot might have given him this important task out of recognition of his success, eight years earlier, in Ratanakiri, in providing him a continuous supply of rice. He came also to be responsible for all the logistics associated with the comfort and security of foreign visitors. The leadership of an entire district, as we shall see, was also the highest position these tribesmen were granted. Even this was in Preah Vihear Province, at the periphery of the country. Never were the highlanders allowed to serve the interests of their own folk and culture. In this way they were the first victims of the regime, and perhaps only a minority of those who had enrolled into the revolution were able to survive some thirty years of revolutionary struggle, 1968–1998.

As early as 1968, the hostilities against Sihanouk's troops were planned and led by three KR leaders – Ta Pouk (Pol Pot), Ieng Sary and Son Sen – who had settled their central committee in the province the previous year, aided by the Viet Cong (VC). I very much doubt that this rebellion was an initiative of the hill tribes themselves, as is often claimed by analysts. They formed independent tribal groups, not in a position to launch concerted attacks, as anthropologists themselves explained since they formed separate and independent communities. An important trait underlined by Frédéric Bourdier is that 'there existed no higher social and political unit above the hamlet or village.'[14] So, how could they have launched a concerted attack against the government troops just by themselves?

The Khmer Rouge leadership epiphany in Ratanakiri

During the First Indochinese War (1946–1954), the protracted and widespread presence of the Vietminh troops had a lasting influence on the highlanders. And it was from the entire Khmer territory, with some 10 per cent Montagnards [15] too, that some 1,700 Khmer-Vietminh were, for nearly two decades, relocated to Hanoi for further training and use for the Vietnamese communists in later days, after the July 1954 Geneva Accords. Among them was Pen Sovann (1936–2016), then aged only eighteen, who was later

---

14 *From Padi States to Commercial States: Reflections on Identity and the Social Construction Space in the Borderlands of Cambodia, Vietnam, Thailand and Myanmar*, International Institute for Asian Studies (IIAS), Amsterdam University Press, 2015, p. 53.

15 'Montagnards' is the French version of the English word 'highlanders'.

married to a Vietnamese girl by his sponsors and would serve as the prime minister of the Hanoi-backed People's Republic of Kampuchea from 27 June to 5 December 1981, having been the general secretary of the Kampuchean People's Revolutionary Party from 1979 to 1981. He was then arrested for a lack of discipline, as he had dared to go to Moscow for negotiations without the express permission of his supervisors, and was sent back to Hanoi for further 're-education'. He re-emerged in 1991 and later joined Sam Rainsy's Cambodian National Rescue Party (CNRP).

Interestingly however, using the figures from the last official census of 1962, Bourdier notes that the total population of the province was 49,306 at the time, representing a low population density of 4.5 inhabitants per km².[16] Earlier, in this study, we find that, in 1994–1995, the time of our investigation, Bourdier calculated that the total population of the province was 69,599, among which the indigenous population were 52,793 (68.27% of the total) and 16,806 lowland people.[17] At the same period, the Jaraï were 14,000, the Tampuon 18,000, the Krâchok 2,200, the Brao/Brou and Krœung 23,800.[18] Today, the province hosts around 185,000 people, of whom approximately 50 per cent are of indigenous origin.[19]

On the other hand, Sara Colm,[20] an American researcher from Human Rights Watch, offered us a carefully investigated 21-page study about the impact of the KR revolution on the indigenous inhabitants of Ratanakiri Province and vice-versa their influence on the KR leadership. She, also, interviewed numerous highlanders in the 1990s. As expected, many of her findings tally with mine. She did not fail to notice that Pot Pot 'idealized the untarnished nature of highland society ... together with his admiration for their never having been colonized.'[21] She adds that the tribal people 'would be working for a classless society, where all ethnicities would be fairly treated and society as a whole

16 Ibid., p. 223.

17 Ibid., p 148.

18 Ibid., p 132.

19 'Indigenous People and Land Issues in Ratanakiri', Thol Dina and land titling, April 2021.

20 Chapter 5 'The Khmer Rouge's legacy for highland Culture and religion in Northeastern Cambodia' in Frédéric Bourdier (ed.), *Development and Dominion: Indigenous Peoples of Cambodia, Vietnam and Laos*, Bangkok: White Lotus, 2009. See also Sara Colm, 'The Highland Minorities and the Khmer Rouge, 1969–1979', unpublished manuscript produced for the Documentation Center of Cambodia, Phnom Penh, in 1996.

21 Colm, 'The Khmer Rouge's legacy', p. 142.

would prosper.'[22] But the reverse side of the coin was that 'Whoever opposed them was killed: they charged they were the arms and the legs of Vietnam and the CIA.'[23] Hence she also confirms that 'close to 5,000 highlanders fled from Ratanakiri to Laos and Vietnam ..., before the communists officially took power in Phnom Penh.'[24] In her conclusion she writes:

> Pol Pot's early affinity with the highlanders never faded despite rarely having been seen in the northeast after 1970. According to his aides, one of Pol Pot's final wishes was to have a portion of his ashes spread in the Northeast after his death.[25]

The most interesting of her findings, which happens to be consistent with mine, is that:

> The estimated number of deaths from all causes in the KR's Northeast region (Ratanakiri, Mondolkiri, Stung Treng and Kracheh provinces) from 1975–79 is relatively low compared to other areas: *about 7 per cent of the population died.* The difference in the treatment of highland groups in the Northeast region, compared to other regions in DK, is reflected in the fact that highland leaders from every ethnic groups were promoted into the KR leadership up to the level of district secretary and regional Party committee member; there were no large-scale population transfers in the [region] other than in Mondolkiri; and the death toll does not approach the toll of any other [region].[26]

This being said, some of my conclusions diverge from hers, as when she added: 'What was dealt a harsh blow, however, was indigenous culture, traditional livelihood practices, and customary beliefs systems'. But this was not specific to the highlanders and quite similar 'harsh blows' were dealt unto the entire Khmer population by the KR. Not just all their freedoms had been abolished, but all traditional feasts and ceremonies had been banned. The only thing that the tribal people were inflicted upon, beyond what every Cambodian suffered at the time, was forced assimilation through strong encouragements to learn the Khmer language, although I found areas in which local tribal languages were tolerated. I would also question this conclusion of her study:

---

22 Ibid., p. 146.
23 Ibid., p. 148.
24 Ibid., p. 144.
25 Ibid., p. 157.
26 Ibid., p. 143. My emphasis.

I would argue that the Khmer Rouge came to the Northeast with an ideology that was not open for negotiation with the highlanders; they neither accepted nor asked for advice from them. Although they held the highlanders in an exalted position, ultimately the Khmer Rouge showed themselves unwilling or unable to adapt their political framework to the highlanders' social, spiritual, and cultural systems. Like millions of Cambodians throughout the country, it was the highlanders who were forced to adapt – or risk execution – so that the Party could meet its political objectives.[27]

At the end of his memoir, Phi Phuon claims something a little different:

> I think these leaders had been trained to adapt to the national minorities, their living conditions, their customs and habits, their ways of thinking, their ways of conducting their lives. Pol Pot, Ieng Sary, Son Sen, Khieu Ponnary, Khieu Thirith were honest, sincere people who wished us and all Cambodians well. They were full of admiration for our ability to lead a life in harmony with the environment and in harmony with the four elements which are indispensable to all life in our world, namely water, earth, fire and wind. They asked us many questions about our way of life, our customs, our ancestor worship. They were keen to know and understand. As doctors and midwives did not exist, in the face of serious diseases, we could only implore the help of good genii or seek the roots or leaves of trees to heal us.[28]

Still, one can doubt that during the numerous, long training sessions conducted by Ieng Sary or Pol Pot between 1967 and 1971, there was much debate and exchange of ideas. What *Angkar* called 'education' was usually crude propaganda, and everything said by the revolutionary leaders was to be received as Gospel truth. Still, if the exchange was not through words, it certainly was through their way of life that for *Angkar* should serve as a model. I have come to think that Pol Pot, Nuon Chea, Son Sen and Ieng Sary not only adopted some of the highlanders '*traditional livelihood practices*', but struggled to extend them over the entire territory. In particular, as in all tribal groups of Ratanakiri, KR society operated without a judicial system that included written laws. Phi Phuon has noticed and deplored this, in fact. Similarly, in *The Tragedy of the Cambodian History: Politics, War and Revolution Since 1945*, published in 1991, David Chandler, the acclaimed historian of Cambodia, points out that when the leaders were in Ratanakiri:

---

27 Ibid., p. 157–58.
28 See pp. 195–195, below.

Communist Party of Kampuchea (CPK) cadres worked hard to recruit followers and raise the consciousness of tribal people. ... These efforts were crucial in the evolving DK ideology; the CPK cadre, largely urban in background, were deeply impressed by the tribespeople's survival skills, their obedience to their leaders, and their prowess as warriors and hunters.

Pol Pot and Ieng Sary later claimed to have been inspired by the spirit of people who had no private property, no markets and no money. Their way of life and their means of production corresponded to the ability of the highlanders to move their entire village to the communist phase of social evolution in Marxist thinking. Moreover, these men and women were, in Maoist terms, "poor and blank" receptacles for revolutionary doctrine. In 1968–70, hundreds of tribal people from Ratanakiri, especially Tampuon and Jaraï, were recruited into CPK units.[29]

In Ratanakiri at the very beginning of the insurgency, most of the soldiers were highlanders, while the political commissars were from the lowlands. Influence was not just a one-way affair, but a mutual influence and a two-way exchange. And we have a lot of evidence of that: the tools highlanders had made from forest products, their ability to relocate entire villages and manage to find, in the surrounding nature, everything necessary to construct their dwellings with pretty much their bare hands was what was to be inflicted by the KR onto many Cambodian urbanites. Since everything was to be produced locally, in the village or from the surrounding slash-and-burn fields (swidden agriculture), no trade was necessary for everyday survival, and self-sufficiency was the golden rule.

Highlanders approached issues of life and death in ways that might have appealed to the KR leaders. As Phi Phuon recounts in his memoirs, this casual willingness to put an end to a human life can also be seen in the philosophy of the KR, as Phi Phuon explained to Philip Short:

> You're asking me if we took prisoners? No ... and on our side we had orders not to allow ourselves to be taken alive. If we captured a villager, and it was someone from the area, we sent him back home. But if we caught a government soldier, we killed him. There wasn't an explicit guideline to that effect, but everyone understood it was what we should do. It was a

---

29 Yale University Press, New Haven and London, 1991, p.175.

struggle without pity. We had to draw a clear line of demarcation between the enemy and ourselves. That was the guiding principle.[30]

Similarly, putting to death a living creature (man or animal) by slitting the throat and bleeding might have been inspired by what the KR leaders witnessed in Ratanakiri. Finally, laying the corpses of the deceased in shallow graves, rather than incinerating them as in Buddhist culture, might have also been borrowed from the highlanders. This of course was also more expedient when having to deal with so many human remains at the same time.

Finally, the communal house at the centre of every indigenous village in Ratanakiri, the village meeting place where quarrels were settled, punishments doled out and decisions made, was replicated at the heart of every people's commune with what was just called *sahakor*.[31] *Sahakor* also is the word for the large building in which communal meals were served, and where compulsory evening meetings took place. The KR had developed elaborate models for these lengthy public confession and mutual criticism sessions.

More importantly, one cannot fail to see the uncanny parallel between the remarkably brief 1976 Constitution of Democratic Kampuchea and the customs and mores of the hill tribes of Ratanakiri – in particular about the place of the death penalty and the absence of a comprehensive judicial system. Both systems – DK's and tribal – clearly distinguish serious misdeeds that lead to a death verdict, and more minor ones that lead to re-education or an extra arduous practical task to perform.

Article 10, Chapter Seven: Justice

Action violating the laws of the people's State are as follows:

– Hostile and destructive activities that threaten the popular State shall be subject to the severest form of punishment.

– Other cases shall be handled by means of constructive education in the framework of the State or people's organizations.

---

30 Short, *Pol Pot*, p. 191.

31 Usually inaccurately translated into English as 'cooperative'. In fact, there was not a single real one under DK, but just 'people's communes' as in China, the model for the KR, or literally 'collectives', a production unit in which absolutely everything belonged to the collective, private property having been totally abolished. Unlike all proper 'cooperatives', these were created by the Maoist State and not by the people concerned.

In spite of the understatement, the severest form of punishment cannot but be understood as 'the death penalty'. On the other hand, for more minor offences, re-education would be the norm. And in a way, that was how things worked in pre-modern tribal societies: 'the accused was arrested and brought before all the men assembled to try him. [For serious offences against the village community] he is sentenced to be sold as slave, or killed and massacred straightaway ... The death is inflicted outside the village, far from all habitats, but without any cruelty, without any torture, for the Phnong kills to be rid of a dangerous individual.'[32] As in societies without a legal superstructure, informal assemblies of villagers or people's commune members met as 'judges of the People's Representative Assembly'[33] at the local level. The DK constitution is silent about how this (or these) assembly (ies) shall be created. Cannot they simply be the almost daily evening meetings during which the 'masses' were made to listen to the voice of the local *Angkar* and each poor soul was to 'confess' his daily failings and strong points, while denouncing also the weaknesses of others? So, there was no need to specify in the constitution how these local People's Representative Assemblies would be appointed.

The BBC journalist-cum-historian Philip Short also points to the far-reaching impact on Pol Pot's mindset of his three-year's activism in the province from 1967 to 1970.[34] In particular, thanks to his long interviews with precisely Phi Phuon, he was able to explain how this long stay in the forest radically changed Pol Pot's frame of mind. Born in a fairly affluent farming family from the countryside, but educated from a very early age in a bourgeois-aristocratic environment around the Royal Palace in Phnom Penh and then Paris, 'the City of Light', he was regenerated and 'purified' in the prey, the forest, 'the Heart of Darkness', where he solidified his inclusive meaning of the Khmer *chet* – meaning both 'race' and 'nation' to include all peoples whose origins were in Cambodia. In his 'explosive' contact with the indigenous tribal people, he and his close associates came out as New Men, as instructed by Mao.[35] After Paris, Hanoi and Beijing, Pol Pot completed his ideological pilgrimage in Munthy (Office) 100, deep inside the dense forest of Ratanakiri. He became besotted with what he saw as perfect, imagined, primitive communism. In a way, he

---

32 Michel Tranet, ed., *Les Pro-Khmer au Cambodge*, Adhémard Leclère, fin XIXe-Début XXe, Phnom Penh : Atelier d'Impression Khmère, 2002, p. 47–48.

33 DK Constitution.

34 Short, *Pol Pot*.

35 See Ibid. in particular Chapter 5, 'Germinal', and Chapter 6, 'The Sudden Death of Reason'.

thought he had found the key to what, along with his accomplice Nuon Chea, they saw as a guaranteed success for a Khmer way to achieve communism *hic et nunc*. And he was to achieve this feat (unparalleled in human history) from that primeval form of communism they inflicted on the entire population. Highlanders, who seemed to have bypassed the hated feudalist and the capitalist eras imagined by Marx, were fit to become the spearhead of their epic journey into paradise on earth here and now.

The revolutionary regime in the province lasted an entire decade, from 1968 to 1978, and not just the three years, eight months and twenty days it reigned over all the cities and townships in Cambodia. This is why, in this birthplace of the revolution, the identity of one[36] of its two paramount leaders, Ta Pouk[37] or Saloth Sâr, who later became Pol Pot, was known to all the people here, contrary to the rest of the country. In the province, as early as 17 April 1976, during the celebrations of the first anniversary of the victory of the KR, Pol Pot was presented as the general secretary of the Communist Party of Kampuchea, and the names Van (Ieng Sary), and Hem (Khieu Samphân) were also mentioned. The rest of the country, apart from the narrow inner circle of leaders, was informed of these identities only on 27 September 1977, when Pol Pot 'came out' and publicly proclaimed that *Angkar* was in actual fact the Communist Party of Kampuchea, led by himself. The regime had become the beacon of total world revolution and, thanks to the creation of a blanket irrigation system, the country was about to surpass its Angkorian past.

It is of course geography that explains the choice of this strategic province, far from the capital, for the launch the KR revolution in March–April 1968.[38] Not only had this tri-border region (Vietnam–Laos-Cambodia) been vital for the Vietnamese communist revolution, with its multi-branch Hô Chi Minh trails, but also its almost totally forested expanses which lent themselves perfectly to guerrilla warfare. Besides, the *Khmer Lœu*, or 'Upper Khmers', were stirred by a multi-secular resentment against lowland Khmers who had traditionally considered these non-Indianized ethnic groups as just a source of

---

36 The other being Nuon Chea.

37 It has been confirmed to us locally, after Philip Short presented the definition in his *Pol Pot*, that *'pouk'* indeed means 'mattress' in Khmer. It is true that Pol Pot has always appeared as an unctuous and smooth-tongued persona who, apparently, always tried to cushion conflicts. Each was supposed to find peace and tranquillity around him with his perpetual, enigmatic smile.

38 Nuon Chea, the regime's chief ideologue then in charge of the Party in Phnom Penh and the rest of the country – the West in particular – had started it as early as January in Battambang, his native province.

elephants and slaves. Vietminh propaganda during the First Indochinese War (1946–1954) developed on fertile ground and the population was already well prepared to support revolution when Pol Pot arrived: the new revolutionary regime would bring the end of enslavement, exploitation and contempt.

Secret American bombings – starting in the province as early as 1962[39] and becoming public from 1968 – drove the people to take refuge into the forest, willy-nilly, for their own survival. Once there, they joined the followers of total revolution. In fact, the various ethnic groups, centred around their individual villages, reacted radically differently, from village to village when faced with revolutionary perspectives.

If relatively high numbers of Jaraï or Tampuon, previously converted by the Vietminh invaders in the course of the first Indochinese War (1946–1954), welcomed Phnom Penh revolutionaries with open arms, others were more suspicious and even ran away to join their respective tribes in Laos or in Vietnam as soon as collectivization, along with repression, was inflicted on them from about 1972. On the other hand, for the KR leadership (*Angkar*), hill tribes were the very embodiment of honesty, loyalty and blind obedience, and provided the most secure foundations of revolution. Their way of life – their self-sufficiency at the village level and their use of barter for a few essential possessions that could not be produced locally (like bronze gongs) – became an ideal of communitarianism and solidarity in harmony with nature. It was the Rousseauistic myth of the good savage, along with Mao's 'blank page'. And this was how the KR leadership saw the new province.

Indeed, from the dismissal of Sihanouk on 18 March 1970 by the two Assemblies[40] that had appointed him Head of State in 1960, our KR apparatchiks launched, with the enthusiasm of Maoist neophytes, the entire province along the path of total collectivization. This was easy as the young Khmer Republic then removed its six thousand troops[41] from the entire province – and even the entire northeast region (*Eisan*) – because, as the Americans advised them,

---

39 This is what Phi Phuon claimed, and credibly, since he was living close to the border, in the far north-eastern corner of Ratanakiri province. It appears in his memoir (p. 58), and he repeated it at the Court.

40 The National Assembly and the Council of the Kingdom, in accordance with article 122 of the 1947 constitution, withdrew their confidence from Norodom Sihanouk as Head of State. Lon Nol remained the Prime Minister and Cheng Heng, the President of the National Assembly, became the interim Head of State before the election of a new regime or a change of institutional form – into a Republic, in this case.

41 David Chandler, *The Tragedy of Cambodia: History, Politics, War and Revolution since 1945*, Yale University Press, 1991, p. 202.

21

the blanket of forest cover made it uncontrollable. The KR proclaimed this as a big victory, drafted – often forcibly – adolescents from the region, and armed these new soldiers with Chinese weapons (mostly Kalashnikovs) that were coming down the Hô Chi Minh Trail.

'Solidarity' groups were first created among ethnicities that had been used to living entirely free in the forest. Then gradually, by enforcing the Khmer language to the detriment of vernacular dialects, our sorcerer's apprentices of a radical social revolution engineered an absolute ethnocide, not only controlling local languages but abolishing all the customs and mores of the hill people – in brief, annihilating their entire cultural identity. Still, few were those who saw their fate, and that of their families, improve in any way. Too many were to give their own lives in combat after enrolling in the movement as adolescents.

As a very young man in early 1968, Phi Phuon,[42] a Jaraï, was proud to have been the first highlander to dare to shoot (with an antiquated rifle) at Sihanouk's soldiers, along Road No. 19 near the Vietnamese border. After having vanished into the forest, this audacity could have kicked-off of the civil war. For a Jaraï, 'civil war' might not be the proper phrase, for a large section of the Annamite Range was their turf and it was being colonized by usurpers coming from the plains: both Vietnamese and Cambodians were seen as invaders and modern colonial borders had little meaning.

Pol Pot was filled with admiration for their sense of community and their solidarity before the challenges of everyday life. They were also able to survive in almost total autarchy, solving everyday problems. With the forced[43] evacuation of all cities on 17 April 1975, the KR inflicted this model on the entire urban – and even the farming population. After the first rice harvest in early 1976 from newly created 'advanced people's communes', *Angkar* established self-sufficient economic units throughout the country that were supposed to make the entire territory leap into an affluent society. The country would also soon be industrialized in a Super Great Leap Forward to produce abundant wealth that had before been squandered for the exclusive benefit of feudalists and capitalists. With perfect equality, everyone would become wealthy and happy.

---

42 Born in 1947 and interviewed in Phnom Malay between 2001 and 2015. See his autobiography below.

43 'Forced' for the urbanite victims, of course, but also compulsory for the KR too, as they were too few at the time to exercise an absolute control on the population. If the people had stayed in their familiar environments in the cities, the KR could easily have been robbed of its victory.

This idealized vision of the tribal way of life served as the exact model for the future KR society. Ieng Sary, in the very last days of the regime, in late 1978, at the Bœung Trabek B–32 re-education camp for returnees, lectured about how to become perfect revolutionaries and therefore how to complete their re-education. As Ong Thon Hœung explains in his autobiography:

> He then speaks about the hill tribes from the North, pure and faithful people who do not hesitate to sacrifice their lives for those they guard. He himself saw three of his guards die in front of him to defend him. That is why he is convinced, like the other Khmer Rouge leaders, that the hill tribe people (Montagnards) are more trustworthy that the lowland Khmers. Here are people who live in utter destitution and totally ignorant of what is taught in the schools, people who have always rejected colonisation – while those from the lowland in general, and the townsfolk in particular, if they are educated and with a better standard of living, have accepted foreign domination. According to Ieng Sary, the hill tribes had long lived under a primitive communist regime: they have no private property, do no use currency, do not know about profit and naturally move on directly to modern communism with no problem. Objectively the most devoted to the revolution, they must be taken as models.[44]

Marie-Alexandrine Martin, an anthropologist and renowned Cambodian specialist, puts this clearly in her *Cambodia: A Shattered Society*:

> The Khmer Rouge leaders considered the Montagnards as pure elements and, as their way of life appealed to them, *they decided to generalize tribal society to the whole of Cambodia*. We must develop mutual help, abolish the capitalist concept of private property, accept Spartan living conditions and semi-nomadism, learn to live from hand to mouth, flout formal education, vow an unconditional fidelity to the leader … [45]

The vision was economically and historically inept, but it became criminal with its brutal implementation, through terror after 17 April 1975.

It was Sihanouk himself who, after 1959 and the creation of the new province of Ratanakiri, proclaimed that all the motley ethnicities were to be known simply as 'upper Khmers' or *Khmer Lœu*, implying that in a new province in which lowland Khmers were nonexistent, with hill tribes on the

---

44 Ong Thong Hœung, *J'ai cru aux Khmers rouges*, Buchet/Chastel, 2003, p. 216.
45 *Le Mal cambodgien*, Hachette, 1989, p. 201, my emphasis. An English edition was published in 1994 by the University of California Press.

plateau and Lao in the valleys, the province suddenly was peopled with vast majority of Khmers. That was the first step towards forced assimilation that was to accelerate dramatically in the DK days. Under the Sihanouk's Sangkum regime,[46] women were instructed to cover their breasts, men to wear trousers instead of loincloths and the children to attend schools giving instruction in Khmer. And lowland Khmers started to arrive, as authorities regarded the land as just up for grabs. But by 1967 and the arrival of Pol Pot, the policy had yet to be implemented on a grand scale and the presence of Khmers and their administration was mainly through its army, as we shall mention later.

On the other hand, Jan Ovesen and Ing-Britt Trankell are more perceptive: they noticed that the indigenous peoples of the northeast were the darlings of the Khmer revolutionaries and were not really submitted to the most horrendous living conditions as the lowland inhabitants were.[47] Along with all cultural communities in Cambodia, including the Khmer, tribal people were required to make some adjustments. Swidden farming, for example, was prohibitied and Khmer language became obligatory for tribal people who were moved onto the plains. Still, it is fair to conclude that these minorities were not just more spared than the rest of the population, but they served as role models for their radical regime:

> The indigenous upland minorities in the northeast held a special place in Pol Pot's revolutionary imagination. They represented the Khmer ideal of purity because they were the least contaminated by foreign influences; their society could be taken as an example of the "primitive communism" of Karl Marx's fantasies, not yet touched by the slavery and feudalism stages in the universal historical materialist scheme. Pol Pot actually spent a year or so in the late 1960s among these people ... while he imbibed the "Ur -communist" tenor of their social institutions. Khmer Rouge ad-miration of the uplanders did not go so far as general cultural acceptance, however, and most of their religious institutions, notably animal sacrifices accompanied by large quantities of rice wine – concrete manifestations of the social and ecological solidarity that characterizes their worldview – were rigorously suppressed.[48]

---

46   1953–1970 was the historical period of political control by Sihanouk

47   Jan Ovesen and Ing-Britt Trankell, 'Foreigners and honorary Khmers: ethnic minorities in Cambodia', in C. Duncan, ed., *Civilizing the Margins: Southeast Asian Government Policies for the Development of Minorities*, Ithaca: Cornell U. Press, p. 246.

48   Ibid: pp 248–9.

In doing this, Pol Pot and his group, to a large extent, misread their way of life and degree of collectivization, which was just mutual help in case of difficulties.

It does not seem that the indigenous minorities from Ratanakiri were at all involved in the cruel repression policies of the leadership – and least of all in the decisions of arrests. To a large extent, the unfortunate ethnic minorities from Ratanakiri, although they were continuously favoured by the leadership, in actual fact just served as praetorian guards used by lowland revolutionaries to grab power. Once they were in power, they became reliable handymen to serve their 'Excellencies'. After the fall of the regime, they were – again – the most professional soldiers, feared by the Vietnamese, as Phi Phoun explains. They were not really allowed to serve the interests of their own folk and culture. In this way they were the first victims of the regime, although a few managed to survive some thirty years of revolutionary struggle, 1968 to 1998.

Charles Meyer, a Maoist sympathizer and long-time personal advisor to Sihanouk,[49] was optimistic about the prospects of a revolution that combined peasants and their pithy countryside common sense with the unalloyed Marxism-Leninism of so-called 'foreign-trained intellectuals'. One month after the fall of Phnom Penh, and after refugees from the first massacres poured into Thailand, he was still expecting the KR to work wonders in the country of his election and bring Heaven on earth here and now. In an article entitled 'Rebuilding Cambodia: A Daring Gamble', published by *The New York Times* on 16 May 1975, he wrote the following lines, in polar contradiction to all other observers:

> From a Maoist point of view, the victorious Cambodian revolution is exemplary. Long before moving to action, the Marxist intellectuals were learning from the peasants. A political line was patiently worked out, rectified when circumstances demanded, and applied with a minimum of compromise, all in the context of the peasants' experience and with their participation.
>
> In Cambodia, where oral tradition is more important than writing, the fruits of the intellectual-and-peasant political education didn't need to be fixed in texts that would guarantee ideological orthodoxy or in five- or eight- or ten-point programs.

Then, speaking of the brutal evacuation of Phnom Penh, he writes:

> In other times, the peasant army would undoubtedly have razed it, after having exterminated part of the population. In 1975, they were content

---

49 Charles Meyer, 1923–2004, was Sihanouk's closest advisor from 1946 until 1970.

to empty it of its citizens, who will be purified and re-educated by hard work in the rice fields ...

The peasant revolutionaries' ambition is to reconstruct their country on the foundations they have freely chosen. They think they will only be able to do so if they totally destroy all the material symbols of foreign domination and create a "new man" within a peasant socialist society that is authentically Cambodian.

This is a political, economic and cultural revolution that certainly re-calls the Chinese experience. It is perhaps even more radical, and certainly has a distinct style. Its nationalist character could lead to total indifference to the outside world. This is a daring gamble for little Cambodia – not the first in its long history.

Conversely, Philip Short[50] rightly explains that it was this fiery combina-tion of illiterate countryfolk and Maoist pseudo-intellectuals that set the poor country ablaze and caused the cruel death of a quarter of the population in three years, eight months and twenty days. What an achievement, poles apart from Meyer's dreams, not to speak of the complete collapse of the economy and the reduction of the survivors to utter destitution after unspeakable sufferings! Additionally, the invading 'liberators', who occupied the poor country from 1979 for another twelve years, shipped to Vietnam all moveable equipment, mainly from the capital but from many provinces, too. I personally was dismayed by the destitution and the filth of the capital when I returned to Cambodia in the summer of 1989. It gave the impression that the KR had only just been defeated. Westerners were received with open arms – contrary to the erroneous assertions of Charles Meyer – with this reservation: 'Westerners will once again favour first the rich', as a cyclo-driver told me. I shall never forget this wise prophecy.

---

50 See his *Pol Pot.*

Background to the Memoir

My journey from Lyon to Ratanakiri

*A*s Jared Diamond explains in *Guns, Germs and Steel*, all humanity was originally hunter-gatherers who only started to settle into an agricultural lifestyle some 10,000 years ago.[1] Some still have not done so. Up to the present day, the map of Southeast Asia continues to include a smattering of hilltribe minorities who combine hunting, gathering forest products and swidden agriculture in the peninsula's forested hills. These activities depend on movement, and their villages are best understood as temporary abodes. They form what James C. Scott calls 'Zomias',[2] bypassing the creation of 19th-century nation-states, entities with fixed state borders precisely in the porous areas that separate the region's modern states. From the days of Angkor, the hilly eastern regions have been buffer zones between the Khmer and the Cham realms, as well as sources of elephants, gold, warriors and enslaved people, and forest products.

As we have very few sources about the origins of these indigenous people, they are classified as the first inhabitants of the peninsula, before the arrival from the north of the Viet (or Kinh), the Thais and the Burmese. Khmers are also classified as first inhabitants but, unlike Khmers, hill communities have been looked down upon by the invading newcomers and treated like 'Moi' by the Vietnamese, 'Kha' by the Lao and 'Phnong' by the Khmers. All three words originally meant 'slaves'. Down to the colonial period, and even until the first half of the 20th Century, the rich red volcanic soil of Ratanakiri Province was indeed part of this 'Zomia', or a region to which the Khmers, the Lao, the Siamese and the Annamites attempted to extend their territories, with no one establishing an administration or levying taxes permanently. There was a lot of insecurity in this tri-border area, with slavery and its trade being the region's curse for the local upland inhabitants. Only from the 13 February 1904 Treaty

---

1   Jarred Diamond, *Guns, Germs & Steel: A Short History of Everybody for the Last 13,000 Years.*, Vintage Penguin, 1997. See especially 'Yali's Question', pp. 13–31 in the Prologue.

2   *The Art of Not Being Governed: An Anarchist History of Southeast Asia*, NUS Press, 2009.

with Siam did Cambodia regain the provinces of Stung Treng, Moulapoumok, Melou Prey and Tonlé Repou. Moulapoumok was to become Vœunsay, the main township of this region. Many tribes congregated on the Ratanakiri plateau simply because the soil has always been rich and apparently inexhaustible, provided there was a good water source during the dry season. When I first visited the region in my student days in 1964, it was like a Garden of Eden.

I went to Ratanakiri with my friends Thomas and Danielle White from the British Council in Phnom Penh. I met them at Leicester University during the 1961–1962 academic year. I was a *lecteur* in the French Department, and Thomas was one of my students. After graduation, he did not become a French teacher but took a British Council post in Phnom Penh. The Whites invited me to Phnom Penh in the summer of 1964, and I went there by the French *Messageries Maritimes*: a three-week voyage took me to Marseille, Barcelona, Port Saïd, Aden, Bombay, Colombo, Singapore and Saïgon, where the Second Indochinese War was intensifying. Alternating two days at sea and one on land, the Far East grew on me gradually; I was not suddenly immersed into an exotic environment, as when one steps down from an aeroplane. Being a cash-strapped student, I hitch-hiked my way to Angkor, Ratanakiri, and then the Khone Waterfalls on the Mekong and up to the Boloven Plateau in Laos. I, of course, fell in love with the country and its charming inhabitants and was lucky, the following September 1965, to get a post in the local French Lycée Descartes as an English teacher, in lieu of military service. This suited me perfectly, as I wanted never even to touch a weapon.

For my graduation, my family sent me a new 2 CV Citroën, which I duly collected at Sihanoukville harbour. Every weekend, one or another batch of Khmers joined me as I went to discover another corner of this 'country of wonders', as guidebooks described it. In the dry season of 1966, Khay Matoury and Matoren drove with me to my dear Ratanakiri once again. I was able to hire two elephants from villagers and, in the company of the brothers and our two mahouts, we travelled several days from village to village. We heard the loud reports of American bombings in the distance, on the other side of the Vietnamese border. People sometimes asked, 'Why do the Americans launch such massive bombardments?' I could have replied: 'to contain communist advance in the Cold War', but I doubted they would really understand what that East–West feud was about. So, I lamely replied, 'I don't know', as I thought bombing was not a smart strategy to win the people's sympathy and support for the fight against what I sincerely regarded as a scourge on society – com-

© Henri Locard

Figure 2: Elephants in Ratanakiri, Cambodia.

munism. So, we travelled from village to village, rocked by our elephants' gentle and regular swings.

On one occasion, Khmer police officers popped up from nowhere and flagged us down. They forbade us to travel any further east, giving no reason for this prohibition. Later, I guessed that we had been approaching a Viet Cong sanctuary along the Hô Chi Minh trail; no foreigner was to be a witness to this! At the time, Sihanouk insisted that he had not given them permission to settle all along the border and open logistics trails, yet there they were. Later in the year, Charles De Gaulle delivered his famous September 1966 speech at the Olympic Stadium in Phnom Penh, exhorting the Americans to leave Indochina, as everyone would be happy ever after. But his plea included not a word about the massive Vietnamese presence on Cambodian territory, and he certainly did not suggest that the about 40,000 foreign troops should also leave. That massive presence was the leading cause for Sihanouk's downfall on 18 March 1970, as his compatriots thought he should have done all he could to prevent the Vietnamese communists from using Cambodia as their turf. They had arrived uninvited, but Sihanouk tolerated them. Indeed, as Phi Phuon shows, the Vietnamese never completely vacated the province of Ratanakiri after the Geneva Peace Accords of 21 July 1954, but kept a permanent secret base deep in the forested hills of the far northeastern corner of the province.

I returned to Ratanakiri in 1966 when Chau Seng[3], Sihanouk's chief of cabinet and editor of *Kambuja*, commissioned me to write a report on the new Labansiek State rubber plantation in Ratanakiri entitled '*Ratanakiri ou la montagne aux joyaux*' (Ratanakiri, or the Jewel Mountain). *Kambuja* was a glossy magazine, in both French and English editions, that was distributed through Cambodia's foreign embassies. I travelled to Banlung with a high official from the Ministry of Agriculture, Ho Tong Peng, the brother of then-Minister Ho Tong Lip. My guide and companion for this extraordinary trip was the nicest of men – both for his vast knowledge about agriculture and his attention for the young English teacher I was. This is how, in 1981, Y Phandara, his son-in-law in Paris, later described him after his execution by the KR:

> 'In November 1974, my father-in-law Ho Tong Lip, Director of Agronomic research at the Ministry of Agriculture, a man of sciences, very well-known in intellectual circles, travelled through Paris on his way to a conference in Rome.[4] As well under the Sihanouk regime as under the Lon Nol Republic, amid all kinds of corruptions, hare-brained schemes and political confusions, he had always remained calm and disinterested. He laboriously conducted his research for the benefit of Cambodian agriculture.'[5]

There, I met the Frenchman Georges Bonzon, the plantation director, in his elegant, Japanese-style wooden chalet. Launched in 1960, the plantation was to extend over as many as 12,000 hectares and 2,200 hectares of young

---

3   Chau Seng (1929–1977) was born in Triton, Chaudoc province of Cochinchina. In 1949, he obtained a scholarship to study in a French teachers' training college at Montpelier where he also obtained a BA at the university in French literature. He married a French young lady who was then daughter of a local communist mayor. In 1958, he joined the Sangkum, the newly created Sihanouk political party. He held several ministerial posts, among which education; but his most influential position was to have been a long-time head of Sihanouk's Cabinet. I met him on that occasion. Finding himself on the list of suspicious leftist militants, he preferred to take refuge in France with his family in 1969. From 1970, he became Sihanouk's special FUNK representative in Europe and returned to Cambodia alone in December 1975, with the first batch of returnees, although he knew his life was in danger. After being sent for re-education in Kompon Cham province, and later to Bœung Trabek in Phnom Penh, the special camp for returnees, he was chained and tortured in S-21 under an assumed name to be finally executed on 18 November 1977. He had confessed he had been working all along for the French secret services and was probably the most important politician executed at this Khmer Rouge major prison.

4   The seat of the FAO.

5   *Retour à Phnom Penh : le Cambodge du génocide à la colonisation*, Présentation de Jean Lacouture, a. m. Métaillé, Paris, 1982 ; p. 28. Translation HL.

trees had already been planted by 1966, and their gentle curves followed the bends of the hills. In between the parallel rows of young trees, leguminous creepers had been planted to protect the soil. While in Banlung, I did not sense any hostility to the project among the local population, as some observers later claimed. They wrote that this vast enterprise was at the origin of resentments against the new authorities since the province's creation in 1959, and that these resentments were the root cause of the highlanders' rebellion against Sihanouk's troops in April 1968.[6] Not quite, as the rebellion and the Communist Party of Kampuchea (CPK) headquarters were established in Andoung Meas district, at the other end of the province.

I witnessed a well-organized undertaking that was living in harmony with the local population. The highlanders were welcomed to work for the plantation, which had already enrolled 1,200 staff by 1966. Or, if they preferred, they could start their own private plantation, in which case they were given the young saplings from the vast local nursery. If they did not wish to have anything to do with commercial agriculture, their huts would be dismantled and transported further into the forest, where they could settle on abundant free land.

For those who became employees, the working and living conditions were decent, modelled on the vast French plantation of Chup, in Kompong Cham Province,[7] that sponsored the vast state plantation I was visiting. Workers were paid a minimum of 30 riels a day, enough to buy about six kilograms of rice. On top of that, they had two weeks of paid holidays per year, apart from public holidays and Sundays. Rice was given for free for the workers and their families, and fruit and vegetables would come from Chup twice a week to be sold at the same price as in Kompong Cham Province, transport not being charged. They had the benefit of new wooden houses on stilts, Khmer style, and were given a blanket, a mosquito net and a raincoat, useful during the rainy season. Water and electricity were free. Even *that* was not all. As at Chup, a primary school had already been built, with four grades for some 200 children. There also was an infirmary with twenty beds. The management had encouraged the creation of a workers' committee to organize the favourite sports like football, volleyball and basketball. Sihanouk himself supplied

---

6   For instance, David Chandler writes on p. 174 in *The Tragedy of Cambodian History: Politics, War and Revolution since 1945*, Yale University Press, 1991, that 'an uprising broke out in Ratanakiri [... as] some [Brao] had been displaced by a government-owned rubber plantation.'

7   See Margaret Slocomb's *Colons and Coolies: The Development of Rubber Plantations*, Bangkok: White Lotus, 2007.

money to buy musical instruments for a small band, and even a theatre group, with costumes and props for the scenery. In brief, everything was designed to make people happy and entice Khmers from the plains to settle in what they regarded as utter wilderness. I failed to ask how many local inhabitants had been recruited, but I doubt lowland Khmers could fill all the new posts. I would revisit this question 30 years later.

An anthropologist, Jacqueline Matras-Troubetzkoy, was doing her thesis investigation on a nearby Brao village that had been displaced by the plantation.[8] She noted that there had been some discontent among the displaced Brao when the plantation was first set up. But the situation was calm by 1966–1967, the year of her investigation. She even stayed in Bonzon's comfortable chalet rather than in the Brao village that was the centrepiece of her study. The public rumour was that they were about to get married. Even if entirely untrue, that shows they had at least become friends. Her book does not expand at all on the difficulties of initially establishing the plantation and she is totally unaware that Pol Pot and his crew had settled in the province while she completed her research – not mentioning this even when the book was published 17 years later, in 1983! Her book at least has enabled me to hear two voices around the establishment of this important economic development. Both the official and the unofficial voices described a peaceful situation in 1966.

My report for the magazine ends with a bucolic view from the turquoise-green and transparent waters of Yaklom volcanic lake, some two kilometres east of the plantation: 'How can we imagine that not so far from this serenity, the other side of the border, a fierce war rages and all is hatred, suffering and death, while all here is calm, peace and happiness?' I could not have foreseen, then, that this paradise would be shattered within just two years – and not by a so-called rebellion of the highlanders against lowland invaders, but entirely engineered by Pol Pot, Ieng Sary and Son Sen, and supported by interference and massive aid from the Vietnamese since the days of the First Indochinese War.

During Christmas 1988, some 24 years later, I received a letter at my house in Caluire, five kilometres from the centre of Lyon, addressed simply to 'Henri Locard – Lyon'. The correspondent, who had a good reason to have lost my address, was Khay Matoury, one of the two brothers who had accompanied me

---

8   Jacqueline Matras-Troubetzkoy later published her thesis on the Brao in 1983. *Un Village en Forêt. L'essartage chez les Brou du Cambodge.* SELAF, Paris.

© Henri Locard.

Figure 3: Yaklom lake, Banlung: a highlander musing sunset.

24 years earlier on our elephant trip in Ratanakiri. The letter also surprised his brother Khay Matoren, who had lived in France since obtaining a scholarship in the early 1970s and, in 1988, worked as a chief engineer in Rouen. Neither of us had received any news of him since 1975, nor did we know the fate of his mother or his eight other siblings. Both mother and son had survived the KR regime, but all other members of his immediate family had been engulfed. My wife and I decided on the spot to go to Phnom Penh, but we preferred to wait till the summer, when we could take a more extended trip.

We travelled the following June. At the time, Cambodia granted visas only to members of pro-Soviet communist parties and a few select international NGOs tolerated by communist Vietnam. My wife, Dr Elisabeth Locard, was a paediatrician working for a government agency in preventive medicine for the young and also a member of such an organization, *Médecins du monde*. She had been given a mission to investigate orphanages, as she was involved in international adoptions. I travelled as her prince consort. We had to enter the country through Saigon, which had morphed into Hô Chi Minh City by then, to please the invading Tonkinese in April 1975.

On landing in Phnom Penh, we were reunited with Khay Matoury, who had not merely survived but was thriving and in charge of all military construction. In this connection, he had entered vice prime minister Sok An's inner circle. Our friend regretted to tell us the powers-that-be did not allow private citizens to host foreigners, so we booked a room at Sokhalay Hotel on Monivong Boulevard, which had been renamed Achar Mean[9] in memory of the first president of the Khmer People's Revolutionary Party in 1951, while Norodom Boulevard had become Tou Samouth, in honour of the man who succeeded Achar Mean in 1954.

Elisabeth and I made a long visit to the main orphanage set up by the state along Achar Mean Boulevard, one of many orphanages throughout the country, as so many parents had not survived. This one was the showroom for visitors: children here were treated decently and some had indeed been put up for adoption. We did not fail to notice that the vast majority were boys, and asked why. It was because better-off families who could afford to feed an extra mouth were happy to have a maid for free to do all the household chores. Out of this short mission, adoptions in Vietnam and Cambodia became legal, under the sponsorship of the relevant Ministries of Foreign Affairs.

My wife soon had to return to France for her full-time job and look after our four children, twin girls then aged 18 and boys of 16 and 14. I stayed and explored the revival of higher education in the country. My first destination was of course the French Department at the Royal University of Phnom Penh, a vast teacher's training college for all upper-secondary school teachers. Along with an English Department, it had just opened the preceding September (1988) and I met a dozen students from the first cohort of students. One of their teachers soon organized a seminar for me.

I had anticipated the possibility that such a seminar might be proposed and had come with a number of articles from well-known columnists that served as a base for our discussions. Students also had much to say about

---

9   Or Son Ngoc Minh, 1920–1972, founder of the pro-Vietminh Khmer People's Revolutionary Party in 1951.

France, then celebrating the 200th anniversary of the French revolution. For President Mitterrand, the celebration was all about human rights, and certainly not the Terror! The students were less interested in the squabble between Mitterrand and Thatcher, each claiming their country to have been the inventor of democracy and human rights, preferring to argue about the meanings of 'revolution'. After a few seminars, the Faculty dean popped in and suggested it might be better if we put an end to such prattle. He offered to put me on a plane to Siemreap-Angkor with a French delegation that was planning to launch an arts and crafts school in the city. It later became the famous 'Artisans d'Angkor'. We had to fly, as the road between Kompong Thom and Siemreap was not safe at the time; the KR insurgency was still threatening. One student, a Sino-Khmer named Sok Phal, the only survivor of a factory owner (the factory of course had been appropriated by the state, but soon would be transferred to the well-connected) was surprisingly articulate in French and had agreed to be my interpreter during the seminars.

I thoroughly enjoyed the trip, all the more so since Siemreap city was still off limits to ordinary citizens. Why the desperately poor PRK government chose not to develop tourism at that time remains a mystery to me. The centre was deserted, as in DK days, and a new market had been established on the main road to Phnom Penh some 2–3 km to the east. I also had the whole of Angkor Wat temple to myself, nearly, but as I was walking back along the grand alley leading to the temple, I passed a small group of students with whom I exchanged a few words. They had come by boat along the Tonlé Sap led by Hem Borith, their Khmer teacher from Sisowath High School in Phnom Penh, who had learnt some French during the Republic. We exchanged addresses and met again in 1993 at l'Alliance française, where Borith was refreshing his French and I was on sabbatical. Later he would help me considerably with the Khmer portions of my collection of KR slogans.[10]

Returning to Phnom Penh, I went to the Higher Education division of the Ministry of Education, where I was received with open arms as I explained what had happened with my seminar. They said they would see to it and ring me later. The same day, I received a call asking me to resume my seminar the very next afternoon. As always inside authoritarian regimes, the traditional wing is constantly vying with the modernist wing. Some juggling is required.

---

10 Le Petit Livre rouge de Plo Pot, Paris: L'Harmattan, 1996. A second, enlarged English edition is published as Pol Pot's Little Red Book: The Sayings of Angkar, Chiang Mai: Silkworm, 2004.

I also heard that all higher education branches had been re-started in the last decade, thanks to Soviet and Vietnamese assistance. Hallways echoed with the sounds of lecturers speaking in Russian, Vietnamese, Khmer or French – in all disciplines except law, not a surprise for a communist regime that demands blind obedience. Without asking permission from anyone, I rode my bicycle to what had been the Law Faculty in the *Sangkum* days. I was again received warmly by Lœung Chay, the rector, who had studied in Bordeaux and could speak French. He was so happy to see me come because he did not know how to start the next academic year now that, along with the military, all Vietnamese lecturers were leaving the country. I also went to my old school, *Le Lycée Descartes*, which had become the Faculty of Economics. The dean greeted me with a smile and we quickly became friends. Later, we organised a twinning between his department and the Law and Economics department at my university, Lumiére Lyon 2. I managed the formalities and contracts were duly signed. An international law course taught in the French language exists to this day.

Still, this was not all. When I returned to Lyon after my usual one month in Oxford that summer, I was interviewed for a local free radio programme run by Cambodian refugees. I spoke about the renewal of arts and crafts, mainly traditional silk weaving and silversmithing. A listener named Mœung Sonn called in and invited Elisabeth and me to come straight to his house for lunch after the programme, and we were delighted to oblige. He was there with his wife Phally, and their three young children. They had been imprisoned in the KR detention/torture centres, had lost four young children and absolutely wished to share their extraordinary, painful story. Sonn had started to compose a chapter with a journalist from *Le Progrès*, the local newspaper. But the work was stalled as the journalist knew nothing about Cambodia and the region, and Sonn was not in a position to write in more elaborate French. So, I soon started recording the husband and wife as they narrated tribulations that took me to the heart of the brutal regime: the prison-extermination centres where Sonn spent half of those blazing years. This led to the publication of *Prisonnier de l'Angkar* by a reputable Paris publisher, Fayard, in 1993 and consequently to a long-term research interest in KR prisons in the entire territory. Everywhere, the same stories of massive arrests, interrogations under torture and executions identical to Mœung Sonn's original district of Prey Nup, near Sihanoukville, were repeated.

I returned to Cambodia in 1991, when visas were easily available, and travelled round the entire Tonlé Sap lake in search of similar institutions. In each province, indeed each district, I was told '*mean*', 'there were'. Sonn's truth had been replicated throughout the territory. I persevered throughout the 1990s, including all of 1993–1994, a sabbatical year granted by the French Ministry of Education, and several long summer trips. At the same time, I became affiliated with the Royal University of Phnom Penh as a visiting professor. Of course, I extended my research to Ratanakiri Province in 1994, precisely when it was opened to the world. Identifying the main prison in Banlung was easy as it was the only permanent institution of its kind in the entire province. I had therefore the time and opportunity to spread my investigation to all aspects of the DK regime there – in particular to reactions of the indigenous people in the late 1960s, when the KR leadership claimed they were on the cusp of paradise, here and now. I compiled my insights into a dissertation on the KR repression system and KR ideology, and was awarded a PhD in 2000. My shift of focus was thus sanctioned by academia. My dual competency in English and now History proved a boon when I reached retirement age – early, thanks to my four children. And I could stand on my feet and do what I pleased from the year 2000.

Collaboration with Phi Phuon

How did I meet Phi Phuon, the protagonist of this study? This story begins in the 1990s, when I crossed paths with Stéphane Courtois shortly before he became a leading light in intellectual circles in France with the bombshell publication of *The Black Book of Communism*. Courtois and his collaborators convinced the scholarly community (and much of the general public) that DK represented the climax of communism in the world: the last, the most lethal and the most totalitarian regime the world has ever known. Courtois enthusiastically encouraged me in my research. His journal, *Communisme*, published a relatively long summary of my analysis of the KR prison system under the title 'Le Goulag khmer.[11] Subsequently he agreed to be a member of the panel during my PhD viva. Since then, my intellectual journey has progressed along the trail that he began to blaze.

In 2000, Parisian publisher *Autrement* invited me to write a composite portrait of a KR intellectual trained in France. I immediately thought: why imagine a composite, artificial portrait when a living persona probably exists in the flesh, here and now? I soon thought of Thiounn Mumm, scion of one of

---

11 '*Le goulag khmer rouge*', Revue *Communisme: La Question du Totalitarisme*, No. 47–48, 1996.

the most renowned families in Cambodia and, to boot, the first Cambodian *Polytechnicien*. He had joined the Khmer revolutionaries in his student days in Paris in 1949, even before Pol Pot. As Minister of Industry under DK, he had been very active in the opening (or re-opening) of a host of factories and workshops with Chinese aid. I approached him at his residence in Rouen (Normandy) where he had retired. The man had a reputation for being very secluded, but he welcomed me, invited me to a restaurant and immediately liked the idea of collaborating on his memoirs.

I again turned to Stéphane Courtois, who suggested that his publisher, Robert Laffont (much bigger than *Autrement*) might be interested, as such a book would be a complete novelty – and yet in line with his own research and publications. Thiounn Mumm and I were soon invited to an elegant restaurant, near *l'Étoile* and not far from the Laffont offices, by Charles Ronsac, an old gentleman who had been the *éminence grise* behind *The Black Book of Communism*. Ronsac was even prepared to give an advance to Mumm, provided that he wrote an outline of his memoirs (like a table of contents) and one chapter, and that he was a '*repenti*'. The last request did not worry me much; in a Cambodian religious context, 'repentance' does not make much sense. I thought that if Mumm was not yet ready to state that he had become 'a reformed man', self-realization would come naturally with the writing. Alas, Mumm was the victim of a stroke that left him half-paralysed. The specific project had to be dropped, but the general idea continued to interest me.

Mumm suggested that I approach Suong Sikœun, another prominent KR 'intellectual'. Sikœun also was a child of Paris-VIII, a hotbed of Maoism, where he had become a junior assistant of the then-called Vincennes University, and his ex-wife, Laurence Picq, the notorious author of *Beyond the Horizon*, lived in eastern France. I went to Dijon to meet her and she obliged me by giving Sikœun's address and telephone number in Phnom Malay, where Sikœun now was living with his new wife and son. I was lucky to meet a man in full possession of his intellectual abilities and most desirous to explain how he fell into the trap of becoming an ardent worshipper of the Maoist brand of communism.

By then I had just retired from my post at *l'Université Lumière-Lyon 2* and was settled in Phnom Penh, where I taught Cambodian history. In early 2001, I made a journey of 400 kilometres, or two decades by a different reckoning, to Phnom Malay, where Sikœun was an informal leader. A few survivors, like Ieng Sary, So Hong (Pol Pot's nephew) and Tep Khunnal (who married Pol Pot's young widow), had managed to play their games well enough to become businessmen. But most had divided the rich, deforested land into reasonably sized holdings and squeezed enough out of it to survive with their families. We did not see utter poverty, as is often the case in the country's far reaches, away from the capital.

Living close to Sikœun's modest wooden house, another man was willing to open his heart and explain to the younger generations how and why he could have been involved in this criminal regime for three entire decades. He was a Jaraï who now went by the name Phi Phuon, but had also been known as Vy Cheam and Comrade Cheam. On the other hand, his real name at birth was Rochœm Tvin. It was no coincidence that those two personalities lived close to each other in Phnom Malay. Both had been zealous staffers at the large Ministry of Foreign Affairs, from its creation early in the regime to its fall on 7 January 1979. They represent the extreme poles of the broad spectrum of people attracted to a regime that operated much like a cult. Sikœun, the 'intellectual', had been conditioned by the most radical Maoist and post-May 1968 French thought, and later in Beijing and Hanoi; Phi Phuon, as David Chandler notes, was the ideal-typical 'blank page'[12] of Mao's musings. Unlike his friend Sikœun, Phi Phuon did not consider his life to have been ruined: from being an unschooled, illiterate adolescent, a member of a minority community who could not speak a word of the national language, he had risen to become the deputy-governor of an affluent district in western Cambodia. The revolution had been a kind of emancipation that, sadly, had degenerated into raw violence. In his view, cruel leaders like Ta Mok or imperialist nations like Vietnam had turned an inspiring adventure into a disaster. Even in the 1970s, he deplored the absence of a fair justice system, without which the path toward death for innumerable innocent victims was almost necessarily short and brutal.

From the experience he gained while managing the logistics for the Ministry of Foreign Affairs, DK's largest ministry, and arranging the visits of numerous foreign delegations, mainly in 1977 and 1978, he had enough know-how to contribute to the smooth development of Phnom Malay, including resolving land ownership conflicts. But above all, he was one of the very few ex-KR leaders who talked candidly with researchers. Already, he had been interviewed by Philip Short for *Pol Pot, the History of a Nightmare*, Long Dany of the Documentation Center of Cambodia (DC-Cam), and others. Most KR

---

12 *The Tragedy of Cambodian History*, Yale University Press, 1991, p. 175.

leaders either blankly refused, like Nikân, Son Sen's younger brother, or evaded the issues, or even – like Nuon Chea, Brother No. 2, or Khieu Samphân, the ex-Head of State of the regime – followed the advice of their defence teams and remained practically silent at the Khmer Rouge Tribunal (ECCC).[13] Jacques Vergès's ghost continued to haunt the ECCC hearings after his sudden death in 2013, and the French defence lawyers of the accused continued to deny the historical responsibilities of their clients.

By the time of my interviews, both had been de-conditioned and distanced from their tragic experiences. Our first recordings were made in 2001, but the real work did not get going until Sikœun's memoirs had been fully completed and published.

The process

To interview Phi Phuon, I would travel from Phnom Penh, where I was lecturing at the History Department of the Royal University of Phnom Penh, to Phnom Malay for two-day interview sessions. I rewarded my interpreter/translator financially, while Phi Phuon generously donated entire days to the project. The first interviews took place at Sikœun's house, and we later used the spacious residence of So Hong.[14]

To tape the interviews with Phi Phuon, we settled most comfortably in So Hong's large garden, under the shade of a tin roof. So Hong's wife, who had cooked for Prime Minister Pol Pot in Phnom Penh, prepared the most exquisite Cambodian recipes. My oral questions were put in French and translated into Khmer by Sikœun, who then translated Phi Phuon's Khmer answers into French. At the same time, I took abundant notes in French. Sikœun first transcribed the interviews and then transformed them into a coherent narrative in French. I divided the narrative into chapters and chose titles for each. Later, I translated the full manuscript into English, which all educated citizens know today in Cambodia.

I have in my possession some 50 tapes on which Phi Phuon's memoirs were recorded. We started in 2001 (7 tapes), but the project went dormant

---

13 Most of those, like Arthur Vercken and Victor Coppe, were disciples of the notorious negation-ist Jacques Vergès (1925–2013), who represented Klaus Barbie in Lyon, before leading Khieu Samphàn's defence.

14 I also interviewed So Hong (1945–) extensively in his Phnom Malay home between 2013 and 2015, as he had been close to his uncle, Pol Pot, who partly educated him. He is, with his children, one of the clear economic beneficiaries of the revolutionary regimes.

© Henri Locard 2018

Figure 4: Interview tapes.

until Suong Sikœun's own autobiography was completed and published.[15] We started again from the beginning on 14 April 2014 and completed the interviews (50 tapes) on 21 March 2015, so just over a period of one year, interrupted by three months I spent in France. We completed the interviews exactly 25 days before Phi Phuon's tragic and sudden death on 15 April 2015.

I am very grateful to both Phi Phuon and Suong Sikœun. They persevered over many months to complete a task that promises to facilitate insights into Cambodia's recent tragic history. We have attempted to remain as close to reality as possible and to leave aside ideological or purely academic speculations. This, in the hope of contributing to a better understanding of why those horrendous sufferings had been inflicted onto the Cambodians in the course of an experiment in total communism, an ideology that has always been most alien to the Cambodian cultural tradition.

---

15 It was published in 2013 by Les Éditions du Cerf under the title: *Itinéraire d'un intellectuel Khmer rouge*, preface and biographical notes of KR officials by Henri Locard.

Part II

The other side of the mirror:
Memoirs of Phi Phuon,
Pol Pot's aide-de-camp

*Interpretation and translation from Khmer into French by Suong Sikœun,
and then into English by Henri Locard*

Figure 5: Kappa tribal basket, given to the author by Rochœm
Tveng.

– I –

A childhood in harmony with nature

I, Phi Phuon, born Rochœm Tvin (រ៉ូ ម៉ ទ្វិន) alias Vi Cheam,[1] was born on 18 August 1947, in Chây village, Talao commune, Bokham District (currently Andoung Meas), in Ratanakiri Province (then part of Stung Treng Province), located about ten kilometres north of the Tonlé San river. The second child in a family of five children, I came just after Rochœm Tveng (រ៉ូ ទ្វេង), born in 1945, and before another brother (now a medical officer) living in Khsan village, district of O'Yadao, and two sisters. In fact, I have had nine brothers and sisters in all, but four died 2–3 months after birth and others when they were 4–5 years old. My father, Aèt,[2] was born in 1923 and died in 2011; my mother died in 2003. My maternal grandfather was an ethnic Jaraï national, but my paternal grandfather was a Krâchok. At home, the entire family spoke Jaraï. There was not a single Khmer in the district, but there was one Vietnamese merchant, in the middle of the bush on the road to Bokéo, the main township in north-eastern Ratanakiri Province.

At the time, there was no school in the area; but in the future province of Ratanakiri, created in 1959 during the *Sangkum*[3] era of Norodom Sihanouk, the first school was opened in Lumphat, the new capital of the province on the Tonlé Srèpok. When I grew up, I learned the Lao language, because there were itinerant Lao teachers who taught from one village to another.[4] They gave evening classes, and we studied by torchlight. I was maybe thirteen years old.

---

1   This revolutionary alias was given to him by Pol Pot in 1970.

2   At the ECCC, he reported his father's name as Pa Tout Kvek and his mother's as Ros Chambeck. His Khmer wife is named Sreng Kim Ly (elsewhere referred to as Sréng Bunly).

3   *Sangkum Reastr Niyum* (People's Socialist Community) is the name given by Sihanouk to the political regime he dominated from 1955 to 1970.

4   For the influence of the Lao revolution during the First and the Second Indochinese Wars, as well as its role in Ratanakiri and Stung Treng provinces, read Martin Rathie's thoroughly researched, 'The Lao Long of Cambodia Ethnic Lao in the Cambodian Revolutions', in Desley Goldston (ed.), *Engaging Asia: Essays on Laos and Beyond in Honour of Martin Stuart Fox*, NIAS Press, 2019, pp. 190–229.

Vietnam was close by, but there were no Vietnamese teachers, nor Khmer. I learned to write Jaraï language with the Latin alphabet. I practised at home for two years. It was the only way to learn. I began to learn Khmer in 1963, first memorizing terms like 'American imperialists', 'struggle movement', and 'resistance movement'. By 1967, my understanding of this language was about 30 per cent, which was good enough for me to perform my work (1 August, p. 18).[5] At that time, Jaraï revolutionaries were very committed to speaking Khmer, and tried not to communicate with each other in our Jaraï language (1 August, p. 21).

In 1963, the neighbourhood included five other villages, named Nhang, Ta Nha, Nay, Châng, and finally Chây, a large village of about sixty houses and maybe 250 inhabitants, all Jaraï. At its head was a chief, elected by both men and women. The village lived in perfect harmony and avoided ethnic conflict.

1 – Jaraï customs and mores

The Jaraï are one of the largest ethnic minorities in the far northeast of Cambodia. They live on both sides of the Cambodia–Vietnamese border, and are far more numerous in Vietnam. They have a spoken and Latin script written language, unlike minorities who only know a spoken language. The Jaraï of Cambodia and Vietnam have always maintained fraternal relations. Today, these relations are more restricted than in the past because of the administrative formalities that are required of all citizens from both sovereign countries. For example, nowadays, the Jaraïs of Cambodia cannot stay in Vietnam for more than a week or ten days, whereas they had been allowed to stay as long as they pleased.

In general, each village occupies the same field for four years. Jaraï villages change their location if an ill-fated event – an epidemic, a fire or a crime – occurs there. The case of a girl from Mondolkiri (a neighbouring province), who became pregnant before being married, can be mentioned in this respect. To avoid a curse over her family, she went to the river and aborted the foetus. When informed of this news, the chief of the village, positioned along the

---

5   Details of Phi Phuon's knowledge of the Khmer language are drawn from his testimony at the Extraordinary Chambers in the Courts of Cambodia (ECCC), the tribunal where senior DK leaders were tried for crimes against humanity. Phi Phuon testified for six days in July–August 2012. Since all testimony was in the year 2012, citations will refer to the page number of testimony on a particular day and month, in this case, (1 August, p. 18).

river, decided to move it to a new place to ward off the wrath of the gods caused by the staining of the water of the river by blood from the abortion.

My first village was called Chak Krala, the second was Kaun, the third Han Yang and the fourth Yabi. There were ill-fated events in Chak Krala, including many old people dying there. So, we left and created Kaun, hoping to exorcise the misfortune. People also move on after the soil nutrients on the territory that had been selected for slash-and-burn agriculture becomes depleted. But most often, villagers are forced to find a new place to settle because they are powerless to curb the rapid growth of weeds that invade their fields after three or four consecutive years of cultivation. When moving a village, it may happen that two clan leaders will disagree about where to move. Then, the original village will split and two will be established.

Each funeral ceremony lasts five to ten days, after which a final ceremony is held with the killing of a buffalo. One announces a death either by sounding gongs or by communicating the news from house to house. The gongs also serve other functions. From the sound and the melody, people know whether it is a happy or ill-fated announcement. These gongs are expensive, today from twenty to more than a thousand US dollars. Generally, the north-western corner of each village is reserved for a cemetery. There are offerings for a period that can last up to ten years before the final ceremony is celebrated. In general, this is organized to conclude a suitable period – not just a single death, but for a series of deaths in the family. For each death, there is a choice of three types of coffins: the first is made of precious wood called *tatrav*[6], the second in *chheu kram* wood and the third in ordinary wood. Coffins made of *tatrav* wood are wide, deep and airtight. Around the tomb, a sort of fence is erected, on which are hung wooden carvings of symbolic representations such as those of a couple, a monkey, an elephant, an owl or an airplane. The couple symbolizes marital happiness, the monkey a quick movement and the elephant transport, while the owl is intended to warn us of an unfortunate event and the airplane means a trip out of the country. Family and friends from surrounding villages come and take part in the funeral ceremony. The duration of the ceremony, or the choice of coffin, does not depend on the age of the deceased, but only on the social level of his family. If a specific one has several heads of buffalo to sacrifice,

---

6   *Tatrav* (taeRtA), Aida cochinchinensis or Nauclea speciosa, is a very hard, durable wood, Cambodia-English Dictionary, Catholic University of America Press, 1977, p. 318.

then the funeral ceremony lasts longer. Each guest donates a pig's head and a jar of rice alcohol.

After leaving Ratanakiri Province in May 1970, I did not return until August 1997. Previously, I had received, through the Red Cross, a letter from my elder brother, telling me that my parents were still alive. To visit them after almost three decades of separation, I flew with my Aunt Thea from Phnom Penh to Banlung before going to my home village, where I stayed for more than a fortnight. In April 2003, I visited my parents and other family members a second time. My mother died in December of the same year. In 2004, on the first anniversary of her death, all members of my extended family, including my grandchildren, went to my home district to take part in the funeral. We slaughtered six heads of buffalo and three heads of oxen on this occasion, and the guests made an offering of sixty heads of pigs. A French journalist filmed the ceremony from start to finish. In 2012, for a similar ceremony dedicated to my father's memory, we slaughtered the same number of buffaloes and oxen, and the guests brought the heads of forty hogs. Compatriots from the 'Rochœm' clan living in Vietnam also attended my father's funeral ceremony. At least three hundred guests attended.

Among the Jaraï and other ethnic minorities in northeast Cambodia, the inhabitants of each village regularly organize celebrations on the first, fifth and tenth year after a death. My paternal grandfather died in 1965. He left about twenty grandchildren. The funeral ceremony lasted five days and five nights in a row.

Relationships between boys and girls are quite free. Marriage is prohibited between a boy and a girl from the same clan and living in the same village. For a boy and girl who violate this prohibition but admit to being in the wrong, the clan leader imposes a fine of one buffalo for each offender. The villagers then slaughter the two buffaloes, make a variety of dishes, and eat together. In the past, the two perpetrators were banned from the village and forbidden to marry. Their child was jointly entrusted to the care of the father or the mother. However, if they lived in two different villages, the boy could marry the girl, even if they belonged to the same clan. To my knowledge, my parents' case is unique: my father, who is of the 'Krâchok' nationality, married my mother, who is a Jaraï. My mother also speaks Krâchok. The Jaraï tribe is founded on the matrilineal kinship principle and therefore I count as a Jaraï. Besides, I also speak Jaraï, live like a Jaraï and think like a Jaraï. I am a Jaraï.

In the vast majority of cases, people decide to marry after living together for at least one year. If the girl becomes pregnant during the courtship, they marry after the birth and the fertilization is deemed a divine blessing. There are no contraceptives. In the not-too-distant past, it was customary for first-born children to be put to death because the identity of the father was uncertain. There is no minimum age for marriage. In general, women get married at the age of 16 or 17.

From the age of 12 to 15, I lived with my maternal grandfather, most of the time in the fields, while my grandmother stayed in the village. I often remember the stories of animals that my maternal grandfather told me. These related to monkeys, hares, tigers, snakes, deer, bears, etc.. I also remember the happy days when my comrades and I went fishing. We used creels in drying ponds to catch the fish or set traps to capture the wild beasts. But at the same time, painful memories come to my mind when hunger gnawed, and we had to make do with a single tuber of cassava, without salt or sugar. I also remember when our clothes were reduced to rags or even worse, sometimes without even a loincloth covering us.

As soon as I entered the age of adolescence, my father and my grandfathers began to teach me the ways of life: how to cultivate fields, how to make hunting instruments and how to hunt, how to make fishing tools and how to fish. When you became an adult, you must acquire all of this knowledge and know how to behave. You also learnt that two things must be avoided for sure: living in servitude and becoming a thief. In our community, every thief caught red-handed is simply executed.

Thus, from my earliest childhood, I knew how to make bows, crossbows and arrows, essential for hunting, as well as fishing nets. I also knew how to build houses for spirits, for chickens, for pigs, I knew how to make them all. The houses were built from bamboo; the supports were trees. A henhouse can last ten to twenty years: the house becomes dirty, but the birds cannot destroy it. Personally, I had two bows and three categories of arrows: the first was tipped with iron and poisoned, the second tipped with bamboo, that was also poisoned, while the third was made of wood or bamboo and is only for the slaughter of birds such as wild cocks, turtledoves, sparrows, quails, partridges, water hens and peacocks, as well as squirrels. The people of my village also went hunting for tigers and panthers, but no one ever took part in the elephant hunt. In general, they shared the products of hunting or fishing.

2 – A Jaraï village

The inhabitants of a village form several clans. In mine, there were three, including Rochœm, Sev and Sâl. The Rochœm clan, my clan, was the most powerful and our leader ran the village. We also joined the revolutionary movement in the largest numbers. My family also hosted Rochœm from Vietnam, who came to live among us. Today, in Thailand, there is still a Rochœm who raises shrimps for sale in Trat Province.

Each clan adopted its own traditions and customs. In general, each clan consisted of ten to twenty families and occupied the same long house. A long house was between 100–200 meters in length, including a central space with a large hall that served as both a meeting place and a ritual site – to exorcise evil spirits and pray to *va tao* (good spirits), which took the form of shining stones that watched over the village and its inhabitants. These dark yellow stones, probably amber, came from residues left by lightning and had the configuration of a pickaxe. For the protection of poultry houses, we put the head and wings of a chicken on a plate sprayed with its blood, and exposed it in front of the *yeak tao* (male spirit) and the *ta tao* (female spirit). Sometime during the incessant wars, these stones disappeared. Rooms were on both sides of the median space. The older ones lived at the ends, while the youngsters lived in the middle.

The piles of the houses were made from wood; the roof frame was covered with *khanma* leaves, large and resistant to the elements. Each house could last from 5 to 10 years. Each village was home to 150 to 200 families and each family had an average of 5 people. Planting without ploughing was done on cleared forest land[7] of about one hectare. Several families divided the land into elongated rectangular strips going from one end of the cleared land to the other. So, rectangular strips of about 1,000 square metres could be cultivated by individual families without trespassing the neighbouring strips.[8]

Although younger than my older brother, Rochœm Tveng, it was I who dared to take the initiative and decide everything, without fear. I made polished arrows to kill wild beasts and had a dagger. There were many beautiful peacocks and ibises, and other birds like turkeys and hoopoes. In addition, there were roosters, wild ducks, partridges, and even *kong aèng* (a large lizard species) and squirrels. We caught a multitude of turtle doves and other smaller

7　'*Essart*' in French.
8　For details of the careful organization of planted land, see Jacqueline Matras-Troubetzkoy's *Un village en forêt: l'essartage chez les Brou du Cambodge*, pp. 341–71, CNRS, Paris, 1983.

birds by putting resin around the watering holes where they would drink and bathe. We also caught deer and wild boars.

There were *præh* (buck), *chhlouh* (deer), wild boars, and also saw *rokhan* (panther/leopard with spots) and *khlah dombong* (tigers with stripes). One year, a tiger ate a resident of our village; people had become his usual diet and it had killed three since it was identified: a woman and two men, named Blaœum and Phnat. I don't remember the woman's name. One year, the tiger came to our village in March, when there was no water and the rainy season had not started. It just sat under a mango tree, and no one dared leave their house. They could have shot it with a poisoned arrow or a gun, but the people believed in the spirits and thought they should allow the tiger to go away happily.

By the time I was fifteen years old, I was more willing, more audacious. I decided everything. I dared to do things without fear. I had a dagger and an arrow the length of two arms. And I could shoot small animals or birds, like turkeys and peacocks. We sprayed water that had been mixed with a special kind of resin. When the birds came to drink, they would get stuck and could be captured. We captured from 100 to 200 small birds a day: doves, *popek* (turtledoves) or *popul* (a sort of grey-green turtledove), hens and wild cocks. All of these rested on the resin and we captured them. There were several types of doves: some were very beautiful, as they had tufts, or hoopoes, on their heads. These birds loved to bathe. Wild partridges and ducks ran and flew away. There were many fruits in the forest (*kacho, kachâs*), but no wild buffaloes.

There were wild elephants, but nobody in my village knew how to catch them. As for my village, we were not good at training, catching or even feeding them. We did not hunt them for food, either. There were some in Phum Vœu village. They knew how to feed the elephants and train them.

There were all kinds of snakes, such as *thlann* (pythons), *puvék* (cobras) *vey krobey* (another variety of cobra), black snakes, and the *lahang* snake found in mountain caves. The cruellest type of snake is the *pophléak* (cobra). One killed a man and a woman when I was an adult.

In my village, there was no Buddhist religion at all. Under the leadership of my grandfather, Lok Ta Ot, we believed in the spirits of trees and the earth. In a Jaraï village, there is normally a *sala* (hall) built for the worship of spirits. A stone that had been struck by lightning was placed in the sala. A ritual involved the washing of this sacred stone. During the ceremony, a pig's or a chicken's head was used as an offering. The chicken wings, the liver and all the entrails of the chicken or pig were used to make offerings and given in prayers to the spirits for happiness and progress in the village, so that any danger or bad thing was spared from the village. The spirits of the earth heard our prayers and brought happiness and progress to our village. So, I have never known malaria. If we had a fever, we used traditional medicine, usually the root of a tree.[9] We also used traditional medicine if we had diarrhoea, and we said a prayer for healing. You could also sacrifice a buffalo as an offering for more serious cases. Those are the beliefs of the community. We organized customary ceremonies with many decorations and structures, accompanied by rice alcohol brewed in large earthen pots. To the spirits, who are the owners of the land and water, we asked them to give us happiness and wealth.

The Jaraï did not live in collectivized structures, but there were five of their villages: Phum Chok, Phum Touch, Phum Khlang, Phum Lamam, and Phum Seuv. There was solidarity among the villagers, but they could not marry each other. They lived only in their village communities. In the village, they built rows of very long houses, with passages between the rows. Food was shared. If someone had something in abundance, they gave it to others. If someone killed a deer, he shared it. The same was true if you slaughtered a pig. For husked rice, we could ask to borrow from each other. Next time, they would borrow from us. Children ate together as a group. Once married, couples ate separately.

We know tales and legends about our Jaraï ancestors. My mother is Jaraï, my father Krâchok. My mother's father was also Jaraï. He liked to tell stories about hares. These reminded us not to be fooled by others and suggested tactics to get out of predicaments. This was to form our judgment and help us to gain experience through learning.

What was the origin of the Jaraï? We did not know. We came from the east, from Vietnam. There were many Jaraï languages: Radhe, Bunong, Piyang, Kuey, Tchang and Pdae. Who was the king of the Jaraï? I never saw him. Tampuon, Krâchok, Kravet, Brao, Lao, Khmer and Poa also were there.

For each family, there was no collective farming. Each slash and burn field belonged to an individual family. There were still four elephants in our village, but we did not know how to capture young ones in the forest to train them. At that time, the land problem did not exist yet. Those who wanted some, and were in a position to develop the land of their choice, could do it. No land title deed was required of them.

---

9   Traditional medicines in the NE were very effective against malaria. Chinese doctors came to study them during the DK period.

3 – Khmer 'colonization': The creation of Ratanakiri Province in 1959

The government of the *Sangkum Reastr Niyum* (People's Socialist Community) of Prince Norodom Sihanouk, with the help of the French, built the Bokéo airport and the rubber plantation in the area. It was also a Frenchman, Georges Bonzon, who headed the rubber plantation at Labansiek (now Banlung), the whole of which belonged to the Cambodian state. As for the inhabitants, they began to cultivate small areas of cabbages, gingers, oranges and rambutans.

It was also the *Sangkum* administration that, in 1959, decided to create the new provinces of Ratanakiri and Mondolkiri out of Stung Treng and Kratieh provinces. It also installed a chief at the head of each village, assisted by two deputies, and a garrison directed by a station chief in each commune. But it lacked a health service and schools, except for one in Bokéo, intended for children of the Khmer and Lao, and of Vietnamese settlers from Stung Treng.

The creation of the new province of Ratanakiri attracted traders and new inhabitants who came to settle in towns and surrounding areas, including Lumphat, its capital, located on the banks of the Tonlé Srèpok. Four new districts were created at the same time: Lumphat, Vœunsay, Bokham (Andoung Meas) and Bokéo (Andoung Pech). In Bokéo (literally 'gem mine'), precious stones were exploited at Bo Nhok and Bo Lay. Nowadays, the Bo Nhok and Bo Lay deposits remain exploited while those of Bo Kham have been abandoned or exhausted. At the time, the Forestry Commission was not yet created. The exploitation of forests and its corollary, the timber trade, were therefore on a very modest scale.

My village was entirely populated with Jaraï, but there were Krœungs and Krâchoks in neighbouring villages. The Lao lived mainly on the banks of the Tonlé San and Tonlé Srèpok, especially in Talavo, along the Tonlé San – hence the origin of the name of the village. Lao also had long settled the district of Vœunsay, also on the Tonlé San.

Before entering the revolution, I saw with my own eyes Sihanouk soldiers arriving with their weapons. They threatened us: they were demanding chickens, ducks and pigs. If they wanted something, they would take it, even if we did not give it to them. If we did not obey, they would shoot at us. This caused our anger. Nothing was paid. If I had not joined the fight, life would have become impossible. They came to oppress us. They came to destroy us, to subjugate us. I

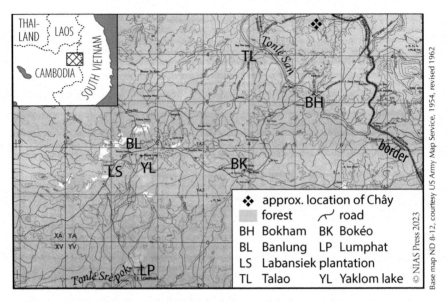

Map 2: Central Ratanakiri Province prior to the revolution.

had to join the fight. I entered the *maquis*[10] because of rubber plantations. I was not directly a victim, but I had witnessed the condition of the coolies in Bokéo. They worked for the plantations, cut the forests and planted the young trees for the smaller plantations. In one day, if the coolie worked well, he earned sixty riels,[11] but sometimes he earned only twenty riels. If weeds invaded the young plants, and especially if the plants were damaged as weeds were removed, the salary was cut. Coolies could be fired from one day or one month to the next. That's why they had to be careful.

---

10 'Maquis', or 'prey maquis' is a reference to de Gaulle and the résistance against the Pétinists during WWII in France and its colonies. It describes the forests where guerrilla fighters hid themselves from the dominating Nazi 'collaborators'. The original *maquis* was the impenetrable evergreen oak forest of Corsica, where outcasts or bandits went into hiding.

11 One kilogram of rice cost five riels at the time.

– II –

My political training

*M*y father guided my first steps into politics, when I was 13 or 14. In 1947, he joined the resistance movement against French colonialism, under the auspices of the Vietminh. This is why he educated me to continue his struggle for the revolution, for independence and liberty. 'Don't allow anyone to look down on us. They despise us; they regard us like rubbish.' This is why my father urged us to get involved in the revolution.

He had served as a messenger and escorted Vietnamese cadres, and also Jaraï, Tampuon or Lao, when they went from village to village to make political propaganda and agitation. He was also in contact with the Jaraïs of Vietnam. My dad told me he was trying to recruit his family and friends. They knew there would be fighting, so they hid in the bush to preserve their strength. When I was a child, I heard the elders talk about the Issarak[1] struggle for the camp at Châk Yuk on the Lao border. It was an old French base, taken by the Issarak in 1954. Their leader was a Lao tribal chief whose name was Ta Khang. My father explained to me that the Issarak believed that we would be freer with independence, and we could improve our standard of living.

My father instilled in me patriotism and the ideals of freedom, equality and social justice. He received his Vietnamese political training with five other comrades, named Eng, La, Theun, Ang and Im. He told us that life in the *maquis* was full of difficulties and dangers. Two days a week, in the evenings, on Saturdays and Sundays, he would learn the rudiments of the written Jaraï language, taught by Jaraï of Vietnamese origin. The lessons lasted one year. They wrote with charcoal on bamboo tubes. They were taught the concept of sacrifice, both of oneself and of one's children and the whole family.

He sometimes worked together with Eng, La, Theung, Ang and Seung, while at other times, Bong Im, Bong Lao, Bong Thon and Bong Mou were his

---

1 Khmer Issarak literally means 'free Khmer'. It was made up of a series of groups created in the wake of WWII, led by charismatic leaders and initiated by either Thailand or Vietnam. In spite of its name, the 'United Issarak' never were united: some were communists, others not-at-all. Those who referred to themselves as United Issarak were in actually members of the Khmer-Vietminh which operated mainly in eastern Cambodia from 1950 to 1954 under the auspices of the Vietminh.

fighting companions. Out of twenty people who joined the fight, only three managed to stay in the ranks; the others gave up the struggle and returned to their family homes. Only single volunteers went to complete their training in Vietnam. Out of one hundred people at the time, only two survivors remain today, generals Bou Thang[2] and Seuy Keo. At that time, Seuy Keo served as a messenger and escorted the cadres when they went from village to village, like my father did. Ong[3] Savaing, one of the Vietnamese cadres who accompanied the first Khmer revolutionaries in Ratanakiri, told me in 1967 that, among the three thousand former resistance fighters who left in 1954 for North Vietnam, including 300 came from the national minorities, the vast majority returned to their homeland in May 1970.

After my father, my uncle Lav (alias Lern) Poy Hlœun was an important influence on my understanding of the political situation. He had joined the revolutionary movement in 1951 and his political ideas were much more advanced. He started talking politics when I was 15 or 16, about 1963. He was a Jaraï, like me. He asked me to join the revolutionary movement.

In the early 1960s, the revolutionary movement in Ratanakiri – or at least in our district – was entirely Jaraï. Before the arrival of the Khmer revolutionaries, we used the Lao language to communicate between different nationalities.[4]

In 1954, after the Geneva Agreements stipulating the evacuation of all Vietminh troops from Cambodia, Laos and South Vietnam, I had another uncle who volunteered to leave for North Vietnam. He never returned, having succumbed to malaria in 1967 while he was in Laos.[5] The returnees from Hanoi, after 1970, were assigned to positions of responsibility in the military, political, cultural and health fields, but, from 1973, were very early victims of the discriminatory and repressive measures on the part of the KR leadership.[6]

---

2   Bou Thang, 1938–2019, became a senator in the present regime. He had fled to Vietnam in 1974 or 1975. See Ian G. Baird, *Rise of the Brao: Ethnic Minorities in Northeastern Cambodia During Vietnamese Occupation,* University of Wisconsin Press, 2020.

3   Ong is a title meaning Uncle or Elder Brother in Vietnamese.

4   Lao was the common language before the Khmers settled in greater numbers under the French. Lao were riparian and tribes lived on the plateau.

5   Phi Phuon explained that he had a wide and varied career, including two years in Laos, 1965–1967.

6   More than that: they were simply purged as Vietnamese spies, if they did not manage to escape back to Vietnam, like Pen Sovann (see below).

My father returned to the village in 1954 with a shotgun, when arrests of Issarak fighters stopped after the signing of the Geneva Peace Accords for Indochina. He urged his children to engage in the revolutionary struggle. He told us that we, poor peasants, suffered a great deal and, as national minorities, we suffered a much worse fate, especially since we were forbidden to access the knowledge each of us was entitled to. Not only were we deprived of basic freedoms, but we also had no democratic rights. We were despised and looked down upon like dust.

Between 1954 and 1963, my father urged us to engage in the revolution. In particular, he told his children that the struggle would be fraught with difficulties and obstacles and that finally we would win and liberate our country and our people. To do this, we needed:

First: to define the objectives to be achieved;

Secondly: the struggle requires strict discipline;

Third: it was necessary to put the interests of the country and the people above our own interests;

Fourth: abnegation, dedication and sacrifice were the watchwords that guided and inspired any revolutionary worthy of the name.[7]

He told us that life in the forest was full of risks and difficulties. He did not go to Vietnam for his training, but the trainers came from Vietnam to the village for the night and the weekends. He stole food at night in the villages. It was during the Japanese occupation, but he never saw Japanese, only French and Khmer. He was known to have entered the struggle movement, but the authorities never spotted him.

My father urged his children to engage in the revolutionary struggle. Society held us in contempt and considered us as waste. He went on to explain:

1. The struggle would be difficult, success would be assured if we kept to the strategic aim. We were clearly going to win.

2. Discipline was necessary and we had to be patient, even when we had nothing to eat. We had to manage even with bare hands and know how to find wild vegetables, fruits and animals in the forest, in order to continue the fight until the victory.

---

7   Here Phi Phuon mimics his father's lecturing style, like a schoolteacher using a blackboard.

After the 1954 Geneva Conference, the first North Vietnamese came to us in 1960, while the first American bombings affected us from 1962. It was also the year when, when I was fifteen, the chief of my village asked me to become a messenger and guard the village permanently, day and night for five days, when it was my turn. I was initially attached to three villages: first Phum Yang, then Phum Chay and finally, Phum Ta. In 1963, at the age of 16, I decided to follow my father's example by joining the ranks of the revolution despite the reluctance of my mother, as well as the idea of following Poy Hlœun (ព្យ ហ្លឺ ន), whose revolutionary name was Ta Lav. He had married my father's elder sister, Rochœm Phjing (រ៉ូ ឈឹ ង). He urged people to rebel and especially young people to be brave in the struggle for the revolution. During the period of DK, Ta Lav would become a member of the Central Committee.

I served as messenger, carrying the letters in bamboo tubes from Cambodia to Vietnam and vice versa. It was a high position that required the confidence of the highest leaders, because I carried secret documents and was in regular contact with the various cadres responsible for bases and regions. Under the revolution, there were different types of messengers, from those of villages, communes, districts, sectors and regions to those of the Central Committee of the Party. I knew three of them: the Loy brothers, Maly, Tuy and Say, belonging to the Jaraï, Tampuon and Krâchok ethnic minorities. Only the first is still alive. At the time when I served as a messenger in Ratanakiri, there were also two women messengers: Teunh, a Jaraï who still lives, and Pleik, a Krâchok who is now deceased. They carried messages over short distances, for example between the village of Chây and my village, south of the Tonlé San. They never crossed the river.

At the time, we were twenty people including three young girls who wanted to go to Vietnam. At the border, we were not accepted because the planned number had already entered. Most returned to the village, but five of us decided to live in the forest around Phnom Nga, in the mountainous village of Chây, in Talao commune on the Vietnamese border. The others were Comrades Im, Lao, Thon, and Mou Ang. We were all 16 or 17 at the time. I was the leader. We built our camp following the model of the Vietnamese camps, with a dormitory, a kitchen, a courtyard (all thatched straw and bamboo huts) and latrines. We dug our kitchen into the ground, so as not to let the smoke escape. We stayed there for a year. We cultivated fields and paddy fields and raised pigs and poultry, but not oxen or buffaloes. We must be autonomous, not steal the property of others, nor become the slaves of anyone. We were equipped with AK–47 light rifles from Czechoslovakia or the Soviet Union, and Ampiel hunting rifles. They could only use one bullet and were therefore not automatic; but when enemy planes flew low in these mountainous regions, they were easier to shoot down.

I had seen Vietnamese camps because they had come to settle on our soil. And, by the way, I had crossed the border too. At the time we did not really know where the real border line was, but now that we know it, I can say that the Vietnamese had established themselves well inside our territory, at least 10 kilometres from the border. We held a political meeting once a month. The Vietnamese who were responsible for our political education asked us, 'Where do you plan to go after living here for a year?' We answered, 'It depends only on you. We will go wherever you want!' So, the Vietnamese decided to reveal that 'the Khmer representatives will not be long in coming. Our three Vietnamese, Cambodian and Lao peoples must unite to fight together the American imperialists'. We were in regular contact with the Vietnamese. They had set up camps in our territory, so we went to their homes. We continually came and went between the two countries. We set traps and hunted for game, which we bartered for salt. We needed the salt. The Vietnamese told us to wait until our leadership gives us a plan, a mission. But they added that if we could not wait, we could go back to our village. We listened to them, but we did not know who our 'leadership' were. We did not know anything at all.

From 1965, our compatriots from Ratanakiri, especially the young people, were impressed and even fascinated by the Vietnamese fighters, all well-armed, well-disciplined and determined to dedicate themselves body and soul to the revolution. The clever propaganda they developed undoubtedly contributed to the development and acceleration of the revolutionary process in Ratanakiri, as in the whole country.

The Vietnamese did not tire of repeating to us that 'the three Vietnamese, Cambodian and Lao people are brothers who share the same grain of rice and the same clove of chilly, and who unite to fight against a common enemy: American imperialism and its lackeys.' And they added that 'After the liberation of South Vietnam, we will help you to liberate the Cambodian people from exploitation.' Finally, they did not fail to warn us: 'Your country will experience the same kind of war as at home.' The inhabitants welcomed these good words and many volunteered to serve in their ranks. The Vietnamese did not hesitate to organize themselves as in a conquered country. They set up their own camps, their own administrative structure, their own hospitals, their own production units, rice fields and vegetable gardens, and their own pig, poultry and dog farms.

In 1964, I was hospitalized in a Viétnamese hospital – Hospital No. 10. I had been injured by the strafing from US aircraft. They had strafed our village and I was hit by bomb shrapnel. I was a 'secret bodyguard'. The inhabitants had been evacuated to the forest, and the 'secret bodyguards' were preparing for the possibility of a landing of American commandos. Such operations began from the end of 1964, in order to pursue Viet Cong who took refuge in Ratanakiri. Our village was in the area next to the border. There was bombing and machine-gunning from that time. There were even deaths: in our village, many people perished. Prince Sihanouk sent planes to take the wounded civilians and have them treated in Phnom Penh. Hospital No. 10 was in the forest. I stayed there for 10 days, and when I had almost fully recovered, I came out – to return to our camp – and then continued the treatment by swallowing tablets.

We had various forms of ongoing relationships with the villagers. Through them, we learned about the general situation, especially when the enemy was preparing to launch a search operation, carried out on land by Lon Nol's[8] troops and in the air by the American Air Force, which took off from its South Vietnamese or Thai bases. The enemy was confined to the south of the Tonlé San, precisely in Kanglé, in the district of Andoung Pech, but nowadays in that of O'Yadao. Our group did not separate until mid-1967.

When Ieng Sary arrived in Ratanakiri in May 1967, I was still staying in Chây village. More precisely we were at the foot of Mount Bak Touk, where I had just settled. In December of the same year came Pol Pot, who was sick and transported in a hammock from the village of Kanglé to that of Nay. We had to walk a whole day to get from Chây to Nay.

In May, a demonstration was held in Andoung Meas district. Under the protection of our village militia, three deputy district governors, Linn, Lau and Long, led a protest against the rising price of rice and salt. More than five hundred people participated. The Phnom Penh army, commanded by a corporal, served as an intermediary, but their attempt to use force and break up the demonstration provoked the anger of the population. That happened before I met Ieng Sary and Pol Pot. In villages where people do not produce

---

8 At the time (1964), General Lon Nol (1913–1985) was both defense minister in the *Sangkum* regime (1955–1970) and chief of staff of the *Forces Armées Royales Khmères* (FARK).

enough rice, they traded with neighbouring villagers for sesame, rice and salt.

Jaraï leaders of the resistance in Vietnam came to Cambodia in 1964 and 1965 to talk to our leaders about the fate of their compatriots who were taking refuge in our country, fleeing the American bombings. They were also looking to buy edible cassava, with red grooves in their leaves, which our villagers produced in abundant quantities.

– III –

First meetings with Pol Pot and Ieng Sary

1 – Arrival of the first Khmer revolutionaries in Ratanakiri in 1964

*A*s early as 1964, the first representatives of the Workers Party of Kampuchea (WPK) arrived in Ratanakiri. This was the first time I met Khmers from the plains. They came specifically to work with the movement. What did we think about Cambodians? At that time, we did not know what it was to be a Cambodian, a Vietnamese, or a Lao. For us, these labels did not mean anything. There was no hostility. I had seen Frenchmen once as well. A dozen men on the Vietnamese border: perhaps prospectors. But I do not remember it very well. I did not know at that time that there was a revolutionary party. Nothing was clear: we were talking at that time about leading the Indochinese revolution. I did not learn of the existence of a Cambodian revolutionary movement until 1965.

We met two representatives of the Cambodian party, who arrived in Ratanakiri after passing through Mondolkiri. Bong Sim (father of Mrs Samm, who currently lives in Malay) from the province of Prey Véng, and Bong Vy were about thirty years old. The first was tall but thin, while the second was tall and strong. They were accompanied by three older Vietnamese cadres, Ong Savaing, Ong Leaing and Ong Beuk. The Vietnamese had played the role of intermediaries for the two men, who had come to establish contacts with us. The party representatives told us that, from now on, we had our own leaders, and that we were going to lead the Cambodian revolution. They said that the Cambodian, Vietnamese and Lao peoples had a common enemy: US imperialism.

Sim and Vy summoned activists from Vœunsay, Lumphat, and Bokéo districts to my camp, along with the Vietnamese. It was early in 1965. There were thirteen people for the first meeting: two from Lumphat, two from Vœunsay, two from Bokéo, myself (and the other four) and Sim and Vy – and three Vietnamese: Ong Savaing, Ong Leaing, and Ong Beuk.

Comrade Sim had a separate office built near an inexhaustible spring, three kilometres from the village. He lived there with his wife, along with two daughters (Samm and Sam) and a boy (Doh). As for Comrade Vy, he first lived in Vœunsay, then settled in Bokéo. They lived from agriculture. They first grew rice and sweet potatoes, and secondly bananas, papayas and sugar cane. At the same time, they raised pigs and poultry. They also set traps to catch game. Finally, they hunted deer. They had no cars or bicycles. Everyone walked. Comrade Sim and his family spoke Jaraï.

I did not understand Khmer, but Comrade Lae, a Jaraï who knew Khmer, served as an interpreter. I was useful because I knew the geography of this region and knew where to find the Vietnamese. At the time, I was at the O'Ampor-Kuliv office at Phnom Ngak, located in the Naga's Tail region, at the junction of Cambodia, Laos and Vietnam. In 1979, three thousand KR fighters would find refuge in Chak York. The region is dominated by high mountains, and currently is uninhabited.

Immediately after they had settled in early 1965, these revolutionaries convened a three-day seminar during which were taught lessons on politics, health and guerrilla warfare. They urged us to prepare for a long-term political struggle, closely associated with guerrilla activities. When I first met them at the end of 1964, they told me, 'Now, with us, the revolution comes to your home. Be ready to raise your banner and resolutely fight to make it triumph!' They also took the initiative to set up messenger rest stations in the villages of Châk and Nay. They hid the messages in bamboo tubes, which we carried to the Vietnamese. These, in return, entrusted to us theirs that they put in the same tubes and intended for our leaders. To go from one rest station to another, it took two days' walk.

Sim and Vy asked me to set up three offices for meetings, two north of the Tonlé San and the third southwest of the Tonlé San. For security reasons, we did not settle in one place, but our specific task was to extend geographically the influence of the movement. The southwest office was in Malik village, Bokéo District, south of the river. Since Vœunsay is in the north, there was an office on the edge of both banks. The third was on the site of our office of origin, near the Vietnamese border. This place is called Phnom Ngork; it was there, formerly, that the French had raised a flag.

In each office, a covered area had been built for study – a room for political meetings, six houses – as dormitories, a school, a refectory and a kitchen. Among us five, one person ran each office. Myself, I stayed one more year, until the end of 1966, in Phnom Ngork – but I travelled from one office to another. In these three offices, the main activity – the main goal – was to arouse and extend the revolutionary movement, to formulate propaganda slogans and make them known to the population. Slogans like 'For an independent Cambodia!' 'National forces are the essential forces for independence!' 'We must also mobilize international support for independence!' There was talk of independence in the sense of independence from the Americans, and from American imperialism. We were already predicting a coup d'état, and a civil war would not fail to occur after that.

We also studied a paper on class struggle between the rich and the poor. I saw this document in 1965, after Vy's arrival. It said, 'The poor must rise up against exploitation. The forces of the poor must be mobilized to rise up against the domination of the rich. The rich were the capitalists, the compradors, the landowners, and so on – no matter where we were'. For us, there was no land problem, except for the existence of a state rubber plantation at Labansiek, led by a Frenchman.[1] The document was in Khmer, translated into Lao – and we translated it from Lao into Jaraï, Tampuon, Krœung and Brao, the languages of the region. It was translated by my aunt's husband, Ta Lav, who spoke Khmer, Lao, Jaraï, Krâchok, Krœung, and Brao. He was in Malik's office, where Va also lived, but Ta Lav was mobile; he moved a lot. Another polyglot, named Thin, was of Tampuon nationality and also spoke Vietnamese. He would participate in the liberation of Phnom Penh, but in 1976 he would leave for Vœunsay, where he would belong to the regional committee. After 1979, he became military leader of the Northeast region. Now he is a colonel in the Royal Army, and deputy chief of staff of Military Sector 101.

At that time, in 1966, there was still no talk of the Party, but of the revolutionary movement; and we did not use the word 'Angkar'; we were talking about 'the top echelon'. That year, three delegates were sent to a national meeting in Kompong Cham, near the Vietnamese border – Ta Lav, my aunt's husband, Lann and Ing – but they have all died since. At the time, I did not know they had gone there or that it was a Central Committee meeting, or that

---

1   Named Georges Bonzon. He later became the head of the state coffee plantation at Païlin and was assassinated by the KR in 1979.

they had decided to move the headquarters to Ratanakiri. However, I think they made that decision for security reasons, because there was American bombing. They wanted to have a secure base, surrounded by a safe population – this was the case of national minorities – and a fairly large living space. A base in a region of forests and mountains was favourable in all these respects. They were also aware that there was a hidden insurgency of national minorities against Phnom Penh. So, the terrain was favourable.

2 – Arrival of Vietnamese regulars and the beginning of American bombings

Around 1965, the first Viet Cong fighters arrived in my village. At first, they were not very numerous and they settled near the village of Nhang, about 16 km from the border, and also near the villages of Ta Nga, Chây and Chhay. Today, Vietnam has fully annexed the village of Nhang and half of the villages of Chây and Ta Nga. However, the Vietnamese revolutionaries did not settle inside our villages, but in the surrounding forest. They were in Phnom Voa, Phum Chae, Khum[2] Talao, in Andoung Meas District. Soon, they arrived in large numbers, thousands or even tens of thousands, and with new weapons. They told us they wanted to free 'Prey Nokor',[3] and then they would liberate Cambodia. These troops lived on their own and did not mix with the tribal populations. At first, they only discreetly transited through the territory. They recruited people to clear footpaths in the forest that later broadened into bicycle paths, to transport rice to feed the soldiers. Then they penetrated as much as 30 kilometres into Cambodia, and the Americans tracked them; there were bombings as far as Bokéo and Banlung. At first, we did not have any weapons, but the Vietnamese soldiers walking through were exhausted and short of food. They needed pork and dogs that we exchanged for arms. From the beginning, the Americans targeted these Vietnamese troops. I explained all of this to the Tribunal (31 July, pp. 33–34).

---

2   *Phum* is the Khmer word for 'village' and *khum* means 'commune'; Talao was a township of Lao on the Tonlé San. I went there at Christmas 1965 and was impressed by the beautiful wooden houses, reminiscent of those in Laos. I was invited there by my landlord, Colonel Srey Meas, who was in charge of the region. On the way, we saw the rusty remains of tanks from the First Indochina War. Srey Meas, by then a general, and his wife and four children, were massacred by the KR at the beginning of the DK regime.

3   Prey Nokor is the Cambodian name of Saïgon before the Đại Việt conquered it in the early 17th Century.

The first American bombardments on my village began in February 1962. In October of the same year, these bombings caused twelve dead and wounded. They were intended to free the South Vietnamese forces from Viet Cong attacks. Between 1962 and 1967, the Americans continued their bombings, but on the Vietnamese side. At the same time, they raided the valleys and plains, forcing the inhabitants to seek refuge in the forests. The Vietnamese told us that soon these bombings would spread to Cambodia. From 1965, the inhabitants of my village, Phum Koet, commune of Talao, Andoung Meas District in Ratanakiri, ten kilometres from Vietnam, all returned to the forest to escape the raids. First, we took refuge in the *chamkar* (slash-and-burn fields) whose harvest we picked up. Then we took refuge in the forest with the products from this harvest.

The Americans intensified the bombings in late 1965 destroying homes and killing livestock. Towards the end of 1967 and the beginning of 1968, it was mainly the giant B–52 bombers that were at work, especially between the villages of Koet and Chê, and between the villages of Ta Nga and Nhang, where all the inhabitants sought refuge in the forest. Americans were also bombing rivers because they were mistaking mist for smoke from kitchens. We dug the ground to install our kitchens, taking care not to let the smoke escape. In the forest where the villagers had taken refuge, they took good care to hide in trenches they had dug with their own hands.

The US bombardments surged in 1969 and early 1970. Those of March 1970 killed 31 villagers and injured one. I saw the helicopters of the Phnom Penh government come to evacuate the dead and wounded towards Phnom Penh. After the overthrow of Sihanouk on 18 March, they paused before resuming even more intensely in 1972 and 1973. The USA threw a huge number of bombs during 200 days in 1973, as I told the Tribunal (31 July, p. 36). No casualties were reported in my own village. But in neighbouring villages, Ta Nga and Nhang (now a commune), there were two deaths. That commune was made up of twelve villages, each of which had more than fifty families. Mine, for example, was home to more than two hundred families, so more than a thousand people. For a long time, there had been no elephants. It was the same for all the communes in the entire district.

Some inhabitants joined the revolutionary movement after the American bombardments in 1965, but not that many. Moreover, from 1965, our compatriots from Ratanakiri, especially the young people, were particularly impressed, even fascinated by Vietnamese fighters: all well-armed, well-disciplined and determined to devote themselves body and soul to the revolution. The example they represented, as well as the clever propaganda they conducted, undoubtedly contributed to the development and speeding up of the revolutionary process in Ratanakiri Province, as in the whole country. Besides, our first modern weapons were acquired from the Vietnamese fighters. We exchanged food for guns. The number increased exponentially from 1968 and especially after 23 March 1970, when Prince Norodom Sihanouk called for our compatriots to join him in the *maquis* to fight the US-supported government of Lon Nol.

3 – First meetings with Ieng Sary and Pol Pot

In the years 1967 and 1968, there were only four Khmers in Ratanakiri: Comrade Pouk (Pol Pot), Comrade Van (Ieng Sary), after Comrades Sim and Bâng (Brother) Vy, who were already on the spot. At the beginning of the rainy season in May 1967, and to establish relations with the Vietnamese, Ieng Sary arrived for the first time at Ngork in Ratanakiri, accompanied by Comrade Thin, his bodyguard. There were rain showers all the time. He was welcomed by Comrade Len, a Tampuon from Stung Treng. On Len's suggestion, we established a Jaraï base near Talao commune in 1966, having as its staff myself, then aged 19 and from the village of Malik, Bong Mali, aged 30, and Bong Phéng a 22-year-old, both from the village of Chây. I, myself, had my uncle-in-law, named Ta Lav, while the others received the political influence of Ong Savaing, one of the Vietnamese cadres who accompanied the first representatives of the WPK in Ratanakiri.

Ieng Sary came from the village of Krâleng, in Bokéo District – where they were going to set up *Munthi Muey Roy*, 'Office 100'. At first, I did not know about it because it was secret. But afterwards, I learned that he came from Mondolkiri and Kratieh. After arriving in Krâleng in July, he went up to my place and gave me a message in a bamboo tube. He told me to take it to the Vietnamese. It was only after reading this message that the Vietnamese came to see him in Ngork. After contacting the Vietnamese, Ieng Sary returned to Office 102, which was also in Krâleng.

From July 1967 until December – when Pol Pot arrived – Ieng Sary organized the region and became its regional secretary. Office 100 and Office 102 were close to each other, one kilometre apart. There was a stream called O'Tœk Chrap (or O'Kap), and both offices were on the bank of the stream.

Office 100 was upstream and 102 downstream. A third base was between the two, named the Office of Ta Krit. Kamphay and Thang Si lived there, both cadres of the Lao minority. They are dead now. The Ta Krit Office was a reception centre, a 'reception' office, for people coming from outside, base cadres who came from elsewhere, the cadres of the security contingents – the units that constituted the nucleus of the eventual KR revolutionary army. Initially, they were secret bodyguards.

Around November 1967, I came to live with Sim at Malik's office. I became his bodyguard. Sim and Vy comprised the Northeast Regional Committee until the arrival of Ieng Sary. I was with Sim only three months. Then, in 1968, the armed uprising got started following the combing by the government troops along the road through Andoung Meas District.

Tall and rather slim, Ieng Sary had a fair complexion and was easily taken for a foreigner, especially when he spoke with the strong accent characteristic of Cambodians from South Vietnam.[4] He wore black pants and a white shirt whose pocket always was filled with a small notebook and two ballpoint pens, one in blue ink and the other in red. He did not smoke. He walked with a stick, swinging his arms, his back slightly arched, a rucksack on his back. Under a somewhat severe appearance (we rarely saw him smile and even less joke), he favoured persuasion over coercion, preferring to convince rather than compel. He regularly listened to news from around the world, especially the BBC broadcasts in Vietnamese. He did not fail to note in his notebook the main international events. He did the same when I reported my actions during my five-day mission. He lived a simple and well-regulated life, getting up very early in the morning and going to bed very late. He had normal relations with his collaborators, villagers and ethnic minorities. He liked to ask questions about the living and working conditions of the villagers. He listened attentively and noted meticulously in his little notebook all that we reported to him. He visited my office, located in Lvang Sos, in May 1967. That is when I first met him. He inquired first of all about my state of health and that of my comrades, before asking how long we had settled there. As I did not yet understand Khmer, he communicated through his interpreter, Comrade Lon, a Jaraï like me. I soon became Lon's bodyguard. I told Ieng Sary we had been there for over a year. So, he went on to ask if we knew the geography of this place and the surrounding area.

---

4   Ieng Sary was born in Cochinchina and his Khmer accent was closer to Phi Phuon's than to those of Pol Pot and other Phnom Penh-based intellectuals.

Two months after his arrival, Ieng Sary summoned some sixty cadres from all the northeast ethnic minorities (Jaraï, Lao, Krâchok, Krœung, Brao, Tampuon), including only one woman, to a political seminar at his office. He asked us if we knew where the headquarters of the Vietnamese revolutionary forces were. As I responded positively and said that I knew the geography of the region well, he told me that he would give me an important mission: to carry a message to the Vietnamese leaders, placed in a tube of bamboo. He insisted on confirming that I knew them well, and especially where they lived, because there were many Vietnamese in the area. As I was sure of nothing, he instructed me to memorize their four-digit code, adding that 'it is important to recognize that the mission certainly is difficult but, with diligence and perseverance, you will eventually achieve the desired result.' Then he said, 'If you succeed in this mission, I will give you others, because there is a lot of work to be done! The mission you have to carry out requires five days to complete.' My cousin was my interpreter since I did not speak Khmer yet. At that time, I knew some Vietnamese words like 'eat' or 'where are you going?' Or 'I got lost' and especially 'I want to go to the headquarters'.

The first day, I came back empty-handed because I forgot the four-digit number. The second day was like the first: it was a failure too. On the third and fourth day, it was still impossible for me to reach the goal. I took two days to search along the right side of the Hô Chi Minh Trail and two more along the left side, but to no avail. Ieng Sary, on the fifth day, recommended that I go further north on this multi-branched trail to find the central base of the Vietnamese, which I finally managed to find north of the Tonlé San.

It extended some 300 meters on both sides of the road in the middle of the forest and several kilometres inside our territory, and it was inaccessible to villagers. It was protected like a garrison, with a line of trenches dug one and a half meters deep in a kind of no-man's-land sandy clay soil. They had cleared all the undergrowth and kept only all the tall trees. There were many tents and hammocks, and also underground facilities, but no straw huts or cabins. In fact, Vietnamese guerrillas were stationed all along the Hô Chi Minh Trail, about 5,000 men in 1967, but had been there long before, in bases surrounded by deep trenches and barbed wire. We can still see these trenches today.

I recognized the place according to the four-digit code and handed the bamboo, about forty centimetres long, to a tall Vietnamese with light skin that revealed his North Vietnamese origin. I could not know his name or his age. I was given the response about an hour later. After receiving the message, he simply told me that tomorrow morning at around 9 o'clock, he would go in person to the place chosen by mutual agreement, in this case O'Thong Chvê (or O'Tang Chnaè), located three kilometres from our headquarters. But instead of the Vietnamese official, it was rather his bodyguard who came to carry the promised message, contained, like ours, in a bamboo tube. This camp, established in 1965, still exists today despite our repeated requests and serves as the headquarters of the 5th or 7th Military District of the Vietnamese People's Army. Ieng Sary stayed only one week at my office before returning to his, located in the village of Krâleng.

I did not really know Ieng Sary until after the liberation of Phnom Penh, while I was in charge of security at the Ministry of Foreign Affairs. When he gave directions, he usually did it succinctly without going too much into the details, leaving us with a broad possibility for creativity in applying a decision. He often insisted on the art of directing, namely strictly respecting the main steps to follow before arriving at any conclusion or decision. The first step was to apprehend a concrete situation as it actually was, without altering or distorting it. The second consisted of a concrete analysis of the facts in an objective way, taking into account the favourable aspects and the negative factors before putting forward a proposal worthy of the name, in order to arrive at a solution.

Ieng Sary moved to Office 102, a couple of kilometres from Office 100 where Pol Pot, then known as Ta Pouk, settled. He came from the village of Krâleng, south of the Tonlé San to my new office north of the river. Pol Pot, surrounded by bodyguards armed with rifles and AK–47 Kalashnikovs, arrived in Ratanakiri in December 1967 with comrades Vin,[5] Khan and Thin, a Tampuon; Bong Dam, his Cambodian personal physician and the brother of Kheang Kaonn (who now lives in Païlin); and bodyguards Bong Youn, Bong Souey and Bong Khon, all ethnic minorities. From my office, it took four days to walk to Office 100.

I first met Ta Pouk in December 1967, when he had malaria. Normally, Pol Pot and Ieng Sary walked on foot, like the others. But Pol Pot was sick the first time I saw him, and he was carried in a hammock (we did not use stretchers) to a Vietnamese hospital for treatment. 'Hospital No. 5' was next to Mount Ngork, in

---

5   In fact, Chhim Sam Aok had been recruited by Son Sen at age 17, while a schoolboy, and later took the revolutionary name of Pâng but was also known as Vin. He became Pol Pot's chief administrative assistant at Office 870, the Party Centre in Phnom Penh. He was arrested in 1978, interrogated, tortured and executed at S–21.

the forest. I was one of his porters. He was seriously ill. Ieng Sary, accompanied by two bodyguards, was also travelling. He stayed almost one month before being discharged from hospital in mid-January 1968. After the Vietnamese informed us of his recovery, we went to the hospital to escort him back to Office 100. He was walking, but let himself be carried as he felt too tired. He did not want to be carried, but when he was too tired, he had to resign himself to it.

He rested on a bamboo bed without a mattress, using his bundle as a pillow. He had brought with him a blanket, a mosquito net, a towel and a *krâma* (traditional scarf). He also had his own hammock. He ate only rice soup with cooked dry fish and drank only boiled water. Dam, a nurse from the *Sangkum* era, served him as a personal physician.

At that time, I spoke a few words of Khmer – but not very well. And with him, I did not say anything. Not a word. I just carried him. If someone asked me something, I would answer. But other than that, I remained mum. I only remember that he asked me, 'Are you tired?' And I said, 'it does not matter.'

I had already been told that he was the main leader. He was very handsome, white-skinned,[6] and I thought he looked like a Chinese. Later, when I saw him again, he asked me my name and where I lived – which village, which district, what minority, how long I had spent in the bush. I told him, 'Since 1963'. He had an interpreter with him. He visited my 'office' to see the different facilities I had set up. Wild fruits were picked: *kuy*, red fruits, and *makprey*, like little wild mangos. We had traps to catch fish, and I dug a well to keep the fish alive. I had also set traps to catch wild fowl and deer. I salted the meat and gave it to him. He really enjoyed it all. He was very happy, and between him and me, bonds of friendship and affection were forged.

Pol Pot lived in Office 100, with his wife and Vin. At 102 lived Ieng Sary and his wife, along with Keo Meas,[7] who was a Central Committee member, and his wife, Yem. Those two, I did not see them after 1968 or 1969, and I do not know where they went. To protect them, there were heaps of traps all around – with bamboo spikes, spears, and snares hanging over the heads.

6   This is why he was named 'Sâr' = 'white' in Khmer, when he was born.

7   From 1954, Keo Meas (1926–1976), an ex-Issarak, was head of the revolutionary committee in Phnom Penh. He met Mao in Beijing in 1952 and co-founded the Pracheachon Party, the official branch of the clandestine Khmer People's Revolutionary Party. He accompanied Pol Pot to Hanoi in 1965 and stayed there, a victim of malaria. A member of the Central Committee, from 1969 he was the KR representative in Hanoi until 1975. Accused of being pro-Vietnamese, he was arrested on 20 September 1976, taken to S–21, and executed one month later.

We did not have mines – not yet. There were guards: groups of five people. And patrols around, with bows and poisoned arrows. We had guns – Enfield carbines, some MAS 36,[8] and AK–47s too – but very few. We also had powder guns, which were used to hunt.

Aged 43 at that time, Pol Pot was a handsome man, well-built, relatively tall, but rather slim and with a broad face. He never raised his voice when he spoke. He articulated his words slowly, often accompanied by a slight smile. His voice was soft and he spoke clearly, which allowed me to quickly understand him. He wore a black shirt with white buttons, and carried a notebook and two ballpoint pens, one red and one black. He had a sense of humour and sometimes joked. He was a *bon vivant*.

When we heard the turtledoves cooing, he did not fail to ask us if we knew them well. Sometimes, in the face of the privations and hardships we were exposed to, he could not help worrying about the effects they might have on us while expressing his admiration for our compatriots of ethnic minorities who had succeeded, in the face of such a situation, in preserving, by themselves, a life in the natural state while preserving their identity. He cited as an example the construction of houses whose different elements were tied not with the help of nails but with creepers. In the same way, we collected all our daily food from nature: leaves, fruits, meat and fish. Even more, women could give birth even without midwives or doctors. His presentations and comments on a particular situation or topic were put into notes that could serve as lessons for us. For example: how to defend a support base? We just had to dig traps, plant piles and mount snares, and erect a protective enclosure. He wrote down in a booklet all our ways of life and abilities that he wished his compatriots to emulate. Every newcomer would be given a copy of these instructions.[9]

From 1967 to 1970, I met Pol Pot only four times. The first was at Office 100; the second on the banks of the Tonlé San; the third when he gave me instructions on guerrilla warfare, and the last on the occasion of the awarding of the prize given to me when I got first place in the competition for the best guerrilla soldier in the year 1969. On each of these occasions, he was always affable and eager, being the first in front of us to shake hands and inquire about our health before asking if we were tired after such a long walk.

---

8   The MAS Modèle 36, also known as the *Fusil à répétition 7 mm S M. 36*, is a military rifle. First adopted in 1936 by France, it was in use long past the World War II period.

9   Unfortunately, this booklet has long been lost and no investigator has ever seen it.

I would not really know Pol Pot until after 1970, when I accompanied him during the long march that took us from Ratanakiri to Stœung Chinit in the province of Kompong Cham, on the edge of Kompong Thom. On his return from Beijing in May 1970, when we met again, he remembered me well and asked if I would agree to serve him as a bodyguard and go down with him 'below', that is to say, towards the plain. I noticed that Ratanakiri people respected him and loved him very much. I was a messenger at first, because I had mastered geography. I was filled with a sense of responsibility and I loved him. I considered him a comrade in arms. Before giving us a task, he made sure we were able to do it. He was imbued with a spirit of gentleness and politeness. He was very affable and not at all abrupt or rude. His words were mesmerizing and revealed his goodness, while showing a lot of modesty. We had full confidence in him and were ready to put our lives in his hands. We did everything to accomplish the tasks he asked of us and we could never blame him or find that he was wrong.

He was a born orator who captivated his audience with sober yet persuasive eloquence. When he spoke, he was very careful not to hurt anyone. He preferred irony to controversy. If he ever submitted a document, he was unparalleled when it came to identifying what it really meant and making it real. He was often seen leaning on his desk, absorbed in writing, always writing. When he listened to the radio for news, he moved from time to time to take notes. He did not complain about anything, neither of the weather nor of the food. His simplicity, kindness and courtesy were worthy of the affection and respect given by those around him. During meals, he avoided addressing political issues; instead, he preferred to tell anecdotes or funny stories, relaxing the atmosphere, making us forget for a time the nuisances of everyday life. In Ratanakiri, Pol Pot never left his headquarters to visit the inhabitants.

From 1971 to 1979, I attended a total of five political study seminars that he organized. These re-education or 'life' seminars were organized by alternating presentations addressed to all trainees present and sessions in small groups. Written documents would later be distributed to all participants. They were addressed to all civilian and military cadres in the country from regions, sectors and districts. Participants could reach up to 100. During the civil war, these seminars took place during the rainy season, the dry season being taken by the armed struggle. One would choose a person who would voice his self-criticism in front of everyone, detailing his strengths and weaknesses. In this first period of national and democratic revolution, the *yothea* (soldier) must show a fighting spirit and resolve in the struggle to win. Civilian cadres (*kamaphibal*) must work to consolidate the rear bases at all levels. I was considered a civilian and I did not understand military issues, although I had followed three months of strategy courses with the Vietnamese and in Vietnamese language. As a bodyguard, I took care of Pol Pot's close protection while attending the conferences he conducted. Likewise, I also listened carefully to what was said on the platform and to the views expressed by cadres and combatants.

The purpose of these indoctrination sessions was to make us aware of what we must do and what we should not do in carrying out our tasks. Action by free consent must take precedence over that obtained by constraint or coercion. The political leader would assume responsibility in all areas and in all aspects, while the commander would deal only with military techniques, that is, problems related to combat at the front.

Pol Pot would speak in the morning from 7:30 to 11:00. To sustain attention for so long, he knew how to intersperse his speech with humorous notes and many real-world examples. Whether it was Nuon Chea, Khieu Samphân, Ieng Sary, Son Sen or Ta Mok, none had this ability to fascinate us for so long. All laughed and were happy to listen to him: they fell under the charm and magic of his words. He had a prodigious memory. He could remember the names of all the localities he once visited. Similarly, on a military map, he could accurately indicate where the posts and fortifications of the enemy were installed and when they had been installed.

When it came to revolutionary introspection, before we heard him explain its meaning, we did not know what to do. But once we had learnt it, we were able to comply with it accordingly. He was unrivalled when it came to telling an anecdote or a funny story, raising the hilarity of the audience. He often insisted on the prevalence of dialectic materialism: everything was connected, everything evolved, everything was governed by the law of the unity of opposites, every quantitative change was eventually transformed into a qualitative change. A given action would lead to a result that had both positive and negative aspects. It was important for us to identify the objective and subjective causes, to be able to propose appropriate solutions. It required in advance a thorough and comprehensive analysis of all the data connected to the problem.

After the general lectures, we had small-group introspection sessions. For example, we chose a person first, who practised it in front of everyone, detailing his strengths and weaknesses, and so on with each person present.

In concluding his reflections, Pol Pot emphasized that every human being can make mistakes, but the most important thing was that he would recognize them and be determined to correct them. While the vast majority managed to adapt, there were still some who failed and decided to put an end to their lives.

He would cite the example of Vietnam, which surpassed us both in terms of area and number of its population. In addition, the northern part of the country, which had already regained its independence, constituted a solid base.[10] The situations prevailing in the three countries – Cambodia, Laos and Vietnam – were different from one another. It was the same for their respective populations as regards the development of the revolutionary movement. Following the example of certain peoples who had already managed to emancipate themselves by their own efforts, he said, ours is determined to follow the same path and not to shrink from this responsibility. Since then, especially since the coup d'état of 1970, the revolutionary movement in our country had continued to develop and gain in magnitude and power, like the tumultuous waves that, in their hurried course, break dikes and dams. The liberated territory then continued to expand from the original five provinces to include the entire country, except for the larger cities.

It was from this period that the key principles that constitute the foundations of the KR ideology were formulated and elaborated: to be independent and sovereign, to count only on one's own strength and to support one's own needs. This concept was concretely translated on the ground by 'attacking the enemy to snatch their arms and with these weapons to fight them'. With the vast newly liberated area, having gotten rid of the human obstacles – of feudal and other landowners and agents of the enemy – the revolutionary forces now had a larger and more secure base to move forward in their struggle. When the Vietnamese wanted to launch their attacks against South Vietnam, we told them: go ahead! 'We shall fend for ourselves without your assistance.'

It is instructive, in this respect, to draw a parallel between the positions of the two protagonists: the Cambodian Communists and the Vietnamese Communists. The former would stick to their independence and sovereignty, while the latter would feed a hegemonic ambition towards their neighbour. Before 1975, the Vietnamese asked the Cambodians for permission to establish sanctuaries on their territory. But they refused to evacuate their

---

10 Note here that Pol Pot did not consider that South Vietnam had achieved its independence, but that it had become 'a colony' of the USA.

troops once Vietnam was liberated. Furthermore, in 1973, the Vietnamese negotiated peace in Paris with the Americans, leaving them free to spread havoc in Cambodia with their bombings. In addition to this characteristic treachery, they exerted on us incessant pressures to follow their example. But our refusal to negotiate and our determination to continue the fight alone culminated in victory on 17 April 1975, demonstrating that we were right. From January 1975, the Vietnamese admitted to having been wrong to negotiate with the Americans and resumed the war, which they certainly won – but we Cambodians won our war first!

Moreover, during the years 1971 and 1972, during the Chenla I and Chenla II operations that took place on National Road No. 6, the revolutionary Cambodians and their Vietnamese comrades had divided sectors of the front to fight the enemy. While Cambodians generally succeeded in their operations, the same cannot be said of the Vietnamese. The latter were only really effective in the vicinity of large cities populated by large numbers of their compatriots. The Cambodians held the Road No. 6 section at Prek Kdam, as well as Road No. 5 at Prey Khmer in Kompong Chhnang Province. In 1973, we managed to cut all linkages between Prek Phneou and Prek Kdam. Lon Nol's troops then remained entrenched at Sala Lek Pram, Longvek and Oudong. This illustrates the effectiveness of the strategy of guerrilla war and popular war developed by Pol Pot who, like Mao, advocated the encircling of the city by the countryside.

– IV –

Other revolutionary leaders arrive; the civil war begins

1 – Nuon Chea

I did not have the opportunity to meet Nuon Chea[1] when he went on a short visit to Ratanakiri in 1969. I saw him for the first time in 1971, when he came alone to Office 870.[2] We only got there two days before. He lived apart from Pol Pot, but worked with him all the time.

He is tall and light-skinned, and has a sturdy constitution; he is readily taken for a Chinese businessman – which is not surprising since his father was an immigrant from China. It was also under this appearance that he had acted as Brother Number Two for decades in the entire country, while constantly hiding to conceal his true identity.[3] 'Since I met him, I have considered him

---

1   Nuon Chea (1926–2019) or 'Brother Number Two', whose real name was Long Bunrot, was the son of a Chinese immigrant businessman who sent him to Thailand for his secondary and higher education during WWII. During the years Pol Pot was in Ratanakiri to launch the revolution, Nuon Chea was in charge of the rest of the country. He is the one who set his country ablaze, before Pol Pot, by starting the civil war in Battambang in January 1968. Although he was Pol Pot's equal partner at the apex of power in the DK regime, this was not widely known beyond the inner circles of the leadership. He ended his tumultuous life in August 2019, at the ECCC prison in Phnom Penh after having been sentenced to life for genocide and crimes against humanity.

2   Office 870, along the Chinit River, on the border of the provinces of Kompong Cham and Kompong Thom, was the code number of the secret base of Pol Pot and the KR leadership during the civil war, a code that was kept after the KR victory of 17 April 1975 in Phnom Penh.

3   Unlike all other communist regimes, no one – inside or outside the country – knew at the time who the leaders were, except the Vietnameses communists. The only public person was Ieng Sary, the Minister of Foreign Affairs. Fr Ponchaud, who listened to the KR radio in Khmer while they were in power, was the first Westerner to identify the leader as Pol Pot-Saloth Sâr, in 1976. Most people did not believe him. Even inside the country, most people could never listen to the radio; essentially, its broadcasts were intended for cadres.

After 7 January 1979, the Communist Party of Vietnam announced that the regime had been led by 'the Pol Pot-Ieng Sary clique'. Its members were tried in absentia in Phnom Penh and sentenced to death. Except perhaps in the Ratanakiri days (1967–1970), and in Ratanakiri only, as reported by Phi Phuon, Ieng Sary was *never* the Khmer Rouge's No. 2, as the Vietnamese claimed for propaganda reasons. They knew it was Nuon Chea, but did

one of the leaders I have loved and respected. I was devoted to him. As for his personality, he was an educated man. He was humble and gentle, and knew the Buddhist discipline. He knew the Buddhist religion well. That was what I noticed.'[4]

In January 1972, along with three other bodyguards, I had the opportunity to accompany him when he visited his wife, who had remained in Sraê Andaung, her native village, located in Kompong Tralach District in the province of Kompong Chhnang. She was living at Office 24 with their children, a boy and two girls. We visited them as we returned from a trip to Samlaut and the northwest. All around their house were fields of sugar cane and orange groves. His wife, Ly Kim Seng (aka Sorn), lived surrounded by her son, her two daughters and her old parents. She warmly received us, but was surprised that I and another guard, Tuon, who was Krœung, did not speak Khmer correctly. We stayed with them for five days before returning to our base.

We went as far as Samlaut, where Nuon Chea met with Ros Nhim,[5] president of the Northwest region and his deputy, Kong Sophâl alias Keu, and Tol, Vanh, Samay, San and Khek Pèn (aka Sou), all members of the Regional

not take him to court in 1979 because they thought Nuon Chea was their friend (he had been educated in revolutionary lore by Lé Duan, spoke excellent Vietnamese and had been their chief negotiating partner from 1960 to 1977) and they hoped to put him at the head of the PRK, the new pro-Viet regime. In actual fact, Nuon Chea had always been very deft at hiding his true feelings and was virulently anti-Viet. He knew that only imperialist Vietnam could grab power from the KR to recreate French Indochina under their auspices. As I explain below in Part III, Nuon Chea was the main conceiver of the most exotic tenets of DK ideology, more than Pol Pot, as he confessed in 1978 to the Communist Party of Denmark. There, he underlined too that absolute *secrecy* was the path to victory. When Tou Samouth (No. 1 in the movement) was killed by Sihanouk's police in 1962, Nuon Chea was already No. 2. He refused to become No. 1 and pushed forward No. 3 – Saloth Sâr – for the sake of remaining safely in the dark. Moreover, it was his uncle who had betrayed Tou Samouth to Sihanouk's secret police. He placed Saloth Sâr on the front line, promising him to be always by his side while taking together all major decisions. Nuon Chea indeed launched the violent revolution from Battambang in January 1968, while Ta Pouk launched it in Ratanakiri only in April – with the contribution of Phi Phuon. To this very day, and even after his death in 2019, Nuon Chea remains a blurry figure of the KR revolution and only Pol Pot's name is branded by all analysts, thus privileging the Vietnamese propagandists and ignoring reality. Nuon Chea also managed to say almost nothing at the Tribunal. Finally, he was the one in charge of the entire prison-extermination centres, above Son Sen, and therefore primarily responsible for the widespread massacres under DK.

4   Portrait by Phi Phuon given at the ECCC on 31 July 2012, in answer to a question by Son Arun, Nuon Chea's national defence lawyer, p. 45.

5   Ros Nhim, 1922–1978, joined the Khmer Issarak in 1946 (and also the Communist Party of Thailand) and the CPK Central Committee in 1963 as secretary of the Northwest region and is said to have instigated the 1967 Samlaut Rebellion. He became a member of the Party's

Committee. The journey was through the dense forests of the Cardamoms, avoiding the usual paths for security reasons. We did not meet any living soul except the Pors, the only ethnic minority in the region. They are quite tall and light in colour, like Chinese. They speak a language that is incomprehensible to us. Like us, they practice slash and burn cultivation. They dress normally and are busy picking up cardamom seeds for sale in Thailand.

We moved mostly on foot, sometimes on elephant backs or on a tractor. We had two elephants, each under the control of two mahouts and that could carry four people. During the trip, I happened to play mahout for part of the journey. When you tap on the right, it turns left and when you tap on the left, it goes to the right. In the morning, the elephant got started at five o'clock. At nine o'clock, we must let him rest. At four o'clock in the afternoon, he resumed the road until seven o'clock in the evening. On such a long trip, it was recommended not to force the elephant too much. Overworked, if he ever stumbled and fell, he would never get up again. At night, you had to chain it to a tree and light up a fire; otherwise it would not sleep. It was given food, especially at night, but it kept throwing its trunk right and left to catch and chew bamboo and other foliage along the way. To prevent it from eating too much, we just hit him in the head with the mahout stick.

Before heading to Office 24, we made a detour to visit Ta Mok,[6] president of the Southwest region, who had settled north of Mount Pis and west of Amleang in Kompong Speu Province. He was surrounded by Sèm Pal, Chong, Sé, Soeung, Sary and Srâh, all members of this regional committee. As soon as he met us, Ta Mok asked me dryly: 'What is your ethnic origin?' I answered him on the spot: 'We belong to the minorities', but without specifying which ones. And without waiting for the answer, he continued in a tone not devoid of nastiness: 'What do you want to eat?' And I told him that we ate what we were given to eat. We stayed five days at the headquarters of the Southwest

standing committee in 1975 and was purged at S–21 in June 1978, accused by Nuon Chea of having formed a secret plot with Sao Phœm to overturn the regime.

6   Ta Mok or Chhit Chhœun (1924–2006) has become a symbol of KR ferocity, along with Duch. Acting much as a warlord since the days of the First Indochina War (1946–1954) and under the direct leadership of Nuon Chea, he orchestrated murderous purges in all regions during the DK regime, beyond his own Southwest (*Nirdey*) region. Nuon Chea, the ultimate authority of S–21 prison (now Tuol Sleng Museum), was an arch-believer in vast plots to destroy the revolutionary leadership. Ta Mok was arrested by the Cambodian authorities in March 1999, before the ECCC was established, and died in a military prison in 2006 without going on trial. Of Chinese descent, he was buried, and not incinerated, in a lavish funeral ceremony organized by his sizable extended family.

region before continuing our journey. I cannot know what the discussions between Nuon Chea and Ta Mok were, for the simple reason that I was in no way qualified to attend the meetings.

Returning from the northwest, we stopped at Mount Aural pagoda, where we spent the night by the river that bears the same name and flows into the great Tonlé Sap Lake through Oudong, in the province of Kompong Speu. From Office 24, a car from Sector 304 took us directly to Kompong Thmâr, from where we continued the trip by boat to Office 870. We did not arrive there until April 1972.

During the trip, Nuon Chea told us that the Party had given us a mission to fulfil. It was about getting in touch with the leaders of the Northwest region and making them understand the main problem of the day: it was holding the enemy forces in the West to prevent them from sending reinforcements to Phnom Penh. To achieve this goal, it was imperative to cut portions of National Road No. 5 and sections of the Railways, both between Battambang and Pursat and between Pursat and Kompong Chhnang. In addition, the second-secretary of the Party told us about one thing and another, just as instructive as funny. But what was special about him was that he would eat well, sleep well and always remain in a good mood. He had a special preference for *prahoc*, a kind of fermented fish that he grabbed with both hands to carry to his mouth. On the road, as soon as he saw leaves or edible fruits, he never failed to stop to pick them. He carried with him a bottle of something that could have been alcohol, from which he usually swallowed a sip at the beginning of each meal. He practised gymnastics every morning after waking up, around five o'clock. He did the same in the evening.

2 – Son Sen and his wife Yun Yat

In mid-1968, Office 102 moved to Kralaeng village. Towards the end of 1968, Son Sen[7] arrived with his wife, Yun Yat. They settled at Office K–1, located in the Jaraï village of Krachak. Mrs Khieu Ponnary and Ieng Thirith also came

---

7   Son Sen (1927–1997) alias Khieu and Kham, a schoolteacher, studied at a teachers' training college in Melun, France, and became head of studies at the Institute of Pedagogy in Phnom Penh. This enabled him to recruit many young men and women into the revolution. He became minister of defence during the civil war and retained the position under DK. He was the head of both external and internal security systems, as the regime did not deploy a police force. Son Sen was the boss of all the KR prisons in the country, under the direct authority of Nuon Chea. Son Sen and his wife were assassinated on Pol Pot's orders, his last crime, on 15 June 1997.

with them. The Son Sen couple held the national minorities in contempt, and on several occasions the latter refused to serve under their orders, especially in 1969. I met Son Sen for the first time at the K–1 office while he lived there with Tiv Ol and Chet. Of dark complexion, he did not shave regularly, unlike Ieng Sary, who shaved every morning. He was always wearing glasses, which was at the origin of his nickname 'Ta Venta', 'glasses-wearing grandfather'. Tall but of rather frail constitution, he looked like a climbing vine. He was an anxious, nervous man who worried about trifles and easily lost his self-control. At first, he only lived at K–1 and was not assigned to any particular task.

He had regular and frequent working relations with Pol Pot, not only on military matters but also on political issues. After coming down from Ratana-kiri, these close relations developed in 1973 during the siege of the city of Kompong Thom by resistance forces deployed from Siemreap. First, he provid-ed the party secretary with a detailed account of the situation at the front, and then rigorously applied the directives and recommendations that he received. The same was true for the execution of the Party's military line, namely the principles of guerrilla warfare and people's war with a view to achieving the national and democratic revolution, while bringing together as many national and international forces as possible. If we hit the enemy with the right blow, the enemy will not fail to react. In this case, it sufficed to redouble the blows until he was unable to fight back. In guerrilla warfare, which would lead the Revolutionary Party to victory in April 1975, the real military commander would be Pol Pot, whom Son Sen would scrupulously follow.

I am not very familiar with Son Sen's wife, Yun Yat[8] alias At, who settled in an office other than mine. When she moved, I was called, with other guards, to carry her. She could not walk because of a heart problem. Medium-sized and with a light complexion, she spoke with the characteristic accent of our

---

8   Yun Yat (1934–1997) was a primary school teacher from Siemreap and joined her husband in the *maquis* in 1965, two years after he had joined it. After the new constitution and the formation of a government, she became minister of education. She was the main writer of the articles of *Tung Yuveakchun Padevoat* (*Flag of Revolutionary Youth*). After the arrest of Hu Nim in 1977, she was also given the Ministry of Information and Propaganda. She was then responsible for the programmes of DK radio. A hard-liner, she exercised a strong influence on her husband, who headed the DK security establishment. It was said that she singled out those who should be arrested in her ministry. She, her husband and their daughter's family were murdered on 10 June 1997 at Anlong Veng, on Pol Pot's orders. He accused them of betrayal and negotiating to join the Hun Sèn government. The killers, some of his generals, took their fierce revenge over Son Sen's cruelty by killing all his family members and running a tank over their bodies. This had not been Pol Pot's wish.

compatriots from Siemreap, her hometown. She had very strict relations with people, but she was criticized for being somewhat fussy and especially finicky. For example, if someone she received had inadvertently badly buttoned his shirt, she did not fail to accuse him of disrespect for her and she never failed to criticize him. She was angry about a trifle and was very hard on those around her for everything related to discipline, relationships with people and the smallest details of everyday life, such as clothing, food or hygiene. Her hair always looked nice. She did not hold in high esteem our compatriots of the ethnic minorities, whom she did not hesitate to accuse of ignorance and lack of culture, while reproaching us for not knowing how to dress. She criticized the way we cooked, peeled vegetables and cut meat. She refused to eat when presented with dishes that did not conform to her tastes. This made everyday life with her impossible, because she could only be surrounded by slaves.

I had the opportunity to attend a seminar of political studies that she directed with Khieu Samphân. She stated in particular: 'Now that we have completed the national and democratic revolution, we are now preparing to undertake the socialist revolution with a view to achieving communism. The main task today is for each of us to arm ourselves on the ideological as well as political and organizational levels to serve the Party, the Revolution and the People without ever deviating to the right or left.' She insisted particularly on the importance of not forgetting our class origins in the ideological and political outlook of each of us. If we were from the peasantry, we must never deny our original class. She added that, by nature, every peasant was more or less liberal.[9] On the other hand, the worker is more disciplined, and accustomed by his work to follow a well-defined and rigorous timetable, while the petty bourgeois like the students tend to be forgiven for all their acts. Each one of us must build on the working model, that is to say, lead a life by following a strict schedule, (for example getting up at a set time in the morning and going to bed at a set time in the evening). Studies and work, political work and manual work, should be conducted together.

Yun Yat exercised an undeniable political influence over Son Sen, her husband. When the latter was about to make a reasonable decision, she usually intervened to dissuade him and have him adopt an opposite measure.

---

9 'Liberal' has consistently negative connotations in Khmer Rouge parlance. It meant you did not blindly obey *Angkar* – the most unforgivable failing. See slogans 416 to 421 in Locard, *Pol Pot's Little Red Book*, pp. 296–8. This indicates that this doctrinarian might have been the author of some of those slogans.

When her husband declared that in the implementation of the Party line, it was necessary to be flexible, considering the reality of the situation as well as the contingent things, Yun Yat retorted that the Party line must be respected to the letter, like an absolute rule, that is to say, forthright. She always wanted to have the last word over her husband.

The couple had two children, a boy and a girl, both deceased now. The son attended a fighter pilot training course in China. He died in 1979 at Phnom Thippadey, in Battambang, during a fight with People's Army of Vietnam troops. The girl, her two children and her parents were killed by Pol Pot's men in June 1997, in Anlong Véng. When Son Sen and his wife joined the *maquis*, first in 1963 with Pol Pot and Ieng Sary and again in 1965 with Khieu Ponnary and Ieng Thirith, they entrusted their children to the care of Yun Yat's older sister, Mrs Kim Lon, living at the time in Kompong Cham with her husband, Kœn Run, a teacher. People found Yun Yat not very friendly, and nobody wanted to be part of her family or work with her.

3 – Khieu Ponnary, Pol Pot's wife

Khieu Ponnary[10] (aka Yim) accompanied Yun Yat to Ratanakiri. She was of medium height, thin, and had a brown complexion; she always weighed her words as she addressed people and kept a certain reserve in her relations. With our ethnic minority compatriots, she advised the Khmer from the plains 'to learn from their experiences and listen to their opinions'. She held them in high esteem and admiration. She praised in particular their ability to develop the land without carts and oxen, and without having to plough it. They planted

---

10 Khieu Ponnary (1920–2003) became Saloth Sâr's wife on 14 July 1956, although she was four years his senior. Because of a gynaecological problem (ovarian cancer), she could not have children. She had been operated on by the revolutionary surgeon Thiounn Thiœun. She was one of the first female students at Lycée Sisowath in Phnom Penh and became a Khmer language and literature teacher there. She had a reputation for being a competent but demanding teacher. She became a member of the Democratic Party in the early 1950s. She went to Paris together with her younger sister Khieu Thirith, who studied for a BA in English at the Sorbonne, and met Saloth Sâr while she was studying at a teachers' training college. After her return to Phnom Penh, she founded the first clandestine women's association. Like Yun Yat, she joined her husband in the *maquis*, where she mainly collected information on the way of life of ethnic minorities and taught the women Khmer and hygiene. Like her husband, she greatly admired their fortitude and ability to survive in the most difficult circumstances. She started to lose her mind after the KR victory, becoming obsessed with the idea that the Vietnamese were determined to poison the entire KR leadership.

pumpkins, squash, eggplants and cabbages during the rainy season. In the dry season, they consumed wild vegetables, bamboo, coconuts and wild pepper shoots, which are tasty ingredients for Cambodian ratatouille. She loved hand-husked rice. She was not fussy about food and not shy about helping in the kitchen. During the trip to Stœung Chinit in 1970, she stubbornly refused to ride on the back of an elephant, or in a car or on a cart. She absolutely wanted to do what everyone else did, that is, walk on foot. Throughout the trip south, Khieu Ponnary continued to encourage us and comfort us. During the moments of rest between Mondolkiri and Kratieh, she showed us, on a map, the places that we crossed. She kept stimulating us during this long walk, encouraging everyone. She was very optimistic about the outcome of the struggle.

As soon as she arrived at Stœung Chinit, she went to the surrounding villages to begin her work as an educator and propagandist. She did not stay at the office. She was tirelessly dedicated to training women cadres, and organized meetings for women and girls. She attracted the esteem, respect and affection of those around her and those who knew her. In this work, she was assisted by In Sokan[11] (aka Yon), and Sim, the wife of Koy Thuon,[12] then-president of Sector 304 (North, then Centre). Sim would be arrested and eliminated soon after her husband. The couple left three children: two girls and a boy whose fate is totally unknown to me. She also was the younger sister of Ul Sophoan (aka Rong), wife of Sim Son,[13] who was the DK ambassador to North Korea from 1976 to 1981.

---

11 In Sokan, 1929–1979, alias Yem, studied phthisiology in France and married a French woman. From 1959, he worked in the large Khmer–Soviet Friendship Hospital in Phnom Penh with the surgeon Thiounn Thiœun and taught at the Medical Faculty. After Sihanouk's fall from power in 1970, he became his representative in Paris and returned to Cambodia after 17 April 1975 to work in the same hospital that had become the Hospital of 17th April. He died in the Cardamom Mountains after the KR flight on 7 January 1979.

12 Koy Thuon (1933–1977) met Tiv Ol and Son Sen at the Institute of Pedagogy, where they studied to become schoolteachers. He joined the Party in 1960, entered the *maquis* in 1963 in Siemreap province, and then became Secretary of the Northern region in 1967. He played an important role during the civil war (1968–1975) and, in 1970, set up base 870 for the KR leadership at Stœung Chinit. He was minister of the economy in the FUNK and, from 1975, in the DK government (Commerce). He was notorious for liking young ladies, and for opposing rigorous collectivization and the abolition of currency. He was first put under house arrest in Phnom Penh in April 1976, ostensibly for crimes against women, and sent to S–21 on 25 January 1977, where he was executed in March. His purge set the DK killing machine in motion and all regions were radically purged, one after the other – except Ta Mok's Southwest region.

13 Sim Son (1928–1990) had been a primary school teacher before joining the *maquis* in the late 1960s and becoming head of the Kratieh autonomous region 505. Later, he was a civilian cadre

In February 1972, I accompanied her to the southwest, notably to Amleang in Kompong Speu, where she chaired a seminar for the women and girls of the region. She stayed there for one month before going to the northwest, from where she did not return to Stœung Chinit until April of the same year. She was full of vigour and initiative at the time. She continued her work as an educator after the takeover in April 1975. She exerted a certain influence on her husband, as she showed herself more practical than him, having her feet firmly planted on the ground and apprehending things in every minute detail. She fell ill in late 1976, suffering from Alzheimer's disease.[14] With the disease, she changed dramatically. The warm and welcoming lady she had always been made room for a scowling woman, disillusioned and easily angered. She did not recognize us anymore. As time went by, the condition got worse and proved incurable. The remedies could only act on the symptoms, but not on the illness itself.

4 – Ieng Thirith, Ieng Sary's wife

Khieu Ponnary's younger sister, Ieng Thirith[15] (aka Phea), was of the same size and complexion, but she was more beautiful and more plump. The two had a similar way of speaking, with carefully chosen words. In Ratanakiri, she lived with her husband at Office 102, first established in the south, then transferred north of the Tonlé San. In 1965 she joined the *maquis*, leaving her four children, three daughters and a boy, with her elderly mother, who was living in the family home on Dr Hanh Street in Phnom Penh. Later, in 1975, embassies for Albania, Romania, Laos and Cuba were set up there. In 1971,

---

at Malay, where he was killed by a falling tree in 1990.

14 She suffered rather from chronic paranoid schizophrenia 'whose focus was Vietnam, but which would progressively invade every aspect of Cambodian life' (Philip Short, *Pol Pot*, p. 211). I would add that the entire revolutionary regime suffered from a similar paranoia. It was probably the result of not receiving hormone replacement therapy after undergoing the hysterectomy for her cancer treatment.

15 Khieu Thirith (1930–2015) married Ieng Sary in Paris in 1953 and joined him in the *maquis* in 1965. She was DK's Minister of Social Affairs, in charge of the population's well-being! With her husband, to whom she was very close, she practised what the KR denounced as 'familialism', that is, giving special treatment and especially inheritances to offspring. Very much a political animal, after the fall of the regime, she was very vocal in denying wrongdoing by the KR, shifting blame for the hundreds of thousands of massacre and starvation victims onto the invading Vietnamese army. All these lies were uttered with a winning smile to the interviewing journalists. She was arrested in 2007 by the ECCC for crimes against humanity, but was released from prison in 2011 being declared by doctors mentally unfit to stand trial.

she left for Hanoi, where she directed the Radio 'Voice of the United National Front of Kampuchea' until April 1975.

Often busy with her job as Pol Pot's special secretary, she had little time to get in touch with the villagers. But she had cordial relations with her collaborators and her acquaintances developed real friendships with her. During leisure time, she liked to mingle with people and inquire about their living and working conditions. She took a special interest in the way cooks prepared dishes or made treats and other delicacies. She regularly listened to the news on the radio. She was interested in politics, and she admired the way of life of national minorities as much as her sister. One day, she went to Kang Kham, where she was treated to a soup with bamboo shoots and a kind of fish called *andèng*. After tasting it, she kept repeating, 'It is really delicious! It's *really* delicious!' She also enjoyed a sauté of leaves of a kind of vine called *vor yeav* wrapped in rice flour.

5 – Tiv Ol and Ney Sarann

Around 1969, Tiv Ol[16] and his wife, Léng Kim Hak, along with Sin Phâl Kun, Pâk (a single woman) and Ney Sarann,[17] arrived from Mondolkiri, his initial base, followed by Chanthy (another woman) and many others. The latter were divided into two groups: the first was to teach Khmer to villagers, the second to teach them courses on hygiene or health care.

---

16 Tiv Ol (1933–1977), a teacher of Khmer language and literature and party member after 1958, was among the many teachers introduced to communism by their trainer, Son Sen. He taught in Cambodia's most progressive private secondary schools, Chamraen Vichea and Kambuboth, in the early 1950s and at Preah Sihanouk College in Kompong Cham from 1955 to 1960. Because of his revolutionary ideas, the authorities moved him into an administrative position at the Ministry of Education. He was involved in the creation of a teachers' trade union and a students' association. Feeling threatened by Sihanouk after the dissolution of the Sino–Khmer Friendship Association, he joined the *maquis* in 1967. In 1975, he became vice-minister of information and propaganda. He was arrested on 6 June 1977 and sent to S–21, where he was executed in September of the same year.

17 Ney Sarann (1925–1976) joined the Indochinese Communist Party in 1950. He also joined the Khmer Issarak rebels, who practised guerrilla warfare in Cambodia during the First Indochina War. He was among about 2,000 revolutionaries who were taken to Hanoi after the July 1954 Geneva Agreements, but he returned home on foot a few months later, along with Nuon Chea and Sao Phœm. He became chief supervisor at the private college of Chamraen Vichea. He joined Saloth Sâr in the *maquis* in 1964, along with Ieng Sary and Sao Phœm at their Office 100, a secret base near Mimot. In the July 1971 Party Congress, he opposed the most radical elements of full collectivization. He was named head of the *Eisan* (Northeast) region, but was arrested on 20 September 1976, along with Keo Meas, taken to S–21 and executed at the end of the year.

I met Tiv Ol, alias Penh and revolutionary name Saom, during the Long March. He was an open and warm man. Voluble, he would speak with a fast and jerky flow. There was no shortage of funny stories to make us laugh. Once, when he saw a creeper along the way, he asked himself aloud: 'Why do lianas wrap the trunk of trees from right to left?' Strange question! At another time, he pondered, 'Fish live in every pond in the mountains. I thought they only existed in the plains...' We answered that fish move upriver as long as there are streams. As soon as they reach a new channel, they stay at the entry for a while before continuing on their way. This is especially true for the fish called *khsan*, masters in the art of making their way, even through mud. Shortly after, Tiv Ol mused, 'I have lived in the city for a long time. Here, I find that many things are different from those existing in the city. I do not know anything at all. I cannot know if the fruits of such a tree are edible or are not, or if such leaves or vegetables are edible or not.' Tiv Ol kept us good company from start to finish, from the Naga's Tail to Stœung Chinit.

In Ratanakiri, Tiv Ol taught the basics of the Khmer language to our ethnic minority compatriots. He had been a teacher, and even wrote a book to teach Khmer to foreigners. During the trip, he told us that before embarking on a long journey, one must learn to use maps. He had a teacher's mentality, and this is probably why he took an interest in all that was new to him and especially to communicate his knowledge to those around him. Once in Stœung Chinit, Tiv Ol joined Hou Yuon and Hu Nim at the L–8 Office, which published propaganda materials from the Kampuchea National United Front (FUNK). The trio was responsible for writing articles and texts before submitting them to Khieu Samphân for review. Later, Tiv Ol would be appointed deputy minister of information of the Royal Government of National Union of Kampuchea (GRUNK). After 1975, I never had the opportunity to meet him again. Much later, I learned of his arrest or his liquidation in September 1977.

Tiv Ol was married to Léng Kim Hak alias Phâl and Sey, also a teacher. She joined him in Ratanakiri at the same time as Madame Pâk and Sin Phâl Kun alias Sou and wife of So Phân.[18] In 1975, Sey became head of the Office of the Ministry of Social Affairs and Health headed by Mrs Ieng Thirith. But

---

18 After the 1954 Geneva Agreements, So Phân (1936–2004) was among those who went to Hanoi, where he learnt the Vietnamese language. He became Ieng Sary's private secretary and, in 1977, Sary's deputy in the press and information department of the Ministry of Foreign Affairs. After 1979, he was at the head of the radio of the Voice of Democratic Kampuchea at Païlin. He died in Samlaut in 2004.

despite being trained in China, she would be arrested and liquidated on 20 September 1976, at the same time as her husband.

I briefly met Ney Sarann alias Ya, of Khmer nationality, fortuitously for the first time around December 1967 in the village of Krâlèng, when I came from the village of Rumlich. Surrounded by two bodyguards, a Jaraï named Yam and Khon, a Lao, he was probably going for a meeting in the neighbouring village of Chamcar Trâdèng, more exactly at the Kâng Dèn (Kâng Daeng) office, named after the Tampuon-nationality district chief of Bokéo. He told me that he was coming from Mondolkiri. He was tall, light-skinned and sturdy, with brush-cut hair and a deep voice. I met him again in 1971, when he came to attend a political seminar held at Office 22, near Phâky Damrei Neak, located in the Prey Lang forest, not far from Dâng Kda, in Stœng Trâng District, Kompong Cham.

The president of the Northeast region, Ney Sarann was assisted by four members of the regional committee: comrade Vy, a Khmer, and three Jaraï, comrades Ta Lav, Ing, and Khiou. Khiou was chairman of the O'Yadao District Committee, Ing was district chief of Andoung Meas, and Lav was responsible for the Bokéo District Committee. In addition, military responsibilities were assigned to members of the northeast ethnic minorities: to Hâm, a Krâchok, Thau, a Jaraï, and Keo Huon, also a Jaraï. After 17 April 1975, a special battalion of 300 minority soldiers succeeded to take Preah Vihear temple from the hands of the Republicans.[19] The tribal inhabitants were not yet organized into people's communes, but they had practised mutual aid according to their ancestral tradition since time immemorial. For example, for clearing the forest for agriculture, they divided themselves into groups of ten people and each group would be allocated a portion of land. It was only after 1970 that the people's communes were gradually constituted and self-help teams systematically organized. The communal kitchen and communal meals were only instituted after the first harvest of 1975.

In June 1976, Ney Sarann led a DK delegation in negotiations on border issues with the Vietnamese delegation led by Deputy Foreign Minister Phan Hien. Accused of having delivered information to Vietnam, Ney Sarann was arrested on 20 September 1976 and interned at S–21 before being eliminated at the end of the same year. Vy, his assistant, was not targeted but, feeling threatened, he put an end to his life a year later.[20] The other three members

---

19 See also Chapter XXII, below.
20 Philip Short notes in *Pol Pot*, p. 384, that he was purged only in 1978, after having become the *Eisan* regional secretary.

of the Northeast region committee would do the same in 1978. The real problem was that all these leaders were powerless against the Vietnamese attacks. Since liberation in 1975, the Vietnamese had been attacking all the time. Looking for scapegoats, the KR leadership accused them of connivance with the Vietnamese.

6 – The beginning of the civil war

In Ratanakiri, after the victory of 17 April 1975, the Vietnamese had been constantly harassing us in the Naga's Tail, O'Yadao and along the Tonlé San. But they concentrated their strongest attacks in the Eastern region, especially after 1977. As preventive measures, Cambodian forces had been carrying out their attacks deep inside Vietnamese territory, up to Tay Ninh. This was a serious mistake. If it was possible during the anti-American war, it proved highly adventurous when it came to fighting the Vietnamese for the simple reason that they could dispatch reinforcements more quickly and more massively. The Americans relied on their planes, tanks and firepower, and not man-to-man combat, while the Vietnamese counted on their huge infantry, one of the best in the world and experienced with guerrilla warfare and people's war. Although I was a civilian, I was somewhat familiar with military matters. I had studied the theory for three months in Ratanakiri, taught by the Vietnamese in 1967. One year earlier, a commando group of 100 American soldiers arrived by helicopter at Ta Nga, north of the Tonlé San, to take the Vietnamese from the rear. They camped one night and flew away again the next day without fighting.

This is when Comrade Sim entrusted me with the position of chief of Pol Pot's bodyguards. We had to ensure the protection of cadres in their propaganda and agitation work. We took care of the installation of offices and revolutionary bases. Sim, who had settled in Vœunsay in 1964, only came to Andoung Pech in 1967. He then took charge of political work among the population and was responsible for the clandestine guards. After a certain period, I was entrusted with the responsibility of logistics and supplies. I would go to the Bokéo market every day to buy salt, cloth and mosquito nets. In 1967, the village of O'Ampor, where I lived, was the object of violent bombings by American B–52 aircraft, which also unrelentingly strafed neighbouring Tœk Chap, leaving deep craters that are still visible today. From my office, I walked alone to the villages of Kak, Malik, Kè and Kanlèng, and often slept alone at the edge of the Tonlé San if there was no boat to cross it.

In February 1968, Samdech Norodom Sihanouk, then Head of State, toured Ratanakiri. At the time, we had all settled on the banks of the Tonlé San in Andoung Meas District. A distribution of clothing was from up on high and the helicopter in which the prince sat. The craft landed at Bokéo airport. He announced that the traitors would be treated with great severity. Indeed, to avenge the murder of a district chief who was accused of being a double agent, a certain Donn, some 200 hostages of ethnic minorities went through the firing squad.[21] Sihanouk admitted three months later that he himself had ordered these executions: '*I do not care if I have to go to hell: I will submit the appropriate documents to the Devil himself.*' On their side, the revolutionaries also did not spare their prisoners of war.

In 1968, I was in the village of Sangkê between Andoung Meas and Bokéo. Government troops launched a large-scale sweep on National Road No. 19 and the Andoung Meas Road (Bokham) to extend their zone of control. Comrade Kiev, of Tampuon nationality, with whom I had an appointment, told me: 'Now that the enemy is attacking us, we cannot do nothing.' I said, 'I'm going to do something!' I then went to the head of the commune, named Man, and I took his Enfield and a shotgun. With Pheng, one of my comrades, I attacked the government soldiers on the Andoung Meas Road, causing them one death and three wounded. This feat of arms did not fail to be noticed by the leadership of the revolutionary movement. My supervisor, Sim, summoned me and said: 'Our forces must remain underground and engage in guerrilla activities.' He asked me to return to my former role, that is, to be his bodyguard again. He was responsible at that time to set up revolutionary guard units. In 1969, he stated that the present situation requires the reorganization of the revolutionary guards into three groups: one at O'Chheu Ni, another at O'Chheu Kram in the village of Koep, and the last in the village of Lo. These guards defended the revolutionary bases and took care of setting traps and planting stakes and pikes around these bases. The inhabitants cut the trees and put them across the roads to slow the advance of the enemy troops. As for our guards, they moved constantly while remaining continuously vigilant.

The hostilities against the government troops began as early as December 1967 and lasted until May 1968. Those in limited number launched combing operations, with a view to extending their area of control on both sides of

---

21 See the references to this massacre in Milton Osborne's *Sihanouk, Prince of Light, Prince of Darkness*, Chiang Mai: Silkworm Books, 1994, p. 197, and in Philip Short's *Pol Pot*, p. 176.

National Road No. 19, from Bokéo to O'Yadao and Andoung Meas. They had trucks and road rollers for transport. We attacked them with bows and crossbows in skirmishes, using guerrilla tactics. I was not present when Sihanouk came to Bokéo and distributed clothes in February 1968. It was also the time when district or provincial government officials were murdered, which was the cause of the bloody repression. It also corresponded to the influx of Vietnamese soldiers to the province, to protect themselves from the fighting in their country after the failed Tet offensive. They settled in the forest on the side of the Naga's Tail, as usual. In particular, Nun, head of Andoung Meas District, in the resistance since the Issarak, a double agent, was arrested by the Sihanouk army. At the time, there were no prisoners: they were executed – on both sides.

Only offices 100 and 102 had numbers. Later, there was another office, named K–5, north of the Tonlé San in Noy, a Krâchok village in Andoung Meas District. Noy was 10 kilometres north of the Tonlé San, and nearly 10 kilometres from the Vietnamese border in the very top of the Naga's Tail. This was where the military headquarters were installed and Pol Pot, Ieng Sary, Koy Thuon and Son Sen lived there. I was responsible for the development of the base. It was built at the foot of a mountain, Phnom Bak Touk, bordered by a river with its source in Vietnam and encased in a deep valley, surrounded on all sides by wooded peaks. All the cadres from the plains lived there. In mid-1968, everyone lived together at K–5, the northernmost headquarters. Like offices 100 and 102, K–5 was well-organized and clean. All offices and houses were always clean and well laid out. By the way, it was the same in Vietnamese camps. Office K–5 operated until 1971 and covered a much larger area than Office 100.

Regarding the decision to start the armed struggle, I do not remember exactly, but we started to organize the 'secret bodyguards' as defence forces. There were enemy combings on the road from Andoung Meas to Bokéo, which endangered Office K–5, and on the road from Bokéo to O'Yadao, which endangered offices 100 and 102. Government forces were positioned every two to ten 10 kilometres along the road in the forest, while villages were only accessible by trails. The population was used to making itself invisible: since 1964, they avoided emitting smoke, so as not to attract American aviation. So, we mobilized the villagers to cut trees and obstruct the roads, and we organized guerrilla units to target them.

As I mentioned before, while I was Vin's bodyguard in early 1968, I left with two others. They had powder guns and I had an Enfield. We attacked a tracked vehicle on the road from Bokéo to Andoung Meas. My shots injured two soldiers, including the driver, and put the vehicle out of action because I had targeted the tank. They fought back violently, but I had run away about 500 meters before they started shooting at us. I was mentioned in dispatches as a model in guerrilla warfare, because, before this attack, no one dared to attack the enemy. It was the first attack in our area. When I took the initiative to do so, the other bodyguards and the villagers realized that the enemy was not so strong! Immediately after, we organized ourselves into groups of five. All this was well before the arrival of Son Sen. Some in these groups were armed with AK-47s or powder guns; or bows with poisoned arrows, or Enfields. But we had only a few guns. The government commune chiefs and their deputies had Enfields – and we seized them.[22]

You ask me if we took prisoners? No. On our side, we never had prisoners – and there were no captured revolutionaries, either. Fortunately. We had orders not to be captured. If we captured a villager who had been recruited into the government troops, and he was someone from the area, we would send him home. But if he was a government soldier from the plains, he was killed. At first, there were no explicit instructions regarding prisoners, but everyone understood that it was the way we should act. It was a merciless struggle. We had to establish a clear demarcation line between the enemy and ourselves. That was the guideline.[23] After this attack, I was transferred to the logistics department to take care of the supply. So, I dressed like ordinary villagers to buy provisions from Bokéo for the local bases. I spent six months doing that. I bought pipes to make powder guns, and some rice.

This is when I became a Party member. On 8 January 1968, I was accepted as a candidate member for a 'probationary period' of three months. Officially, I became a member of the Communist Youth League, the first step towards becoming a full member of the Party. That would happen three years later, in 1971, at the S–71 base in Stœung Chinit. This short probationary period was due to my successful guerrilla attack against the tracked vehicle. From

---

22 Phi Phuon recounted this event twice during our interviews. His accounts are at odds with each other, so I present both.

23 This was to become Democratic Kampuchea's paramount policy and mantra, applied through-out its regime. For instance, Khieu Samphân, the then head of State, proclaimed in Colombo, at the Non-aligned conference in August 1976: 'we must continue to fight and suppress all stripes of enemy at all times. Everything must be done neatly and thoroughly.'

this time onward, I received a small stipend. Not much, but something, until 1975, when money was abolished (26 July, p. 7).

In the middle of 1968 came Koy Thuon alias Thuch. He was in charge of all base activities throughout the region, from Ratanakiri and Mondolkiri to Kratieh. He was responsible for guiding – or rather arranging guides for – all the many, many revolutionaries who left the city to go to Ratanakiri. In 1969, Sim and Vy went to Vœunsay to establish new offices.

Nikân,[24] real name Son Nhan, arrived in 1968. He was Son Sen's younger brother and a schoolteacher, and did clerical work at K–5, stencils and documents. His revolutionary name was Kân (i.e., Nikân) and he worked with another, who was called Kim. Kim has now disappeared. Son Sen arrived in late 1968. He first lived at Office K–1 and worked at K–5, then he joined the others, and settled permanently at K–5. Son Sen was in charge of the army, and security. Towards the end of 1968, at the same time as Son Sen, Sou Phân arrived with his wife, who became Ieng Sary's personal secretary. Later, Sou Phân became my deputy in the Ministry of Foreign Affairs together with Mrs Moeun, Pich Chhean's wife. I have known them since 1968.

There were also others who arrived in the course of 1968: Sim Son, who later became the DK Ambassador in Pyongyang; Tum (not the same man as Dam's brother), who later became secretary of the Kratieh region (i.e., Siet Chhê[25]); and Tiv Ol and his wife. Tum and Dam, the brothers of Khieng Kaonn, were already there, having arrived with Pol Pot at the end of 1967. Dam was a nurse.

In 1969, we continued our guerrilla activities and at the same time cultivated about ten hectares of rice fields. Government troops were confined along Road No. 19 and the Andoung Meas Road, with our forces stationed in the middle. After the rice matured and we were busy harvesting it, the Americans took the opportunity to submit us to heavy shelling, killing all of our 24 cattle and causing death and injury among the civilian population, as well as a great deal of material damage. A large part of the revolutionary forces stationed south of the Tonlé San rushed to safety north of the river. Given the scale of enemy

---

24 Nikân, born in 1940, became head of protocol in the Ministry of Foreign Affairs after the KR victory. After the 1979 Vietnamese invasion, he became a KR commander in the Sampov Lun area of Banteay Meanchey Province and defected to Hun Sèn in 1996, along with Ieng Sary. He now lives on the Thai border near Sampov Lun. He is rarely interviewed.

25 Siet Chhê (1932–1977) was a schoolteacher in Phnom Penh from 1954 to 1964. He became Eastern region secretary (only for a sector) and accompanied Pol Pot to see Mao in 1975. He served in the General Staff of the Army. He was arrested and killed at S–21 in 1977.

search operations, Ieng Sary, then in charge of the Northeast region, seconded by his deputy Son Sen, urgently convened a meeting of civilian and military cadres to deal with the attack. This is when Pol Pot began the long trek along the Hô Chi Minh Trail to North Vietnam, from where he then flew to Beijing.

Following the vote of the two chambers (The National Assembly and the Supreme Council of the Throne) on 18 March 1970 to withdraw its confidence in Prince Norodom Sihanouk, the revolutionary forces seized the entirety of Ratanakiri, Mondolkiri, Stung Treng, Kratieh and Preah Vihear Provinces, a vast unbroken part of the Cambodian territory.[26] From May of the same year, almost all former Khmer resistance fighters who had been in North Vietnam since 1954 gradually returned to the country. Ieng Sary wrote a letter and I took it to the Vietnamese. From that day, the two sides maintained close and cordial relations. As for armaments, we only had kalashnikov rifles, some 36 Enfields, and basic rifles. Only the bodyguards were armed with AK-47s. At the end of 1968, the Vietnamese donated 200 old rifles.

Also living in Office 102 with the Ieng Sary couple, were Mrs Chanthy, Mrs Vin, wife of Phong, Loey, Ngin, Phè, Tham, Ing and Yan. About ten people including Bong Sim, Phy, Khân, Seuy, Mong and Phâng, all single, lived with the Pol Pot couple at Office 100, located on the edge of a small stream with water in every season. The base was one kilometre wide by three kilometres in length. The house of Pol Pot and Khieu Ponnary, contiguous to a bathroom and a toilet, was adjacent to that of Comrade Sim, with the same facilities. All around, a fence made of half-timbered tree trunks was raised and surrounded by bamboo stakes and traps. Behind was a large room that served as both meeting room and refectory, and a kitchen. In front of and facing a larger stream, named O'Kap, was built a sort of shed housing the office staff, including comrades Vin, Mong, Phâng, Thin, Khân and Seuy. On the other side of the brook were the houses and fields of the village inhabitants.

Office 102, where Ieng Sary and Ieng Thirith lived, was as extensive as Pol Pot's. In the village of Kanlèng, there was a kind of district committee, consisting of Dèng, Dang and Kham, who were in charge of recruiting new members. In December 1968, I became a member of the Party, sponsored by Comrade Sim, a Khmer, and Comrade Ban, a Jaraï and health officer. On this occasion, I swore loyalty to the Party's statutes in front of its flag.

---

26 In actual fact, the Americans had advised the new Republican regime to give up control of this large, sparsely populated, entirely forested, utterly indefensible region. Nonetheless, the KR celebrated this departure of the government troops as a great victory.

In 1968, Pol Pot left Office 100, which would be definitively abandoned from March 1969, to settle at Office K–5, five kilometres north of the Tonlé San in the village of Nay, Talao Commune, Andoung Meas District. Ten kilometres further south on the other side of the river is the village of Kanlèng, and the village of Kak was established on the same bank, a little to the north. In December 1969, accompanied by his wife and Vin (later Pâng), Pol Pot made a long journey on foot to Hanoi, from where he flew in March of the following year to Beijing. As for Ieng Sary, he left Office 102 to settle at K–5 before leaving for North Vietnam and China in early 1971.

During the time he lived in Ratanakiri, Pol Pot bore the revolutionary name of Ta Pouk.[27] Once he returned to the plain in 1970, he took the name of Pot and, after liberation on 17 April, 1975, Pol Pot became his official name.[28] As for Nuon Chea, known as Nuon in hiding, he had by then become the second character of the new regime. Everyone did the same. So instead of Choeun, my name became Cheam and Vin became Pâng.

In 1970, immediately after the fall of Sihanouk on 18 March, Lumphat was liberated by the KR, assisted by Vietnamese troops. The Cambodians alone seized Andoung Meas.

---

27 Here, Phi Phuon confirms Philip Short's description of Saloth Sâr's aliases: in Ratanakiri, he chose to be called 'Ta Pouk' which literally means 'Grandfather Mattress' – not a very revolutionary name! This was meant to explain that he was the one who would soften all conflicts.

28 'Pol' is traditionally the name of a slave in Khmer, and Saloth Sâr presented himself as the most proletarian of proletarians. 'Pot' was added for the alliteration, like Vorn Vet or Phi Phuon.

– V –

Pol Pot's Long March

Headquarters moved to the centre of the country

*I*n May 1970, in the company of my uncle Ta Lav, I was in charge of welcoming Pol Pot at the Naga's Tail (more exactly at Tavéng) on his return from China. He was accompanied by Mong, his bodyguard and Sat, his personal physician and Vin's wife, from South Vietnam. At the same time, about 100 others, both Khmer and ethnic minorities, also arrived at Andoung Meas and Vœunsay, where they were welcomed at Office D–12.

Pol Pot was about to embark on his long walk from the Naga's Tail, a region along the borders of Cambodia, Laos and Vietnam. He also returned to Cambodia through the Naga's Tail, to Office O'Kapak, where I was waiting. We were on the banks of the Tonlé San, all occupied by Vietnamese troops at the time. His march would last for seven months, from May to December 1970, when he arrived close to the Stœung Chinit River on the border between the provinces of Kompong Cham and Kompong Thom. During the first three months, the Vietnamese taught a team of three young students from France to use the radio for telecommunications, as Pol Pot did not understand much about this mode of communication.[1] Most of the time, he travelled on a motorcycle or in a palanquin carried by his helpers, or on an elephant. We moved slowly through the forest, clearing the tall grass and creepers that were in our way. We fed on forest products and animals we hunted. We only carried salt. Pol Pot told us that the situation was now more favourable than before, so all lowland cadres hastened to leave the northeast and return to the plains.

Before departure, Pol Pot dispatched a reconnaissance team of five people including myself and my elder brother, Rochœm Tveng. The journey started from Office K–12 and passed successively through Office 15 in Nay Village,

---

1 This is a surprising statement about someone who was supposed to have followed a two-year training course at the Violet School of radio-electricity in Paris from 1949 to 1951 – although he failed his exams and left without a degree.

Office K–7 in Kong Lê commune (Andoung Meas District), and villages On, Kracha (Bokéo District), Khtang and Khteang (both in O'Yadao District) before arriving in Lumphat District. From O'Yadao, we took nearly a month to reach Lumphat. After that, we were always in the forest. Then the rise of the water level on the Srèpok prevented our progress for nearly two weeks. During the crossing of the flooded river at K–12, we lost a comrade, drowned as he was carried away by the powerful current.

During the months of June, July and August, we were still in Ratanakiri Province. At the time, the revolutionaries already controlled the territory between the dense and clear forests that extended throughout four provinces: Stung Treng, Preah Vihear, Kratieh and Kompong Thom, as well as the districts of Stung Trang and Chamkar Lœu in Kompong Cham Province. We did not go through any villages except Tbèng, where we were supplied with a car, a 'Land Rover', to continue our journey. Khmer people, like the ethnic minorities, were engaged in slash-and-burn agriculture in this dense forest, and only benefitted from cart tracks. They built shelters in the form of huts made of *phaav* leaves from the treetops. We went mostly through forests, sometimes very dense, always avoiding inhabited areas and identified tracks, not to be detected by American bombers.

Our group of about eighty people, most from minority ethnic groups, crossed the Srèpok River north of Roveat, Koh Nhiek District in Mondolkiri Province. Between Mondolkiri and Kratieh, we remained stuck in the forest and the mountains more than two months. In 1970, Pol Pot chose Koh Nhiek, on fertile black soil and served by a river, to become the capital of Mondolkiri, instead of Sen Monorom, which was too close to Vietnam. The crossing of the Mekong was done upstream from Sambaur in Kratieh Province by canoes during the night, from eleven in the evening to four in the morning the next day. Pol Pot also crossed in a small boat, accompanied by Yèm (Sim Son), Pâng, Yi and Seuy.

Throughout the trip, from the Naga's Tail to Stung Trang, communications were provided by a team of Vietnamese technicians, who also trained Cambodians to send telex code transmissions. They stayed in Stung Trang for three months before returning to Vietnam. The newly formed team of Cambodian technicians included comrades Phâng, Pon and a third whose name I do not remember, all aged thirty and coming from France. Office 80 already existed when we arrived. It was comprised of three buildings: a dwelling house, a kitchen and a dining room, all covered with thatch, and was surrounded by a fence about one kilometre away. A guard post was on each side.

Koy Thuon and his wife joined our marching column between Mondolkiri and Kratieh and continued throughout the trip to Office 870, located near the Stung Chinit River, which the committee of Sector 304 had built to host us. We found most of what we needed, such as food and other kitchen and office equipment. Pol Pot brought a few documents with him. In general, he would start his presentations without any paper in front of him. It was only after a month's stay that he began to write the ideas and reflections he had developed during his political seminars, the first of which took place after our installation in May 1971.

Khieu Samphân,[2] Hou Yuon[3] and Hu Nim[4] also lived in Office 870 when Pol Pot arrived, but in another dwelling, half a kilometre away from ours.

---

2   Born in 1931, Khieu Samphân studied in France from 1954 to 1959 and obtained a University Doctorate in economics. He was president of the Marxist-Leninist Circle in Paris and became a member of the French Communist Party. Back in Cambodia in 1959, he became a member of Parliament in 1962 and 1966, and briefly was secretary of state for foreign trade. He also published a popular magazine *l'Observateur*, in which he described the living conditions of ordinary people. He fled into the *maquis* in 1967 after the Samlaut rebellion and became one of the so-called 'Three Ghosts', along with Hu Nim and Hou Yuon.

  After the three went into the *maquis,* they were believed to have been assassinated by the powers-that-be. This is why they were dubbed 'the Three Ghosts' when they reappeared as major leaders of the FUNK and the GRUNK, created by Sihanouk shortly after he lost power in March 1970. Apart from Khieu Samphân, they were mainly figureheads to fool international public opinion, while the real leaders of the rebellion were Saloth Sâr (then Ta Pouk) and Nuon Chea, along with Ieng Sary and Son Sen. One of the major DK leaders, Khieu Samphân officially became head of state in April 1976, after Sihanouk's resignation. A main ideologue of the regime, he was party to all major decisions – a role he strenuously denied in his autobiography and at the Tribunal after he was arrested in November 2007. He claimed he was never in the least involved in the criminal policies of DK. Among all accused by the ECCC, he is today the only survivor, imprisoned for life for crimes against humanity and genocide. He lost his final appeal in September 2022.

3   Hou Yuon (1930–1976) also studied from 1949 to 1955 in Paris, obtaining a doctorate in economics and joining the Communist Party of France. A member of the National Assembly, he joined the *maquis* in 1967. A strong partisan of the cooperative movement, a very popular speaker with the farmers and a strong opponent to total collectivization imposed from up above by *Angkar*, he was not allowed to enter Phnom Penh in 1975. He was seen in a re-education camp in Kompong Cham Province in April 1976, but disappeared soon after.

4   Hu Nim (1932–1977) studied in France from 1955 to 1957, obtaining a BA in Law, and took a Law Doctorate in Phnom Penh in 1966. He became a member of Parliament in 1958 and in 1965 was involved in the Khmer–Chinese Friendship Association, which Sihanouk dissolved in 1967. Fearing arrest, he joined the *maquis* on 7 October 1967. He became minister of information for the GRUNK in 1970, a position he retained after the KR victory. He was arrested

Having two to four kilometres of perimeter, it was installed right in the middle of the forest, hidden from everyone. In early 1972, they all moved to the newly established Office 24, located in Prek Sangkê village, Stung Trang District, Kompong Cham Province, 30 kilometres away from Office 80. Khieu Samphân had a small hut with a bed and a small writing table, where he wrote large volumes in Khmer and translated texts into French. That's what I saw him do. I knew that, after the coup d'état and after the establishment of the FUNK, at least theoretically, he was the commander-in-chief of the army and controlled the work of the Front. I respected him. I loved him because it was great to have an intellectual on our side in the jungle.[5]

It was at Office 24 that Khieu Samphân was married, aged 40, with So Socheat (aka Rinn), from Preah Vihear, who was some twenty years younger than him. Previously, he told Pâng about his desire to create a family and asked him to arrange a marriage with a girl from the base. On Pol Pot's approval, Pâng addressed Man, then chairman of the Preah Vihear region committee. So Socheat worked at Man's office. After a few months of observation, the marriage took place in December 1972. The wedding ceremony began with a salute to the Party flag. The bride and the bridegroom then took turns in swearing fidelity to the Party and the revolution, and expressing their determination to create a new family devoted body and soul to the homeland and the people. To close the ritual, all the participants broke into singing the *Internationale*.

Only Hu Nim alias Phoâs, Poc Deuskomar[6] alias Pach, and Tiv Ol were permanently established at Office 24, while Hou Yuon would move from one village to another to hold political meetings. Tall, of dark complexion and of robust constitution, Hou Yuon had the appearance of a businessman who embodied very well the role of representative of the people. Open, welcoming and warm, he spoke easily, frankly and directly. During the war of resistance

---

on 10 April 1977 and executed on 6 July after writing a long confession, which was published in 1988 in Chandler, et al. (eds) *Pol Pot Plans the Future*, 227–317.

5   See the ECCC reports of Phi Phuon's testimony at the Khmer Rouge Tribunal, 1 August 2012, pp. 102–3.

6   Poc Deuskomar was a young banker when he joined the revolution in July 1968, becoming deputy minister for foreign affairs in the Royal Government of National Union (GRUNK) formed by Sihanouk after his fall on 18 March 1970. He left the movement at some point between 1973 and 1975, probably because he resented the KR's brutal methods (see Milton Osborne's *Before Kampuchea*, Bangkok: Orchid Press, 2004, pp. 77–83). He was also connected with the Thiounn family described in Ben Kiernan's *How Pol Pot Came to Power*, Yale University Press, 2004, p. 31.

from 1970 to 1975, he moved relentlessly, day and night, both in the rear and at the front, to bring the good news to the people and the combatants, comforting and encouraging them to persevere in the fight. He enjoyed a great popularity among ordinary people and especially young people, who really loved him. Each time he came home, about every three months, he would visit Pol Pot and Khieu Samphân. He would not stay at the office for more than three days before regrasping his pilgrim's baton to go about preaching. He came to the office at night and left at night, too. As for Hu Nim, he lived at Office S–8, located near the Stung Chinit, with other intellectuals such as Hou Yuon, Tiv Ol and Poc Deuskomar.

All newcomers settled under canvases stretched between the trees. Each canvas was four meters long and three meters wide. Each of us only had a tent, a hammock, a mosquito net and a blanket, as well as three spare sets of clothes, three underpants, three long-sleeved shirts and three short-sleeved shirts, as well as two khaki caps, a *krâma*[7] and two pairs of sandals cut from car tyres. All this equipment was provided by China and Vietnam. The bodyguards were armed with Type 56 rifles while I carried an automatic Chinese rifle that used Kalashnikov bullets and had a coconut-shaped bandolier. It weighed about seven kilograms and was particularly effective when it came to defeating an enemy attack. From 1967 to 1975, I received a monthly salary of 30 riels, while women received 40. Each month, with this salary, I could buy two long tubes of bamboo filled with dried bananas, which could be kept very long. At that time, a *kapha*[8] of rice sold for fifty riels. So, we progressed extremely slowly, secrecy being paramount.

As Pol Pot had told us that the situation was more favourable than before, all cadres hastened to leave the northeast and return to the plains. During our trip, the Americans continued their aerial bombardments. In particular, they targeted the villages of O'Ta Sek, Hoeng Prarmar, Kiri Andet, Sre Veal, Speu, Thnal Bek, Rokar Khnor, Meak, and Dey Kram, located in the districts of Stung Trang, Chamkar Leu, Krauch Chhmar and Batheay in Kompong Cham Province as well as Baray District in Kompong Thom Province. These bombings caused some casualties among the civilian population, but did not worry the resistance leadership. For its part, the Lon Nol government was pursuing its own bombardment with its aircraft, including the T–28s (we call them 'cut wings'). These were more efficient than American planes and left nothing in their paths but

---

7   The all-purpose traditional checkered scarf of Khmer farmers that became a symbol of revolutionary outfit.

8   A tribal basket worn on the back that could contain about 10 kilos of rice.

devastation and ruin. Ships, barges and other boats, and *sampan*[9] rarely escaped their deadly strike. They perpetrated their crimes at Peam Chhkok, Daun Veal, Prek Kry, Ta Ches, Phum Tuol, and Kompong Luong, causing hundreds of casualties among the riverside population's of the Mekong, the Bassac, the Tonlé Sap and the Tonlé Toch. But these bombings, as intensive and as devastating as they were, did not disturb the determination of the KR leaders in their pursuit and realization of their final plan of attack against the last nest of resistance of the Lon Nol forces, entrenched in the capital. After leaving Cambodia in 1973, Vietnamese troops left spies and even entire families in some places, particularly in the flooded forests of the Great Tonlé Sap Lake.

After the leadership left Ratanakiri, they settled at Office 23, northeast of Kompong Thmâr on National Road No. 5 and north of Dang Khdar village, to which it was connected by a road. A little further south was Office 33, where Pol Pot and his wife, Nuon Chea, and Koy Thuon (aka Thuch), president of Sector 304, were located. East of the road facing Office 23 was Office 22, which served as Koy Thuon's headquarters. In the same perimeter, a little further south, a large meeting room was built for the Party Congress held in 1971. Further south was a logging operation, on the edge of which Office K–25 was located. K–25 was considered the Party School of Sector 304. To the east flows the Stung Chinit. On its western shore spread from north to south was a whole series of villages including Phum Tbeng, Phum Trapeaing Prey, Phum Trapeaing Khtim, Phum Bœng, Phum Sayon, Phum Baky Taing and Phum Ren. We were worried about the outside enemy but most concerned about spies, infiltrators who found a reason to enter the office and who then asked about the work of the great uncles.[10] We, ethnic minorities from Ratanakiri serving in Office 870, had been formed as a group of bodyguards to ensure their protection. The S–71 base was in Stung Trang District of Kompong Cham. We had no concerns about security at S–71. The place was 100 per cent secure. The guard group was posted at all four cardinal points. At each of the four cardinal points, there was a group of three men at S–71, and later, in 1973, at B–5, Sdok Taol, when we were closer to Phnom Penh. From then on, both bases were used. Pol Pot was at the front at Office 23, directing the attacks and Nuon Chea and Khieu Samphân remained at the rear, at S–71.

---

9   A rather narrow, elongated and elegant wooden Cambodian boat moved by an oar at the stern. Sampan is a Chinese-Malay term.

10 The 'great uncles', of course, were Pol Pot, Nuon Chea and Khieu Samphân. See ECCC reports, 1 August 2012, p. 108.

– VI –

The civil war on political and military fronts

1 – The political front

The Political Seminar of May 1971

*I*n May 1971, in preparation for the Party Congress, Pol Pot convened a political seminar that lasted more than one month and was attended by more than 100 cadres from all over the country. The seminar was held at Office 23 in Sector 304 (Kompong Thom Province), in a room decorated with portraits of Karl Marx, Friedrich Engels, Lenin and Stalin. The participants were members of district (*srok*) committees, sectors (*dambon*) and regions (*phumphea*), and the Centre was represented by Pol Pot, Nuon Chea and Khieu Samphân.[1] I also attended the seminar, while ensuring its security with 100 other guards. All the guards belonged to ethnic minorities. Security for the Centre was provided by ten guards: four Jaraï (myself, Lin, Sin and Phon), three Tampuon (Ty, Toang and Chuon) and three Krœung (Huon, Noeun and Tan). The general conference was followed by group discussions and closed with revolutionary introspection sessions of all participants. The individual introspections were preceded by two model introspections.

The General Conference was held by Pol Pot, in the morning from half-past seven to eleven o'clock and in the afternoon from two o'clock to four o'clock. He focused on the domestic situation in three areas: political, military and economic. He then discussed the international situation, relating to the development of the current revolution. Our policy was aimed at bringing together all sections of the population, especially the workers and peasants in the united struggle against the American imperialists and their valets. The peasants were the nucleus and the workers played the role of vanguard. When the population understood the need for a people's war, it would be more

---

1   Note that Phi Phuon confirms here that these three characters – Pol Pot, Nuon Chea and Khieu Samphân – were indeed at the core of the *Angkar Lœu* (Upper Organization).

determined than ever to give it its full support and to take an active part in it. Pol Pot spent almost ten days on his political presentation. It was up to each cadre to fully assimilate the Party's policy, so as to be able to apply it properly and effectively among the masses.

Regarding the military, the presentation focused on the technical aspects of people's war: what strategy should be adopted and which tactics would be best in practice, on the ground? In the economic sphere, after the coup d'état of 18 March 1970, the liberated zone extended over a vast, unbroken region, favourable to the development of a national economy that would be based mainly on rice production. On this occasion, Pol Pot also addressed the problem of conquering new agricultural territories to plant bananas, maize and cassava,[2] which would form the basis of a self-sufficient economy. Speaking of the international situation, which was addressed in only a single day, Pol Pot emphasized the importance of the substantial support provided by the socialist countries, particularly China. But the delivery of aid presented many difficulties and depended on the goodwill of the Vietnamese and the Lao. For all these reasons, it was more important than ever to take from the enemy in order to fight on the ground.

At the time of the seminar, the enemy had already begun their combing operations at Kompong Thmâr (Chenla II). But the Stung Chinit region did not undergo US bombing. It was rather the villages of Chan Kiri and Kiri Andet in the Baray region and Chamkar Andoung in Chamkar Leu District that had suffered. Pol Pot did not miss the opportunity to criticize the Americans for supporting Lon Nol to foment the coup d'état of 18 March 1970.[3] At the same time, he paid tribute to the anti-war activities of the peoples of Europe and America, especially their youth and students. But he insisted

---

2   These would later be called 'strategic crops'.

3   As the now-open American archives show, the USA and the CIA did not 'foment a coup d'état' on 18 March 1970: this is communist propaganda and Phi Phuon naturally believed in this propaganda. The Khmers dismissed Sihanouk by themselves and legally, according to the 1947 constitution, revised in 1960 to create the position of Head of State. Sihanouk had been at the country's helm since 1945 – for 25 years, enough for a country leader. Besides, his economic policy had become inadequate; he had turned to Mao, to the dismay of most educated Cambodians, and finally granted parts of the national territory for the sanctuaries of the VC, secretly and without informing his parliament. Yes, after Sihanouk was dismissed by his compatriots alone, the US supported the Lon Nol Republic, legally too, as it wished to contain the spread of communism in Southeast Asia.

on the importance of the struggle led by the Vietnamese and Lao peoples, underlining that their contribution was vital to our own struggle.[4]

As for the discussion groups, they would meet from half-past seven to eleven in the morning and from two to four in the afternoon, following the same schedule as the general conference. Each group consisted of ten people, including a chair who led discussions related to the content of the general conference. At the end of the discussions, two revolutionary-model introspections were held. After that, there were individual introspection sessions in which each group member engaged in their own ideological, political and organizational self-examination. The person concerned was first required to communicate the level of his ideological and political training, the degree of ideological maturity he had acquired, and his sense of organization. He was then submitted to various questions posed by participants who, in turn, took the floor to 'construct' the person concerned by highlighting his qualities as well as his defects and their respective causes, as well as the means that seemed appropriate to them to strengthen their good points and eliminate or at least reduce their weak points.

The introspection session for each group member ended after the person had expressed his thoughts on the remarks attributed to them. It was a rule that he should accept them willingly, without seeking to refute those he considered unjust or defamatory. There were, however, cases when the person concerned found these remarks so unacceptable that he ended his own life. It is not an exaggeration to say that instead of helping to make people more aware and more determined to serve the country and the people, some introspection sessions only confused people, and disoriented and further discouraged them. They were harmful because they dehumanized people by robbing them of the ability to distinguish right from wrong and what was just from what was not.

When everyone had completed his revolutionary introspection session, it was up to the group president to draw the lessons that emerged from these days of work by focusing on the negative aspects without forgetting

---

4   We have here a confirmation that youth demonstrations across the West against the Second Indochina War – known as "the American War in Vietnam" – sugar-coated communist propaganda and helped the VC and the KR to win the war. They had first won the international propaganda war before seizing Saigon and Phnom Penh. This testimony demonstrates that Americans had very poor information. They were not at all aware that the entire KR leadership had been meeting for weeks at Stung Chinit and that the leadership was conducting the civil war from there. They never bombed it. If they had, the *Angkar* likely would have disappeared and there would have been no DK regime.

to conclude on a generally optimistic note. The discussion sessions lasted as long as the General Conference, depending on the number of topics covered. Similarly, the revolutionary introspection sessions were held for as many days as there were members of each focus group. It is interesting to note that the first seminar lasted more than one month while those in each of the next four years did not take more than two weeks. Those were held on the background of the national and democratic revolution before proceeding to a higher stage, that is, the socialist revolution in order to achieve communism.

At that time, the headquarters of VC troops was established between Prek Prasap in Kratieh Province and Stung Trang District in Kompong Cham Province. Pol Pot did not raise this as a problem, much less ask them to leave Cambodia. Nor did he did talk about the return of the former Khmer resistance fighters who left for North Vietnam in 1954. The urgent problem of the hour was to unite to fight the common enemy, together.

The Third Party Congress of September 1971

About twenty delegates, including all members of the regional committees, participated in the Third Party Congress, which was held in the first half of September 1971 and lasted no more than ten days. The Northeast (including the provinces of Stung Treng, Ratanakiri and Mondolkiri) was represented by Ney Sarann alias Ya, Vong, Ta Lav, Hâm, Yi, and Yèm; the East by Sao Phœm,[5] Phuong, Siet Chhê, alias Tum and Sok Khnol; the North region (comprising the provinces of Kompong Cham, Kompong Thom, Siemreap and Oddar Meanchey) by Koy Thuon, Kaè Pauk[6] and Sua Vasi alias Dœun;[7]

---

5   Sao Phœm, c. 1925–1978, an ex-Khmer Issarak military leader in the Eastern region, was one of the founding members of the Khmer People's Revolutionary Party (PRPK) in 1951. Secretary of the Eastern region, he became a full member of the standing committee in 1963. He died in mysterious circumstances on 3 June 1978, while on his way to meet Pol Pot (he tried but then retreated). It might have been a suicide. He was accused of colluding with the Vietnamese.

6   Kaè Pauk, 1933–2002, an ex-Khmer Issarak, joined the movement as an adolescent but re-entered civilian life in 1954. He went again into the forest in 1964. By the early 1970s, he was a military commander of the KR's Northern region, quickly establishing a reputation as one of the most brutal of KR figures, becoming vice-secretary of the North region under Koy Thuon. After Koy Thuon's arrest, he was appointed secretary of the Northern and Central regions. He and Ta Mok, from the southwest, are the only known survivors of Pol Pot's purges of regional leaders. As regime regional secretaries, the pair worked together to form their own ruthless purges. These two figures are most responsible for the bloodbath that DK was to become, especially in the Eastern (*Bophea*) region in 1978.

7   Dœun later became head of Pol Pot's Office 870 before being purged in S–21.

the Northwest by Ros Nhim,[8] Kong Sophal (aka Keu) and Tol (chief of the Phnom Veay Chap base); the Southwest by Ta Mok[9] and Sè; the West by Chou Chet[10] (aka Xi), Chong and Sam Pal; the Special Region around Phnom Penh by Vorn Vet;[11] Autonomous Region 103 (Preah Vihear) by Man; Autonomous Region 106 (Siemreap) by Soth; Autonomous Region 505 (Kratieh) by Sim Son; the Centre by Pol Pot, Nuon Chea, Khieu Samphân, Khieu Ponnary and Son Sen, who then commanded the Central Committee troops. But neither Yun Yat, nor Hou Yuon, Hu Nim or Poc Deuskomar attended. It was the same for Ieng Sary and Son Ngoc Minh, the first on a mission to China and the second hospitalized in Beijing. We also note the absence of the guests of the brotherly parties, those of China and those of Vietnam.

Pol Pot and Nuon Chea were the only ones to address the Congress. Those present preferred the charismatic presence and eloquence of the former to

---

8 Ros Nhim (1922–1978) joined the ICP in Battambang in 1946 under the authority of Sieu Heng, where Nuon Chea later joined him. He entered the CPK Central Committee in 1963 and became head of the Northwest region in 1967, at the time of the Samlaut Rebellion, a position he held until his arrest on 11 June 1978, when he was taken to S–21 and executed.

9 Ta Mok (1925–2006) whose real name was Chhit Chhœun and was sometimes known as Brother No. 15, trained as a Buddhist monk, like most boys of his generation. He joined the revolution in 1952 and became a member of the CPK Central Committee and secretary of the Southwest (*Nirdey*) region from 1968. He gradually rose in the Party and, by 1978, ranked high in the standing committee after having taken part, with Kaè Pauk, in the cruel purges of cadres and the population throughout the country, placing his men (and women), the notorious *Nirdey*, as new cadres on the entire territory. He played a leading role in the fight against the Vietnamese occupation in the 1980s in the northern region of Cambodia. He was arrested in 1999 and an ECCC trial was expected, but he died in 2006. Based in Takeo-city under DK, he was close to Chinese advisors both during and after the DK regime.

10 After being trained at a pagoda, Chou Chet (1926–1978) entered an ICP school in South Vietnam in 1950 and joined the Party in 1951. After a year-long stay in Hanoi from 1954 to 1955, he returned to Phnom Penh, where he contributed to left-wing newspapers. After a lengthy prison sentence in 1962, he joined the CPK in Takéo in 1973 and obtained positions in the GRUNK, first in social affairs and then in religious affairs. In 1975, he was promoted to secretary of the Western region, but was arrested on 26 March 1978 and executed two months later at S–21, after writing a 427-page confession.

11 Vorn Vet, 1934–1978, whose real name was Pen Thuok, dropped out of school to join the Khmer Issarak in 1954 and soon met with Saloth Sâr. After the Geneva Agreement, he returned to Phnom Penh to become a teacher at Chamroen Vichea, a progressive school. From 1963 to 1968, he was head of the Phnom Penh Party Committee and from 1971 head of the Special Zone around Phnom Penh. A member of the standing committee, he became vice-premier for the economy in 1976. Accused of plotting with the Vietnamese and Ros Nhim to overturn the DK regime, he was the highest dignitary of the revolutionary regime to be arrested and taken to S–21, on 2 December 1978, and was executed a few days later. The regime was then devouring its own children.

the vehement rhetoric of the latter. The Congress chose 30 September 1960 as the official date of the founding of the Communist Party of Kampuchea, thus breaking all affiliation with the Indochinese Communist Party and disengaging itself from Vietnamese influence. It also reorganized its governing bodies, from the Central Committee to the base, to launch the final assault on the city of Phnom Penh.

At the end of this Congress, Pol Pot emphasized that from 1960 to 1970, our country had gone through the first stage of the National and Democratic Revolution, and 1970 had marked the beginning of a second stage, during which all efforts must be deployed to mobilize all forces inside and outside the country to fully liberate our country and our people. A national-level movement of emulation was launched on the theme, 'seize weapons from the enemy to turn against the enemy'. The vice-presidents of the regions, in collaboration with the presidents of the sectors and the districts, were assigned the task of encircling the enemy in the chief towns, while regional presidents were in charge of encircling the enemy in the regional capitals and in Phnom Penh. The ultimate goal was to fully liberate the country within five years at most.

2 – The military front: The management of the civil war from Stœng Chinit

Pol Pot obtained daily information from several sources. First, he regularly listened to foreign radio broadcasts. Then, his personal secretary, Phuok Chhay[12] alias Touch, former president of the General Association of Khmer Students (AGEK), regularly made a daily newsletter, a kind of succinct summary of news from within the country and from abroad. Finally, he had the reports that the military commanders on the front as well as regional officials sent him every day. All leaders must be at the front to guide operations directly.

In March 1972, I accompanied Nuon Chea on his journey from Stung Trang to Samlaut. We spent more than one month on the journey.[13] We travelled by car or motorbikes, or by boat. Sometimes we rode on ox carts. We also travelled on elephant backs. We returned to Stung Trang in April

---

12 Born in 1936, Phuok Chhay studied along with Hu Nim and Chau Seng at the Law Faculty in Phnom Penh. After the revolutionaries' victory in April 1975, he was in charge of welcoming Chinese experts to Pochentong. On 14 March 1977, he was arrested and sent to S–21, where he was executed on 6 July 1977.

13 See above, pp. 195–195, for details of the journey.

of the same year. The Samlaut trip aimed to neutralize the Thai troops and prevent them from opening a new front to the west, which would pose a real threat to our plan to capture the capital. In contrast to the behaviour of the South Vietnamese army, the Thai army remained rather passive in its support of Lon Nol's troops. The Northwest region committee, chaired by Ros Nhim, included Héng Tiev (aka Tol), Vanh, San (Battambang, Païlin and Pursat), Khek Pén (aka Sou, Poipet), Hoeng (Sisophon), and Samay (Samlaut).

After my return to Stung Trang, I moved from one place to another. In 1971, I accompanied Pol Pot on his journey through the country, from Krauch Chhmar in Kompong Cham Province to Stung Treng via Kratieh and Preah Vihear to hold seminars on political studies. We travelled in a convoy of three motorcycles. It was Saloth Ban (aka So Hong), his nephew and private secretary, who drove the motorbike on which Pol Pot was riding with his bodyguard, a Krœung named Huon.

At the time, no discordant voice was heard within the Party; everyone agreed on the objective to liberate of the country in less than five years. During the same period, the Centre sent Hou Yuon to the northwest to hold meetings and rallies to convince the population of the need for the people's war in order to gain its support and participation.

I married on 28 November 1972 with a girl of my choice, Sréng Bunly, a female cadre from Chœung Prey District in Kompong Cham Province. I knew her because, with Nuon Chea's wife and Khieu Samphân's wife, she was on the team of cooks for the Party Central Committee at K–5. I then told Pâng, who was responsible for Office K–5, that I intended to marry her. After asking the opinion of the interested party and consulting Pol Pot, Pâng agreed. The wedding ceremony at Office B–30 began with a salute to the Party flag, followed by the oath of the newlyweds to achieve marital happiness in accordance with Party objectives. On this occasion, Pol Pot had given us a pig for the banquet, but other traditional wedding elements like drinks, desserts, music and songs were missing. Only Pâng, Kèn, head of Pol Pot's bodyguards and So Hong's wife were involved. From this union would be born five children, four of whom are still alive. Two other guards celebrated their marriage at the same time. They were Chhun, a Tampuon national and former head of the Office of the Ministry of Social Affairs and Muon, a Jaraï. The first and his wife currently live in Ratanakiri while the second is dead, leaving a widow living in Samlaut.

Figure 6: Phi Phuon's Khmer wife, Sréng Bunly, at the time of their wedding

In 1973, I moved with Pol Pot to Y–1, on the road from Kompong Thmâr in Kompong Thom to Chamkar Andoung in Kompong Cham Province. At that time, our forces managed to seize half of the city of Kompong Cham, including the textile factory, and the Phnom Proh and Phnom Srey hills. During this battle, about 60 of my ethnic minority comrades from Ratanakiri, who formed a special unit, died under attacks by the enemy navy. The latter landed from the Mekong at Prek Krey, in Chœung Prey District. Prek Krey's garrison, along with those in Andoung Veat and Prek Chhkok, located in Kompong Chhnang Province, formed a line of defence for the Republican troops that were in charge of monitoring the supply route of the resistance forces.

Although the American bombardments stopped in 1973, those of the Lon Nol army continued nonetheless. I served as liaison officer between Pol Pot and Son Sen, who was based in Bos Khnor while commanding the KR troops engaged in the attack on Kompong Cham city. Still, throughout the five years of the civil war, whether or not American troops were on the ground[14] or in

---

14 American troops, on the specific request of the new Republican authorities (they did this without Lon Nol's approval), entered the provinces along the Vietnamese border to clear Vietnamese sanctuaries on 30 April 1970. President Nixon promised they would not penetrate more than 30 kilometres into Cambodia and would leave by 30 June. So, the VC troops simply moved swiftly westwards, as far as occupying the Angkor park, near Siemreap. After 30 June, there were never more than 30 military advisors, and never in combat positions. By 17 April

the air, our leaders kept repeating that America was our paramount enemy. America had invaded many countries in the world and had bombed us cease-lessly for 200 days and 200 nights in 1973. The secondary enemies were those who refused to join the revolution. As to the clandestine enemies, they were CIA and KGB agents, and we needed to make a clear distinction between the last two categories: open and hidden.

After occupying half of the city, the resistance forces withdrew under ene-my fire, taking part of the population with them to the north, to the liberated areas of Treung, Bos Khnor, Thnal Bek, Srè Veal and Stung Trang, all in the same province.

In 1973, the Vietnamese left Cambodia to participate in the general elections envisaged by the Peace Agreements signed with the Americans in January 1973 in Paris. As a result, Nuon Chea had to travel to Vietnam in 1974 to negotiate with them. Previously, I had accompanied Nuon Chea to negotiations that took place at the border between the two countries, specifi-cally in the district of Ponhea Krèk in Kompong Cham Province. Sao Phœm had also been present. After leaving Cambodia in 1973, Vietnamese troops left spies and even entire families in some places, particularly in the flooded forests around the Great Tonlé Sap Lake.[15]

In 1974, a large delegation of the Provisional Revolutionary Government of the Republic of South Vietnam, led by Prime Minister Nguyen Tan Phat, made an official friendly visit to the liberated area of Cambodia. Pol Pot, accompanied by Khieu Samphân, Hou Yuon and Hu Nim, travelled through Stung Trang to the Bœng Ket rubber plantation in Khtuoy, where they wel-comed the delegation. At the time, Héng Samrin[16] was commander of the 4th Division of the Eastern region, which had more than 3,000 men, including about 2,000 responsible for transport and supply and 1,000 fighting forces.

1975, all had left, a fact that the KR combatants totally ignored, convinced that they were still fighting (and therefore defeating) the Americans. See the testimony of first-hand witness Fr François Ponchaud on 17 April 1975, in *L'Impertinent au Cambodge*, Paris: Magellan & Cie, 2013, p. 69.

15 This last sentence is repetitious, but the point bears repeating. The belief that all Vietnamese people in Cambodia were spies is ludicrous, but it was widespread and deeply held, and led to disastrous, endless and increasingly intense purges.

16 Héng Samrin, born in 1934, became the flag-bearer of the Vietnam-imposed People's Republic of Kampuchea (1979–1989), as he was the most senior KR officer who had defected to Vietnam. Today, aged 89, he is still President of the Cambodian National Assembly and No..2 member of the CPP (The Cambodian People's Party). The body, usually without any debate, merely endorses all the decisions of the executive and its leader, Hun Sèn, as in communist countries.

In July 1974, we had a big meeting at S–71 at the village of Meak, in Stung Trang District, not far from the Mekong River, just south of what would become the Dey Krâhâm re-education camp for returnees late in the following year. The meeting lasted more than a week. Ieng Sary had come back from Beijing to attend, and it was presided over by the two 'uncles', Pol Pot and Nuon Chea. The international situation was discussed and the progress in the liberated zones. We also had 'life sessions'.[17] I was again in charge of logistics, including feeding the one hundred or so participants. There was a big blackboard on which the issues discussed were detailed and diagrams of the troops converging on Phnom Penh were drawn. This is the time when the evacuation of Phnom Penh was first discussed. It is also the time when I heard that Hou Yuon did not agree with the evacuation plan.

---

17 Meaning introspection or mutual criticism and self-criticism sessions.

– VII –

The last years of the civil war

In October 1973, Pol Pot left Stung Chinit and settled in Meak, located in the district of Stung Trang, where he conducted another seminar of political studies in May 1974. He moved closer to Phnom Penh in October 1974, settling at Office B–5 in Taing Paun Village, Kompong Tralach Leu District in Kompong Chhnang Province. He stayed there for seven months, until the liberation of Phnom Penh on 17 April 1975. Son Sen, meanwhile, moved to Dok Tol on National Road No. 5, Ta Mok to National Road No. 4 and Koy Thuon to Prek Kdam, also along Road No. 5. By motorcycle, from Meak in Stung Trang District to Tracheh-Sala Lek Pram, on National Road No. 5, Kompong Chhnang district, it takes a whole day.

1 – The Chinese film: The Heroic People of Kampuchea

In March 1974, a team of four Chinese filmmakers began filming the film *The Heroic People of Kampuchea*, assisted by four Cambodian colleagues, including comrade Chan, a former resistance refugee in Hanoi, and Kim. Ieng Sary also returned from Beijing at the time of the filming. They first arrived in the province of Ratanakiri, then travelled by road through Siempang, Stung Treng, Kratieh and Kompong Cham. From there, they headed to Skoun and Prek Kdam to reach the B–5 office near Oudong, where they met Pol Pot. The latter and the other KR leaders were present in the film, as well as the women's regiment taking part in the attacks on Phnom Penh. This regiment appeared on the banknotes of DK (which were never distributed). It was headed by two commanders: one, named Vin, is the wife of General San, head of the Central Committee's 920 Division, who would be taken prisoner by Ta Mok and executed at the same time as So Sarœun and Khorn, in 1997. The other is Yeay Maen, a protégée of Ta Mok, president of the Southwest region, where she came from. The film shows workers actively building a dam and water tank on the Stung Chinit in Kompong Thom Province. During the filming, the Chinese newspapermen went as far as Kep[1] to swim: I saw them!

---

1   The sea resort of Kep had fallen to the revolutionaries on 16 March 1974.

The film was screened in 1976 for the accredited diplomatic corps in Phnom Penh. We saw images of our fighters firing shells on Phnom Penh. Also present in the film were images of the enemy navy and barges whose advance was blocked by mines hanging from railroad bridges spanning the Mekong between Kompong Cham and Phnom Penh.

In March 1974, accompanied by a few bodyguards including myself, Pol Pot went to Kep, a famous seaside resort dating from the colonial era that had just been liberated. Starting from Office B–5, he crossed national roads No. 4, No. 3 and No. 2 before reaching the coast. He wanted to visit the liberated areas of the region. The trip, made alternately by motorcycle and car, lasted less than a week, exactly three days to go and three more to return. Our convoy included twelve bodyguards, including myself.

Lin, Huon, Mong, Ban, and Pon were on five motorcycles and an American 4x4 car owned by the Southwest region office was available for the leaders. From National Road No. 4, Ta Mok, President of the region joined us. Sê, the head of Kampot, did the same. At lunch, we were served plenty of seafood: shrimp, lobster, crab, squid and mussels. We did not stay more than three hours in Kep, subject from time to time to the artillery fire of the enemy stationed in Kampot. Pol Pot took advantage of this brief visit to swim in the sea water. He would return to Kep regulary, twice a year, and loved to float on the water for hours after a few swimming exercises. In the same year 1974, I also accompanied him when he, along with the ambassador and military attaché from China, visited the islands Koh Rong, Poulo Wai and Koh Tang. We left Kep in the evening to spend the night at Phnom Vor, nearby. This was the first time I had been able to see the sea and bathe there, but not swim. I did not know how to swim. And it was also the first time I visited the salt marshes.

In 1974, the Battle of Oudong forced us to transfer the population of some 30,000 people west to Amleang,[2] to save their lives. It was the time when Pol Pot approached the capital and installed his headquarters at B-5, in the forest, west of the railway, at the edge of a small river which comes down from Phnom Aural. This was the only time I intervened in the fighting. Indeed, finding myself near the Tonlé Sap, our group was fired on by sailors escorting a barge that was carrying sugar, dried fish and *prahok* to the capital. I asked permission to answer with B-40, then B-50 rocket grenades to aim

---

2   It was near this village that Duch established the prison-extermination centre M–13, a proto-type of S–21, in 1971.

at the barge's head. But I did not see any victims and the boat was able to continue on its way.

2 – The last weeks before the fall of Phnom Penh

From January to March 1975, the tension continued to grow. The first phase of the final assault plan against Phnom Penh included the second capture of Oudong and the interruption of navigation on the lower Mekong, including attacks on Neak Luong's Republican naval base and on National Road No. 4 between Kompong Speu and Phnom Penh. The Special Region was responsible for the assault launched from National Road No. 2 towards the south, on the west bank of the Mekong and the islands in front of Phnom Penh. Pol Pot managed the military operations personally, assisted by Son Sen, who directly commanded the troops at Dok Tol, a KR outpost. Every two or three days. Son Sen travelled by motorcycle to Pol Pot, to consult and receive instructions. He followed the track that connected Dok Tol, Kraing Khdoep and Ang Praleung Pagoda to Amleang in Kompong Speu Province. The two also communicated with each other by T.O.25 and T.O.46 [radios]. The enemy sometimes succeeded in intercepting our coded communications, while we did the same with theirs. In order to avoid any decoding, we used double security messages, but we mostly used passwords. For example, the number 500 meant that Pol Pot summoned Sen to his headquarters, 350 indicated that the encounter would occur at Dok Tol. Self-taught in the art of war, Son Sen had not attended any military academy. It was the same for Pol Pot.[3] It was important to understand the situation of the enemy and follow his movements step by step. Our outposts were constantly subjected to heavy bombardments by the enemy, who continued to resist fiercely on the northern and western fronts. From January 1975, our forces and those of Lon Nol fought to the death, but no side had managed to win. On the enemy side, General Ith Suong[4] directed the operations.

In March, the military situation changed dramatically. The enemy was by then completely paralyzed: all its land, river and air supply routes had been

---

3   In fact, Pol Pot received military training in China during 1965–66.

4   It seems here that Phi Phuon is not quite aware that Lt Gen. Sak Sutsakhan was in charge of the entire military operation on the Republican side at the end of the civil war, while General Ith Suong's purview was limited to the capital. Ith Suong was known to be a merciless foe.

cut. It mainly used savage bombardments, not even sparing Oudong's Buddha pagodas or the statues on Phnom Chettareus.

Throughout the country, revolutionary leaders were erecting monuments in honour of fallen fighters and cadres. One such monument in Stung Trang honours the memory of more than 60 ethnic-minority fighters who died in the fighting around the city of Kompong Cham in 1974.[5] For each death, a tomb was erected registering his name, date of birth and the day he was killed. Opposite, a vast monument for the commemorative ceremony was built three hundred meters from the banks of the Mekong River. To the west of Kraing Lovea railway station in Kompong Chhnang Province, a monument of the same kind was also erected. In Siemreap, north of Sras Srâng, on the road to Banteay Srey, a similar monument was being built. Pol Pot, on behalf of the Central Committee of the Party, chose June 30th as the date to commemorate all of our ancestors who died for the sake of the homeland. He directed all Party and Government officials to come to Wat Phnom (Phnom Penh) every year. So Hong, who wrote this directive, asked Pol Pot why he chose the date of June 30th. He replied, 'Because it's the longest day of the year – the summer solstice.'

Some preparations were made for when the KR took power. Bank notes had been printed in 1974 and were stored near Wat Phnom after liberation, but were never used as there was no network of markets (30 July, p. 78–79). There was a strong desire to abolish private property and fight against corruption. We wished ownership to become collective and even oxen and buffaloes belonged to the community.[6]

A final meeting took place at B–5, at Tan Poun village, Kompong Tralach District, where Om (Uncle) Pol Pot, Om Nuon Chea, Om Khieu Samphân, Ta Mok, Son Sen, Koy Thuon, Vorn Vet, and Sao Phœm were present. Victory was now possible and we could attack from all sides. It was agreed that we had to evacuate the entire capital because our experience of the evacuation of other district capitals, like Oudong, Neak Luong, Skoun and Angtasom in Tramkâk District of Takeo Province, had been very positive. All the military leaders said that if the inhabitants remained, the Party would find it difficult to control them. Otherwise, they said, they did not know how long we could remain in power.[7]

---

5   Phi Phuon also spoke of this during his ECCC testimony, 31 July, p. 39.

6   Phi Phuon made this point at the ECCC, 30 July, pp. 79–80.

7   This was emphasized again by Phi Phuon at the ECCC on 30 July 2012, answering a question by Elisabeth Simoneau-Fort, the co-lawyer for the civil parties, p. 91. If the KR leadership had

Nuon Chea stood up and was the first to say the evacuations were necessary and we should all approve this plan. And then Khieu Samphân said he agreed,[8] and all applauded to mark their unanimous approbation. It was unanimous and none present expressed any reservations openly.

---

not taken that drastic decision, the radical revolution, as they conceived it, could not have taken place. *Angkar* and its guerrilla soldiers just could not control the cities at all.

8   Khieu Samphân has always claimed that he had always disapproved of the total evacuation of the capital and therefore was not responsible for that decision.

– VIII –

Angkar enters Phnom Penh, 17 April 1975

1 – The first days in the capital

*I*t was the military leaders who first liberated Phnom Penh: Son Sen, Ta Mok, Koy Thuon and Sao Phœm entered the city from all sides. After ensuring maximum security, they let Pol Pot take his turn.

I was first ordered to go into Phnom Penh on 19 April with Son Sen, and we arrived along Road No. 4.[1] There were many people leaving the city, all along the road, some bare-footed. One family was transporting two bags; they were sweating. I approached and asked what they were carrying. They would not tell me, so I inspected the bags and saw banknotes. I told them that, in the liberated zones, there was no currency and money was no longer in use. They burst into tears. I tried to console them, saying that the situation was evolving and that they should not be upset.[2] Later, I heard from soldiers that the population in the people's communes was suffering. They also remarked that it served them right because they'd had an easy life in Phnom Penh, and now they must endure the same difficulties as those suffered by soldiers in the civil war.

There were also corpses, some decomposing, at the crossroads between National Road No. 3 and No. 4, and near the Pochentong Airport. Son Sen told me there was fierce opposition at certain places and some soldiers had to be shot. Almost no inhabitants remained.

It was the first time I ever entered the capital. Son Sen took me round to all the strategic places: the Olympic Stadium, the Royal Palace, the Monivong Bridge and, in the end, the Chruy Changwar Bridge, which was broken at the time. The French Embassy, where all the remaining foreigners had taken refuge – except those of communist countries, Vietnam and China in particular – was in the area under the responsibility of Koy Thuon and Kaè Pauk, both from the Northern region. The first aircraft from China, with its delegation of officials,

---

1   This is the main road, built with American aid in 1959, from Phnom Penh to Sihanoukville.
2   Phi Phuon also reported this anecdote at the Khmer Rouge Tribunal on 30 July 2012, p. 72.

along with Ieng Sary, disembarked at Pochentong one week after liberation, while the foreign European refugees were still at the French embassy. I was tasked to find suitable accommodation for these 'guests', in the area behind the Royal Palace.

As for Pol Pot himself, he entered the capital only on 20 April 1975, in a convoy of three cars along National Road No. 4. He sat in a jeep driven by Meal, a Khmer, with Ban, Pon and his two bodyguards, Huon, a Krœung and Lin, a Jaraï, and Pâng. I was in a four-wheel drive and the others in a Land Rover. From Dok Tol, the convoy took the highway to Thnâl Totung and reached the Phnom Penh railway station. The city was completely empty, occupied only by soldiers. Debris of cars, trucks and burnt motorbikes strewed the streets of Phnom Penh, where dogs and abandoned cats roamed. In Bey Chan, east of Pochentong, we saw soldiers burning dead bodies. There was no looting or damage. At that time, Nuon Chea remained at Office 74, in Meak, directing the evacuation operations of the urban population. He arrived in Phnom Penh only on 24 April, the day before Ieng Sary arrived from Beijing. The latter arrived at Pochentong International Airport in a Chinese special plane, accompanied by Shen Chia, deputy head of the International Liaison Department of the Central Committee of the Chinese Communist Party.[3]

The leaders of the Communist Party of Kampuchea chose to come to the railway station first, partly because it was easier to ensure security, but especially to commemorate the holding of the Founding Party Congress there in 1960. We stayed at the Phnom Penh Railway Station three days before moving to the Royal Palace and settling at the adjoining Silver Pagoda.

Pol Pot lodged inside the Silver Pagoda, where he had a bed and a desk. Not all the buildings of the Royal Palace were used and the objects there remained untouched. Some of the future Office 870[4] staff and guards, a total of more than 300 people, moved into the middle space. These staff and guards would later be shifted to Office 870 on the site of the former National Assembly building, which would become Pol Pot and Nuon Chea's centre of operations. Others were at the railway station, the Ministry of National Defence, the Presidency of the Council of Ministers, Wat Phnom and Chamkar Mon. At that time, Pol Pot held no political meetings at the pagoda. Only cadres came in turn to consult him on issues that concerned them directly. As a security

---

3   The foreign community was still in the French Embassy.
4   Code name of the office from which Pol Pot and Nuon Chea directed the regime.

measure, he spent the night either at the Silver Pagoda or at K–3, a villa located at the corner formed by Pasteur Street and the old Dr Hanh Street.[5]

During the transfer, Pol Pot was visiting the Trapeaing Ang Doeng dam in Tram Kak District (Takeo Province), accompanied by Ta Mok, in charge of the building site.

Employees in the capital's power plants and drinking water plants were not evacuated, but all hospital staff were evacuated and all hospitals were renamed. The Khmer–Soviet Friendship Hospital became 'April 17' and was directed by Dr Thiounn Thiœun (aka Pen), assisted by Dy Phon (aka Thok), a dentist trained in Paris. They led a staff that had served the revolutionary movement. Shortly after, in May. Phthisiology specialist Dr In Sokan (aka Ni), arrived from Paris. There were also doctors trained in the *maquis*, Hong and Poeun, Ieng Sary's eldest daughter and Ieng Vany's husband. From the industrial point of view, the foundry in Kbal Thnâl would not be created until around 1977. But the car tyre factory in Takhmau, the glass factory in Stung Meanchey and the distillery of Prek Phneou, which produced a kind of wine from sticky rice, as well as Kompong Som's beer brewery, were soon started again, thanks to the help of Chinese experts who arrived in Phnom Penh in the early days of the new regime.

2 – First meeting after the capture of Phnom Penh

The first important meeting after the capture of Phnom Penh was held in May 1975 in the Silver Pagoda compound. It lasted ten days and secretaries from all regions attended. The Centre was represented by Pol Pot, Nuon Chea, Ieng Sary, Son Sen and Khieu Samphân; Sector 304 by Koy Thuon, Kaè Pauk and Sua Vasi (aka Dœun)[6]; the Northeast by Ney Sarann (aka Ya), Vy, Lav and Hâm; the Special region by Vorn Vet and Chéng An;[7] the Southwest by Ta Mok, Sé, and Kâng Chap;[8] the West by Chou Chet, Chong and Sèm Pal; the

---

5 Now Street 214.

6 So Dœun alias Sua Vasi, became president of Office 870 in October 1975, but was arrested on 12 February 1977, sent to S–21 and executed. Khieu Samphân replaced him as Office 870 president.

7 Chéng An was secretary of Sector 15, in the Special Zone just north of Phnom Penh in Kandal province. In 1976, he was placed in charge of industry. He was arrested in early November 1978, accused of fomenting a plot with the Vietnamese, then taken to S–21 and executed in early December.

8 Kâng Chap (–1978) was an associate of Ta Mok in the Southwest region and participated, with Kaè Pauk, in the purge of the Northern region in 1977. He was arrested on 2 August 1978 and sent to S–21.

Northwest by Ros Nhim, Kong Sophal and Eng Teav; and the East by Sao Phœm, Phuong[9] and Siet Chhê[10] (aka Tum). Note, however, the absence of Hu Nim and especially Hou Yuon, who was banned from entering Phnom Penh, because he was against total collectivization, in opposition to the creation of real 'cooperatives' created and managed by the collectives' members. He also opposed the evacuation of all cities.

The meeting, which lasted about ten days, began like all the meetings of this kind, with Pol Pot's assessment of the general political, military and economic situations. He spoke for the first four days, followed by group discussion sessions, but without individual introspection sessions. The Party secretary took more than four hours to develop his ideas on seven subjects relating to: 1) the general situation; 2) Party-building; 3) population control; 4) building a self-sufficient economy; 5) 'grasping and holding' the population in people's communes based on rice production; 6) managing foreign affairs, including dealing with accredited foreign embassies in Phnom Penh; and 7) setting up the government and establishing an assembly of people's representatives.

Nuon Chea then spoke as the second secretary of the Party, followed by each regional secretary. After that, Son Sen and Ieng Sary spoke in the names of the Revolutionary Army and the Ministry of Foreign Affairs, but Khieu Samphân was silent.[11] Of course, as always, no discordant voice was heard. Finally, the meeting ended by deciding that the country had passed the stage of the national and democratic revolution and that, from now on, the Party would strive to achieve communism by beginning a socialist revolution. After this meeting, the Party's two main journals, the *Revolutionary Flag* and the *Revolutionary Youth* were launched, both edited by Yun Yat under the super-

---

9   Phuong was born in Takeo province. He joined the Khmer Issarak but returned to civilian life as a carpenter in Phnom Penh in 1954. He again joined the *maquis* in 1962, when he was named secretary of Sector 21, in Kamchay Meas district. He became adjunct secretary of the Eastern region in 1971 and, in April 1976, took charge of rubber plantations. He was arrested on 6 June 1978, taken to S–21 and executed shortly after.

10 Siet Chhê (1932–1977), a schoolteacher in Phnom Penh from 1954 to 1964, joined Saloth Sâr at Office 100 near the Vietnamese border. He was in Pol Pot's Beijing delegation, which met Mao in 1975, and then was appointed logistics chief at the General Staff Headquarters in Phnom Penh. In March 1977 he fell a victim to the purge that swept those associated with the former Khmer–Chinese Friendship Association and was taken to S–21 for execution, together with Hu Nim.

11 Khieu Samphân's silence is quite logical: first, he did not represent any region; second, Sihanouk had not resigned. Therefore, he had no official position in the regime – yet. He was just a kind of *éminence grise*.

vision of Nuon Chea. The meeting's decisions emphasised that the economy must be based on the massive production of rice. To achieve this result, it would be necessary to develop a whole system of hydraulic development, with networks of canals and dikes throughout the country.[12]

---

12 Here, Phi Phuon does not mention another big meeting at the Institute of Technology during the same month with more officials from all over the country, to which he was neither invited nor asked to be part of its security. This omission is unsurprising: he was neither a local nor a national leader, and he was no longer directly responsible for Pol Pot's security. Nonetheless, he told the ECCC Tribunal that he was aware that it had taken place. During this big meeting, the leadership allocated, or confirmed, all local leadership positions down to the district level. See Bun Chan's description on p. 293, below. During this meeting, Pol Pot claimed that the civil war had caused some 600,000 victims among the Cambodian population. The number was written on a large blackboard in the main amphitheatre. That spurious figure (I think it includes victims from both sides of the conflict), which is based on no investigation of any sort that we know of, has served as a base for many historians of DK.

– IX –

In charge of safety and logistics at the Ministry of Foreign Affairs (B–1)

1 – My last days with Pol Pot

*A*fter liberation, I lived for two weeks at K–3, a building located in the centre of the foreign embassy district. The Vietnamese Embassy was not in this district, located instead at Chamkar Mon. Office 870 was then an eight-building complex around what had been Khieu Ponnary's house in Dr Hanh Street. Or maybe it was bigger. I only knew where I was sent on duty. Those who knew kept the secret well; I had no right to know and I had no intention of knowing. Pol Pot did not always live in the same place. Sometimes, he slept in K–3, sometimes the Silver Pagoda and sometimes K–1, located near the Tonlé Bassac. Nuon Chea and Pol Pot always moved together, but never lived in the same building. For their security, a battalion of 300 to 350 soldiers was assigned to them. By the end of 1975, the Office 870 moved permanently to the buildings of the former Buddhist Institute.[1]

After returning from Beijing, where she had accompanied Pol Pot in 1970, Khieu Ponnary was still in a normal state. She devoted herself body and soul to her role as president of the Democratic Kampuchean Women's Association, assisted in her work by the wife of Koy Thuon. Her activities were deployed in Sector 304 (North), in the Southwest and also in Poeng village in Baray District and Sandan District in Kompong Thom Province. Towards the end of 1975 and early in 1976, she began to develop Alzheimer's disease.[2] She then placed with Mrs Phan Thik, the wife of her nephew, Srey Chanthoeun. Phan Thik served as her companion and helped her settle in a villa in Boeng Kéng Kâng, near the current Bokor junction.[3] Without being totally deranged, she lost her memory and did not even recognize the people who were closest to her. The slightest annoyance made her angry. She accused Chhim Sam Ok

---

1 The Buddhist Institute and the National Assembly were next to each other at the time.
2 Most analysts speak of paranoia.
3 This is the big intersection of Monivong Boulevard and Mao Zedong Boulevard.

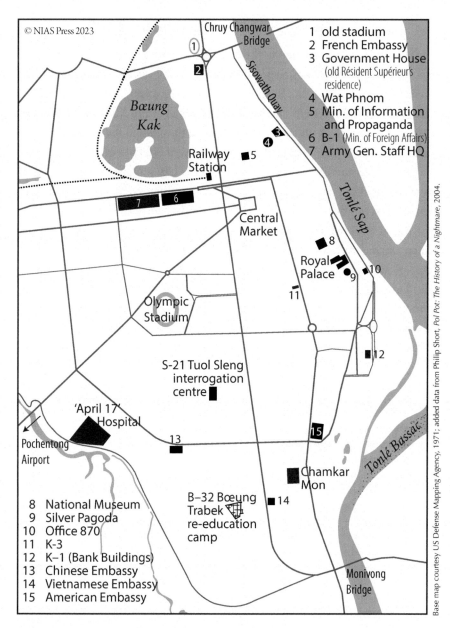

© NIAS Press 2023

Base map courtesy US Defense Mapping Agency, 1971; added data from Philip Short, *Pol Pot: The History of a Nightmare*, 2004.

1 old stadium
2 French Embassy
3 Government House
   (old Résident Supérieur's
   residence)
4 Wat Phnom
5 Min. of Information
   and Propaganda
6 B-1 (Min. of Foreign Affairs)
7 Army Gen. Staff HQ

Chruy Changwar Bridge

Bœung Kak

Railway Station

Central Market

Royal Palace

Olympic Stadium

S-21 Tuol Sleng interrogation centre

'April 17' Hospital

Pochentong Airport

Chamkar Mon

B–32 Bœung Trabek re-education camp

Monivong Bridge

Sisowath Quay

Tonlé Sap

Tonlé Bassac

8   National Museum
9   Silver Pagoda
10 Office 870
11 K-3
12 K-1 (Bank Buildings)
13 Chinese Embassy
14 Vietnamese Embassy
15 American Embassy

Map 3: Phnom Penh during the Khmer Rouge period

(aka Pång) of being a Vietnamese agent and having her vaccinated to drive her crazy. After this, she was permanently separated from her husband, who lived most of the time at K–1, but frequently went on working visits to the provinces.

2 – The Ministry of Foreign Affairs (B–1)[4]

In May 1975, I was assigned to the Ministry of Foreign Affairs, B-1,[5] where I settled permanently. I was responsible for both staff safety and logistics. I was assisted in my work at B–1 by Comrade Tuon, a Krœung, and Comrade Sin, the future Mrs Mâk Ben[6] and head of the cooks at the Ministry of Foreign Affairs. I would go to Office 870 from time to time, when Pol Pot summoned me there. Kèn, a Jaraï, replaced me as the head of Pol Pot's guards.

Security issues at B–1 were minimal, as the city was almost empty and all forms of delinquency had disappeared. The only major incident would be the mysterious murder of Malcolm Caldwell.[7] And, again, it took place more than two kilometres from our Ministry and I was not informed until several hours later. During my hours of service, like all the guards, I carried a pistol and an AK–47 with a folding butt. I was never given the opportunity to use them.

Two major concerns required the full attention of the Party leadership: production and security. Diplomatic and information work at B–1 were of course not part of my duties. For instance, Comrade Mut, revolutionary name Keat Chhon,[8] was tasked with writing the official speeches, like those to the

---

4   It was established in the former Council of Ministers building, designed by Vann Molyvann, on Pochentong Boulevard. It has now been demolished and replaced by a new Chinese-style Council of Ministers building. Next to it, Hun Sèn had his 'Peace Palace' constructed. Office 870, the seat of the Party's standing committee and the centre of power, was situated at the former Buddhist Institute near the Royal Palace. There was no operating Council of Ministers under DK.

5   'B' from the the word *boroteh*, meaning 'foreign'.

6   Mâk Ben went to France in 1966 and obtained a doctorate in public administration in 1972. He joined the FUNK, then the *maquis* and the Ministry of Foreign Affairs in 1976, where he worked in the press department. In 1979, he went to Beijing with Yun Yat to work at Radio DK. He became DK ambassador to Yugoslavia in 1987 and played a role in the negotiations that led to the 1991 Paris agreement. He joined the Phnom Penh government in 1998.

7   Malcolm Caldwell (1931–1978), a British academic from the School of Oriental and African Studies at the University of London, was sympathetic to the KR regime. He was accidentally shot in late December 1979 during a visit to DK. See below, pp. 157–158.

8   Keat Chhon (1934–) became a well-known politician who served all regimes, from Sihanouk's to Hun Sèn's (1994–2013), as minister of finance. During his scientific studies in France at *L'École Nationale supérieure de génie civil* and at the *Centre nucléaire de Saclay* outside Paris from 1954 to 1961, he joined the French Communist Party and the Marxist-Leninist Circle. While in France, he married a Vietnamese student who had been brought up at *Le Couvent des oiseaux*, at Dalat in South Vietnam. In 1961, he first worked as an engineer at the Ministry of Industry and Public Works, and then was appointed rector of the newly created University of Kompong Cham (1965–1968), in fact an engineering school. He was minister of industry and commerce from 1967 until 1969. As vice-minister in the Council of Ministers under Penn Nouth. he rallied to the GRUNK in Beijing. He returned to Phnom Penh in a special

UN or the non-aligned countries conferences.[9]

It had been explained to me, firstly, that we must undergo a revolution in order to achieve communism. Secondly, this could only be achieved through an inevitable class struggle. In China, I was shown a film with Mao Zedong and also with Lenin and the workers. Thirdly, I must be disciplined vis-à-vis the Party, totally devoted to the Party. To die or live, it does not matter: we only breathe through the Party; we must not look for anything other than that. I joined the Communist Youth in July 1968 in Ratanakiri and the Party as a candidate in 1971 at Stung Chinit. I am a full member of the Party.

I was not responsible for any arrest, change of position or appointments – except for some low-level technical staff such as cooks, gardeners and drivers. What took up most of my time would be what we call logistics: taking care of supplying the Ministry with everything it needed. It was my responsibility to verify that all material goods were properly sorted out and stored, especially food. I would go to the Central Market[10] to stock up on rice and other foodstuffs for the Ministry of Foreign Affairs. It was Pang, then Dœun, then Khieu Samphân who, from Office 870, took charge of supplying the Central Market with salt, sugar, fruits, vegetables, and so on. We made an accounting of everything that was taken away for this or that.

For me, like all Party members, revolutionary duty was more important than married life. I lived separated from my wife. I only visited her when I had the time. From this union, three boys and two girls were born. The eldest child, a boy named Phuon Thirakvann but known as Chek, was born on 1 January 1975 at B–17 in Stung Trang District, Kompong Cham Province. The second child is also a boy, Phi Sakkada, called Da, born in November 1976 at the April 17 Hospital (ex-Soviet-Cambodia Friendship Hospital) while I was accompanying Pol Pot to Beijing. He is now a Lieutenant Colonel of the Royal Cambodian Armed Forces in Military District No. 5 (Battambang).

---

convoy of Vietnamese jeeps on 22 April 1975, after travelling down the Hô Chi Minh Trail.

Under the DK regime, he was in charge of general policy at the Ministry of Foreign Affairs, holding a post second only to Ieng Sary and So Hong. He had the privilege of travelling on the Chinese plane that took Sihanouk and his wife to Beijing on 6 January 1979, the day before the arrival of the Vietnamese in Phnom Penh. He also was part of the DK delegation to New York a few days later, where he pleaded for support for the overturned DK government and for help to ensure that Sihanouk did not remain in the West. He refused to testify at the ECCC.

9   See ECCC daily reports 31 July 2012, p. 64.

10 Also called the 'New Market', built in the 1930s.

The third child is a daughter, Vi Sutheara, called Mom, born at B–1 in March 1978; she now lives with her husband in Anlong Véng. The fourth child, a boy, died in Anlong Véng of a relapse of typhoid fever when he was one year old. The youngest, Vi Vathana, called Noy, was born in January 1989 in Phnom Malay, where she currently lives with her husband.

My wife cooked for the leaders of the 870 Office, with Mrs. Nuon Chea and Mrs. Khieu Samphân, as well as a certain Yin, a niece of Nuon Chea. Yin was married to Chen, who was in charge of the security in the Kratieh special sector. These women were also responsible for tasting all their dishes to ensure that Party leadership would not be poisoned. We had three meals a day, starting with thick rice porridge for breakfast, as is the habit in Cambodia. For the other two meals, they had all sorts of sour soups, fried vegetables, and meat and fried fish. They also had fruits and sweets.

For the efficiency of my work, I placed in each unit a security cell that reported to me daily. No act of theft, delinquency or vandalism was reported to me; no thefts of bicycles or motorcycles, or even vegetables. It was the same for night-time encounters between boys and girls: nobody sneaked for private meetings at night. Everyone scrupulously fulfilled the tasks demanded by the Party, as best as they could.

I very much regretted the arrest and killing of Koy Thuon. I did not know if the accusations were true or if he had been framed. Called back to Phnom Penh on 14 March 1976, he was first appointed Minister of Commerce before being placed, towards the end of the year, under house arrest in a villa located between K–1 and the old American Embassy. He had a bad reputation for loving good cheer and was known for having had many love affairs with pretty girls, whom he made marry his officers once they stopped enjoying his favour. Arrested for sex cases on the orders of Pol Pot and taken by Pâng to S–21 on 25 January 1977, he was later accused of being the brain of a pro-American opposition and executed on 17 March of the same year.

Arrests were surprising for everyone, but senior leaders said nothing about these. We just knew that people had disappeared. Similarly, nobody mentioned any killings.

Our movement was called the National Democratic Revolution during the resistance period. However, after liberation on 17 April 1975, it was called the Socialist Revolutionary Party, with the purpose of creating a communist state. Communism was the goal of the regime. It was true that during the national resistance, we fought against the American imperialists and their servants, while under the democratic resistance, we fought the feudalists, capitalists and reactionaries. The resistance was against the former regime, not any particular groups of people. However, it was implemented in an extreme manner that took many innocent lives. Everyone was petrified, including me! I might have been arrested or even executed if the Vietnamese troops had not overthrown the regime.[11]

3 – My duties outside the Ministry

In Phnom Penh, I enjoyed complete freedom of movement. I travelled either by motorcycle or in a French car, a Peugeot 403. At the time of Prince Norodom Sihanouk's *Sangkum Reastr Niyum*, Cambodia abounded in French cars. Also, in 1975, we had no fewer than 4,000 German Mercedes cars, collected from all over the country and stored in Phnom Penh. I reported this information to Pol Pot, who recommended that I maintain them well so that we would not have to import any for twenty years. All car drivers for the foreign embassies based in Phnom Penh were to learn to drive at the Technical School of Russey Keo, under the responsibility of Thiounn Mumm.[12]

I did not go to S–21 unless I was on duty, and I was not allowed to go inside. Each time, I collected at the door some documents that I was responsible for bringing to Ieng Sary. During DK, I went there only three times. The outer perimeter was fenced with vertical, corrugated iron plates. I could not suspect whether it was a prison because, at that time, I did not know what a prison was, having never seen one in my life.

I counted two close friends at B–1, Seang Huor Long alias Phat, an engineer trained in the German Democratic Republic and married to Lin, and Héng Pich alias Chhân, an engineer trained in the Soviet Union and married to Vi. I told them, 'You will be appointed ambassadors to a foreign country while I am going to vegetate here, ignorant as I am!' They taught me the basics of the English language. Both were accused of being agents of the Soviet KGB and would be liquidated after being interned at S–21.

---

11 This paragraph is extracted from Long Dany's interview of Phi Phuon for DC-CAM, 19 December 2010, p. 15.

12 Thiounn Mumm (1925–2022), the grandson of Thiounn, the well-known interpreter and then-long-serving Minister of the Palace under the Protectorate, became the first Cambodian to enter *l'École polytechnique* in Paris. Mumm joined the KR revolution in Beijing in the early 1970s. Under the KR regime, he was in charge of rehabilitating the entire industrial network of the country and creating a technical education programme, essentially from scratch.

All artistic performances and film screenings took place at the Chatomuk Theatre, which seats about 300. Each performance was filled with people selected from the staff of ministries and departments and military units, as well as factory workers. Thus, I attended the projection of the Chinese documentary film realized in the liberated zones in 1974. The comments were made in Khmer by the services of Propaganda Minister Hu Nim. I was also present there two or three times while ensuring the security of visiting foreign delegations.

Meetings and other large gatherings were held at the Olympic Stadium. On 1 January 1976, I attended the meeting marking the anniversary of the founding of the Revolutionary Army of Kampuchea (RAK). One thousand people were there and Pol Pot reviewed the troops in his capacity as secretary of the Military Committee of the Party Central Committee. Son Sen, Nuon Chea, Ieng Sary and Khieu Samphân were also present. I also took part in the rally on 7 July of the same year, celebrating the victory of 17 April 1975. This was a sort of dress rehearsal for future celebrations; the regime had not yet the means to give it all the desired lustre. Victory anniversaries were to be celebrated in 1976, 1977 and 1978, always on 17 April.

In June 1975, while Pol Pot was secretly visiting China, I went to Kompong Som[13] to welcome about thirty Chinese military experts, including mine clearance experts. Some would work at the Ministry of National Defence while others would stay in Kompong Som.

In October 1975, Ieng Sary commissioned me to make an exploratory trip to open Bavet Pass, in Svay Rieng Province, for trade with the Socialist Republic of Vietnam. Ban, a former high school teacher and at that time Pol Pot's personal secretary, accompanied me. I took this opportunity to go to Saigon-Prey Nokor,[14] recently re-named Hô Chi Minh City. The trip from Bavet did not last more than an hour. Traffic was light on National Road No. 1, which connects Phnom Penh to Saigon. The city itself seemed calm to me;[15] on the whole, it had been little affected by the war. I made contact with Duong Chinh of the Vietnamese Liaison Committee. Duong Chinh had maintained official relations with us in the *maquis* since 1974. Upon my return, I gave Ieng Sary a detailed account of my trip.

---

13 Or Sihanoukville, its French name.
14 Prey Nokor is the Khmer name used before the Vietnamese occupied it around 1620. Saigon is the literal translation of 'Prey Nokor' into the Vietnamese language.
15 Unsurprisingly, after their victory on 30 April 1975, the VC authorities ruralized hundreds of thousands of city dwellers into re-education camps. Unlike their Cambodian neighbours, though, they never evacuated the entire population.

Photo © Martin Rathie

Figure 7: Laotian President Souphanouvong with Ieng Sary and Khieu Samphân at Banteay Srey, 1977; also present (far right) is Suong Sikœun, translator for this memoir.

In March 1976, elections were held for the Assembly of People's Representatives. I did not take part for the simple reason that nobody told me to go to vote. Instead, I accompanied a Chinese delegation to the rubber plantations in Stung Trang. Mrs. Bo Vèn, then secretary of the Party cell at B–1, Mrs. So Saè, then head of the Secretariat of the Ministry, and So Hong voted.

Whenever a large foreign delegation made an official visit to Cambodia, Pol Pot would summon me to his residence for a one-on-one meeting where he gave me recommendations concerning the safety of the guests. This was the case for the visit of the Burmese President Ne Win in November 1977 and President Souphanouvong of Laos in December 1977. Ne Win visited the Silver Pagoda, the Albert Sarraut Museum (now the National Museum) and Angkor Wat, while Souphanouvong visited Kompong Som, Angkor Wat, Banteay Srey and the Western Baray near Siemreap. In general, foreign delegations returned home in their own aircraft, directly from Siemreap. At first, official receptions for the delegations of heads of State were held at the Government House (the former residence of the French *Résident Supérieur*) and then, at the Palace de Chamkar Mon.

In 1977, I became responsible for the security of all foreign delegations visiting Cambodia, whether official or unofficial, public or clandestine. Previ-

Figure 8: Visit of a Chinese delegation to Angkor Wat – front row, left to right: Koy Thuon, Wang Shangrong (PLA deputy chief of staff), Ieng Sary, Zhang Chunqiao, Pol Pot, Geng Biao (Director of International links at the CCP Central Committee), Son Sen, Sun Hao (Chinese Ambassador), Khieu Thirith, Siet Chhê. (Koy Thuon and Siet Chhê were later tortured and executed at S-21.) People in the back row are chauffeurs and guards.

ously, only Office 870 dealt with visits like the secret visit of Zhang Chunqiao,[16] member of the Political Bureau of the Central Committee of the CCP, on 22–26 December 1975 to Phnom Penh and Siemreap.

---

16 Zhang Chunqiao (1917–2005), also nicknamed 'The Cobra', was considered the head of the notorious 'Gang of Four' at the time of the Cultural Revolution. He wrote the first draft of the DK constitution at about the same time. Note the absence of Nuon Chea, who always remained in the capital while Pol Pot was touring Cambodia or in China. Koy Thuon and Siet Chhê were exterminated at S–21 in 1977 and 1978.

– X –

Pol Pot's 19-day secret tour of China, meeting with Chen Yonggui and visiting his model people's commune

*I*n November 1976, shortly after Mao's death, a visit took place in utmost secrecy. A special plane with a ten-person delegation led by Pol Pot took off at noon from Phnom Penh and arrived in Beijing at about half-past six on the same day. The delegation included political cadres: Pol Pot himself, Ieng Sary, Vorn Vet, Ros Nhim and Toch Kham Doeun.[1] Also present were Mong, his personal physician, his private secretary, Ban, and Heng Sila, his Chinese interpreter, all Khmer. Finally, his security team included myself and Kèn, his bodyguard, a Jaraï who came from near my village on the edge of the Tonlé San and had accompanied us during Pol Pot's 'long march' to Stung Chinit. Our trip was kept secret.[2]

In Beijing, we stayed at the Residence Hall of the Central Committee of the CCP, located in the Zhongnanhai[3] compound, where we were greeted by

---

1 Toch Kham Doeun (1935–1977) left for France in 1954 to study mathematics up to the doctoral level. He was the president of the *Union des Étudiants Khmers* (UEK) in Paris from 1960 to 1968, and a member of the Marxist-Leninist Circle. He became the GRUNK ambassador to Cuba (1970–1972) and then to China (1971–1975) and worked under Ieng Sary in the Ministry of Foreign Affairs. Accused of being a CIA agent, he was imprisoned at S–21 on 14 March 1977 and executed in May, along with his wife.

2 We noticed the absence of two big names: Nuon Chea and Son Sen. It should be noted that Pol Pot would never attend an important meeting or launch on a journey with his alter ego, Nuon Chea, the latter being the country's high political commissar in his absence. This was also the case in late 1976, when Nuon Chea was temporarily named Prime Minister; Pol Pot was supposedly on sick leave, but in fact was in China. For his part, Son Sen had the upper hand on the army and internal security; he could not be absent, either.

3 Located near the Forbidden City, the Zhongnanhai compound serves as the headquarters of the CCP and the Central Government of the PRC.

newly elevated Prime Minister Hua Guofeng.[4] The whole of the next day was devoted to talks between the Pol Pot's DK delegation and Hua Guofeng's Chinese delegation. All subjects of political and military cooperation after Mao's death were discussed. I, of course, could not attend the secret political discussions. During that time, while three of my fellow bodyguards were resting at the guest residence, I went to the market looking for fabrics for blankets, mattresses, pillows and bolsters, for the residences of foreign guests to our country. In the evening, we were invited to a sumptuous welcoming banquet in our honour, organized by President Hua Guofeng in the Great Hall of the People. While returning to our residence, Heng Sila talked about a demonstration in favour of Deng Xiaoping.

The next day, we were accompanied by Chen Yonggui,[5] a member of the Political Bureau of the CCP, to his famous 'Dazhai', the model people's commune in Shanxi province, southwest of Beijing. We were informed of this municipality's history since its foundation, starting from scratch, with its current development, structure and functioning, along the lines indicated by Chairman Mao Zedong and according to wishes expressed by its members. His presentation covered roughly four areas: politics, economics, security and foreign relations.

Numbering 300 cadres and more than 10,000 members living in an area of more than one thousand hectares, this people's commune was devoted to the cultivation of rice and cabbage at the same time, and to the breeding of ducks, geese, oxen, sheep, goats and pigs, all of which appeared to be well-nourished. We went around by car and could see that it was well-served by an excellent irrigation network. All this production was destined not for trade but to cover

---

4   Hua Guofeng (1921–2008) was party chairman and premier from 1976 to 1978. Although he had had the Gang of Four arrested shortly after the death of Mao, he insisted on continuing the Maoist line. This is why, in December 1978, a group of party veterans led by Deng Xiaoping forced him from power. And this is probably also why, at this very time, the Chinese leadership refused to send soldiers to Cambodia, even though the Vietnamese invasion was looming large.

5   Chen Yonggui (1915–1986) was known by the revolutionary name of Dazhai, also the name of his model people's commune. From 1953, he led a peasant movement to turn the harsh environment surrounding the Dazhai commune into one favourable to agriculture. The plan was a success and grain output increased steadily, but surely did not meet the propaganda claims of passing from 237 kg per *mu* in 1952 to 774 kg per *mu* in 1962 – parallel to the KR slogan, 'One hectare three tons' of rice, thus tripling the yield, due to massive irrigation works. This was taken as a model of self-reliance and Mao launched the directive 'Learn from Dazhai in agriculture'. In 1969, he was elected to the CCP Central Committee and in 1973, a member of the CCP Politburo. He became vice-premier in 1978, the year after he visited DK.

Figure 9: Dazhai as represented in a poster in the early 1970s. The image captures the Maoist slogan, 'Industry learns from Daqing, agriculture learns from Dazhai.'

the needs of the commune itself. It also had a forge and a power station, a nursery school and a primary school, and several health centres. A model clinic was doing research on malaria. Its members took their meals collectively, in groups of 100 people. We were there in November and the paddy was almost mature, so the commune was preparing for the upcoming harvest. Some people were working to stop the flow of water into the rice fields. We returned to Beijing for lunch, and talks between the two parties resumed in the afternoon.

The whole next day was spent visiting the Great Wall. We felt that the population was still in a difficult situation. Some walked; there were many bicycles, but no motorcycles. We also saw carts pulled by horses, but not by oxen as in Cambodia. There were a lot of sheep and goats. There were very few cars, all official, and quite-small buses.

The fourth day was occupied by a visit to a metal plant, a one-hour drive west of Beijing. Iron wire and iron rods were made for reinforced concrete, some of which was exported. These were the same bars used to make the *khnoh* (or bars and rings that chained the prisoners in DK). We were not told about the socialist organization of work, all explanations being in Chinese. But we were struck by the rapid industrialization of the country after less than twenty years of revolutionary rule. The workers looked very fit. All nearby buildings were factories and the workers' homes were far away. We returned to Beijing for lunch, after which the two-party discussions continued.

The next morning, the fifth day, our delegation flew to Changchun, capital of Jilin Province, northeast of Beijing, which we reached after a two-hour flight. We were greeted by the provincial governor, who spoke with our delegation as soon as we arrived. After lunch at a restaurant situated just at the entrance of a tunnel, discussions continued all afternoon. In the evening, we were the guests of a banquet organized by the governor in our honour. We were served game, including perfumed fox, and treated to an artistic evening filled with revolutionary songs and dances that were strikingly similar to those offered to us in Beijing. Some songs and dances were modern and others were traditional, all performed by worker-actors. Overall, the songs seemed more traditional than our revolutionary songs. We were introduced to ethnic minorities who had joined the revolution very early. Revolutionary films showed us the role of the class struggle in China's history, emphasising the importance of consistency and perseverance to achieve victory.

The sixth day was still devoted to the political talks among the political delegates. It can be easily imagined that the new authorities, after the recent death of the Great Helmsman, were anxious to reassure the DK leadership that nothing would be changed in the close relations between the two revolutions, that all contracts would be scrupulously respected, and that even new projects would be launched. In short, the Cambodians could count on the continued political, diplomatic, technical, industrial, agricultural, commercial, humanitarian and even financial support from timeless China.

In the evening, after the required banquet, we were made to attend an artistic representation of a dozen scenes or films. These portrayed landowners who exploited the peasants, as we had learnt to do with our staged revolutionary songs. One film was about class struggles to get rid of capitalists. Another portrayed Zhou Enlai engaged in precisely this fight. We were therefore witnessing the rehabilitation, after death, of a hero who had fallen somewhat out of favour at the end of Mao's reign. On this day, my wife gave birth to a second boy, Phi Sakkada (aka Da), but I would not know this until later.

During the seventh day, our delegation visited a unit of the People's Liberation Army of China (PLA), stationed more than an hour's drive northeast of Beijing. It was an outpost in the defence belt of the Chinese capital. The camp had a large field for military training and a shooting range for many soldiers. There were also sheds with several tanks and guns, and a helicopter airfield, but we did not see fighter jets. In the afternoon, we returned to Beijing to meet a military delegation that congratulated us on our victory of 17 April 1975.

On the eighth day, we left the capital to go three hours away, to a military school specially dedicated to the training of some 350 KR soldiers and cadres by a unit of the PLA. Pol Pot spoke to them, encouraging them to apply all the concepts learned as accurately as possible and as quickly as possible, so as to shorten their training period as much as possible.

The next day, day nine, talks between the two parties proceeded throughout the day. In the evening, President Hua Guofeng held a farewell banquet in our honour. In his speech, President Hua reaffirmed the total support of the CCP, the government and the Chinese people to the just struggle waged by the government and the people of DK, under the far-sighted leadership of the *Angkar Padevoat* (Revolutionary Organization). The President promised forcefully that his country would continue to work for the rapid training of all the cadets that Cambodia needs for its construction and defence. Pol Pot responded by thanking the Party, the Army and the Chinese people for their invaluable help. This would end the more political part of our journey.

On the tenth day, Chen Yonggui joined us as we left Beijing at 9:00 am to fly to Changsha, the capital of Hunan Province, where we arrived around noon. We stayed there for five hours. As a souvenir, the aircraft crew offered each delegation member a travel bag. Returning to Phnom Penh, Ieng Sary, myself and Heng Sila, the interpreter who also represented the Ministry of Foreign Affairs, handed over our three bags to Office 870, as evidence of our commitment to the Party. Unfortunately, we had no cash to buy souvenirs for our family.

The next morning, day 11, we went to Shaoshan, Mao Zedong's home village, where we visited his house and spent the night. The next day, we went to a museum that narrated the stages in Chairman Mao's revolutionary life, and the primary school where he had been a teacher. We also admired the rice fields and their irrigation network before returning to Changsha for the night. On the thirteenth day, we visited a factory that produced AK47-style bullets, where more than 700 workers worked in the morning from 8:00 am to 10:30 am and from 14:00 to 16:30 in the afternoon. They also rest on Saturdays and Sundays. They only work five hours a day, 5 days a week, or 25 hours in all! Or so we were told.

The fourteenth day was occupied by visits to a rubber plantation, a banana plantation and an orange grove in the vicinity of Shaoshan. However, I found our Cambodian plantations more beautiful and on more fertile land. On the fifteenth day the entire Cambodian delegation paid a courtesy call on the governor of Hunan Province in Changsha, with whom Pol Pot then held talks throughout the day. In the evening, we attended a banquet, of course, followed by an artistic performance very similar to those in Beijing, organized in our honour by the governor.

The next morning, the sixteenth day, at nine o'clock, we flew to Nanning, the capital of Guangxi Province, where we arrived after more than an hour of flight. The rest of the day, we rested in the guest residence. The next morning, we were taken to a confectionery factory located in the Nanning area. We returned to lunch in the city. In the afternoon we were busy visiting a factory making jams and canning oranges, pineapples, rambutans and lychees. The next day we flew to Kunming, capital of Yunnan Province, where we stayed for two days waiting for the plane that had to come from Beijing to take us back to Phnom Penh. While we rested at the hotel, our leaders continued their discussions with Chinese officials.

After these almost three weeks of visiting China, how did I feel? The Chinese people have led the same revolution as the Cambodian people; they suffered as much and consented to as many sacrifices as we had. Finally, they managed to achieve remarkable exploits in all economic fields. I felt fully confident in the victorious outcome of our revolution, which was following the same path as the Chinese revolution and would not fail to achieve the same results. Admittedly, misery and poverty still remained in China. Life was still especially difficult for peasants who were struggling to exploit their small plots of land at the foot of arid mountains. The roads were still narrow, with little traffic. In Beijing, we saw mostly bicycles. But the hope of seeing the socialist revolution triumph and transform into communism remained intact in the hearts and minds of millions of poor people.

In China, the people have realized Chinese-style socialism. In Cambodia, we are therefore allowed to hope that we can build Cambodian socialism. I feel that people trust the communist revolution and dialectical materialism. Where China has succeeded, why not Cambodia? If China triumphs, Cambodia can triumph, too. Concretely, economic development must be based on agricultural development, which in turn relies on rice production. Agricultural development products must be invested in developing the industrial sector, which in turn helps to diversify agriculture to increase production. Everywhere we see self-sufficient people's communes, demonstrating that the need to help ourselves is more than just a slogan.

Throughout our visit, it never came to our mind to ask our guests anything. All members of our delegation, including those assigned to the security of our leaders, were fully aware of the extreme importance for Cambodia's survival of friendship and solidarity with the people and the government of China. So, they refrained from behaving in a way that could annoy our guests in any way. Moreover, we had been designated by the Party to accomplish a revolutionary mission and to represent our people's struggle with dignity. We came back tired but happy with our visit. My wife did not even know I was in China, and I did not bring her any presents. I did not tell her when I returned.

– XI –

Pol Pot's tours in the provinces

1 – Tour around the Tonlé Sap

*I*n October 1977, I was in charge of escorting Pol Pot in his inspection tour across the northwest. Ta Mok had just tightened his control of the region after the arrest and elimination of Ros Nhim and his associates Kong Sophal, Chea, Ham, Sou, San, Samay and Vanh. This was the only time I accompanied Pol Pot on his visit to the provinces without foreign guests. The Party secretary sat in a jeep at the head of a four-car convoy moving towards Battambang. Ieng Sary and two bodyguards were in another car. The journey lasted a whole day, including a stop at Kompong Chhnang where Pol Pot met Ta Yim, the father of General Yan, future commander at Phnom Chhat.[1] On the way, we had lunch in Pursat with the deputy secretary of the Northwest region. We saw some rice fields, already ripe, and people digging a canal in other places.

In Battambang, where we spent the night in a house on National Road No. 10 that would serve as the seat of the DK delegation in 1992 during the UNTAC (United Nations Transitional Authority in Cambodia) period. We were the dinner guests of Ta Mok.

The following day, we drove to Phnom Sampov and then to the just-finished Kamping Puey Dam. A large crowd selected from among the members of the vanguard people's communes, dressed in black and waving national flags and those of the Party, lined up along the road to greet the Party secretary. The dam inauguration ceremony began with a report of the site construction work by the chief technician, a North Korean of about forty years. Next spoke the ambassador of North Korea, who reiterated the support of his government to DK and promised constant help in all areas. Pol Pot spoke last, thanking the North Korean government and its great leader, Field Marshal Kim Il-sung, for the invaluable help given to DK, and the North Korean technicians for helping to build the dam. He then exalted the friendship and solidarity between the two governments and the Khmer and Korean peoples, lauding

---

1   Phnom Chhat is nestled on a hillside near the Thai border in Banteay Meanchey Province. Troops of the KR and State of Cambodia/RGC confronted each other here in August 1993.

their determination to work together to develop and further strengthen the ties that unite them.

The next morning, on the road that leads to Sisophon, we stopped at the agricultural station of Mé Chbar in Thmar Kôl, where we were greeted by Khuong, formerly Ros Nhim's bodyguard and now the head of the place. Mé Chbar was a trial centre for rice, created by the French and covering an area of one hundred hectares. At the time, it was in operation thanks to the assistance of about twenty Chinese technical experts, as well as a dozen Chinese tractors. The rice ears were so heavy that they broke. The Chinese said they 'break their necks'. There was also a water pumping station. We stayed there for about an hour to discuss the introduction of new seeds, sown broadcast and not transplanted, the best varieties for export. We also saw the experiment of dry season rice planted in November. On 1 January 1978, when I returned, Khuong had disappeared from the scene.

Ta Mok, along with San, military commander of the Northwest region, made a point to accompany us to Sisophon, where we had lunch. Some places were left fallow; in others people spread compost. We saw people who were skinny and probably hungry; but Pol Pot and Ta Mok said nothing. In other places during my travels, I observed people were only eating clear rice soup with the stems of water lilies. And I saw that people were mistreated. But the Party did not intend to mistreat people! I did not understand and wondered why this abuse persisted. I was convinced that the Party leaders, who were responsible for these people, were not correctly following the policies of the Party and that, in fact, they sought to destroy the Party. And that's why they treated the population in such a way. I observed that this was contrary to the Party line.

From Sisophon, we drove north towards DK's largest irrigation project, Trâpeang Thmâr Dam.[2] A crowd of several thousand people lined up all the way to greet the Party secretary. They had been chosen from among the members of the avant-garde people's communes, all in the prime of life and in good health. They were dressed in black and waved national flags and red Party flags. This inauguration ceremony was much like that for the Kamping Puey Dam, beginning with revolutionary songs. Ta Mok made a short welcoming speech, then a report about the construction of the site was made by the chief technician, a North Korean of about forty years. After, it was the turn of the

---

2   One of the three largest reservoirs created in the era of DK, the Trâpeang Thmâr Dam continues to irrigate a vast territory during the dry season. Many are said to have perished during its construction.

ambassador of North Korea, who reiterated the support of his government to DK and promised its constant help in all areas. Pol Pot spoke last to thank the North Korean government and its great leader, Field Marshal Kim Il-Sung, for the valuable assistance given to DK, as well as the North Korean technicians, for having contributed to the construction of the dam. He thanked North Korea for its promised help with a tractor factory. He then exalted the friendship and solidarity between the two governments and the two Khmer and Korean peoples and their determination to work together to develop and further strengthen the ties that unite them. Loud applause followed after each speech and a relaxed atmosphere prevailed.[3]

We returned to the capital through Siemreap, where we spent only one night in a villa located one kilometre west of Prince Norodom Sihanouk's residence. Pol Pot met with Kâng Chap alias Sae, then secretary of Sector 106 (Siemreap) and minister of justice of DK.

The next day, on the way home, the Party secretary stopped at Kompong Thom for a lunch with Kaè Pauk, the new secretary of the Northern region,[4] who soon afterwards became the secretary of the Central region, too. In the afternoon, together with Kaè Pauk and two members of the regional committee, Sréng and Tol, Pol Pot left for Kompong Cham, where he spent the night. The next morning, he returned to Phnom Penh by boat and landed at K–7, close to Wat Unalom and Sisowath Quay, just north of the Royal Palace.

2 – Inaugurations at Prey Veng and Kompong Thom

The visit to Prey Véng at the end of December 1977 lasted only one day, with the departure from Phnom Penh at nine o'clock and the arrival four hours later in Baphnom, where Pol Pot and the North Korean ambassador, who accompanied him, were welcomed by Chan Séng,[5] secretary of Sector 22 of the

---

3 The word-for-word repetition of the two inaugurations shows that these leaders were just automatons or robots with no human feelings whatsoever. Besides, no mention, of course, is made of the myriad victims who gave up their lives for the sake of the megalomania of the KR leadership. Everything was to be achieved through manual work, as seen in the Chinese propaganda films, but some machinery was deployed. Nonetheless, those slave workers died of overwork and undernourishment.

4 At the time, the previous leader, Koy Thuon, was in the process of being interrogated and then executed at S–21.

5 Seng Hong (aka Chan), and old Khmer Issarak, strongly anti-Vietnamese, took part in the Eastern region (*Bophea*) purge that would spread havoc in 1978. Pol Pot is said (by Solomon

Eastern region.[6] Their purpose was to inaugurate a pumping station. The event was similar to that for the Kamping Puey Dam, but with fewer participants, a thousand at most, chosen as always from the population of avant-garde people's communes. Chan Séng seemed to enjoy a certain popularity in the middle of a healthy population that had enough rice to feed itself. To my knowledge, he was never a victim during the purges that would decimate the Party leaders of the Eastern region. There were four speeches: Chan Séng welcomed the delegation, then the head of the North Korean technicians and then their ambassador spoke, and finally Pol Pot repeated more or less the same speech as at Kamping Puey.

Pol Pot also took a day trip in 1978 to inaugurate the January 6 Dam at Kompong Thmâr, in Kompong Thom Province. This development began in March 1974 and was carried out by Cambodian technicians and workers who had only bulldozers; excavators were still non-existent. Pol Pot was then resident at Y–1, a regional office that would lead the attack on the enemy garrison at Trapeaing Veng in Kompong Thom Province. Sadly, the water evacuation doors were too narrow and the dam burst from water pressure. The ill-fated construction of the dam is featured in the film *The Heroic People of Kampuchea*, produced in 1974 by Chinese filmmakers. It had to be rebuilt in 1977 with the assistance of Chinese technicians; it now bears the name of January 6 instead of the original 'Kompong Thmar Dam – Liberated Zone'.[7]

Having been on duty at Kompong Som, I could not accompany him as usual. I drove there in one day with my driver and Loem, my messenger, to direct the construction work of the reception villas in anticipation of Prince

---

Kane in his *Dictionnaire des Khmers rouges*, Paris: Les Indes savantes, 2011, p. 392) to have ordered his assassination in 1979.

6   The KR divided the territory, first into 'regions' (*phumphea*), then 'sectors' (*dambon*), then 'districts' (*srok*), then 'people's communes' (*sahakâr*) modelled on China, which replaced villages. *Pumphea* and *dambon* only existed during the DK period. *Sahakâr* were not 'cooperatives', as most historians and even Tribunal lawyers have mistranslated. There never was a single 'cooperative' under DK, as a cooperative is created by its members and not by a central State. The model was Mao's China, where these entities were called 'people's communes'. Nobody ever speaks of Soviet or Chinese 'cooperatives'. They are a Cuban creation. The Lao tried to establish cooperatives but they did not last past the early 1980s.

7   Phi Phuon reports, via omission, on the human suffering associated with these projects. Hundreds if not thousands literally worked themselves to death. One might even suggest that Pol Pot celebrated these tragedies in his slogan, *Slap nou lœu karothani*, meaning, 'On the work site until death!' See Locard, *Pol Pot's Little Red Book*, p. 306, slogan number 433.

Norodom Sihanouk's visit. The prince stayed there for five days. I took the opportunity to swim at the small beach in front of Serpent Island.

3 –Chen Yonggui visits Pol Pot in Cambodia

During 3–5 December 1977, I ensured the security of a Chinese delegation led by Chen Yonggui, aka Dazhai in Chinese or Ta Chai for the Khmers, a member of the Political Bureau of the Central Committee of the CCP and deputy prime minister of the PRC at the time of this official friendship visit to DK. Pol Pot wished to accompany him personally, testifying to the deep bond of friendship and solidarity that united the two countries and the two peoples. Ieng Sary was also present during the whole trip. Despite his 62 years and his wrinkles, Dazhai was a man who still had plenty of strength. He was a cadre of peasant origin and retained his peasant ways. He did not speak much but did not mince words: he said what he thought.

The day after its arrival in Phnom Penh by special plane on 3 December 1977, the Chinese delegation began its visit to the Eastern region, where they were received in Tonlé Bet[8] by Sao Phœm, a member of the Standing Committee of the Central Committee of the CPK and President of the Eastern region, surrounded by members of the Regional Committee, Phuong and Chan, as well as Sok Khnol (aka Lin), president of the Regional Office. After spending the night in Suong, the guests returned to Phnom Penh to leave the next day, 5 December, for a visit to the Chup Rubber Plantation, reputed to be one of the largest in the world. At noon, the delegation arrived in Kompong Cham city, where it was received by Kaè Pauk, president of the Central region. The afternoon was spent visiting a textile factory built with Chinese help in the *Sangkum* days. The next morning, the delegation visited the paddy fields and cotton fields of Speu-Srê Veal and, in the afternoon, the January 1 Dike and the rice fields in Baray Kompong Thom. In the evening, Kaè Pauk organized a welcoming banquet in Dazhai's honour.

On 7 December, Ta Chai visited the Trâpeang Thmâr Reservoir in Phnom Srok District in the morning and in the afternoon, he left for Siemreap, to be received by Kâng Chap. The following morning, he toured Angkor Wat, Angkor Thom and Banteay Srey before heading to the Baray Toek Thla Reservoir,

---

8   Tonlé Bet is the township opposite Kompong Cham City, on the left bank of the Mekong. The two towns are now joined by a bridge built by China.

Figure 10: Chen Yonggui

where Ros Nhim, chief of the zone, was present to greet the guest, who at the same time said goodbye to Kâng Chap and his collaborators. After spending the night in Sisophon, the delegation left for Battambang on 9 December before going to the agricultural research centre in Bœng Pring, Bovel District. The afternoon of the same day was devoted to the January 17 Reservoir[9] in Kamping Puey and a cotton plantation in Andoek Hep.

The next day, the hosts left Battambang by train to go to the Western region, where they were greeted by Chou Chet, president of the region. In the afternoon, they visited the people's commune of Phnom Popork and participated in rice threshing with some peasants. They then went to Kompong Chhnang, where they spent the night. The next morning, they visited the Krang Leav military airfield, where, with the help of Chinese technicians,

---

9   Cambodia's second-largest reservoir, Trâpeang Thmâr, constructed by DK.

the DK government was undertaking to build a military air base. Under an adjacent hill, it was planned to dig a large space for the parking of combat aircraft. Five hundred meters from vast water tanks dug into another hill, the Chinese had been digging a long tunnel of several hundred metres with a succession of rooms, larger or smaller, all concreted inside. There was to be a concrete floor and everything was to be electrified and ventilated. All this was meant to become a military command centre,[10] but the Vietnamese pushed into Cambodia in late 1978, just before the vast system could be completed.

More than 100 Chinese engineers and technicians were housed in the city and brought to the site by coach. Sou Meth,[11] chief of the 502 Division and DK Air Force, was responsible for the work. The Cambodian labourers who worked there had been sentenced to more or less heavy penalties, and were fed and housed on site. They seemed malnourished and badly dressed in torn clothes, and had ruffled hair like convicts.In January 1979, when the Vietnamese troops seized the airfield, these prisoners fled by the thousands to regroup in Leach, in Pursat, where they armed themselves and joined the forces of DK, who were fighting the invaders along National Road No. 5.

In the afternoon, the Chinese guests continued by train to Phnom Penh. The following day, the delegation left by National Road No. 4 for Kompong Som, where it was greeted by Meas Muth,[12] Commander of the DK Navy, Thuch Rinn[13], Port Manager and his deputy Chap Lonh. The afternoon was devoted to visiting the city's harbour and shipyard(s), and the beaches. Ta Chai did not visit the site of the new Phnom Penh–Kompong Som Railway Line, which follows Road No. 4, nor the site of the big Kompong Som oil refinery, which was being rebuilt by China.

---

10 One can understand the concern of the Vietnamese, who must have feared being caught in a vice by the ambitious Chinese. All the more so as the latter had also started to build a new naval base near the bottom of the Gulf of Kompong Som. Vietnam had many reasons to overthrow the KR regime.

11 Sou Meth died in June 2013 while he was one of the accused of the ECCC's trial 003, along with Meas Muth. Sou Meth was among the accused mainly because of the crimes he had committed in the construction of the Krang Leav base.

12 Meas Muth (1938–) was indicted by the international component of the ECCC on 3 March 2015 for war crimes, genocide and crimes against humanity, but Hun Sèn and his government refused to have him arrested.

13 Thuch Rinn (1940–2002), see below during Sihanouk's visit to Sihanoukville-Kompong-Som.

On 13 December, Ta Chai, as always accompanied by Pol Pot and Ieng Sary, went to the Southwest zone, where Ta Mok expected him at Veal Rinh. In Kampot Province, he visited a durian plantation in Tœk Chhou and the Chakrei Ting Cement Factory[14] where rehabilitation work had been carried out by Chinese technicians. In the afternoon, Ta Chai went to Takéo, where he was greeted by Sam Bit,[15] a member of the Southwest region committee. The next day, 14 December, the delegation left Takéo where Chen had slept in the 'palace' of Ta Mok at the edge of an artificial lake, to return to Phnom Penh. Ta Mok did not take care of anything to entertain his guests. I myself had the rooms and the meals prepared.

On the way, the delegation stopped at Leay Bo,[16] a model people's commune in Tramkak District, Ta Mok's base. Nine thousand families lived in the commune, which had 4,000 hectares of fields, 3,000 of which were devoted to rice cultivation. The dam, cradled in Phnom Domrey Romeal (Skidding Elephant Mountain) to the west of the district, kept the water channels filled all year round. The Chinese were shown the famous rice fields of 100 meters by 100 meters, a perfect hectare. Thus, they could measure exactly the yield per hectare, a yield that was the subject of congratulations from the Party on the official radio, although the soil in the area was not particularly fertile.

Visitors could also admire the poultry and pigs raised on site, which provided the population here with three meals a day (instead of the two elsewhere). The people looked satisfied and healthy. They wore the *de rigueur* black clothes, and brand-new *krâma* (traditional scarves). All the women their hair cut mid-length above the shoulders. There were 100–200 model houses,

---

14 This cement factory would be completely dismantled by the invading Vietnamese, beginning in 1979, and the machinery taken to Vietnam. My sources are the local people during my investigation of the DK prison system. Vietnam, from 1979 into the 1980s, at the time of Do Moi policy for rapid economic expansion, took to all movables from Cambodia, as war booty, in particular in the eastern half ot the country.

15 This local political commissar would gain widespread notoriety in the post-KR regime when his regiment attacked the Phnom Penh – Kompong Som Railway Line on 26 July 1994, killing 13 passengers and taking three Westerners as hostages. He had them executed two months later. After being pardoned by Hun Sèn and appointed major-general in October 1996, he was arrested again on 1 August 1996, and sentenced to life imprisonment in December 2002. He died in prison in February 2008.

16 Leay Bo was a large people's commune of about ten villages covering a fair proportion of Tramkak district and very close to Takéo town. It was a Potemkin village and would be visited by most of the friendly foreign delegations in 1978.

Figure 11: One Leay Bô Primary School, photographed by a Swedish delegation in 1978.

one for each family, and a school consisting of two buildings on the ground, with a tile-covered roof.

Throughout his journey, Ta Chai extolled the achievements of DK, which dared to fully implement the principles defined by Mao. He said he had learnt a lot from Cambodians. Through their application of an ardent class struggle, the Cambodians had achieved modern people's communes in less than three years, whereas China had not been able to achieve them in 30 years.[17]

On the last night, a farewell banquet was held at the Chinese Embassy in honour of the leaders and cadres from the government of DK. The next morning, Chen Yonggui was received in Chamkar Mon by Pol Pot before his afternoon flight to China.

4 – Provincial visits of ambassadors and chargés d'affaires from accredited countries

Towards the end of 1977, just after Chen Yonggui's visit, Ieng Sary accompanied the ambassadors of China, Vietnam, Laos, North Korea, Cuba, Yugo-

17 Julio Jeldres, Sihanouk's official biographer, notes: 'Accompanied by Pol Pot wherever he went, Chen was very excited to see the Khmer Rouge's extremist policies in pushing the country into Communism. Later, when he returned to China, he told his close friends with a sigh: 'Marx, Lenin, and Mao, they all failed to accomplish communism, but in Cambodia they made it.' P. 24 in 'Democratic Kampuchea's foreign policy: a leftover from the Chinese cultural revolution', Documentation Center of Cambodia, *Searching for the Truth*, July 2017, p. 24.

slavia, Albania and Romania's *chargé d'affaires* on a pleasure tour throughout the Cambodian provinces. They travelled from Phnom Penh to Battambang, Siemreap, Kompong Cham and Prey Veng via Kompong Chhnang, Pursat, Kompong Thom, Suong and Neak Luong. The visit lasted only one week.

The representatives of the friendly countries left in the morning from Phnom Penh and spent the night in Battambang. The next day, they travelled to Siemreap and spent two full days visiting the temples of Angkor Wat, Angkor Thom, Banteay Srey and the Baray Toek Thla Reservoir.[18] They spent two nights in Siemreap, one night in Kompong Cham and one night in Prey Veng. Ieng Sary and So Hong, secretary general of the Ministry of Foreign Affairs travelled in a Chevrolet, while diplomats of friendly countries were transported in several white Mercedes. Among them was one woman, the wife of the Albanian ambassador. A jeep with six guards on board opened the convoy and another, also with six guards, closed it. The front jeep was responsible for monitoring the road to prevent people or ox carts from crossing or obstructing traffic as the convoy passed by.

In 1978, I went to Aranyaprathet to prepare for Ieng Sary's visit to Thailand, where he would establish diplomatic relations between the two countries. I met with Chai Chamlak, an official of the Thai Ministry of Foreign Affairs. Sam San alias Rath, our ambassador to Laos, had arrived with him from Bangkok.

---

18 Usually called 'the Western Baray' (or lake), the reservoir dates from Angkorian times and was renovated by Sihanouk.

– XII –

Trip to Kompong Som/ Sihanoukville with Prince Norodom Sihanouk

*P*rince Norodom Sihanouk left the Royal Palace and settled into his new residence near the Independence Monument in March 1977. From this house, with his wife, Princess Monique, Prince Sihamoni, their eldest son, and a lady-in-waiting, he went to Kompong Som, Kep, Angkor Wat, Kompong Cham and Svay Rieng. He travelled in the black Mercedes reserved only for heads of State; white Mercedes were for the diplomatic corps. For the trip to Sihanoukville, I sat next to the driver, while the Prince and the Princess were sitting in the back seat. He visited Kompong Som in September 1978.

Before leaving for this mission, Pol Pot gave me three directives:

Firstly: guarantee the safety of the Prince from the beginning until the end of the trip.

Secondly: ensure that food is both safe and of good quality.

Thirdly: understand the great significance for our country and our people of the irreplaceable contribution brought by the Prince to our struggle in the past and present, and especially in the future. He must be encouraged to continue along the path he has chosen.

I was not unknown to the Prince, since I had accompanied him in March 1973 during his visit to the liberated zone at Phnom Kulen and Angkor Wat. Although I did not know the language of the palace, the important thing was to show our good will and to always be at the disposal of the Prince and the Princess during the trip. Before addressing myself to the Prince, I took great care to apologize for my ignorance of the royal terms and to beg him not to hold it against me. We must always comply with his will and obey all his wishes.

As for the charge against me of having 'a very heavy hand against many innocent Khmer victims,' contained in Norodom Sihanouk's autobiography,

Prisoner of the Khmer Rouge,[1] it is completely false because I did not really participate in the fight – only once in 1968 in Ratanakiri, and in the attack on the Lon Nol Navy in Ta Chès, between Kompong Chhnang and Oudong in 1974.[2] There were no casualties, since all the men had boarded the tugboat. Immediately after the attack, I sped away on a B–5 motorbike to escape enemy bombardment, which was not long in coming, as two hours later Lon Nol's planes came in.

The organization of this visit to Kompong Som city, which was dear to him since it had been his own creation, was part of the policy of relaxation, both internally and internationally, in anticipation of the impending invasion from Vietnam. The Prince was fully aware of the seriousness of the situation and, as the fervent patriot he had always been, quite willing to assume responsibility and to act accordingly.

On leaving Phnom Penh, the princely convoy followed National Road No. 4 and drove through the town of Kompong Speu, which housed an army garrison as well as stores of ammunition and gasoline belonging to the Western region. At the junction of the Kirirom road, we saw the storage of railway tracks intended for a new line whose plan had already been drawn. I knew it because I accompanied the Chinese technicians in discussions with Mey Prang, chairman of the Transport Committee of the Government of DK. The construction of the new line had already started from the Veal Rinh – Pich Nil junction with rails of a width required by the international standard. After 1979–1980, we no longer heard about these rails because they were looted by Vietnamese troops, as were the materials of the Chakrey Ting Cement Factory and the Kompong Som refinery.[3] On the other hand, the Kirirom Hydropower Station was rehabilitated by the North Koreans during the revolutionary era.

In Kompong Som, the Prince divided his time between his former residence at O'Chheu Teal, the Independence Hotel – then called the 'Seven-Storey Hotel' – and another of his former homes, called 'The Treasury'. He also visited the worksite of the old French Elf Oil Refinery that was being

---

1   Norodom Sihanouk, *Prisonnier des Khmers Rouges*, Paris: Hachette, 1986.

2   This is the second time that Phi Phuon recounts this event. See also p. 113.

3   The main point is that the destruction of industrial infrastructure did not occur under DK, but later, from 1979, under the Vietnamese occupation. They de-industrialized Cambodia, claiming the KR revolution was just an agrarian revolution. See for example François Ponchaud's *L'Impertinent du Cambodge*, p. 183, where everything that resembled technical or industrial equipment, and was moveable, was stolen and shipped to Vietnam after 7 January 1979.

rebuilt by the Chinese and the Rolork Dam. But he refused to visit the beer brewery that had been constructed under the Sangkum and designed by his architect Van Molyvann. Everywhere, the workers were dressed in black and did not look malnourished.

At noon he would bathe at O'chheu Teal Beach. In Kompong Som, the Prince enjoyed the services of a special cook and seafood such as langoustines, prawns, crabs, mussels, and squid, as well as all sorts of fruits: longans, lychees, mangosteens, rambutans, durians, custard apples, and perfumed coconut. Pol Pot had instructed me to supply the Prince with all that he ordered. As for drinks, we had at his disposal Chinese mineral water, Dutch Heineken beer, white wine, French red wine and whisky. He spent the night in a wooden cottage on a hill that dominated the treasury on the right and the Hotel 'Independence' on the left.[4] With the members of his suite and accompanied by Thuch Rinn, the harbour manager and myself, the Prince enjoyed a yacht cruise around O'Chheu Teal and Naga Island (*Puek*).

And this is how the Prince narrated the same experience in his memoirs:

> In early September 1978, an important military *kammaphibal* whose name I will never be able to remember, was appointed by the *Angkar* leadership (presumably Pol Pot and Ieng Sary) to accompany me on my travels from Phnom Penh to Kompong Som by car, and organize my stay in the city.
>
> This personality speaks our language with a pronounced *Khmer lœu* (mountain) accent. He probably comes from one of our provinces near the highlands of Laos or Vietnam (the so-called "Three Frontiers" region). Before our departure, President Khieu Samphân[5] informed me that this superior officer was a valiant soldier and that, at the head of his unit, he had been able to annihilate an impressive number of Vietnamese aggressors during the first battles between Democratic Kampuchea and the Socialist Republic of Vietnam.[6] I do not doubt for a moment the military qualities of my companion. But I suspect him of being a very zealous "Polpotian" who, since the coming to power of his political friends, must also have used a very heavy hand against many innocent Khmer victims.
>
> I must still recognize that, during the trip, and during our stay in Kompong Som, this *kammaphibal* behaved very well, even courteously,

---

4 It was the Prince's former bungalow, built for him during the *Sangkum* days.

5 Khieu Samphân, officially the DK Head of State, was in charge of relations with the Prince.

6 This assertion is a pure invention as, at the time, Phi Phuon had no military function whatsoever, nor did he go east to oppose the first Vietnamese incursions. This is an illustration of Khieu Samphân's ability to blurt out brazen lies.

with all the members of my entourage, and was very polite and considerate of me, while striving to conduct with me a fairly measured propaganda for the policy pursued by the Khmer Communist Party. He told me repeatedly and at every opportunity that the leaders, cadres, and people of Democratic Kampuchea hold me in "high regard" because of the "outstanding services" that I delivered to our homeland and its revolution. It is clear that the Polpotians' military difficulties in the border areas of Vietnam influenced this change of language towards me.

... A few kilometres from Kompong Speu, driving towards Kompong Som, I see on the right hangars where, to my great surprise, piles of rails and other elements are piled up for the construction of a new railway line. In the middle of the forest and along the hills and mountains of the region of Pich Nil, I see, like a human anthill, a multitude of workers in the rain, busy with the extremely painful work of the realization of a new rail line from Phnom Penh to Kompong Som. The *kammaphibal* who accompanies me explains that the Vietnamese seek to cut the old line (my work), which crosses the provinces of the southwest (Takéo, Kampot, Kep). This old line, he tells me, runs too close to the border of South Vietnam and may be cut off.

... My car arrives at sunset in Kompong Som-ville. We cross many pedestrians, hundreds of "forced" workers who come out in the late afternoon from factories (built in the 60s by the *Sangkum*) and various sites. Their black clothes, although patched, are not in rags and my compatriots do not seem undernourished.

... I notice that in the port district close to the centre, there are more Chinese (from the People's Republic) than Khmer Rouge. Although I am a nationalist, I do not complain. At least these foreign friends render service to my country. These Chinese are technicians, engineers and workers, and sailors coming from the many boats moored in the harbour.

The *kammaphibal*, who is director of the port of Kompong Som, is careful about his appearance.[7] No black pyjamas (revolutionary), nor khaki uniform (military). He wears elegantly cut trousers with crisp folds, a well-ironed shirt of dazzling whiteness. He travels on a sparkling Japanese motorcycle with sparkling chrome and smokes only luxury American cigarettes that he throws after a few puffs: the height of elegance and waste.

---

7 He was named Thuch Rin (ធុច រិន, aka Krin), and survived and later earned a BA in arts. Like many others, he very much regretted that the printed currency had not been distributed, and he deplored the arrest of Hu Nim. He would flee with his family to Bangkok and then Paris, where he sold newspapers.

... At Kompong Som State Lodge, a team of senior Khmer Rouge wives are responsible for preparing our meals, which include succulent desserts.

The harbour director takes us on a boat – a small luxury yacht offered in the 1960s to my government by Australia, then represented in Phnom Penh by a great friend of our people, Ambassador Noël Saint-Clair De-schamps.[8] ... From the bridge, I can see the activities of the port, which is animated by a swarm of Chinese technicians, labourers and sailors. It is these same Chinese people that I myself see doing their best to rebuild the oil refinery, a Franco-Sihanoukist work that had been 80 per cent destroyed during the 1970–1975 war.[9]

During this trip, I had the opportunity to address Prince Norodom Siha-nouk in these terms: 'Samdech, I am ethnic Jaraï. I got involved very early in the revolutionary struggle. I do not know anything about royal language. If it happens that I address you in unfortunate terms, deign, my Lord, not to be too harsh!' The Prince then took the habit of calling me '*Lok Kammaphibal*', meaning 'Mister Cadre', never being able to remember my name. Nonetheless, it was I who welcomed him to Phnom Kulen and Siempang District, when the Prince made his historic visit to the *maquis* in March 1973. I was trying to be as courteous and deferential as possible with him, in line with the express instructions I had received.

The *Independence Hotel* was home to Chinese technicians working at the oil refinery, but also to Cambodians from Phnom Penh and other parts of the country. At the end of their mission in Cambodia and before returning to China, the Chinese were entitled to a visit to Angkor Wat and a stay in Kompong Som.

At that time, Kompong Som city and its port were led by Thuch Rin (aka Krin), a philologist, graduate of the Royal University of Phnom Penh and for-mer member of the Southwest region committee. At the port, a group of young people loading imported ore into the train carriages recognized the Prince and spontaneously gathered around him, uninvited, braving the official ban.[10]

---

8   Noël St. Clair Deschamps (1908–2005) was Ambassador of Australia to Cambodia from 1962 to–1969, also representing the United States and Great Britain at the time when Sihanouk had broken diplomatic relations with those two countries. I suspect the US bankrolled the purchase of the yacht. I wonder if they bugged it?

9   Sihanouk, *Prisonnier des Khmers Rouges*, pp. 269–277 (my translation).

10   Under DK, no one was allowed to interact with anyone outside the immediate family or working environment – least of all with foreigners or national heroes. You were supposed to ignore everyone.

– XIII –

Was there any internal resistance to the Democratic Kampuchea leadership?[1]

*D*id anyone secretly resist the government? First, during the coup d'état of 18 March 1970, we didn't have many members. During the five-year war, we gathered adequate forces and, for instance, created a *Snaèng* unit,[2] a transportation unit based in the battlefield. During the revolution that led up to the founding of National Democratic Kampuchea, hundreds of villagers volunteered, and they all were committed to liberating the country. On the one hand, this revolution was known as the revolution of National Democratic Kampuchea, which won a complete victory on 17 April 1975. Let me answer your question directly. No, there was no resistance movement to overthrow the KR regime, except in 1977.

Does that mean that there had never been traitorous groups aiming at overthrowing the revolution? No! Of course, some wanted to overthrow the revolution and they looked for ways to cause trouble, particularly by throwing accusations against the Southwestern and Eastern regions. In fact, it was overcrowded in the Southwest region and everyone was desperate for power. Another problem was that Ta Mok had been continually promoted by the Centre. Worst of all, the cadres overseeing the Eastern region (*Bophea*) were accused of being the enemy, thus provoking chaos and, as a result, the Vietnamese forces were able to encroach on Cambodia's territory.[3] If the

---

1   Most of Phi Phuon's declarations in this chapter were collected by Dany Long of DC-Cam during their conversation on 19 December 2010.

2   *Snaèng* (ស្នែង), supplies slung on a pole, which is carried on the shoulders of two or more people.

3   Both the Eastern (*Bophea*) and the Southwestern (*Nirdey*) regions raised problems in the eyes of Phi Phuon. The *Bophea* were victims, in 1978, of a sweeping purge conducted by Ta Mok and Kaè Pauk's men; Ta Mok's *Nirdey* troops had purged the entire territory under orders from *Angkar Lœu*, from 1976 to 1978. This turmoil made it possible for the Vietnamese to conquer Cambodia in two weeks.

Vietnamese troops had not captured some areas, our government would not have been overthrown.

As I said at the Tribunal (30 July, p. 82), Ieng Sary told me that, after liberation, there were problems of power struggle in the regions and each wished to become the chief. At the end of 1978, Ieng Sary told me there were even complications at the Centre. At the time there was the arrest and execution at S–21 of Vorn Vet, who had been very close to Pol Pot since the origin of the movement. I noticed that certain regional chiefs had disappeared. Perhaps they were not on good terms with Pol Pot and this is why they disappeared. Koy Thuon was nominated Trade Minister, but then he mysteriously disappeared. I do not know why. (30 July, p. 82)

Ta Mok scattered his *Nirdey* (និរតី; Southwest) forces across every region, causing internal turmoil. For instance, stealing a potato and breaking a spoon were considered crimes. It seemed that everyone viewed everyone else as an enemy, unlike the five resistance years, when the people were unified. Once DK was established, everyone criticized everyone else and dared to kill for power. Did the senior leaders also learn about this? They definitely knew. They knew that the people's communes were not as developed as local leaders claimed. They knew most people had only gruel, with some vegetables. I also witnessed the poor living conditions of people in the Northwest region (ពាយ័ព្យ; *Peayoap*), for instance in Pursat Province. I remember seeing people building dams, canals, and so on. At that time, I teased the elderly Ros Nhim, saying that the fact that villagers ate only gruel showed that the cadre overseeing those people was incapable. Yes, I did. I was just teasing him, but he took it seriously. Based on the Party policy, those cadres who could only provide gruel to their people were incapable and useless.

Of course, the upper brothers were aware of this. That's why in early 1978 they called upon all cadres to tolerate each other and avoid accusing each other of being the enemy. We had to tolerate and learn to forgive others. I heard Pol Pot mention some rebellious movements against the revolution. All the cadres were called to show their stances in their regions. Therefore, we had to be cautious. During the first three years, the first accusations that people were CIA or KGB agents were made. Also, the Kuomintang[4] secretly established its three traitorous lines in Cambodia, aiming to take control over Cambodia.

---

4   This nationalist Chinese party was established in 1912 by Sun Yat-sen (1866–1925), considered the father of modern China. The Kuomintang was eliminated from continental China with Mao's victory in 1949 and retreated to Taiwan with Chiang Kai-shek.

These three lines were tightly unified. Thus, we had to be on an alert for the revolutionary enemy.[5]

The Vietnamese were known for their desire to establish an Indochinese Federation. The Vietnamese government directly asked our government to discuss its Indochinese plan in 1973. But we turned down their entreaties. Then, North Vietnamese troops attacked the southern part of our country. Although we lacked ammunition, we stood firm and attacked back. As one of our slogans said, 'Take the artillery from the enemy to fight the enemy,' 'Where there are people, there are troops.' Then, we refused to negotiate with the Americans. Finally, the Vietnamese government tried to convince the Cambodian government to negotiate with the Americans in June and July of 1973. All of this was troubling. Because of the poor cooperation, we refused to be involved in the negotiations. After our 17 April victory, the Vietnamese were dismayed.

During the five years of fighting in the early seventies, we were independent, but it was difficult to win the war. Nonetheless, we had adequate supplies, including weapons, gunpowder, healthy food, beef, sugar, rice, monosodium glutamate, fish paste, bread, canned fish, oil, and so on. Moreover, the implementation of guerrilla war tactics was running smoothly. At that time, we were able to defend ourselves and struggle to increase our power.

After the liberation, leaders aggressively fought each other for power, especially Ta Mok. I learnt this personally! Why do I say Ta Mok was aggressive? It's because he argued with others while they were having meals. He claimed that comrades Sao Phœm, Koy Thuon and Khieu (Son Sen) didn't arrive in Phnom Penh before him. However, Pol Pot was the one who reached a compromise and suggested that everyone work together. He said that the success of Phnom Penh's liberation was not achieved by any particular individual, but by the unity and solidarity of everyone. Yet Ta Mok was demanding [special treatment] for his own reputation!

After victory, we were aware that some of our members disappeared and maybe they were arrested, including Vorn Vet, Toch Kham Doeun, Toch

---

5   All this is part of the paranoia of the KR who, with Nuon Chea voicing these beliefs, were really convinced that spies and traitors were everywhere. And these traitors were working for three masters: the CIA, the KGB and the Vietnamese, at one and the same time, in the same person. Interestingly, here Phi Phoun adds a fourth: the Kuomintang from Taïwan!!! The paranoia reaches summits and he outdoes Nuon Chea himself. Phi Phoun is projecting back to his own mindset at the time, which likely reflects the state of mind of the average militant.

Phœun,[6] Ta Ya, and so on. The arrests surprised everyone. They didn't say anything about those arrests, but in the case of Koy Thuon, I knew why he was arrested. News of his arrest was published in *The Revolutionary Flag* magazine,[7] explaining that he had confessed to committing a moral offense. I had no idea why others were arrested, except that they disappeared. There were many cadres who disappeared, at both the district and the regional levels. They suddenly disappeared.

The assignment of new cadres all over the country from the Southwestern region caused mass killings. Many of them were proud and rigid. Ta Mok is a bad person, I hate him. In 1979, there seemed to be a heated argument over the management in the Southwestern region, where Ta Mok built up cruel cadres to commit executions. It was true that during the national resistance, we fought against the American imperialists and their servants, while under the Democratic Kampuchea, we fought the feudalists, the capitalists, and the reactionariesists. The five-year resistance was against the former regime, not any particular groups of people. However, in Democratic Kampuchea, the hunt for enemies was implemented in an extreme manner that took many innocent lives. Everyone was petrified, including me!

---

6   Toch Phœun alias Phin (1928–1977) studied in France at *l'École supérieur des Travaux publics de Paris*. He joined the FUNK in November 1971 in the Northern region under the leadership of Koy Thuon. He worked with Hu Nim at the Ministry of Information and Propaganda until 17 April 1975, when he became Minister of Transport. Accused of being part of the Koy Thuon sex plot (more likely being linked to Ta Ya), he was arrested on 17 January 1977, taken to S–21 and executed in May 1977.

7   *Tung Padevoat* (*Revolutionary Flag*) was the Party's official internal newspaper, published monthly from January 1975 until September 1978.

– XIV –

The Vietnamese threat looms larger

1 – Visit of English professor Malcolm Caldwell and American journalists Richard Dudman and Elizabeth Becker[1]

*D*uring 13–23 December 1978, English professor Malcolm Caldwell and American journalists Richard Dudman and Elizabeth Becker made a working visit to Democratic Kampuchea. Nikân (Son Sen's brother), chief of protocol at the Foreign Ministry, and Thiounn Prasith, the English-language interpreter, were in charge of the guests during their stay. As for me, I only accompanied them on the morning of their last day in Cambodia, when they visited the temple of Tonlé Bati in Takéo. They returned to Phnom Penh for lunch. The maintenance of the temple left much to be desired. There was dung everywhere, and bat faeces.[2]

One day before the visit to Tonlé Bati, Pol Pot officially received Richard Dudman and Elizabeth Becker at the former residence of the *Résident Supérieur*, near Wat Phnom. Later, he received Malcolm Caldwell alone, on that last day of the official visit, for a private and confidential lunch at Chamkar Mon, Sihanouk's ex-luxurious residence in the sixties. Afterwards, on that same day, Caldwell and the two journalists were received together by Pol Pot for a last official dinner in their honour at Chamkar Mon. Ieng Sary, Thiounn Prasith and Nikân also participated.[3]

---

1   This visit is placed in this chapter because it took place just one week before the collapse of the regime and the shooting of Caldwell is like the first act of the catastrophic disintegration of *Angkar's* dreams. The regime could not even guarantee the safety of its important visitors and in particular its closest British friend – Malcolm Caldwell!

2   This brief visit is not mentioned in Elizabeth Becker's account of her journey. See her *When the War Was Over: Cambodia and the Khmer Rouge Revolution, New York: Simon & Schuster, 1986.*

3   Elizabeth Becker also does not specify that the interview with Malcolm Caldwell, less solemn and 'between friends', did *not* take place at the French-built *Résident Supérieur's* official residence, but at the less formal Chamkar Mon palace, where the farewell dinner was later arranged.

After that ceremonial and friendly meal, I was summoned in the middle of the night to go the residence I had arranged for the guests, as I was myself in charge of both of their welfare and security. They were housed more than one kilometre from the Ministry of Foreign Affairs where I lived. When I arrived, I was informed Malcolm Caldwell had been shot in circumstances that were difficult for me to investigate, as I was quite far from the drama and therefore not a direct witness. Two possible explanations have been given by Elizabeth Becker and historians. The first was that, in their private dinner with Pol Pot, Caldwell might have raised the issue of the well-being of the Cambodian citizens he met during the long trip. He could have blamed the ultimate leader for the cruel treatment they suffered and that Elizabeth Becker also noticed. But Becker wrote that Caldwell returned from his private dinner relaxed and happy with his conversation with his host. Besides, an abrupt conversion of Caldwell to the gospel of Western democracy is most unlikely. The second hypothesis was that a secret Vietnamese commando unit had sneaked into Phnom Penh in the middle of the night to assassinate Pol Pot's friend and so discredit the regime they were about to overrun. This, again, is most unlikely as security was very tight in Phnom Penh around the leadership and its guests.

No, indeed the most likely reason was a personal conflict between two young guards who were in love with the same woman. One of them had given a scarf to the lady as a token of his affection; the rejected lover sought his revenge in the middle of the night, which led to that exchange of bullets. A stray bullet could have hit Caldwell in a bloody accident. The guards were from the special Y–10 top-security unit (Y for *yothea*, or KR soldiers), which often brought the accused to S–21 and had a reputation for being very brutal.[4] In his autobiography, Ong Thong Hœung[5] tells precisely the same story, which he claims to have heard from one of the guards that same night.

---

4 Contrary to the rest of the population, as far as we know, neither the political nor the military wings of the KR were victims of forced marriages, but freely chose their partners, at least from the men's side. Once the choice had been made, the Party was to give its formal approval. This state of affairs is illustrated in this autobiography by the examples of none other than Phi Phuon himself, Nuon Chea and Khieu Samphân. So, the exchange of bullets between the two young men was most likely a private issue. Malcolm Coldwell, when he heard the cracks of guns, would have been wise to crawl under his bed, like Elizabeth Becker under her bath, rather than open his door into the passage. But he was bold and confident; as a champion of the regime, he imagined himself to be perfectly safe.

5 *J'ai cru aux Khmers rouges*, p. 224.

2 – Vietnamese troops stationed since 1964 in the northeast refused to leave after 1975

Once the KR took power in Phnom Penh, skirmishes with Vietnamese troops increased and, by 1975, the DK government was preparing for an armed confrontation with its powerful eastern neighbour. Vietnamese troops continued to occupy the areas where they had been stationed since 1964 or 1965, extending from the Tonlé San to the Naga's Tail in the northeast. This was despite our repeated requests to quit. They annexed the entire village of Nhang and half of the villages of Tung Nghè, Chang and Chan in Andoung Meas District in Ratanakiri. We had tried to dislodge them more than once, but to no avail: they were well entrenched in strong fortifications. From Memot in the province of Kompong Cham to Svay Rieng, armed confrontations and other skirmishes between the two countries had been countless. According to the information provided by our compatriots from *Kampuchea Krom*,[6] we took the initiative to bring the attacks deep inside the Vietnamese territory to the city of Tay Ninh itself. All this information was reported to me by the wounded who were driven at night from the battlefields to April 17 Hospital in Phnom Penh.

The tension prevailing at the border made the internal situation even more complicated. While during the war against Lon Nol, unity and unanimity in our ranks posed no problem, now everywhere there was confusion, and no region of the country escaped internal dissensions and repressions. The war we were about to fight against Vietnam would be long and difficult. But I was fully confident that we would be victorious.

When certain leaders, whom I know well, were accused of treason, when we were informed that Sao Phœm was a traitor, I asked myself the question: 'How can such loyal comrades fight against each other? But perhaps there is some truth to these accusations, because Vietnamese troops often managed to carry their attacks very deep inside our territory, sometimes even behind our lines.'

3 – I accompany Prince Norodom Sihanouk during his retreat in Battambang

On 1 January 1979, I accompanied Prince Sihanouk and his entourage to Sisophon, near the Thai border. Sihanouk and his close family were in one Mercedes; former Prime Minister Penn Nouth and his family were in an-

---

6   Meaning the information given by the Khmer minority in South Vietnam.

other. We left Phnom Penh around ten o'clock in the evening and arrived at Battambang early in the morning, then continued towards Sisophon. So, we travelled mostly at night to avoid being spotted by the Vietnamese air force. I had been ordered to drive the Prince to Thailand, after which he would fly to safety in China. But, after a couple of days, I received new orders from the Party leadership and drove them back to Phnom Penh on 4 January.[7]

4 – I lead the fighting units of the Ministry of Foreign Affairs, Office 870 and other ministries facing the Vietnamese invasion troops

After the break of diplomatic relations with Vietnam on 31 December 1977, military preparations, including the training of ministry staff, were in full swing. As early as 25 December 1978, just about everyone at the Ministry of Foreign Affairs was aware of the massive attacks by Vietnamese troops against Cambodia and, in some places, we were unable to repel them. Moreover, the growing number of wounded fighters brought from the Vietnamese border to various hospitals in the capital alerted people to the seriousness of the situation.

During the first week of January 1979, the ministry organized the evacuation of children and women as well as members of the diplomatic corps stationed in Phnom Penh towards Battambang and Sisophon with a view to a possible exit to Thailand, while all other men remained on the spot, ready to fight the invading forces. Only the ambassadors of Laos and Cuba did not budge and remained in their chancelleries. As the departmental security officer, I was appointed ex officio to lead the department's fighting units. Under my command, were not only the male members of the Ministry of Foreign Affairs, but also elements of the Central Committee Office (870), based in Borey Keila (city of sports), located north of the Olympic Stadium, which served as the Party School (currently the seat of Television No. 5), and the fighting units of K–6, the Ministries of Social Affairs and Public Works. On the instructions of So Hong, secretary-general of the ministry, the male office staff was ready for action as early as the evening of 6 January 1979.

I drove Prince Norodom Sihanouk, accompanied by Princess Monique, and the former Premier Penn Nouth and his wife, as well as Thiounn Prasith,

---

7   Read the more detailed narrative of the escape of Sihanouk and his family, together with the regime's leadership, diplomats and the Chinese 'advisors', in Philip Short's *Pol Pot*, pp. 395–401.

Keat Chhon and Madame Poc Mona[8], to Pochentong International Airport. While waiting for a flight that left for Beijing at 8:00 pm, the Prince was mad with rage. He said that the Vietnamese invasion was our fault and he did not want to go and plead our cause to the UN. Through that night after, I could not sleep. I was busy contacting the army staff for permission to obtain weapons and ammunition from the state-owned Tuol Kork armoury. I was able to secure more than 800 rifles, consisting of 500 AK-47s, 200 B–40 and B–41 rocket grenade launchers and ten 60mm mortars and 100 hand grenades.

On the same evening of 6 January 1979, the Party's four most senior leaders also left the capital. Pol Pot, Nuon Chea, Ieng Sary and Khieu Samphân, as well as the Chinese ambassador Sun Hao, accompanied by their wives, travelled separately in their own cars before meeting near the Thai border. The factory workers in Phnom Penh and surrounding areas were evacuated mainly via National Road No. 5, and also National Road No. 4 towards Phnom Aural. On the morning of 7 January, members of the other departments left in droves in hundreds of trucks and cars. Only the fighting units of the Ministry of Foreign Affairs and the Phnom Penh defence remained in the capital. The latter consisted of a few young soldiers armed only with handguns. I deployed my forces first on Sisowath Quay, in front of the Royal Palace.

---

8   Dr. Thiounn Thiœun's wife, like a sort of lady-in-waiting, as she came from an aristocvratic family.

– XV –

The arrival of the Vietnamese and the second resistance

On 7 January 1979, at eight o'clock in the morning, Ta Mok came to see me at B–1 to tell me that he was joining Sou Meth, commander of the DK Air Force, at the Army General Staff Headquarters. I also met So Hong, who was riding a motorcycle while I prepared a car for him. Ta Mok asked me how many men were in the units under my command.

I had more than three hundred. He promised to supply me with seven tanks and asked me to contain the Vietnamese advance at Neak Luong. But it was a hollow promise since Chen, the head of the tank unit, had betrayed us. The next day, 8 January, I deployed my units along National Road No. 4, ready to engage in combat and protect anti-aircraft batteries at the Samrong railway Station. The fighters of Air Force Division 502 were unaware of any entry of Vietnamese troops into Phnom Penh. They told me that their commander had not informed them. I urged them to bomb the Central Market. But they refused to do so unless ordered by their commander, who had already run away.

At eleven o'clock on 7 January 1979, the first fighting broke out at the Monivong Bridge in Kbal Thnâl, where Vietnamese troops launched attacks with DCA 37 cannons and 12–7 machine guns. At that moment, all the vehicles carrying factory workers could leave the capital. In the meantime, I travelled by jeep to Pochentong, where I noted that the Vietnamese invasion troops came from the east. I then returned to Phnom Penh and ordered all units based at B–1 and the Olympic Stadium to withdraw and regroup at Tuol Kork. At half-past eleven, the first three tanks, carrying the flags of the Vanguard unit and of the Kampuchea United Front for National Salvation (KUFNS), signalled the beginning of the final assault on Phnom Penh. Clashes then erupted, but our forces were powerless to destroy the Vietnamese T–54 tanks. I dispatched a group of fighters for news from the Central Market side, which was already fully occupied by the invading troops. In a panic, the driver rolled over the jeep as he sped along Kampuchea Krom Boulevard, killing three passengers. I had the dead brought to Chéng Héng's villa and the wounded to Anlong Chrey Hospital. By now, the Central Market side was fully occupied by invading troops. I then deployed the rest of my forces on the road to Pochentong and, at half-past three in the afternoon, I gave the order to attack the international airport. Enemy forces there were trying to join the forces at the Central Market, but our attacks prevented them and they were forced to withdraw.

On the same day, many Vietnamese helicopters continued to land their forces all along National Road No. 4. I stayed there all day. As other DK units had not moved and had not engaged in the fight, I thought it was wiser to preserve my strength. In the evening of the next day, 8 January 1979, I decided to orchestrate an orderly retreat for my units, which returned, having walked all night from Thmat Porng on Road No. 26. Calm had returned in the night and, at eight o'clock, I decided to begin a long and difficult orderly retreat from the capital, marked by a series of attacks against the enemy. We initiated our retreat by the dikes of Toul Kork and from there we started a long walk to Samrong. But halfway we found rice and dishes ready to be served and still hot. Our forces, more than a thousand fighters, rested at the Samrong train station.[1]

On 9 January, my forces took up positions along the road that connects Thmâr Porng with Oudong, in anticipation of a Vietnamese attack. The region lacked nothing to supply the combatants: oxen, pigs and poultry. Here, all the villages were deserted. I did not know where their people had gone. That night, I decided to evacuate my units. I knew this region well, having been there during the war from 1970 to 1975. On 10 January, we camped in the Ang Prâlung Pagoda, next to Dok Peang and Tong Krê villages, Ponhea Leu District, Kompong Speu Province.

On 12 January, I met with General Ponlork, previously military commander of the city of Phnom Penh, currently a member of the Veal Veng District Council in Pursat Province. He told me that the Party leadership was ordering us to contain the enemy on Road No. 26 so that they would not move further. I then deployed my units from Smach Station on National Road No. 4 at Amleang in Kompong Speu. There, the forces of several military cadres, including division chiefs Suy, Boeun, Thoem, Thim and Run, joined from the east, having fled the Vietnamese advance. Many of our forces had died while crossing the Mekong because they could not swim.

---

1   Samrong station is some ten kilometres west of the capital. As to finding food for up to 1,000 soldiers at a people's commune, this was quite possible, as members of those communes numbered into the thousands.

On 15 January, Vietnamese troops launched a combing operation from Oudong on National Road No. 5 and Thnâl Totung on Road No. 4 to put our forces in a pincer movement on Road No. 26. Some twenty of our tanks were immobilized there, abandoned by their drivers as a result of the treachery of their commander.

I remained in this region until 15 March, when I led my forces to Samlaut, in the province of Battambang, where the KR leadership had first taken refuge. Samlaut had become the focus of the exploitation of iron ore under DK, thanks to Chinese aid. For two and a half months, entrenched at Bat Dœng Station on Road No. 26, we managed to hold in the face of Vietnamese attacks launched from Chrâk Sdach Pagoda, in the district of Kompong Tralach, province of Kompong Chhnang and Chbar Mon in Kompong Speu Province. Our ammunition was provided by Ta Mok and Sèm Pal, President of the Western region after Chou Chet's purge. Our forces were reinforced by six divisions coming from the east, commanded by Huy, Tuon, Thim, Nget, Sim and Riem. During a major enemy attack at Bat Dœng in late March 1979, we lost 30 men and several dozen wounded.

Once the bulk of our fighting forces on the Vietnamese border had been routed, no serious resistance existed inside the country and the invading troops could advance at will. On 15 January 1979, I visited the wounded at Anlong Chrey Hospital in Aural District, Kompong Speu Province. By chance in a forest, I meet Ta Mok, who was with wounded, hungry fighters. But Ta Mok's concern was elsewhere. He was only worried about preparing the land for the next dry season rice crop. When I asked him what I must do, he ordered me to withdraw my forces from the battlefield to protect the leadership of the Party. He then had 20 General Motors trucks brought to transport all my men, close to 2,000, from Phnom Aural through Leach to Pursat, Phnom Thippadei, the hydroelectric dam at Kang Hoat, Phnom Veal Chap and Chamlâng Kuoy in Battambang to drop them near the iron mine, exactly in the village called Ta Mok in the district of Samlaut.[2] The more than 10,000 townspeople who had survived rallied to me. I told them, 'We are fighters who are constantly moving. You cannot follow us.' They said, 'It does not matter! We will follow you, and we can serve in transport and supply units!' I then assigned a company to their protection.

---

2   Samlaut was an important settlement as *many* ex-KR and their descendants have survived there to this very day.

Shortly after Koh Krâlor, I met Hor Nam Hong.[3] He was very angry because someone had stolen his radio. I told him, 'Do not worry too much. Such a thing always happens in a troubled situation like ours. ... The essential thing for us now is to survive!' 'I learned later that he already had a survival plan: he defected to the Vietnamese army, which drove him back to Phnom Penh. This explains why his entire family – his wife, children, parents and parents-in-law – had been with him when we met. They were travelling from Koh Krâlor to Teak Thnim, where they would defect.

From that moment, I took charge of the front on National Road No. 10, from Chi Sang to Treng and Kompong Kol, where there was a sugar refinery. In March, the leadership of the Party, including Pol Pot, Nuon Chea, Ieng Sary and Khieu Samphân, was established with the Chinese Ambassador Sun Hao in Ta Taok, Samlaut District in Battambang. I engaged the enemy only once, on National Road No. 10. We suffered the heaviest losses. Many valiant cadres and combatants were killed in action, comrades Leap, Mon, Téng and Réng. At Samlaut, Kèn, still Pol Pot's chief guard, came to visit me three times and handed me a message from Pol Pot, urging me to hand over the forces under my command to others and to come and provide close security for the top leaders. I asked Kèn to tell Pol Pot: 'I cannot give up on the forces I trained and brought from Phnom Penh. Without me, these forces would soon disband. But it is imperative to ensure the protection of Chinese guests.'[4] After this exchange of notes, Pol Pot again summoned me personally, but I refused to respond.

---

3   Hor Nam Hong was born in 1935. After studies in international relations and diplomacy in Phnom Penh and France, he joined Sihanouk's GRUNK representing it in Paris in 1970 and in Cuba in 1973. He was called back to Phnom Penh in late 1975 and sent to the re-education camp for returnees at Bœung Trabek. He became president of B–32 in 1977. He escaped into the Cardamom Mountains along with most detainees of the Bœung Trabek re-education camp, although already a large number had been killed during DK. After holding various positions in Héng Samrin's PRK regime and a post as ambassador in Paris from 1993 through to 1998, while the FUNCINPEC was in power, he became minister of foreign affairs for successive Hun Sèn governments until his retirement in 2016. He was accused of collaborating with the DK regime by some political opponents and taken to court in France. But the accusation was dismissed by the French court.

4   We must not forget that Sun Hao, the Chinese ambassador and a great friend of Ta Mok, had deliberately remained in Cambodia, together with a few 'advisors' who had failed to leave the country on time. In return, the Chinese sent, through Thailand, abundant weaponry and dollars to make the life of the invading Vietnamese army very insecure. Sun Hao remained with the KR leadership until the Paris October 1991 Agreement, when the Chinese ceased to support the KR. They had to be protected at all costs. By going once more into the *maquis*, the KR were following Beijing's advice.

In the meantime, the enemy was launching a large combing cooperation. To escape, the leaders of DK and the Chinese ambassador, and some advisors, started to cross the Cardamoms to reach the Thai border. Cut off from any relation with the leadership, I regrouped the forces placed under my command. Then, refusing the fight, we began a long and dangerous journey to the Thai border. During the fight on National Road No. 10, we lost five cadres: Ek, Khorn, Leap, Mon and Sem. Left without direction, ammunition and food, we regrouped in a forest on the bank of the Stung O'Chor, an upper tributary of the Sangkê River. We were more than 3,000 civilians and at least 400 combatants.

Among the forces stationed at Kompong Korl, one section led by Chhay, the future police chief of Païlin, returned to this town. With no contact with the leadership and no rear base, I never ventured to engage my men in a fight. As soon we arrived at the Stung O'Chor, I urgently called a meeting in which I asked this question: 'Now we are short of food and ammunition. If we head east, we will run into the Vietnamese. If we head the west, we will end up at the Thai border, where we will be given the opportunity to rebuild our forces and resume the fight to liberate our country from the Vietnamese. In a situation like ours right now, we must never procrastinate. Any hesitation is equivalent to death.' As the participants in the meeting remained perplexed, I added: 'If we decide to walk west, we can reach the border in three days. We shall be able to keep hope, if we choose the west. Our leaders have also gone west.'

Thus, fully convinced, the participants opted to go west. I urged them 'to start straightaway, as long as everyone is in good health. If some of us fall ill, crossing such a dense and extensive forest would become an impossible endeavour.' As expected, we reached O'Chor three days later, and could see Thai territory. Then while walking along the border, we arrived at Bo Taing Sou, but we did not meet anyone. We continued our journey, guided by a map, always worried that we would meet the Vietnamese face-to-face at any moment. I ordered the rest of our forces to hasten the pace.

On the way from O'Chor, I met Ieng Vuth, Ieng Sary's son, alone in the middle of the forest, on the top of the highest mountain in the area, west of Païlin. He shared his last cassava and sugar cane with me. I asked about the forces under his command. He informed me that they had disbanded and vanished. He had no news of the sons of Vorn Vet or Son Sen. Son Sen's son had attended a military pilot's course in China along with Ieng Vuth in during 1977–1978.

After we arrived at Païlin, we felt relatively safe. From there, we reached Kamrieng in the afternoon of 4 April 1979, already arranged thanks to Ieng Sary. Here we met forces led by General Thim, a Tampuon who was responsible for the logistics of the army staff. The general told me that Ieng Sary had told him that Kamrieng had been chosen to become our rear base.

Thim provided me with a Chinese jeep, commonly called a 'command car', and informed me that So Hong was currently in Say Samân (Malay) and Chê, a Krœung, president of the Office of the Ministry of Public Works and Transport, had settled at Kamrieng while Nikân directed operations at Mâk Heun on the Sisophon road west of Malay. I also met Y Chhean.[5] He had reached Kamrieng the night before I arrived. When I drove the car to Mâk Heun, Nikân had just routed the Vietnamese troops coming from Poipet and seized a sizeable war booty, including three two-watt radio transmitters. Nikân gave me one, for all intents and purposes. Generals Sok Pheap,[6] Phœng Phon and So Dân, from Division 450, were also among us.

At this time, Malay became a support base for the forces of DK. The Thai military told me that our leaders were on their territory and they were willing to drive me to them, if I wished.[7] After I told them that I wanted to see Ieng Sary, they then drove me to Boeng Chhnang, near Kamrieng, where Sary welcomed me warmly. I gave him a report on my activities since the fall of Phnom Penh, including the size of my civilian and military contingents.

---

5   Y Chhean was then Ieng Sary's bodyguard and chauffeur in Phnom Penh after 1975. Under DK, his most important contribution was in Siemreap in 1978, when he shut down the local ex-colonial prison, together with Phnom Krom prison near the Great Lake, and cleaned up the city in preparation for receiving tourists. After the fall of the regime, he became a commander at Païlin. He joined the Hun Sèn government in February 1996 with his boss Ieng Sary and preserved his position.

6   Sok Pheap was head of Division 450 around Païlin and joined the Hun Sèn government at the same time as Y Chhean. He was promoted to be a four-star general by Hun Sèn in January 2014.

7   The Thais still believed in the domino theory and feared that a powerful Vietnamese army of more than 100,000 men would be in Bangkok within a few days or weeks. But the Thai army never really had to fight in modern times. It was essentially a ceremonial army! So, they treated the wounds, fed, and armed the remaining and totally decrepit elements of the KR army to contain the advances of their enemies the Vietnamese communists. They succeeded beautifully, as Phi Phuon further explains in his memoirs. The Thai military, thanks also to Chinese dollars and weapons, enabled the KR army to block the Vietnamese army on the Cambodian side of the border, without having much to fight themselves. And, on top of it all, the Thai army became even richer by drawing their percentage from Chinese aid, plus from the international humanitarian aid that soon fed the KR troops together with the Cambodian civilian refugees.

Ieng Sary had assigned So Hong and Nikân the responsibility of the Sisophon-Poipet-Bovel Front, while Thim and I were made responsible for a front extending from Ampil Pram Dœm and Kompong Ley in the province of Battambang to Bœng Acheang (currently Stung Koy) in Païlin. Y Chhean and Théng (So Hong's younger brother) were to defend the Païlin region. As for me, I established my headquarters in Kamrieng. For their part, Ieng Sary, Ieng Thirith, Khieu Ponnary and Dr. Thiounn Thiœun selected Phnom Rang, near Bœng Chhnang, on the Thai border. Sar Kim Lomuth,[8] Ok Sakun,[9] Pech Bunreth[10] and Kor Bun Héng[11] also ended up nearby, while Pol Pot settled at Pass 505 near the Thai border town of Trat.

During our retreat from Mâk Heun to Kamrieng in April 1979, the deaths caused by sickness and famine became innumerable. Among them were the more than 300 girls and young women from the transport unit in Phum Daung (Malay). In May 1979, while we were in the midst of a reorganization, the Vi-

---

8   Sar Kim Lomuth (1930–) joined the Democratic Party from 1946 to 1955 and was director of the Indiana Jati Bank in Phnom Penh under the Khmer Republic, but also a member of the clandestine CPK. In 1975, he was not relocated and Pol Pot kept him as a financial cadre in the ghostly Bank of Foreign Trade. In Khieu Samphân's shadow government in the 1980s, he was in charge of transport and supplies. He joined the Hun Sèn government in 1995 and testified at the ECCC in June 2012.

9   Ok Sakun, 1932–2003, a Sisowath School alumnus, obtained a Cambodian government scholarship for France in 1950. His academic career was short, as he failed the entrance examination at the École Centrale de Paris, but he became a member of the Marxist-Leninist Circle and married a French woman before returning to Cambodia in 1956. He then became a cadre at the Cambodian Railways. In September 1960, his apartment was the site of a clandestine and later famous 'secret Party Congress', during which the WPK was created as an independent entity. Two years later, Pol Pot became its secretary. Appearing on a list of 34 suspects in 1963, Ok Sakun returned to France, where he obtained a diploma from the École supérieure des Transports. In 1970, he became the FUNK representative to France, returning to Cambodia in December 1975. After a stay at a Bœung Trabek re-education camp, he worked at B–1, the Ministry of Foreign Affairs. He returned to France in 1979 and represented the DK government at UNESCO and at the UN in Geneva. He died of a heart attack after his retirement.

10 Pech Bunreth (1937–2000) attended the Lycée Sisowath and then studied agricultural engineering in France. He joined the FUNK in 1970 and was named the GRUNK ambassador to Albania. From 1975 he worked at the Ministry of Foreign Affairs. In 1979, he became the DK representative at the UN Economic and Social Commission for Asia and the Pacific (ESCAP) in Bangkok.

11 Kor Bun Héng (1946–), a Cambodian of Chinese origin, joined the FUNK in 1970 while studying in Paris. In 1973, he flew to Beijing and then to Hanoi to work with Khieu Thirith at the FUNK Radio. After a period of re-education in a people's commune in the Northern region, he worked at the Ministry of Foreign Affairs. After the regime's fall, he worked at the DK mission in the UN and took part in the negotiations that led to the 1991 Paris agreement. He joined the government in 1998 and later sold telephones near Phnom Penh Central Market.

etnamese troops, leaving us no respite, launched a large-scale search operation, forcing us to withdraw back to Thailand. Virtually all the DK fighting forces retreated into two refugee camps on Thai territory, one south of Khamphut near Trat, and the other north of Sa Keo near Aranyaprathet.[12] The Thai military ordered us to consolidate all of these refugees into a single camp at Ban Laem, on the Thai border in Kamrieng. The camp housed about 100,000 refugees, including those transported from Preah Vihear.[13] Thai navy soldiers were cruel to Cambodian refugees, mistreating them as they pleased. In June 1979, another refugee camp was set up in Ta Ngoc, on the territory of the present district of Sampov Lun in Battambang. There was no international humanitarian aid yet. The International Red Cross did not appear until around October 1979.

In October 1979, Pol Pot summoned me to his headquarters at Pass 505 in the Cardamoms. First, he asked me to report to him on the development of the general situation. I told him that the morale and fighting spirit of our armed forces was not a problem, provided they had a solid rear base of support. The people supported our fight against Vietnamese aggression and actively participated in it. He then inquired about the population's health and living conditions. He told me that the Thai authorities were willing to help us when our patients came for treatment. He also told me to seek help from international humanitarian organizations. Pol Pot recommended that each unit should organize the struggling activities, set up its own support base and send small groups to carry out our efforts to undermine the morale of the enemy and do intelligence work. It was necessary to direct the resolved elements to stay with us and lead the struggle. We must protect our base as we did in Ratanakiri: plant piles, bamboo spikes, and set up booby trap after booby trap. It was important for us to return to our primary principles: people's war and guerrilla war. The existence of a vast rear base stretching from Koh Kong

---

12 At the time, the Vietnamese army could have celebrated their complete victory and opened the devasted country to international organizations and to the West, to facilitate its immediate reconstruction. But such an approach would have hindered their goal of establishing Cambodia as a client state. As a result, Cambodians had to suffer yet another decade of misery.

13 Cambodian refugees transported by the Thai army from the west to the north, near Preah Vihear temple, became a symbol of the total inhumanity of the Thais, who mainly wished to protect their country whatever the human cost for the Khmers. The victims were forced back into Cambodia via the Phnom Dangrek escarpment, and many died in horrendous circumstances as they set off landmines laid by the Thais, KR and the PAVN. See Joan D. Criddle and Teeda Butt Mam, *To Destroy You is no Loss: The Odyssey of a Cambodian Family*, Doubleday, 1987, Chapter 17.

to the Lao border would enable us to carry our actions inside Cambodia, where we could now build resistance nuclei and agents for undermining and destabilizing the enemy.

Pol Pot lived in a hut where he rested in a hammock stretched under his thatched roof. He worked under a plastic tent on a table made of bamboo. Kèn was responsible for his security and commanded about fifty guards, ten of whom were national minorities. Khieu Ponnary did not live with him. In April 1979, she left Thai territory and moved to Kamrieng with her sister along with Dr. Thiounn Thiœun and his wife, Poc Mala.

From the moment I set up my command base in Kamrieng in April 1979, food, ammunition and mines arrived in small quantities from China, through Thailand. Mines were distributed to companies and battalions. We used them ourselves. Accidents could always happen while planting or retrieving them, especially when you hit the line that operated them. There was no map or sketch of mine locations. We simply planted them and left. I settled in Ban Laem from April 1979 until July 1980.

– XVI –

Reconstruction of the Party; stay at Pass 808; return to Phnom Malay

*A*fter July 1980, I left to settle in the north, at Pass 808 on the Dangrêk Range, opposite the Thai village of Ban Travéng in Surin Province. My wife had gone there before me. Also living at Pass 808 were the wives of So Hong and Khieu Samphân. Shortly thereafter, we opened three more passes: 1003, 1002 and 1001. The latter is located where Cambodia, Laos and Thailand meet, and was under the command of Son Sen. Kaè Pauk was responsible for Pass 1002, adjacent to the Preah Vihear Temple, while Pass 1003, located in Anlong Véng in the province of Oddar Meanchey, was protected by General Thim. Pass 808, as well as passes near Tatum and Andèng Mut, were under my responsibility. To move more quickly from one pass to another, I travelled by car, driven on Thai territory by an officer from the Thai Army Operations Department. There were ways of communication in Cambodia, but the journey had to be made on foot for lack of safe roads. Pass 808 received guests from Japan and China, and had a visitors' centre for them.[1]

From Pass 808, we conducted activities in Varin District in Oddar Meanchey Province, and in Prek Chik and Prek Saat in Preah Vihear Province. Pass 808 supported the provinces of Oddar Meanchey, Siemreap, Preah Vihear, Kratieh, Stung Trèng, Ratanakiri, Mondolkiri, Kompong Thom and Kompong Cham. During my stay at Pass 808, I took charge of the comrades sent inside to carry out guerrilla actions. At the same time, I was in charge of supplies, logistics and the distribution of food and ammunition to all units and services. I provided them with clothes, mosquito nets, hammocks, bales, military caps, boots, water bottles, all kinds of consumer products (rice, salt, sugar, coffee, Ovaltine, glutamate etc.) and medicines, as well as agricultural implements (axes, pickaxes, shovels, spades, saws, etc.). I maintained regular radio contacts with Office 870 and Ieng Sary. I reported to them on the situation prevailing at the pass.

---

1   See the description of Pass 808 in Philip Short's *Pol Pot*, pp. 413–14.

1 – Re-education seminars

In June 1981, Nuon Chea came to Pass 808 to conduct a three-day political studies seminar for cadres and fighters living there, including more than 3,000 belonging to the transport unit, with the aim of building a rear base in Koh Kong province. As usual, this seminar was held during the rainy season. In the morning, fifty participants listened to Nuon Chea's presentation on the general situation. He emphasized the political line, the military line, the economic line and the cultural line of DK, defined by Pol Pot. The political line aimed to bring together all possible forces, both nationally and internationally, to liberate the country from the Vietnamese yoke and to build a peaceful, democratic and neutral Cambodia. There would be no question of socialism or communism. Nuon Chea lived in his own office, a tent called 'Tœk Thleak' (waterfall), located at Pass 808. At that time, Pol Pot was at Pass 505 in Koh Kong province.

From 1984 to 1989, Pol Pot organized a total of three seminars on political studies. The first was held in 1984 at O'Suor Sdei, on the Stung Mé Tœk. Intended for 120 cadres of military units operating from Koh Kong to the tri-border area, the seminar lasted half a month. Pol Pot was the only speaker, assisted by Nuon Chea, who sat on the platform with him. Neither Khieu Samphân nor Ieng Sary participated in the seminar. The latter was on Thai territory in charge of diplomatic activities abroad, as well as economic and financial issues. The general conference was held in the morning and lasted ten days. It dealt with the general situation, including political, military, economic, commercial, social, cultural and international issues. The afternoon was devoted to discussions.

The political line was to mobilize all national and international forces in all areas to end the Vietnamese occupation and liberate the country. The military line advocated the use of the people's war and guerrilla warfare to combat the invading forces. If the opportunity arose, we had to launch a frontal attack to destroy an enemy position. We must endeavour to attack enemy supply routes on both land and water. The economic line was to receive help from wherever it came from. In domestic politics, we must stick to a production-based economy with 'roots and stumps', that is to say a family economy aimed mainly at self-subsistence. In 1984, in economic terms, we were totally dependent on Chinese aid, valued at US$ 5 million a month. In areas controlled by DK, there was no market or currency. But the authorities had created a kind of state market where people could buy rice, sugar, salt, glutamate, flour, coffee, tea, Ovaltine, sweets, noodles, pasta, cans and tools for everyday use such as knives, axes, shovels, cutters, harrows etc... During this seminar, Pol Pot invited me to his home. He had just remarried. He lived most of the time at K–1 when he was not on working visits to the provinces.

2 – In charge of logistics at Division 450

In 1979, in Phnom Malay, Ieng Sary, on instructions from Pol Pot, ordered the reorganization of Division 450 of the former Revolutionary Army of Kampuchea, which now became the National Army of Democratic Kampuchea (NADK). Sok Pheap became the military commander, So Hong the political commissar and I was the logistics and supply officer.

At that time, enemy troops made up of 70 per cent Vietnamese and 30 per cent Khmer camped at Phnom Rang, commonly known as Phnom Malay or just Malay, five kilometres from our positions in some places and seven kilometres elsewhere. In 1983, we seized Phnom Rang and destroyed all their shelters in the forest. We chased them off National Road No. 5 and they retreated to Poipet, Mongkol Borey and Sisophon. We then controlled all the forest territory. Every time the enemy tried to attack us, we quickly held them in check.

On 12 February 1985, Vietnamese Division 6 troops launched a large-scale combing operation along the Thai border, starting from Nam Sap on Phnom Ampil, which extends between the districts of Sampov Lun, Phnom Prœk and Bovel in Battambang Province. They attacked from National Road No. 5 with three 130-mm cannons, bringing the entire civilian population of DK along the Thai border to a hasty retreat into Thailand while the fighting units were led by So Hong, Phœng Phon, Mey Muon and myself. General Sok Pheap and Colonel Meas Maung gathered in Païlin, the only stronghold that was not taken.

3 – The Khmer People's National Liberation Front and the United National Front for an Independent, Neutral, Pacific and Cooperative Cambodia

The Khmer People's National Liberation Front (KPNLF), led by former prime minister Son Sann,[2] and the United National Front for an Independent,

---

2   Son Sann (1911–2000) graduated from *Hautes Études Commerciales*, Paris, in 1933. He joined the Democratic Party in 1946 and held several ministerial posts. He was the first governor of the National Bank, from 1955 through to 1968, doubling as Minister of Foreign Affairs from

Neutral, Peaceful and Cooperative Cambodia (FUNCINPEC), led by Prince Norodom Sihanouk, and DK formed an alliance against Vietnamese aggression at the Tripartite Summit Conference in Kuala Lumpur on 22 June 1982. This conference culminated in the formation of the Coalition Government of Democratic Kampuchea (CGDK), with Prince Norodom Sihanouk as president, Son Sann as prime minister and Khieu Samphân as vice-president and in charge of foreign affairs. By May 1983, Prince Sihanouk had received the credentials of three times as many ambassadors of countries that recognized our coalition government as the PRK had. Among these countries were China, Pakistan, Bangladesh, Malaysia, Guinea, Egypt and Senegal. Meanwhile, I was in charge of the security of Division 450 and also that of the perimeter surrounding the space where Prince Sihanouk received the ambassadors of friendly countries. I was designated to guarantee his security from the moment he entered the national road by car from Bangkok and he remembered me very well. I wore the uniform of the National Army of DK. He did not stay for the night at Malay; he arrived there around ten in the morning and left after lunch. Whenever he came, he distributed small souvenirs to the wives of cadres, such as traditional *krâma* scarves. There was plenty to eat; Ieng Thirith would choose the Prince's favourite dishes for his lunch – beef, pork, fish, poultry fruits, wines galore and even champagne, all from Bangkok.

The Site 8 refugee camp was created opposite Sampov Lun in Cambodia, south of Malay. At that time, all KPNLF forces operated north of National Road No. 5. The same was true for most of the FUNCINPEC forces, while two of its 400-man regiments under the command of Colonels Narin and Dara cohabited with my forces, including at Hop Russey, located on the edge of the forest, previously belonging to Monglkol Borey District, but currently in Malay District. They were not fighting units as they did not engage the fight against the People's Revolutionary of Kampuchea-People's Army of Vietnam forces; they only thought of having fun and chasing girls. We could not collaborate with them: they had no experience. I used them to transport food and ammunition. Both Narin and Dara are dead now.

1958 to 1960 and Prime Minister during 1967–1968. After taking refuge in France in 1970, he went to Beijing in a vain attempt to reconcile Sihanouk with his compatriots inside Cambodia. In 1978, he founded the Khmer People's National Liberation Front in an effort to unite all anti-communist Cambodians.

4 – I lead attacks against Vietnam's 'Bamboo Wall'

From 1979 to 1991, Pol Pot lived at Pass 505, at the foot of the Cardamom Range in Koh Kong Province. As for Nuon Chea, he settled in Thmâr Da in the district of Samlaut in Battambâng Province. He moved very often. He went, for example, to Pass 808 in 1982 and to Païlin in 1985.

From Païlin, our forces entered Cambodia through Kamrieng via Ampil Pram Deum and Say Samân to carry our activities further north towards Poipet. It was not until the 1986 that we could open a passage on the Thai border with Malay, to infiltrate our fighters into the interior of the country. The population had told us that no enemy troops were inside because they had all been deployed along the Thai border. I led our attacks against enemy positions at the border, while other units conducted operations against enemy troops stationed in the villages.

As part of the K–5 Campaign in 1987, the enemy erected a barbed wire wall with iron piles all along the Thai border from Poipet to the south. In some places this iron wall was fifty meters from the frontier; in others, only twenty meters, ten meters or even five meters. They defended this territory by placing six categories of Soviet-made mines, including twin mines, corn-kernel mines, battery-powered mines, tapered mines and anti-tank mines. The enemy even laid mines inside Thai territory, and in places where there was no village or cultivation. I organized three-fighter groups to find and explode enemy mines, up to 17 mines in a day. From Nam Sap to the border, we also laid mines. This mine warfare was tragic. Hundreds of thousands of Cambodians from the Phnom Penh side died from exhaustion, illness and famine. From 1986 to 1989, some of our forces attacked enemy positions inside this perimeter. Others, including the 300 men under my command, engaged in harassment on the Thai border by cutting enemy troops in several slices before tearing them to pieces.

From one position to another, enemy troops communicated by telephone. By putting a needle in their telephone wires, we could listen to their conversations and communications. Moreover, we captured more than 300 enemy soldiers, including Vietnamese, who showed us where they laid mines and how to defuse them. At Khla Ngoap on the Sisophon Road, I captured 60 enemy soldiers, some of whom were de-mining experts. When we took them prisoner, we asked them to lay down their arms and let them go home after giving each 50,000 riel and also salt, sugar, rice, soy sauce and fish juice and tin cans. To those who chose to stay with us, we gave the same. On the way that

175

enemy soldiers traversed daily, we put food items and a small note that said, 'Every Khmer worthy of the name does not kill other Khmers. The Khmers must join forces to fight Vietnamese aggression'. In one month, we managed to dismantle and destroy the Vietnamese 'Bamboo Wall'.[3]

Despite the withdrawal of most Vietnamese troops[4] from Cambodia under almost unanimous pressure, mainly from Gorbachev's new Soviet Union, proclaimed in September 1989, several Vietnamese soldiers and officers who spoke Khmer or who had married Cambodian women joined the army of the PRK. Some of their military advisers remained in provincial capitals to organize lightning raids against our forces. Division 286 retreated to Preah Netr Preah on National Road No. 6 in Banteay Meanchey Province and Division 6 to Bovel, on Road No. 578 in Battambang Province. But we were always ready to lie in wait for them out of the towns, from Poipet, Sisophon and Mongkol Borey to Prey Khpous and Kaéng. We knew where enemy troops were moving because the population told us. None of their activities and plans escaped us. In places where we came to an understanding with them, there was no confrontation. Since 1989, our line of defence had stood firm and, on November 15 of the same year, we definitively liberated Malay. From 1990, our compatriots in Thailand returned to their national soil.

5 – Peace negotiations

Although I was constantly on the battlefield, I was regularly briefed on the progress of peace negotiations by our leaders. When the Paris Accords were signed on 23 October 1991, I was at Poy Angkor, a town located on the Malay plain near Kbal Khmoch, Damnak Preah Ang and Nang Kok. Despite the negotiations, the Vietnamese leaders insisted on fighting; they did not believe in the virtue of negotiations but in the force of arms. For them, negotiations were only a moment of respite while their weapons gained ground on the battlefield. In this way, the negotiations could only turn out in their favour.

---

3   See Esmeralda Muciolli, *Le mur de bambou: le Cambodge après Pol Pot*, Paris: Régine Deforges, 1988. What was called by all 'the Bamboo Wall', a derisive echo of the Iron Curtain, consisted mainly of pits, bamboo traps and landmines. It was a big failure and caused thousands of deaths among people forcefully enrolled by the Héng Samrin regime.

4   International pressure to withdraw was almost unanimous. Under Gorbachev's glasnost policy, the Soviet Union also ceased its support for what was becoming Hun Sèn's war.

In the Malay area, the battle was raging on the 'Unity' channel from Prey Khpous in the Bovel area to the Thmenh Trey Bridge in Sisophon District, Banteay Meanchey, across Plain 500, in front of Mongkol Borey and Sisophon. The enemy wanted to force us into the forest and keep its free hand on the plains. After the Paris Agreements, all the KPNLF and FUNCINPEC forces retreated north of National Road No. 5, in the area of Thmar Puok and the former headquarters of Prince Sihanouk at Rumchang, leaving the southern part under our responsibility. The two organizations were preparing to participate in the elections organized by the United Nations Transitional Authority in Cambodia (UNTAC).

Moreover, after the 1991 Paris Agreements, China ceased all forms of aid to DK, and Chinese Ambassador Sun Hao and the Chinese technicians and experts left DK territory. A kind of lull then prevailed on the battlefield. The enemy paused its combing operations. At the end of 1992, in order to take joint responsibility with Ta Mok for the northern part of the front, Pol Pot decided to leave Pass 505, settling first in Chup Koki in Ampil District, Oddar Meanchey Province, while the construction of an office in Phnom Chhat was being completed. He moved to Phnom Chhat in 1993. Nuon Chea lived in Païlin. On 23 September 1993, the combined troops of the Cambodian People's Party, KPNLF and FUNCINPEC launched a massive operation against the NADK forces based in Phnom Chhat, forcing them to retreat to Païlin and Malay. Pol Pot then retired to Anlong Véng, Ta Mok's stronghold (here Tak Mok resided until his capture on 6 March 1999 by the Royal Cambodian Armed Forces).

In the area under DK control, we distributed the land to the people. A family of combatants would receive a field or rice paddy 100 meters wide and one kilometre long, that is to say 100,000 m², which equals ten hectares. When I was in Damnak Preah Ang, located today in Mongkol Borey District in Banteay Meanchey, my unit of 25 families cultivated up to one hundred and fifty hectares of rice fields. It was a particularly rich plain. Land allocation did not take into account military grades. Each family of combatants, whether they were simple soldiers or officers, was entitled to the same portion of land. No hierarchy existed in the NADK. The NADK was constituted of simple fighters, sub-groups (four fighters), groups (three subgroups), sections (three groups), companies (three sections), battalions (three companies), regiments (three battalions), and finally divisions (three regiments). A division also included a special unit, a heavy artillery unit and an intelligence unit. Each unit corresponded to a regiment.

– XVII –

The Situation after the Paris Agreements of 23 October 1991

1 – Democratic Kampuchea and the UNTAC elections

*W*hile the situation of the civilian population changed after the Paris Agreements of 23 October 1991, that of the combatants remained what it had always been. Unlike ordinary citizens, soldiers did not have to worry about carrying out production activities to provide for their families. The person in charge of each region took care of it, in this case Ieng Sary for the region including Malay and Sisophon, north of Païlin. Money came from trade in timber and precious stones. In Malay, we controlled all the forest areas, which began one kilometre from the Thai border and extended from Srâke Yor, Chong Chev, O'Kach, and Thmar Beaing to Phnom Yeay Sam. Thai commercial companies had their own means of exploitation. They called on Cambodian workers to cut wood and paid according to the volume of cut timber, five to ten baht per cubic meter, for example. It was a concession system. But from Malay to Païlin, this kind of trade was not flourishing. Rather, we gave priority to our fighters who cut down trees for beds, desks, plank chairs and small planks, which were mostly sold to Thai people. From Païlin to the south stretched vast areas of forest that abounded in precious woods whose trade was more active and lucrative.[1]

At the time, although all the land was distributed to each family in 1991 after the Paris Agreement, its systematic and large-scale exploitation had not yet taken place. It would begin after the reintegration of about half of the

---

1   We have, in the present paragraphs, some indication about how the KR carved for themselves portions of the Cambodian northwestern territory. First of all, from colonial times, these agricultural regions, with quite rich soil, were practically uninhabited and covered with primeval forest. There were few roads and barely any administrative infrastructure, except along the border with Thailand itself. The second point, as described by Phi Phuon, is that all the business arrangements managed by Ieng Sary to exploit timber and precious stones with Thai companies were quite illegal. Still, developing businesses instead of waging war was a major step towards normality and peace. Both Ieng Sary in the west and Ta Mok, now in the north, became quite wealthy and, paradoxically, the rest of the KR population fared economically better than in most outer reaches of Cambodia.

former DK regime into the government of Phnom Penh in 1996, under the leadership of Ieng Sary. We were satisfied with working in already cleared areas on the plain. We cultivated small plots of land, just to support family needs. Although no land register was yet available, individual properties were well delineated: the rice fields by dikes, the fields by appropriate boundaries – creeks, forests or tracks – and recognized by the administration of the village and commune. Land disputes were rare and always settled amicably. I never heard of recourse to the courts for this kind of dispute.

The situation was getting less tense in 1991 and 1992. But the war resumed after we boycotted the general election in 1993. Ta Mok became chief of staff of the entire Khmer Rouge army – his long-time dream – and this was behind the KR refusal to participate in the elections. In early April 1993, a meeting was held in Phnom Chhat, attended by all the main DK leaders: Pol Pot, Nuon Chea, Ieng Sary, Ta Mok, Son Sen and Khieu Samphân. The commanders of Division 450 Sok Pheap, So Hong and myself (Malay), Division 519 Dul Saroeun, Sok, Voy and Chhean (Phnom Chhat) and Division 415 Y Chhean (Païlin) were also present. Pol Pot chaired the meeting and presented an agenda entitled 'Review of the situation and our forces with a view to participating in the elections of 25 May 1993 in accordance with the terms of application of the Paris Agreements'. At this moment Ta Mok, without being asked, got up and declared: 'No one needs to take part in the elections! After this meeting, all units must attack everywhere and in all places.' The reason given was that UNTAC did not apply points 1 and 2 of the Paris Agreement[2] and insisted on the implementation of point 9, which aimed to disarm the Cambodian parties. Pol Pot asked that the meeting should decide on Ta Mok's proposal. But as no one said a word, he then closed the meeting. Everyone was afraid of Ta Mok. This is how DK decided to boycott elections, organized by the UN. I wanted to protest; but if I had protested, being of lower rank, I would not be alive today.[3]

2 – Representative of Democratic Kampuchea in Mongkol Borey District

In 1992, the Mongkol Borey area was my responsibility. I was promoted Brigadier General with one star. I settled in the village of Shamnom on the

---

2   Point 1 dealt with the transition period and Point 2 with UNTAC. The KR claimed that some Vietnamese troops remained in Cambodia and that the Hun Sèn government troops had not been regrouped and disarmed.

3   Phi Phuon acknowledged this on 20 March 2015, in our penultimate interview session.

Mongkol Borey River. The representative of the State of Cambodia was the chief of Phnom Penh's Regiment 24. The Dutch represented the UNTAC and set up their headquarters at Phnom Thom, on National Road No. 5 between Sisophon and Battambang. The UNTAC leader for Banteay Meanchey Province was a Ghanaian named Reach Koma. At that time, we proposed an administrative organization from the level of the village and the commune on a quadripartite basis. But the representative of the State of Cambodia[4] was opposed. As Son Sen came to understand that this mode of organization would never be realized, he became angry with me. But I was not the only one to have failed. Everyone was in the same situation.

In areas controlled by DK, the elections did not take place. But our activists inside advised the people to vote for the FUNCINPEC, and that was why they won the 1993 elections, particularly in Banteay Meanchey Province in general and Mongkol Borey District in particular. In 1992, residents of areas under the control of DK also joined the repatriation movement organized by the UN. This was for example the case of Mey Mann.[5] After the 1993 elections, many of the returnees returned to our area as a result of discrimination by the authorities in power.

3 – Life after the formation of the two-headed government

After the Phnom Penh government refused to recognize the election results and threatened to secede,[6] DK celebrated its decision to have boycotted the

---

4   That is, Hun Sèn's government in Phnom Penh.

5   Mey Mann (1921–2001) had joined the Marxist-Leninist Circle when he was a student in Paris and went with Saloth Sâr into the *maquis*; as he was too moderate, he was not admitted into the 1960 Congress. In 1975, he and his family were evacuated, along with all Phnom Penh inhabitants. Many family members died, including his wife. In the 1980s he became head of the DK Red Cross and found his ex-revolutionary companions in the refugee camps of Thailand. He told his former companions, 'the Super Great Leap Forward of yours was so great that it took you as far as Thailand!' After UNTAC, he created the first human rights organization in Païlin. He translated Samdech Nhiek Tioulong's history of Cambodia since 1863 into Khmer, but his work was lost and the book is, so far, only to be published in its French version, *Chroniques khmères, 1863–1969*, Paris: Les Indes savantes, forthcoming.

6   Having come only second in the UNTAC-sponsored elections in 1993, Hun Sèn along with his CPP threatened to split the country into two and control only its eastern half, with the support of commmunist Vietnam. The dispute was solved when UNTAC chief Yasushi Akashi installed a two-headed government in Phnom Penh, with two prime ministers – Norodom Ranariddh and Hun Sèn – and Sihanouk as King once again! All this, essentially under the pressure of Sihanouk himself.

elections and called for the fight to continue. The UN had spent more than two billion US dollars for nothing, except for the introduction of AIDS into Cambodia.

After the formation of the two-headed government, with Prince Norodom Ranariddh as prime minister and Hun Sèn as second prime minister, DK called on its fighters and cadres to continue fighting to achieve the following goal: to destroy two things and achieve four others:

Destroy its military power;

Destroy its political power;

Achieve four objectives:

Firstly – Train heads of families;

Secondly – Enlighten and educate the larger family;

Thirdly – Establish power in the village, supported and loved by the people;

Fourthly – Establish military power, loved by the people.

We intended to achieve all these objections within the framework of a liberal regime. We appealed to the goodwill of all Cambodians to stop killing other Cambodians once and for all, and urged everyone to refuse to participate in the K–5 'Bamboo Wall' campaign.

The war continued from 1993 until 1996. In January 1996, from Thailand, paratroopers from Unit 911, trained in Malaysia and Indonesia, attacked us from behind at Nong Ian Pass, near Poipet. About 60 of them were annihilated by our fighters.

But even today, conflicts still arise. In 2003, a royal decree declared that approximately 4,500 hectares of farmland around the mountain of Yeay Sam belonged to the national domain. These farmlands had already been allocated to DK combatants. These people were willing to give their land to the authorities but, in the meantime, anarchic elements grabbed the land. The RGC recognized their right of ownership, which obviously raised the opposition of the DK fighters, their commanders and the whole population. These conflicts occurred in Srake Yor, Damrei Slap, Rotès Bak and Bœng Chung Ruk, located 5–6 kilometres from the Thai border in Malay District, Banteay Meanchey Province. What aggravated the situation was that these intruders, instead of exploiting these farmlands themselves, sold them to private companies. The problem was brought to the National Assembly and the Senate in Phnom Penh.

4 – Malay and Païlin rally to the Phnom Penh Government

The secession of Malay and Païlin from DK had its internal causes. Since Son Sen had taken over the southern front in June 1996, including Division 450 (Malay) and Division 415 (Païlin), the internal situation had continued to deteriorate. Son Sen went to Phnom Penh to sit on the Supreme National Council (SNC) and nothing happened. But when Khieu Samphân went there a month later, he was the victim of typical aggression and received a minor head injury. This sparked Pol Pot's suspicion of Son Sen's loyalty to DK. Upon his return, he was assigned to Office 32, the headquarters of his younger brother Nikân, where he was to take charge of the southern front along with Nuon Chea. As a leader, Son Sen was not impartial. He favoured the people from his family and his faction. He intended to take the place of Sok Pheap at the head of Division 450 and that of Y Chhean at the command of Division 415. He accused those who did not support him of being 'the rotten flesh, the swollen flesh'. He confiscated land that fighters had cleared with their own hands within the authorized quota, accusing them of being 'landowners'. Some had built big houses. He ordered them to demolish these and build smaller houses. He confiscated not only tractors, cars and motorcycles, but also ox carts, which were essential for transport on tracks that were impassable for all other vehicles.

One day, Son Sen convened a Division 450 management meeting at midnight at his headquarters at Site 32, located in Sampov Lun, with the intention of arresting all of them. He practised a discriminatory policy against fighters and cadres loyal to Ieng Sary, including Generals Sok Pheap of Malay and Y Chhean of Païlin. Faced with this situation, Division 450 appealed to Office 870. Son Sen then accused us all of treason. So Hong and his wife left Anlong Véng and found refuge in Division 519, further east. When Pol Pot got wind of the case, he wanted to make the trip to settle the conflict on the spot, in Malay and Païlin. But Ta Mok volunteered to do it.

When Ta Mok came to Malay and Païlin, not only did he fail to solve the problem, but he made matters worse. From the start, he sided with Son Sen. He then ordered Nikân's Division 320 to attack both Division 450 and Division 415. But the fighters and cadres of division 320 refused to obey the order, saying, 'We fought with them, they are like brothers to us. We sleep in the same room, we eat our meals at the same table, we have known each other forever … If they really betrayed, what can we do since we find ourselves in the middle of them, caught in pincers.' But Son Sen did not stop insisting. Division 320 eventually obeyed his orders and fired 12 shots from their DCA 37, into the air to intimidate us.

As we were accused of treason, we turned to the government of Phnom Penh. We then entered into negotiations with General Pol Sarœun,[7] so that the government troops did not attack us. At the same time, we were calling on the cadres and fighters of Division 320 to give up trying to harm us. At this point, Ta Mok was with Son Sen and Nuon Chea at Office 32. Meanwhile, we continued our work of persuasion with the cadres and fighters of Division 320, and we managed to convince generals Rom, Puth, Sobin and Chê to cooperate with us. We informed the Thais that the various Cambodian parties agreed not to fight each other, but still felt threatened by Ta Mok, Son Sen and Nuon Chea. So, we asked the Thais to refrain from helping these three leaders to come to Pailin through Thailand. With the help of the Thais, the three were evacuated to Samlaut, where they found the generals Nikân and Ieng Phan. Ta Mok and Son Sen then ordered these generals to attack us. We got in touch with the generals and tried to convince them to stop the fratricidal fight, but without success. We then asked the Thais to drive the three leaders to Anlong Véng, which they soon did.

---

7   A leading general in the Hun Sèn regime who had been a major military leader in the Eastern region under DK and had rallied Vietnam in 1978.

– XVIII –

The founding of the Movement of the National Democratic Union (MNDU) and the disintegration of Democratic Kampuchea

1 – How Ieng Sary became leader of the secessionist movement

*T*he break with the Pol Pot group, namely Nuon Chea, Ta Mok and Son Sen was thus consummated. The secessionist movement had competent military leaders, but it lacked political leadership. The fighters and cadres in Malay and Païlin fondly remembered the time when they fought under Ieng Sary's leadership, and they thought that he would be the natural leader of the new movement that had emerged from the revolt of the masses against the dictatorship of the group in Anlong Véng. Thus, on August 15, 1996, Ieng Sary presided over the birth in Malay of the Movement of National Democratic Union. From Koh Kong to the tri-border region of Cambodia, Laos and Thailand, the National Democratic Union Movement controlled a vast and connected territory, leaving only the Anlong Véng region as a stronghold for the hard-core KR leaders. General Sam Bit, leader of the KR forces of Phnom Vor sector in Kampot remained the only military leader loyal to Ta Mok, while General Ieng Phan, commander of Division 36 of DK based in Samlaut, rallied to the secessionist movement. Once arrived at Anlong Véng, the trio Ta Mok, Son Sen and Nuon Chea asked to be received by Pol Pot, who refused and instead quarantined them. Since the creation of the Movement of National Democratic Union on 15 August 1996, peace – a real peace – prevailed throughout the previously DK-held territory of Cambodia.

2 – Visit by Norodom Ranariddh and Hun Sèn to Malay

In January 1997, Prince Norodom Ranariddh, prime minister of the Royal Government, paid a working visit to Malay. It was followed by Hun Sèn, second prime minister, on 27 February of the same year. During Ranariddh's visit, a plan was made for the administrative organization of the whole area that DK controlled. We had a three-year grace period to administer ourselves, with the Phnom Penh government promising not to interfere in our internal affairs. This grace period would be extended for another three years. We kept all our movable and immovable properties. We had the same administrative and security structure as in the whole country, but the staff remained entirely of KR origin. Only the name of the country and the national flag changed. If, during this period of grace, the management of public affairs left something to be desired, we should not blame anyone but ourselves.

Customs duties were collected per unit of production. For example, at the beginning, for a cassava truck you had to pay 2,000 Thai baht. There were no fixed tariffs. The money collected went to the district treasury and was used to finance public expenditures for the construction of roads, schools, health centres, and cultural institutions in the district.

3 – Ta Mok rebels, Son Sen is executed

In June 1996, after returning to Anlong Véng, Ta Mok, Son Sen and Nuon Chea were placed under house arrest by Pol Pot in Choam, ten kilometres from Anlong Véng. At that time, I was attending a government administrative training seminar in Sisophon, which took place from 30 June to 4 July 1997. Ta Mok could not forgive Son Sen, whom he saw as the origin of this situation, and devised a plan to liquidate him and his whole family. To carry out this plan, Ta Mok escaped from Choam and contacted his forces in Anlong Véng. His generals, Ngon and Tém, carried out the plot at the beginning of July 1997. Ta Mok then prepared a commando to kidnap Pol Pot and Khieu Samphân, who had moved back to Preah Prâlay, east of Anlong Véng. Meanwhile, Nuon Chea also escaped and found refuge in Thailand. The Thais asked Nuon Chea to come and live with Pol Pot. Faced with such confusion, some forces fled to Thailand. Pol Pot sent Khieu Samphân to negotiate with Ta Mok. As a result, Pol Pot agreed to hand over all power and all economic and financial resources to Ta Mok, including the proceeds from the sale of wood, estimated at 300 million Thai baht. Finally, Pol Pot, Nuon Chea and Khieu Samphân agreed to cease all political activity. Ta Mok accepted all these conditions and held Pol Pot as a prisoner in his house in Anlong Véng, while Nuon Chea and Khieu Samphân fled to Thailand. In the meantime, Ta Mok had Pol Pot's loyal generals executed: San, So Sarœun (Ta 05), Khorn and Kham Vien. Generals Thim, Prâ, and Khœun escaped and returned to Stung Treng while generals Kaè Pauk and Pich Chheang went to Kompong Cham.

Total confusion prevailed in Anlong Véng after the execution of all these brave war chiefs.

4 – Malay under the new administration

After rallying to the Royal Government, Malay was elevated to district status with six communes and was incorporated into Banteay Meanchey Province, whose capital became Sisophon. Malay's administration was placed under the direction of Chhim Bunny, former commander of Division 450's Regiment 107 as governor, assisted by three deputy-governors: Phi Phuon, Ngin Ngon, former commander of Regiment 109 of the same division, and Huy Mân. Militarily, Division 450 became Division 21 of the Royal Cambodian Armed Forces, under the command of Brigadier General Sok Pheap. Finally, Mey Samân, a security officer in Malay, was promoted to district police chief with the rank of captain. So Savy was appointed chief of the military police and Sit Ly became the head of the border police.

5 – My new mission

In August 1997 the Red Cross informed me that my parents were still alive in Ratanakiri, and I decided to visit them. As the roads at that time were in very bad condition, I made the trip by plane. During my visit to Phnom Penh, I received a visit from General Mol Rœup, chief of the Prime Minister's intelligence service, who had been informed of my trip by General Sok Pheap, commander of Malay's new Division 21. This was not our first meeting, as Mol Roeup had visited me at my home in Malay, accompanied by Brigadier General Dom Hak, some time after he had joined the government. Under DK too, without being formally appointed, Mol Rœup had assisted General Thim in his work as a division commander. In 1979, he was taken prisoner by the Vietnamese. During his detention, he did propaganda work and managed to win many friends.

He wished me a pleasant trip to Ratanakiri and asked for my help after I returned. He hoped that I could persuade DK fighting units in nine provinces, namely Preah Vihear, Kompong Thom, Kompong Cham, Stung Treng, Kratieh, Ratanakiri, Mondolkiri, Prey Veng and Svay Rieng to reintegrate into the national community and join the RGC. When he asked if I knew all the commanders of all these units, I replied in the affirmative. At Preah Vihear there was Dy Thin, a Tampuon and Pror, a Krœung; at Kompong Thom, Pich Chheang; in Kompong Cham, Kaè Pauk and Chèm; at Prey Veng, Ach; in Svay Rieng, Noeun; at Kratieh, Koen, a ethnic Lao; in Mondolkiri, Rann Chan, a Bunong; in Ratanakiri, Yâng, a Tampuon; at Stung Treng, Lao and Khœun, Tampuon. The general included these names in a report to Hun Sèn.

I stayed a fortnight in my native village before returning to Malay. Under DK, my parents had lived normally like other villagers. During my stay in Phnom Penh, as agreed, General Mol Roeup arranged for me to visit General Bou Thang,[1] a Tampuon, former Deputy Prime Minister and Minister of National Defence of the PRK, and Seuy Keo, a Krâchok and former Deputy Minister of National Defence and army chief of staff.

Hun Sèn appointed a committee to persuade these KR commanders and their men to return to the national fold and join the RGC. This committee, composed of Bou Thang, Seuy Keo and Brigadier General Thao Kong, an ethnic Krœung and myself, then moved to the headquarters of Military Region No. 1, based in Stung Treng, where Thao Kong served as deputy commander. The committee managed to convince 92 cadres to support the government. These men asked to meet me, knowing that I came from Malay and that Malay was home to the rallying movement. I told them that the government's 'victory, peace and national reconciliation' policy collaborated with the National Democratic Union Movement led by Ieng Sary; it was the only fair policy; there were neither winners nor vanquished. The whole population and the whole nation would come out victorious. The government did not interfere with our possessions or actions. As a result of these policies, Cambodians had stopped fighting other Cambodians. The Cambodians joined forces together, to end the war. The representatives of the nine provinces were unanimous in

---

1 Bou Thang, a Tampuon leader who had fled to Vietnam in the early 1970s and, from 1979, joined Pen Sovann's Kampuchean People's Revolutionary Party. He became chair of the Party's Central Propaganda Committee, served as deputy prime minister from 1982 to 1992 and minister of defence from 1982 to 1986.

supporting these policies and following the example of Malay and Païlin.[2] This was the implementation of Hun Sèn's "Win-Win policy". Every ex-KR leader would keep his military or administrative position, keep his property and automatically become a member of Hun Sèn's Cambodian People's Party.[3]

It was at this time that, by radiotelegraphy, Ta Mok ordered the commanders of the nine provinces to attack the government forces from behind. Exasperated, I answered Ta Mok that 'I have already won the nine provinces. Now, nothing remains for you!' He called me a traitor and heaped all kinds of insults on me. After Pol Pot's death in April 1998, I flew with the 92 KR commanders from Stung Treng to Phnom Penh and spent two nights there before leaving for Kompong Som, where we stayed for another two nights. On our way back to Phnom Penh, we enjoyed a banquet organized in our honour by Prime Minister Hun Sèn at the Chruy Changvar naval base. On this occasion, he said: 'First, the Victory Policy has triumphed. Second, the former members of the Communist Party of Kampuchea will automatically become members of the Cambodian People's Party (CPP). You do not need to apply for membership. We thank you wholeheartedly for your valuable contribution to peace and national reconciliation. In the future, we will remain united and will continue to work hand-in-hand for the good of our country and our people.' Then he went on: 'Concerning Kaè Pauk and Pich Chheang,[4] who are old, we will do as they wish; they can retire or choose something as they please. It's up to them to decide.' In practice, the two men continued to serve in the army because it was necessary to keep the troops well in hand to avoid anarchy. The next day, everyone returned to their units. The government invited me to work, either in Military Region No. 1 or as vice-governor of Ratanakiri province. But I declined the offer and returned to Malay after the elections of 28 July 1998.

---

2 Hun Sèn has since called this policy of pardon and reconciliation the 'Win-Win Policy'. He dates the policy back to 1998, when Nuon Chea and Khieu Samphân were the last two major KR leaders to rally to the government. In actual fact, the 'Win-Win Policy' started as early as 1979, when Hun Sèn, Héng Samrin and Chea Sim practised self-absolution for the crimes they had committed for decades and pardoned all those who joined the new communist regime under the Vietnamese occupation, sometimes after some form of short re-education.

3 Phi Phuon also expressed his support for the 'Win-Win Policy' during his ECCC testimony, 31 July, pp. 75–79. Andrew Ianuzzi, Nuon Chea's lawyer, sought to paint this policy as a whitewashing of history that assigned all blame to the seniormost DK leaders, but he was quickly muzzled by presiding Tribunal President Nil Nonn.

4 Pich Chheang (1938–2006) was DK Ambassador to the PRC during 1976–1985. He died of brain cancer at Anlong Véng.

6 – Ta Mok abandoned by his generals

After the bloody events of 5 and 6 July 1997,[5] Ta Mok, together with Nhiek Bun Chhay,[6] installed a force of 200 men at Preah Vihear temple and visited them every week. As for me, I managed to establish contact with Anlong Véng's military leaders, including Phanna, Ton, Chum and Pim. These kept me regularly informed of events. Ta Mok lost control of the situation after Anlong Véng's military commanders joined the Phnom Penh government. He then decided to assassinate Pol Pot on 15 April 1998, before fleeing to Thailand with generals Ngon, Tem, Nov, Kong, Mean and Pheap. The latter told Ta Mok: 'We must stop fighting and support the government.' This was the end for the latter. The 200 men assigned to Preah Vihear's defence all deserted to Anlong Véng and joined their families, who urged them to lay down their arms and rally to the government. Abandoned by his most loyal and completely isolated from his troops, Ta Mok wanted to withdraw to Thailand. The Thais did not want him and advised him to join the government, but the government was not interested. Ta Mok was arrested in March 1999. The curtain then fell on the last act of the bloody KR drama.

7 – Pol Pot's death

It is obvious that the death of Pol Pot suited everyone. The circumstances of this death are mysterious. Who was present when he expired? Why wasn't an autopsy performed? Why wasn't his body cremated according to the usual rites like everyone else, as Buddhist traditions demanded? And then this monstrous and grotesque scene in which his body was consumed under the flames of burning car tyres. And why did everything go so fast, as if they wanted the thing to remain shrouded in mystery? So much suspicion and responsibility for everyone, especially Americans and Thais, not to name others.[7]

---

5   This is when Hun Sèn launched a coup d'état in Phnom Penh against First Prime Minister Prince Ranariddh, forcing him to flee abroad. Hun Sèn assumed the role of sole prime minister. There was some fighting in the streets of Phnom Penh and some FUNCINPEC leaders fled to the Thai border. About 100 Hun Sèn opponents were assassinated in the process.

6   Nhiek Bun Chhay (1958–) was a member of the FUNCINPEC and, from 1996, was in charge of a committee to make contacts with the KR defectors. He served as member of parliament for Banteay Meanchey from 1993 to 2013.

7   By 1998, Pol Pot had become an embarrassment to all. Still, even if Ta Mok could have ordered his assassination, it is likely that, at the time, no one was prepared to abide by his criminal injunctions. A much more likely reason for Pol Pot's death in the night was that, not wishing at

Both national and international opinion points to Ta Mok for everything that happened under the KR regime: the population relocations, the discrimination against intellectuals and urban citizens, the internal purges, the mass massacres. Everybody knew that by the end of 1977, Ta Mok had placed a huge number Southwestern cadres in positions of responsibility throughout the country. And this was the time of the killings on the largest scale, the greatest tragedy in the history of the country. Ta Mok was a wicked person and I detested him. There is some evidence that during 1977–1978, cadres from the Southwestern region had executed people from all other regions. Innocent cadres were executed by Ta Mok's proud and rigid cadres. People in the east had largely been wiped out. I saw it. We, in Phnom Penh, were on the verge of being killed by Ta Mok's forces, but we managed to be saved. They could not liquidate us. Ta Mok and I had a dispute in 1979. He despised me because belonged to an ethnic minority. I also had arguments with him. I said to him, 'While you are Khmer, why are you executing Khmer cadres?' The debate was lively and we almost mutinied against him. I said that I had nothing to fear from Ta Mok because he was a human being like me.[8]

all to stand trial (the Americans in Thailand were threatening to take him to court), he urged his entourage to give him an overdose of medicine. This enabled him to die peacefully in his sleep.

8   See ECCC daily reports, 31 July 2012, pp. 79–80.

– XIX –

The situation after the 1998 elections – the place of highlanders in the fighting

1 –The political situation

*I*n 1998, I voted in Stung Treng. Out of the six communes in Malay District, the Cambodian People's Party (CPP) gained a majority only in Tuol Pongro. Sam Rainsy's party won the majority. Put in front of this reality, I decided to return to Malay. The province of Banteay Meanchey had four seats in the National Assembly. In the 1998 elections, the CPP won two of these seats, with the FUNCINPEC and the Sam Rainsy Party getting one each.

As vice-governor of Malay, I learned about administrative and criminal laws, the constitution of Cambodia, human rights, and civil society. In all areas, we acted in accordance with the law. We gave priority to improving the living conditions of the population, especially the older people. Now we have roads, electricity, schools and hospitals. We have one high school for the whole district, a lower-secondary school in each commune and a primary school in each village. On average, each family in the district owns three hectares of land and there is no large concentration of land. Only one per cent of district residents are landless. The district-level hospital is known as the Health Centre. The districts of Poipet, Malay and O'Chhrov have support hospitals. The Malay support hospital practices deliveries and surgical operations. As a rule, all surgical operations must be done in support hospitals, which are equipped for these procedures.

Contraband trade and drug trafficking exist in Malay. The district has 500 agricultural tractors, 800 motorized cultivators, 850 motorcycles, 150 cars, more than 400 bicycles and 120 hydraulic pumps. There is no industrial breeding of cattle, pigs or poultry. One hundred and sixty farms are larger than ten hectares. Rice, maize and cassava are the most important crops, and soybeans, beans and sesame are also grown.

In the 2013 parliamentary elections in Malay District, the CPP obtained 12,008 votes, and the Sam Rainsy Party more than 3,000 votes but no seats. This was a huge change from 2003, when the CPP won three seats and the Sam Rainsy Party one seat.

2 – The situation of fighters and ethnic-minorities

Before DK rallied to the Royal Government of Cambodia and peace was restored throughout Cambodia in 1998, many ethnic minorities had been fighting on the Thai border. From Malay to the south, I count myself, Tha (Tampuon), Sith (Jaraï-Tampuon), Lean, (Krœng), Chum (Tampuon), Phaè (Jaraï), Thea (Tampuon) and Madame Than (Tampuon) at O'Ampil, and Sang (Tampuon), Nang (Tampuon). In Kamrieng are Lann (Jaraï), Rinn (Jaraï), and Laye (Tampuon). Further south, at Pass 102, we have Chê, a colonel (Tampuon) and president of the office of public works. In Païlin live Phauk (Krœung) and Kéng, a colonel (Tampuon), and Thuon, a Brao who worked at the Ministry of Foreign Affairs and has become an Evangelical Christian. In Samlaut live Phon (Jaraï) border police, Than (Jaraï) a soldier living in the same village as me, Tan (Krâchok), a village chief who used to be the head of Nuon Chea's bodyguards, and Chieu, a soldier (Tampuon). Sâr, a colonel (Jaraï), who came from my village, Roeu, a soldier (Jaraï), Den, a captain (Jaraï) living in the same village as myself, Madame Peam (Jaraï), settled In Anlong Véng. At Preah Vihear live Keo Huon (Jaraï), from the same village as me, Khoeun, a soldier (Tampuon) and Chheang, captain (Tampuon). In Kandal province settled Mang (Krâchok), living near my village. Executives who engaged in the struggle since 1963 are mostly dead. Among the 80 comrades who joined the struggle from 1967 to 1975 and who participated in the fighting in Kompong Thom, Kompong Cham, Prek Kry-Don Veat-Peam Chhkok in the Kompong Léng District in Kompong Chhnang, Oudong, Phnom Chettereus, Phnom Baset, and Thmat Porng, only two remain.

During the 1968–1975 war, many ethnic minority soldiers died in battle at Kompong Thom, Kompong Cham, Kompong Chhnang, Oudong and Phnom Penh. Highlanders were in the front line and our mortality rate was very high. During the war against the Vietnamese occupation from 1979 to 1998, about

50 per cent of our national minority soldiers were killed in action. During the first war, we attacked an enemy that was entrenched in garrisons or fortified camps, so we suffered more losses. During the second war, it was rather the opposite situation. We defended our positions with a panoply of means of protection. It was the Vietnamese troops who were exposed, so exposed, and this caused them much greater losses than we suffered.

– XX –

My revolutionary career
in retrospect

*D*uring the thirty years I devoted myself body and soul to the service of the revolution, my country and my people, from 1967, when I met Pol Pot and Ieng Sary, and until my retirement in 1998, one could say that I managed to slip through the net. This is partly because I was in charge of logistics and supplies; and I was not a front-line fighter, except at the beginning of the war against the Vietnamese occupation in 1979, so I was rarely exposed to life-threatening danger. Still, I faced countless obstacles. I was wounded twice: first during the war against the Americans[1] and then against the Vietnamese invaders. I managed, despite everything, to preserve my life.

I had a happy childhood. Since there was no school in our villages at that time, a child's duty was to help their parents, work in the fields and defend themselves against whatever life presented. When the first revolutionaries arrived in Ratanakiri, I joined them voluntarily and dedicated my life to the service of the country and the people. I took my first steps in life by learning things on the job, by practice, without asking too many questions and without qualms. On some days, I did not have enough to feed myself. I suffered and I have bad memories of the hunger that gripped me. Also, when I was young, it was as if I had a god of hunting beside me: when I was crossing a forest, he guided us and always brought us game that we could slaughter with a bow: hares, turtles and monkeys.

If one compares the easy things and the difficult things in my life, it is undeniable that the difficult things have prevailed. First, we lived in the midst of nature and were at the mercy of the elements. We did not have a suitable roof to shelter us. Sometimes we slept on the soil, under the stars; sometimes we spent the night in a hammock, hanging from tree branches. We used to walk for kilometres on end in pouring rain, exposed to deadly lightning attacks. Sometimes, while walking in the forest, we lacked water to quench our thirst: those were really difficult conditions to endure.

---

1   He means the civil war, 1968–1975.

After 1979, the war against the Vietnamese was difficult: we crossed the forest or the plains during the night, during 1986–1988. We were tired and had nothing to eat. We set ambushes and we ran away to brave rain, storms, and hunger. We had to transport the wounded, we always wanted to save the sick, even in very critical situations. I comforted the fighters so they did not lack anything.

If I always managed to get through the most serious dangers and overcome seemingly insurmountable obstacles, it was because, according to a soothsayer, I was protected by a supernatural power or lucky star and I was always warned if a major obstacle was going to present itself. Every time I prepared and commanded an attack against an enemy position, I succeeded. So, luck inhabited me.

Since I embarked on the revolution in 1963, I have not regretted anything. I accomplished the missions entrusted to me by the *Angkar* and I saw almost the entire country. It allowed me to broaden the horizons of my acquaintances, to learn new things, to build new relationships and to accumulate experiences that turned out to be useful to me in the future. It enriched me not only as an individual but also as a revolutionary activist. I learned about community life and life itself. For example, I learned that a leader must be flexible, proactive, and considerate of the circumstances, and must not miss opportunities. In addition, we must weigh the pros and cons, know how to encourage goodwill, comfort people and inspire enthusiasm in work.

There were no major clashes between the ethnic minority revolutionaries and the top Khmer leaders, newly arrived from Paris. If we did not know something, we asked them. Each political studies seminar was like a big book for us. Through the seminars, we became aware of our strengths and weaknesses, found the causes and their solutions. I think these leaders had been trained to adapt to the national minorities, their living conditions, their customs and habits, their ways of thinking, and their ways of conducting their lives. Pol Pot, Ieng Sary, Son Sen, Khieu Ponnary, and Khieu Thirith were honest, sincere people who wished us and all Cambodians well. They were full of admiration for our ability to lead a life in harmony with the environment and in harmony with the four elements which are indispensable to all life in our world, namely water, earth, fire and wind. They asked us many questions about our way of life, our customs, and our ancestor worship. They were keen to know and understand. As doctors and midwives did not exist, in the face of serious diseases, we could only implore the help of good genii or seek the roots or leaves of trees to heal us.

Before 1967, I never left my home village. I went to work in the fields in the morning and returned home the same day. Or I left my father's village to go to my mother's, or vice versa. Or I left my village in the morning to visit a nearby village and come back at night. So, when I walked away from home, of course I felt homesick. I missed my parents, my brothers and sisters, my friends, and especially my uncle, the younger brother of my father. He also left home and went far, far away, to North Vietnam to serve the revolutionary cause. He sacrificed everything as we all did, to devote himself, body and soul, to the struggle. His example inspired me and helped me overcome all kinds of difficulties and obstacles. Most importantly, I needed to learn from our leaders, who had given up their comfortable city lives for an existence of sacrifice and danger in the forest, where everything was lacking. I have always felt nostalgia for my parents and my village.

I followed the example of our leaders. From 1966 to 1975, I lived exclusively in the forest. I had no bed to sleep on; a hammock replaced it, or sometimes the ground. My living conditions improved during 1975–1979, when I lived in Phnom Penh. Problems of food and accommodation were only memories. I ate regularly with sufficient and tasty dishes, and sometimes with dessert. I lived in a well-furnished apartment served by electricity and running water, but in rooms that were furnished to serve as offices and not to be lived in. My comfort in Phnom Penh was matched by my responsibilities: I had to take care of the security of the leaders, prepare buildings for the installation of foreign embassies and the accommodation for foreign guests.

When the internal situation became tense during 1976–1978, I did not feel completely safe. Immediately, after the victory of 1975, in front of the Vietnamese threat, I asked myself the question: are we able to defend our country from a Vietnamese invasion? I remember the words of Hua Guofeng, then president of the Chinese Communist Party, who said during our visit to China in November 1976: 'The victory of April 17, 1975, is as easy as removing the skin of a banana before eating it. But to preserve the revolutionary power, defend and build the country, every wrong step can be fatal and must be avoided as much as possible.' From 1979 to 1991, I returned to the forest. I really lived a family life, with my wife by my side and surrounded by my children and grandchildren, only since 1998.

When I returned to my native village, I encountered a former fiancée, a Jaraï named Phean. But she did not serve in our ranks. She remained faithful to me until 1976, deciding to get married after learning that I already had a wife. Her husband is none other than my first cousin, older than me. When I returned to the village after several years of absence, she welcomed me normally, as if nothing had happened between us. She has two boys and several grandchildren.

The border with Vietnam, from the Naga's Tail to Kep is 1,200 kilometres long. In 1977, 14 Vietnamese divisions invaded Cambodia, but we pushed them back. At that time, our country had only seven million inhabitants while Vietnam had more than sixty million, almost ten times more men. If they continued to fuel the ambition to swallow Cambodia, it will be very difficult for us to stop them. In 1977[2] and 1978, after each visit to the provinces, I reported on my mission to Ieng Sary. I often asked myself, 'Is there a causal link between the threat of a Vietnamese invasion and the purges within the Party?'

The disappearances of fighters and cadres I knew began to multiply, but I did not know if they had been executed or not. I was afraid for my own safety. The most disturbing disappearance was that of Pâng,[3] president of Office 870, which happened in July 1978. In my travels, I noticed that the population of Kompong Thom and Battambang provinces was quite miserable; but Ieng Sary had advised me not to interfere with anything that did not concern me. However, the purification affected all the committees of the regions. Still, after the assassination of the English professor Malcolm Caldwell, Office 870 ordered me, at the same time as So Hong and Thiounn Prasith, to write our autobiographies.[4] Ieng Sary told me at the time that he was also asked to write his autobiography too.

1 – Positive points in my life from 1966 to 2015

I have always stood by my first quality, fidelity: fidelity to the revolution, loyalty to the leaders who educated and formed me, and loyalty to friends who are dear to me. I have put myself at the service of the revolution without conditions or demands. My life has gone through innumerable hardships and

---

2   Vietnam's first major incursion was at the end of 1977. Believing they had taught the KR a lesson, the troops returned home in early 1978, but the KR thought they had won a great victory over their ambitious neighbours.

3   Pâng (1944–1978), whose real name was Chhim Sam Ok, was recruited by Son Sen at age 17, when he was a student. He joined Pol Pot at Office 100 in Ratanakiri, as we have seen, and served as his chief of staff until his arrest. His life ended at S–21.

4   Autobiographical updates were regularly requested of all cadres. Information written in autobiographies was often interpreted as evidence of wrongdoing.

obstacles, and I have overcome incredible difficulties as underlined by the Khmer saying: 'Mother's milk is priceless'.[5] I performed my filial duty in 2012 by organizing rituals dedicated to the deaths of my mother (in 2003) and my father (2011) in Ratanakiri.

I have learned the value of taking initiative and showing courage, creativity and flexibility in a changing situation. It is important to have a broad and open mind, and to care about the situation of others. My broad-mindedness has enabled me to establish cooperative relationships with a diverse range of people.

I volunteered to join the revolution; nobody forced me to do it. I was encouraged and comforted by my family members. I am satisfied with the missions that I completed successfully. The advice and training provided by our leaders on all levels was positive for me. They taught me to find in me my weak points and my strengths and how to fix them.

2 – Negative points

Given the low level of my intellectual baggage, I could not claim high responsibility. It required a higher authority that could guide me; otherwise I could not guarantee the accuracy of my actions. There has been a difference between those who attended school and those who did not, and the allocation of positions of responsibility has depended on it. This represents a gap in my ability to understand things, to make a correct analysis and to propose appropriate solutions. This has been specific to national minorities.

I am too impatient. I have tended to have an explosive temperament, and to favour corporal punishment over understanding and education. An old saying from us advises people to avoid the three khô (the second letter of the Khmer alphabet): khœung (anger), khauch (victim of physical damage) and khat (victim of economic loss). It is necessary to bear in mind the three characteristics inherent to the national minorities of northeast Cambodia: strong, valiant and resolutely determined. If we are brave and fearless, however, we also tend to lose our temper easily.

I benefited from the support and encouragement of my parents, siblings, and close and distant friends, and I reciprocated. I have felt comfort with the roles assigned to me and I am happy to have avoided the missions in

---

5   In Cambodia, the bridegroom is supposed to give financial compensation to his bride's family for her mother's milk.

which death can happen from one moment to the next. Thanks to the political and spiritual education that I have received from DK's most senior leaders, Pol Pot and Ieng Sary, I have become what I am. This education allowed me to discover, develop, consolidate and preserve my strengths, and to reduce, correct and finally eliminate the weak points.

3 – Positive and negative aspects of the Democratic Kampuchea regime

What we can notice from the positive things is that the CPK, first and foremost, led the national and democratic revolution with a clear and fair political line. Secondly, it set up an instrument to achieve this revolution, namely a Communist Party with a clear political line that was fair and could be implemented. This Party united and educated its members, and enabled the Association of Democratic Women and the Federation of Communist Youth to become the makers of this policy. This resulted in the victory of 17 April 1975, over the American imperialists and their valets in Phnom Penh as well as over the feudal system of landowners and capitalists. In 1973, we refused to follow the Vietnamese and Lao, who negotiated with the Americans. Instead, we stuck to the principles of 'being independent, self-masters, masters of the situation and of one's own destiny, relying on one's own strength'. From 1975 to 1979, we led the socialist revolution and the construction of socialism by building the country, including the networks of dikes and canals, for the people. The evacuation of the cities has proved to have been a good and reasonable move; otherwise, we would have lost power.

This just and reasonable policy has been internationally recognized. In this process, intellectuals have played an important role, especially in the Ministry of Foreign Affairs. Under the leadership of intellectuals, all layers of the population voluntarily joined the revolution. At the time, living in communities was the desire of the entire population and it was in the best interest of the people. In our relations with neighbouring countries, Vietnam, Laos and Thailand, we had a just foreign policy, that is to say, a policy of non-alignment and living in peaceful coexistence without interfering in the others' internal politics of each country, respecting sovereignty and territorial integrity. We had a fair political line of the united front in all areas.

Moreover, DK abolished the craving for private property and individual property. So, all the wealth of forests, land, subsoil, water and sea was preserved. Likewise, our territorial integrity has remained intact. But what is deplorable is that Vietnam, which shares a long land and maritime border with Cambodia, has always harboured the strategic ambition to swallow us. I do not know why.

DK governed the country for three years, eight months and twenty days. During this very short period we made remarkable achievements, as evidenced by the networks of canals and dikes that crisscross the country. But we achieved this in a rush and without the consent of the people. We assigned a task that was too heavy for the population. We used human forces excessively to dig canals, raise dikes and build dams. We used shovels and pickaxes instead of machinery. We refused foreign aid. And we did not give the people enough to eat.

Enemy elements infiltrated inside our ranks and took advantage of this situation, destroying our regime from inside. The judicial system did not exist. Instead, the security apparatus had the upper hand over the affairs that normally depend on the Ministry of Justice. And they abused their powers to the extreme. The existence of S–21 is an irreparable fault. Security excesses are at the origin of our internal opposition and ultimately were brought under control by Vietnamese intervention. Concretely, 250,000 Vietnamese troops launched a lightning attack that overwhelmed the firepower of DK. Our wrong political line provoked an internal revolt, which called for foreign aid. When one is unable to defend the country, everything falls apart and all the achievements are destroyed, including the people's communes. Vietnamese control has continued to this very day.

After the liberation in 1975, the Party leadership was deeply divided. Each cadre considered his region as a reserved area and wanted to do as he pleased, which led to the result that we know: no one respected anybody and it was general chaos. Across all regions, those who held power, from the top to the base, fiercely and unrelentingly mistreated the people, forcing them to work like convicts. In return, the people nursed a relentless hatred for the regional leaders. All regional leaders were assassinated except Ta Mok. As for Son Sen, he completely failed in his mission as Minister of National Defence.

DK formally disappeared from the Cambodian political scene in 1998. At the time, concerning the situation in Cambodia, only the points of view of the communist countries were taken into account, neglecting the position of the Western countries. So, they have a bad opinion of us. After we achieved victory over Lon Nol and the Americans on 17 April 1975, the United States declared that it would not recognize DK for at least 100 years.[6] The Cambodian people cannot forget this statement. Then, CIA agents infiltrated our ranks, as well as Vietnamese who had remained in the country, marrying Cambodian women and constituting a fifth column of Hanoi within the Khmer population. The same scheme applies to the Soviet espionage service KGB as well as the intelligence agency of the Chinese Kuomintang. All these agents infiltrated the ranks of DK, undermining it from within and eventually destroying it.

DK has lost its leaders, but the ideals the regime embodied survive in the hearts and minds of thousands and thousands of Cambodians throughout the country. At that time, from the regions to the villages, passing through the sectors, districts and people's communes, the infiltrated enemy penetrated into our ranks. The inner enemy was everywhere. The one who ate at night because he was hungry was accused of being an enemy. It was the same for one who broke a spoon as for the one who ate an egg out of turn. There was no judicial system and at the base, village and commune militias were reputed to have had a heavy hand. In short, the control of the population was tainted with unspeakable faults. It has been for all these repeated and multiple mistakes that we suffered a defeat, without a doubt. And Son Sen wanted to return to these practices condemned by the people in 1996 in Malay and Païlin! I travelled to all parts of the country and witnessed all these problems. The socialist revolution, which took place from 1975 to 1979, was a stinging failure.

So, what is the situation today? From 1979 to today, the achievements of the regime are judged differently judged by the population. One party is satisfied, while the vast majority feels aggrieved. The country has been endowed with all institutions and laws. That is, courts and laws exist, but there is no justice. The courts, under the influence of the ruling party, make partial judgments, always in favour of the ruling party and the wealthy. Today is the problem of 99-year land concessions, a policy that is strongly condemned by the population. The government tried to resolve the dispute, but has failed, time and again, and the situation continues to worsen. Likewise, the gap between the rich and the poor continues to increase.

The two main parties – the Cambodian People's Party (CPP) and the Cambodian National Rescue Party (CNRP) – pretend that they can collaborate,

---

6   Of course, US diplomats made no such statement, but this is how America's attitude was presented by the regime and how citizens like Phi Phuon interpreted the situation.

but during the next general elections, in case the CNRP triumphs, will Hun Sèn abide by the results? I very much fear it shall not.

Inside the CPP, if we do not implement what Hun Sèn orders, we are labelled 'anti-Party'. Given this situation, in my opinion, if the leadership does not rectify their policies, they will lose control of the situation and the government will be swept out of office. The Pol Pot regime should serve as a warning: if the people oppose the powers that be, nothing can contain the people's surge.

Interview completed at Malay on 21 March 2015

Part III

Background analysis

Figure 12: Crossbow and rice mortar from Ratanakiri.

– XXI –

Phi Phuon testifies at the Extraordinary Chambers in the Courts of Cambodia

1 – Introduction

The Extraordinary Chambers in the Courts of Cambodia (ECCC) was established in 2006 to prosecute senior KR leaders for crimes against humanity and gross violations of the Geneva Convention dealing with war crimes; charges of genocide against 'the Vietnamese' and 'the Cham' were added later. In all, charge sheets were drawn against nine individuals and a series of investigations and separate trials commenced. During days 84–89 of the trial of Nuon Chea and Khieu Samphân, that is, from 25 July through to 2 August 2012, Phi Phuon faced an array of questions from no fewer than 10 attorneys representing the prosecution, one or the other defendant, or the victims. While the summary judgement covers five pages (16 November 2018, pp. 2173–77), a single paragraph provides the essence:

§4331. The Chamber has found NUON Chea and KHIEU Samphân individually criminally responsible for committing, through a joint criminal enterprise: (a) the crimes against humanity of murder, extermination, deportation, enslavement, imprisonment, torture, persecution on political, religious and racial grounds, and the other inhumane acts through attacks against human dignity, conduct characterised as enforced disappearances, forced transfer, forced marriage and rape in the context of forced marriage; (b) the crime of genocide by killing members of the Vietnamese ethnic, national and racial group; and (c) grave breaches of the Geneva Conventions of wilful killing, torture, inhuman treatment, wilfully causing great suffering or serious injury to body or health, wilfully depriving a prisoner of war or a civilian the rights of a fair and regular trial and unlawful confinement of a civilian under the Geneva Conventions at the S-21 Security Centre (16 November, pp. 2173–74).

Figure 13: Phi Phuon (Cheam) testifying before the Tribunal, 25 July–2 August 2012

This chapter is limited to Tribunal elements that Phi Phuon directly contributed to, or that are associated with Ratanakiri province. From the Tribunal's perspective, Phi Phoun's most important testimony placed the accused at the scenes of various crimes against humanity. He also provided useful context by compellingly describing the paranoid mindset of leaders at critical historical moments, including the leaders' rationale for evacuating cities. These evacuations can be understood as consistent with the presumed goal of creating people's communes, as in Mao's China, and neither country successfully established them in the cities where the population was too diverse. On top of that, and for a pragmatic reason, the KR leaders understood that their forces were too limited to control urban populations. If they had not done so, within a few hours in the capital and a couple of days in the provinces, the revolutionaries could not have resisted onslaughts initiated under the protection of households and the KR could have lost the civil war. This blanket expulsion was also due to their perception that 'foreign agents' were everywhere in the cities – a paranoid preoccupation that underlay atrocities perpetrated throughout the regime. For them, the struggle for survival was just beginning when the KR army entered Phnom Penh. And, most relevant to all of Cambodia is the description of the regime's crimes as 'genocide'; the term 'politicide' would have been a much more accurate description of the atrocities committed during DK's period in power.

2 – Leadership involvement in crimes against humanity

Khieu Samphân always claimed that he was not in the least involved in defining and preaching the KR ideology. In actual fact, he was one of the chief designers of this lethal ideology and a key motivational speaker. For instance, Phi Phuon confirmed that early in the regime, Samphân gave political training courses at the Institute of Technology in Cambodia, which he called the 'Soviet Technical School' (25 July, p. 77; 1 August, p. 96). This placed Samphân at a location where training in brutal techniques was known to have occurred, and undermined Phi Phuon's insistence that Samphân was a unifier who constantly advocated the merger of all Cambodian forces without any class distinction (1 August, p. 87–89) and that Cambodians inside the country unite with Sihanouk.

As for complicity associated with the entry into Phnom Penh in April 1975, Phi Phuon specified that all regional commanders soon congregated at the railway station: Koy Thuon for the North, Sao Phœm for the East, Vorn Vet for the Special Zone around Phnom Penh and Ta Mok for the Southwest. Nuon Chea, the most cautious, along with Khieu Samphân, arrived last in Phnom Penh, perhaps on the 21st, after ensuring security was 100 per cent in place (26 July, p. 62). When Ieng Sary disembarked at Pochentong Airport with 'some Chinese advisors' on 25 April, the leadership was already at the Ministry of Commerce (26 July, p. 64) and stayed there for some two weeks before going to the Silver Pagoda at the Royal Palace in May. The leaders worked from early morning until very late in the night, if necessary (26 July, p. 68).

Phi Phuon also confirmed that decision-making was collective. In the last year of the regime, some activities were open and some secret, like some of Pol Pot's visits to China and the visits of important visitors, like Zhang Chunqiao in December 1975.[1] Phi Phuon testified that all orders coming out of 870 were given by Pol Pot or Nuon Chea and transmitted to all provinces through Office K–7 (30 July, p. 6), clarifying a few minutes later that Khieu Samphân also was active in this process (30 July, p. 9).

Phi Phuon placed the senior leaders at a key event of the regime: a month-long training session in Phnom Penh for some 1,000 cadres from all over Cambodia in December 1976, just as the Four-Year Plan was being launched[2] and clear directives about how to chase 'enemies' were given. Phi Phuon noted that the lion's share of the training was given by Pol Pot and Nuon Chea, and the main subject was how to strengthen the Party by looking, as always, at its strengths and its weaknesses (30 July, p. 23).

He also confirmed that Unit Y–10 was in charge of security at Office 870 and took people away; whereto, he did not know. Phi Phuon never transported anyone to S–21, but took some to Office 870. As to his relations with Bœng Trabek, he repeated there were shortages of everything when B–1 was put in his charge, but he saw to it that plentiful food was supplied, then that the inmates grew their own vegetables, like all offices and ministries in Phnom Penh. Those 'intellectuals' wished to listen to the national and international news, so he brought them a radio. He also gave them coffee – 'they had enough for twenty years'! 'If these people could be re-educated and remodelled to conform to the revolutionary line, they could join our forces.' He did not know where all these people went on 6 January, but he 'met Brother Hor Nam Hong at Koas Krala' in the Cardamoms.

Khieu Samphân has always been in denial about his responsibility for DK's lethal policies, but it was impossible to contradict Phi Phuon's testimony that the three paramount leaders – Pol Pot, Nuon Chea and Khieu Samphân – were always together at the central Office 870, or at K–1, B–5 or K–3 (26 July, p. 91). So, it is hard for Khieu Samphân to claim he was not aware of major decisions or even of the existence of S–21, since all orders for the arrests to this central prison came from Office 870 (30 July, pp. 43–51). He was convicted

---

1   Zhang's visit was also mentioned during Dœun's testimony Dœun was in charge of political affairs at Office 870 until he disappeared and was replaced by Khieu Samphân in mid-1978.

2   See Chandler et al. (eds) *Pol Pot Plans the Future.*

on 7 August 2014 and is serving a life sentence; his final appeal was denied on 22 September 2022.

Phi Phuon reserved his greatest vitriol for Ta Mok, an animosity that dates back to their first meeting in the Ratanakiri forests. Phi Phuon testified that, like Son Sen and his wife Yun Yat, Ta Mok despised him because he was an ethnic minority, and that Ta Mok was a 'bad person.' In 1977 and 1978, Ta Mok's southwest cadres (*Nirdey*) spread throughout Cambodia and executed cadres in the northeast, north, northwest and west, and later the east (*Bophea*). Phi Phuon tried to interfere personally, saying that a Cambodian commander shouldn't have Cambodian cadres executed (31 July, pp. 69–70). At one point, 'the contradiction was intensified. There was almost a kind of riot against him, and I said very clearly that I had nothing to be afraid of. He was a human being like I am' (31 July, p. 70).[3] Phi Phuon reported that many people in his now-home district of Phnom Malay had told him of the *Nirdey's* brutal cruelty and that, in his own assessment, Ta Mok was the worst DK leader (31 July, pp. 71–72).

3 – The evacuation of Phnom Penh

The evacuation of Cambodia's cities constitutes the KR's ultimate crime, a crime no other nation had committed in the modern world, a crime that laid the foundations for all the horrors perpetrated by one of the most criminal regimes of our era. Prosecutor Dale Lysak raised the critical issue of the evacuation of the cities and how the decision was made. He quoted from Philip Short's *Pol Pot, the History of a Nightmare*, in which Short's interviewee, Phi Phuon, mentions that the evacuation of Oudong could have served as a precedent or a model:

> [I]t worked well in the sense that there weren't any big problems [for us] in resettling the evacuees from Udong in the countryside and, on their side, the town-dwellers didn't cause any special difficulties. It was a radical solution designed to foil any attempt by the enemy to destabilize our forces ... Was it so our cadres would avoid the "sugar-coated bullets of the bourgeoisie?" Yes! (26 July, pp. 31–32).

This tells it all: the relocated people could no longer fight back. Once torn away from their possessions and their environment, the population, including

---

3   Ta Mok, 1926–2006. By the end of the DK regime, Pol Pot had more and more confidence in him and, in the 1980s, he competed with Son Sen to lead the KR army.

'foreign agents' among them, could only become wandering paupers that no longer were in a position to corrupt the guerrillas.

Phi Phuon explained to the prosecutors that the KR were guided by revolutionary actions during the civil war. As the movement 'liberated' provincial or district capitals, it learned that 'if [the] population remained in townships, it would be difficult to control them. We had to evacuate them to control the city more easily. If we were to survive, we had to withdraw them all.' And, 'if the enemy wanted to infiltrate them, it was easier to control this' (30 July, p. 68–83). He pointed to places the Tribunal called 'Tram Knar' (in fact Angtasom in Tramkâk District), 'Neak Lœung' on the Mekong, and Skoun in Kompong Cham province (26 July, p. 15). These cities were successfully evacuated in 1974, along with Oudong, and Kratieh, and the aftermath was peaceful: the countryside was a liberated zone and the people 'did not encounter any difficulties … they did not have a problem with food' (30 July, p. 68).

Phi Phuon testified that these successes helped to motivate the decision, taken at a meeting at B–5 in Kompong Chhnang Province in early April 1975, to enthusiastically confirm the decision to evacuate the capital. Nuon Chea spoke first (thus showing his paramount place in the hierarchy) and everyone eagerly applauded their approval, including Khieu Samphân (who has always claimed the contrary, including in his memoirs[4]). No discussions were needed, first because this tactic had worked so well in the past, and second because all the ultimate leaders then assembled knew full well that they had no plausible alternative: they had far too few troops to control the two to three million inhabitants of the capital, including a large number of refugees – even for a single night. Most KR soldiers had never been to Phnom Penh and would be completely lost in the maze of unfamiliar streets, placing them at a terrible disadvantage during any street fight. In a previous interview with investigative judges, Phi Phuon had said,

> beforehand, we were told we had to be vigilant because of enemies buried in the houses, even though the main forces had been smashed. They were equipped with grenades and other ammunitions. They could be a threat for the revolution. There were also enemies and spies hidden in the liberated zones (30 July, p. 86). This is why American bombings could target certain places. Even by evacuating the population, we could keep power only for

---

4   Khieu Samphân, *Cambodia's Recent History* and the *Reasons Behind the Decisions I Made*, trans. Reahoo Translation, Puy Kea, 2004.

three years and eight months. Even by eliminating certain elements, we did not know how long we could keep power. (p. 87)

Here, we have a firm believer in the legitimacy of the revolution who expresses how precarious the situation was for the KR. Their absolute violence resulted from their conviction that, in actual fact, the true believers were a tiny minority and therefore had no choice but to be infinitely merciless and impose their total collectivism by brute force. The decision was *not* taken for ideological reasons – a return to a Rousseau-idealistic rural life – as is too often claimed, but simply for security reasons: evacuating the cities was understood to be necessary if survival was to be ensured (or at least prolonged). The benefit of the evacuation policy to the implementation of people's communes was, at most, a secondary concern. If such a drastic decision had not been taken, Phi Phuon confesses, the revolutionaries were far too small in number to control the cities. The whole grand plan of total revolution could have collapsed, even during the first night after their swift victory.

No testimony indicated that Nuon Chea or anybody else discussed the welfare of the evacuees. Such a discussion would have been useless as the circa 20,000 revolutionary troops were in no position to bring the deportees any kind of help, or even to secure their own welfare. As Phi Phuon said cryptically, 'But when we tried to fight in order to liberate the cities, we also endured a lot of hardship. We risked our lives in order to liberate the cities' (30 July, p. 85) What they wanted was absolute power. They didn't care what happened to the people. Indeed, Phi Phuon testified that they had no reason whatsoever to show any humaneness as they had been told that all these people were traitors, some of them even agents of foreign powers, and therefore they deserved no mercy and certainly no support. The international defence lawyer of the civil parties, Élisabeth Simonneau-Fort, sought to confirm that absolutely no provisions had been made for the welfare of the Phnom Penh evacuees. Phi Phuon answered: 'Those minor details had not been broached. Those people had been used to a luxurious life, to live in air-conditioned rooms, and this is why they sweated all over during the evacuations' (ibid.)

Foreign Agents

Defining and selecting the 'enemy' (*khmang*), came to be of paramount importance under DK. Khmer prosecutor Seng Bunkheang asked about this:

Q. To your knowledge, do you know who were regarded as enemies by the Party?

A. As to what we were told, we determined that we engaged in the popular democratic revolution, and the main enemy was the American imperialists. That's the top enemy who had invaded many countries, and they engaged in bombardments for 200 days and nights. That was in 1973. So, we were educated on this point, and that was the chief enemy.

And another enemy was those who opposed the revolution, who refused to join the revolution. They were a kind of covert enemy, including CIA and KGB agents, and that we needed to know the distinction between these kinds of enemies (26 July, p. 7).

This declaration is of paramount importance as it singles out the *idée fixe* of the KR: American imperialism was the main enemy throughout the regime. And the senior leaders declared victory over the Americans on 17 April 1975. In reality, the last American troops left Cambodia territory on 30 June 1970 and bombings had ceased since by 15 August 1973. It is thus amazing that Phi Phuon called the Americans 'invaders' as he only saw a couple of soldiers in the sixties – and they stayed just for a couple of days – and never after. But that was what the FUNK propaganda machine tirelessly repeated on the radio and to the guerrillas.

The argument resonated for Phi Phuon because he had heard the sounds of American bombs with his own ears. He testified that 'the American bombings started as early as 1962, notably at Nhang, his home village', on the east side of the Tonlé San. 'Bombardments intensified throughout the 1960s and peaked in 1969' (31 July, p. 31). The quite extraordinary memory of the witness enabled him to name four villages that American bombs had entirely or partly destroyed: Lua (phon.), Nhang, Kong (phon.), and Muy. During 1968–1969, 'even the rice fields were abundantly strafed and lots of cattle were killed. I do not understand the anger on the part of Americans or why they deployed those bombs. From 1964, villagers were afraid of staying in their villages and took refuge in the jungle to run away from intensive bombings' (31 July, p. 36). Quite rightly, the defence lawyer makes clear that the massive American bombings in this far northeastern corner of Cambodia incensed the adolescent and drove him to create a rebellion that did not yet exist.

The only explanation for ignorance of the fact that Americans were not physically on the scene might be that the KR movement had been created and initiated by the DRV, which saw its main enemy as the American "invaders", and not the Republican South with which it competed for control of the country. So, the KR just repeated the VC mantra: America aims to re-colonize all of Southeast Asia. The question was repeated by Nuon Chea's lawyer to Elizabeth Becker, when she testified at the ECCC in February 2015: 'Do you believe that, because the USA is a big world power, it can invade a country as it pleases?' Instead of answering that America did *not* invade Cambodia (except again from 30 April to 30 June 1970, and then only to chase the VC in the border region), she answered, 'No, international law bans it' (11 Feb. 2015, p. 6). Inadvertently, Becker's testimony buttresses the paranoid logic used by the KR throughout its regime: the US had flaunted international law in the past and, if this is all that is restraining that giant, then it might well flaunt international law in the future.

Nuon Chea had predicted in 1975 that America would re-conquer Cambodia 'within six months' after its 'defeat', explaining that this is why they had left spies and double agents all over the country: to destroy the revolutionary regime from within.[5] For the KR, the second tier of 'enemies' was the Cambodian population who had refused to support the revolution during the civil war or, worse, had taken refuge in the cities where nests of CIA and KGB agents could influence them. This became the rationale for all future repression campaigns, but Phi Phuon has little to say about this, because

> In the war time, all zones, sectors and district level [officers] were told the enemies were those whom we fought against on the battlefield. Off the battlefield, enemies were those who opposed the revolution. But I, myself, did not witness any measures taken against those who opposed the revolution at the time. I only knew that we fought the <enemies on> the battlefield. (26 July, p. 8)

Phi Phuon reiterates the KR line by saying that, prior to evacuation, there were 'plenty of' KGB and CIA agents in Phnom Penh, but then adds candidly – and in opposition to the KR line and striking a blow against the defense teams: 'After the evacuation, I did not see more enemies. I think there were no more enemies, that's why I could survive and testify before the Chamber. If they lived, I could have been smashed' (30 July, p. 87). Asked about orders concerning Re-

---

5 'Statement of the Communist Party of Kampuchea to the Communist Workers' Party of Denmark, July 1978, by Nuon Chea, Deputy Secretary, CPK', *The Journal of Communist Studies*, 2:1, March 1987, pp. 30–31.

publican soldiers, however, his answer supported the defence positions: 'Those soldiers were defeated, they surrendered. The white flag was raised, so we did not do anything to harm them. People were advised strictly not to do any harm to those people who were defeated' (30 July, p. 88). If this order was ever given, it was totally flouted as, starting with officers, anyone identified as ex-Republican military personnel was executed during the early days of the regime.

Other declarations during his testimony spoke directly to the mindset of the senior leaders, including Phi Phuon's recollection of a Ministry of Foreign Affairs 'congress' that took place only once in the regime and lasted three days (30 July, p. 24). It included some 30 participants, presided over by Ieng Sary and So Hong, and discussions centred on the situation of enemies in Cambodia. The tone of these discussions comprises incontrovertible proof that the KR were taking their miserable country over the precipice. They had already done so with the blanket evacuation of all the cities; now, they spoke not just of eliminating 'enemies' associated with previous ruling regimes (the *Sangkum* and the Republic) in 1975 and 1976, but enemies from all social classes, even those in whose name the revolution had been launched in 1968:

> 1976 is the key year. The enemy was deteriorating. The spy's network was destroyed. There was no longer a class enemy. However, the American imperialists and the CIA and KGB and Vietnam still existed. Although they were defeated, but they still struggled to move on. And the other one is the enemies, the peasants and the workers who were in our rank. And these – also the enemies that needed to be swept clean progressively. (30 July, p. 25)

Less than two years into the obnoxious regime, the leadership's paranoia was reaching new heights. Paramount leaders, psychopaths rather, were travelling further from reality and entering a realm of total hallucination. They now saw 'enemies' everywhere and their delusions would cause the cruel death of hundreds of thousands of innocent victims in the torture-execution centres that dotted the entire territory.

And yet, their rhetoric was compelling. Phi Phuon was utterly convinced that a major duty of all true believers was to combat American imperialism. As he told the Tribunal:

> The enemies were very well identified here. They were the American imperialists. At that time, we had to fight the American imperialists because we were conduct[ing a] national democratic revolution. We attacked

the regime, and we had to build ourselves internally. Everyone had to be absolute and determined so that we could not be bought by the American imperialists. We had to be very clean and proper to achieve this triumph. (30 July, p. 26)

Contrary to the Vietnamese or Chinese communist revolutions, the extreme sense of insecurity of the Cambodian communists was simply because Party members were only a tiny fraction of the population. They knew their position was extremely precarious and they could not in the least govern by consent; the threat of extreme violence was the only way their policies could be implemented, and the fact of violence was the best way to show the genuineness of the threat. Almost the entire population deeply resented and suffered from those radical policies, and resentment alone was sufficient for a person to be identified as an enemy of the state.

The KR were obsessed with the 'cleanliness' or purity of revolutionary ardour. Everything and everyone had to be 'smashed and swept cleanly away': 'At our ministry's conference, it was noted that we have basically smashed and swept cleanly away the enemies[,] who were CIA, KGB, and Yuon Territory swallowers' (30 July, p. 35). This view was presented by Ieng Sary, the ultimate authority in the ministry and, in that respect, a true representative of *Angkar*.

4 – Phi Phuon's duties at the Ministry of Foreign Affairs

Soon, Phi Phuon was entrusted with the logistics to welcome these 'guests', who were first housed behind the Royal Palace, to the west (26 July, p. 68). During Pol Pot and Nuon Chea's meetings with regional commanders, it was decided that, to engage in an advanced form of socialist revolution, it was necessary to create 'advanced people's communes'. All would wear the same black clothes and have the same ideology. Such practices existed in the countryside from 1973, and became more widespread in 1975 (30 July, p. 78). Phi Phuon confirmed that he did not attend the big meeting at the Institute of Technology of Cambodia during which *Angkar* allocated all regional and district leadership posts.

When it came to the establishment of the Ministry of Foreign Affairs, Phi Phuon had widespread duties and responsibilities. He certainly had administrative duties and responsibility for what can be called logistics. He ensured that ministry staff had adequate food, was adequately housed, and had all necessary office equipment. He also had the authority to recruit menial staff, like cooks or women who looked after the children of the senior staff: 'I was the one who had to implement the instruction or advise or instruct people to work at the kitchens and elsewhere concerning administration' (26 July p. 78). To a large extent, this is what he had been doing around the Party leadership since the fall of Sihanouk in 1970. What is less clear was what he called 'the psychological control' (31 July, p. 26) of the staff, and what was meant by 'security'. From his testimony at the Tribunal, it becomes clear that 'psychological control' simply meant to make sure that all the staff was working hard, and that they were working with high morale and revolutionary enthusiasm.

Dale Lysak, a Canadian co-prosecutor, was driving Phi Phuon into a corner as he quoted from another original KR document that detailed the duties of an office: 'We must guarantee security and trace the personal biographies in the entire ministry and must gather weapons and ammunition and send them to the military headquarters. We must always investigate the enemies in the ministry' (quoted in 30 July, p. 29), and Phi Phuon confirmed everyone who worked in the Ministry of Foreign Affairs had to 'memorize' these duties. Dale Lysak continued to quote from another KR document that described the ministry's seven sections: propaganda and education, offices, agriculture, politics, protocol, secretariat of the director, and civil aviation (30 July, p. 33). Like most KR classifications, these are quite confusing. Agriculture, for instance, must only refer to the plot of land north of the capital and along the Tonlé Sap, where the vegetables consumed by B–1 were grown and the fish raised in ponds along the river. As to 'Offices', this is the core of the institution where the entire work of the ministry was performed. And Phi Phuon was, theoretically, in charge of ensuring that this work progressed smoothly. As already mentioned, his duties were essentially twofold. He was in charge of logistics, supplying the wherewithal the 'intellectuals' needed to perform their tasks – essentially writing and translating texts. At the same time, he was responsible for staff 'morale'. Phi Phuon pointed directly to Ieng Sary as the one who spelt out 'the collective political line of *Angkar*' (30 July, p. 33).

As to 'security', did this mean that he was to guarantee the security of the top leadership (*Angkar Lœu*)? That is, did he identify ministry staffers as potential 'traitors' or 'spies' working secretly for imperialist countries? Or did it simply mean that he was to guarantee the safety of all the staff against thieves or delinquents? I am prepared to believe the second alternative, since Phi Phuon claimed that the only 'security' problem he had had during the entire regime was the death[6] of Malcolm Caldwell. In the end, I believe Phi Phuon was *not* a sufficiently high cadre to be in charge of singling out who was to be sent to the countryside for re-education or, worse, to S–21. This was essentially the job of his superior, Ieng Sary, perhaps with some support from So Hong, Pol Pot's nephew and the political commissar of 'political affairs' at B–1 (30 July, p. 14). By the end of 1978, the staff of the most important ministry of the regime – and the only one that acted as a somewhat real ministry – included some 1,000 people (26 July, p. 78).

Pâng, alias Chhim Sam Ok, a young man who had been Pol Pot's private secretary since Ratanakiri days, controlled not only the administration of Office 870, but helped in the selection of staff for all the ministries. A priority was given to peasants and workers from the lowest stratum of society, 'the core force of the revolution' (26 July, p. 82). They were selected according to their autobiographies. Those working in the Ministry of Foreign Affairs needed to be able to work abroad. But they also needed 'to have a pleasant physical appearance, to be tall and well-built' (26 July, p. 84). Throughout the period, Phi Phuon also continued to deliver documents between the ministries and Office 870.

In 1977 and 1978, a number of people disappeared from the ministry; Phi Phuon admits they were sent to production sites for re-education. One in Takhmau, under the authority of B–1, was for people who Ieng Sary determined to have failed to work or to perform all the tasks allocated to them (30 July, p. 41). To the question about the S–21 confessions and whether Ieng Sary received them, Phi Phuon claims that documents were transmitted from Office 870. In his initial interview during the investigation phase of the trial, Phi Phuon specified that the S–21 confessions were annotated by Office 870 before they arrived at B–1, and could arrive at any time. Ieng Sary decided which persons needed to be sent to re-education camps and Office 870 decided who would be sent to S–21. Some were identified as CIA or KGB agents (30 July, p. 47). For his part, Phi Phuon specified that he just escorted suspects outside B–1, where, under Office 870 direction, a Y–10 military unit would come and take them away. Some arrests occurred in the daytime, others at night (30 July, p. 48). After that, 'I did not see them again … I did not know their fate' (30 July, p. 50).

Ieng Sary had launched an appeal to cadres and intellectuals abroad to come back and serve the nation and he was happy to welcome them. He

---

6   See above, pp. 157–158.

welcomed 'intellectuals' as he could not enrol farmers who could neither read nor write. As the work concerned foreign affairs and diplomacy, we needed intellectuals 'to deal with important questions' (30 July, p.51). 'There was also Bœung Trabek and Ta Ley. I did not really know where it was, but I heard about them.'[7] Ta Ley was some 30 kilometres south of Phnom Penh. Phi Phuon was also asked about a place called Chraing Chamres, which depended on B–1. It was just an agricultural locale where food for B–1 was grown, and not a re-education camp. The staff from B–1 could go visit there during weekends, cultivating vegetables and drinking coconut juice. 'Rice was grown and poultry was raised, and there was a fish farm' (31 July, p. 25). This shows that life at B–1 was perhaps not as tragic and the food not as short as Laurence Picq describes in her famous *Beyond the Horizon*.[8]

In mid-1978, Bœung Trabek was placed under the responsibility of B–1, and therefore of Phi Phuon for logistics. From then on, he was in charge of food supplies and the detainees received much more rice and were treated better. The diplomat Hor Nam Hong represented some of the detainees. There were many people with their wives and children. Ieng Sary organized training sessions detailing the international situation and trying to win over all the returnees to the cause of radical revolution by using the traditional KR and communist techniques of public confessions and self-criticism (56). In the last months of the regime, there was a policy change: on the one hand, *Angkar* was trying to gain new friends abroad; on the other, they realized they badly needed the goodwill and services of the returnees rather than having them purged *en masse*. The paradox of the Ministry of Foreign Affairs was that, of course, the staff needed to know English, French and sometimes other languages. And among the poorer classes, who had a priority for the revolutionary regime, none could speak – let alone write – these languages. So, more educated people had to be recruited, including some returnees from abroad. They were called 'intellectuals', a word that had a very elastic meaning in Cambodia at the time. For instance, Ieng Sary, who had merely passed a French baccalaureate, was counted as an 'intellectual'. Phi Phuon explained to the prosecutor that the policy had to be more open and less dogmatic, in order 'to unite' society. The Party had to avoid being 'narrow-minded' and

---

7   For a description of Ta Ley re-education camp for returnees, see Hour Chea, *Quatre ans avec les Khmers rouges*, Paris: Librairie Tchou, 2007, p. 83–94 and 157–192.

8   St Martins, London, 1989.

courtesy Center for Social Development

Figure 14: Some thirty compatriots from Ratanakiri attended Phi Phuon's testimony at the Tribunal

make room for them in the ministry, as they possessed indispensable work experience (30 July, p. 13).

The Court had a document entitled 'Revolutionary Self-Criticism of Comrade Cheam', one of Phi Phuon's several autobiographies. In it, he confesses he had not sufficiently absorbed "'the nature of the proletarian class'" and still desired 'the comforts of private property' (30 July, p. 20). We fully realize the absurdity of this regime – here accusing one of its most dutiful and obedient members, coming from the most destitute section of Cambodian society who suffered from hunger at times in childhood – of not having a sufficiently proletarian outlook on life! Meanwhile, his *Angkar Lœu* accusers were the most corrupt of any politicians in Cambodia, having appropriated the entire wealth of the country for their own enjoyment. They chose as their private residences all the most luxurious villas in Phnom Penh, along with all the possessions they found inside. All house implements and antique furniture at their disposal, the most luxurious cars, not to mention abundant food – the ultimate treat under DK. They, like Long Norin,[9] put on weight while the population was starving. They benefitted from all the sedan cars left by the inhabitants of Phnom Penh.

---

9   Long Norin, 1938–2018, was in charge of Sihanouk's personal security under DK and worked at the Ministry of Foreign Affairs. He therefore had the opportunity– or so he told me – to put on twenty kilos during the regime. He testified at the Tribunal in December 2011.

This interesting document includes annotations by Ieng Sary saying that Phi Phuon was 'loyal and never secret' (30 July, p. 21). Loyalty is the ultimate virtue for the KR leadership, meaning you are entirely reliable for performing any task that is required of you and you are prepared to give your life to protect that of your boss. 'Never secret' probably means you never hide anything, are never double-dealing and are invariably frank. The leaders liked that, as they believed such people were totally malleable. Still, on the more negative side, in the annotations, Ieng Sary accuses Phi Phuon of being 'too independent-minded'. This is paradoxical because *Angkar* also required citizens to take the initiative to solve local problems. A basic slogan or dogma was *hluon ti pœung khluon*,[10] which can be translated as 'Everyone must rely on his own self', like the country must rely on its own strength to survive. This was the so-called *Juche* policy from North Korea, one of the KR models. But, at the same time, you had to strictly obey all orders and never ask questions.

We then came to another written original document concerning a congress of the B–1 Party cell on 18–22 January 1977. Phi Phuon is said to be only Number 5 in the B–1 Party hierarchy (30 July, p. 23), which indicates he could *not* have been the one who selected 'enemies' to be eliminated at B–1.

Élisabeth Simonneau-Fort, the lead co-lawyer of the civil parties, asked Phi Phuon if, at any time, he feared being arrested or for his life.

> Yes, after the murder of Malcolm Caldwell, I was made to re-write my autobiography, like So Hong and even Ieng Sary. If those two persons disappeared, I would disappear too. This is why I was afraid. I had given my life to the revolution and I had done my best to respect the revolutionary cause, and if I was to die for that, I could do nothing. For I had solemnly sworn that I would serve the Party and I had nothing to fear ... I had no idea if the people who disappeared were dead or alive. I do not know. Many high-ranking, like Sao Phœm, Koy Thuon, have disappeared. At Office 870, people who were close to me, like Dœun or Pâng, have also disappeared. Many people have disappeared, like Hu Nim, Hou Yuon, we had lost trace of them, everywhere in the country. We could not help being afraid. (30 July, pp. 90–91)

> Q. Thank you. Now, witness, did you ever fear for your own security in light of those disappearances?

---

10   See my collection of KR slogans, *Pol Pot's Little Red Book*, p. 78 et seq.

A. I think I stated in my statement already that I was afraid, in particular by late 1978. The reason that I had reason to be concerned – because I was asked to re-write my personal biography. By doing so, I felt worried because there was reason behind this. *Om* Ieng Sary said that he, himself, was asked to re-write his own personal biography and that applied to Brother So Hong and to me, so I felt that if the other two people would disappear, and I too would disappear. That's why I was very afraid. However, I was very adamant that I was – I respected and dedicated my life under the revolutionary flag and I did my best for the cause of revolution. If I had to die because of that, there's nothing I could do about it, because I took an oath that I solemnly determined to serve the Party. We had nothing to fear. So that's what I had told myself.

Q. Based on what you've just told this Chamber, am I to gather that to disappear was tantamount to dying?

A. I'm not sure whether people who disappeared died or lived; I don't know. Because a lot of senior people, including Koy Thuon, So Phim, Cheng An, a lot of these senior people disappeared. In Office 870, the very close people to me, including Pang and Doeun, also disappeared. So, the great number of people in the whole country in various zones also had disappeared – Hou Youn, Hu Nim were nowhere to be found. So, with that in mind, I couldn't help but be fearful.

Finally, we come to the murder of Malcolm Caldwell on the eve of the arrival of the Vietnamese. Phi Phuon was at B–1 on that fatal night, more than one kilometre away from the house where the three guests were hosted. He informed the court that, although the security of the guests was the responsibility of B–1, the night guards were from the Y–10 company, which acted as bodyguards for the leadership and took those arrested to S–21. They could have been particularly violent. The murder was definitely not an assassination, but just the result of a quarrel between two of these young men, who were in love with the same woman. One had exchanged a scarf with the lady. The other denounced him to the authorities, who were about to arrest the culprit, as sexual and even sentimental relations were strictly controlled by *Angkar*. In desperation, the rejected rival took advantage of his last night before his arrest to kill his rival. Caldwell came out of his room and the desperate soldier shot him before shooting himself. In his autobiography, Ong Thong Hœung[11]

---

11 *J'ai cru aux Khmers rouges*, Buchet/Chastel, 2003, p. 224.

tells precisely the same story, which he claims he heard from one of the guards that same night. It was not an obscure political plot from one of the leadership enemies, as Elizabeth Becker has suggested.[12]

5 – Politicide in Cambodia

A lot of the international tribunal's energy and time was devoted to the so-called 'genocide' against the Vietnamese despite their small number under DK. The tribunal did not consider the pogrom conducted by Lon Nol's regime during the early days of the Republican regime in 1970, when some hundred – or perhaps even thousands – of Cambodians of Vietnamese origin were killed and 300,000 were expelled. Of the about 300,000 who remained when the KR came to power, the vast majority were quickly expelled *en masse*, a fate so many others of every origin would have loved. It is unlikely that more than 40,000 disregarded the *Angkar's* orders. Even if 50 per cent of these were massacred in the last year of the regime, this accounts for one per cent of all who were exterminated between 1975 and 1979. They could not have *all* been exterminated, as some analysts have maintained. I know of some surviving Vietnamese, including some families in this book, who lived along the Sekong River in Stung Treng province – not to speak of Keat Chhon's wife, whom he had met in his Paris and who was completely Vietnamese and educated at *Le Couvent des Oiseaux* in Dalat. And one must not forget either the mother of my Khmer friends, from the sixties, Khay Mathoury and his brother Khay Matoren whose Saigon-born Vietnamese mother survived the regime and died of old age in 1989.

The Tribunal never looked at what could have been branded as the 'genocide' of Chinese residents who were massacred by the hundreds of thousands, or one-third of their community.[13] This was the same with the Khmers themselves, for that matter. If there was a 'genocide', that of Chinese and Khmers would be of an infinitely larger magnitude than that of the Vietnamese. But the tribunal ignored these experiences. The real reason the Tribunal omitted Chinese victims is that China is a close ally of Cambodia. Without Chinese rifles, trucks, tanks and even planes, there would have been no evacuation of

---

12 And so did the French journalist Jean-François Bouvet, in his *Havre de Guerre*, Fayard, 2018, p. 136.

13 In *Le Génocide Khmer rouge: une analyse démographique*, L'Harmattan, Paris, 1995, p. 77, Marek Sliwinski estimates the total to have been 38.4 per cent of all Chinese citizens in Cambodia.

the cities at all. Even today, China remains a generous donor for all manner of development projects. China and its citizens were off-limits.

Dale Lysak then quoted from the same KR document's discussion of 'enemies' of the revolution: adversaries 'are those [who are] against the revolution. In this case, they must be sent to the security sector ... no need to do things like education. It is [of] no avail' (quoted in 30 July, p. 27). These ominous words echo Article 10 of the DK Constitution: 'Hostile and destructive activities that threaten the popular State shall be subject to the severest form of punishment. Other cases shall be handled by means of constructive education in the framework of the State or people's organizations.' Equally ominous is the fact that this constitution's first draft was written by Zhang Chunqiao, the Gang of Four leader who secretly visited Cambodia in December 1975.[14]

Although we have no evidence that Phi Phuon was in a sufficiently high position to distribute those sanctions, he approved of the strategy, saying that if 'adversarial contradictions' were not removed, 'we could not live or get along well together and we have to take some actions. For example, the actions could be done [by] sending them to the labour camp to work, do farming, because keeping them alive means killing the revolution. So, each individual's performance had to be judged accordingly' (30 July, p. 27).

Still quoting from the document, the prosecutor read: 'The special aspects for 1977 to which the Party cells must pay attention are the increased revolutionary vigilance and a self-mastery in order to eliminate enemies from within and from without the country' and asked, 'Do you remember when ... you first started receiving instructions like this?' Phi Phuon replied: 'This ... kind of instruction ... was given to us from the very beginning' (30 July, p. 28). For those who did not adjust to the radically new revolutionary ideology, the sanction could only be death. And those were many!

Starvation

Phi Phuon later heard that, 'to keep the statistics', relocated townspeople were identified as 'New People' or '17th April People' (30 July, p. 72–74).

So, it was only when we prepared the lists of people could we manage who were present in the villages. And, in addition, we also wanted to ensure

---

14 Ambassador Julio Jeldres makes this claim in 'A Personal Reflection on Norodom Sihanouk and Zhou Enlai: An Extraordinary Friendship on the Fringes of the Cold War', Cross-Currents, no. 4, September 2012.

that we could control the elements in the villages. In some collectives, it was to take charge of them well, while in others there were problems because there were instances of personal revenge. I also observed people were made to dig soil and construct dams while they were only fed with clear rice watery soup (...) This meant that the cadres in that cooperative were not good enough. And then that gentleman was not serious about the matter. And then, actually, the gentleman told me I had to mind my own business because, if I was from the upper authority, I had to mind my own business. But it was my personal character that I would say what I saw, and I told him that in the revolution, we had to ensure equality in our relations. And I told him that if people had watery gruel, it was not a good sign because we were human beings, we have to be treated properly. So that's what I saw at that time. I told the chief of that cooperative.

From 1977 to 1978, I travelled to various provinces more frequently. I went to the provinces and I also noted – or saw the situation of the people and I reported to the upper echelon. I was advised to be a man who calls a spade a spade. So, when I saw this, I had to really report to the upper echelon on what I saw. It doesn't matter which cadre he or she belonged to – or at what level because I was very honest and I knew that, because of that, I was about to be purged, but I think I did well to survive.

Q. You said, when you saw what happened, you reported to the upper echelon? To whom did you report – Pol Pot or other people?

A. I was conscious I worked at the Standing Committee level with Uncle – *Om* Ieng Sary, whom I could talk to. Mostly I talked to him. *Om* Pol Pot would call me to see him every now and then, and I would never hide anything from him – what I saw. On one occasion he said I did not need to tell him about this; I should do that in the self-criticism sessions, instead. When I said self-criticism session, it's more like when I talked about this to *Om* Ieng Sary. I told him about what I saw, and he said I did not need to tell him about this and he asked me to mind my own business and – and also – when I met *Om* Number One, he asked me to wait until the session convened so that I could really express or tell the meeting what I saw. I did not know whether he meant it or [said] it sarcastically.

Q. You said you reported to Ieng Sary on this. After such [a] report, was there any change? Had there been any measures being taken in the areas where you believed to have problems?

A. None of these ideas were taken. I did not know what he said at Standing Committee's meetings I just reported to him at the fields. He normally said that we had to pass and he explained to me that when it comes to transition, he asked me to be patient. However, I could really be patient because what I saw was really painful.

Son Arun, the National Co-Lawyer for Nuon Chea was determined to understand why so many Cambodians had suffered and died from starvation, and the extent to which Nuon Chea was responsible for this. Phi Phoun replied:

> People [were] supposed to have enough food to eat; that was the simple instruction. In Ratanakiri, we did farming and we were told to be self-sufficient, self-mastery and we had to control what we did. For example, like charity begins at home. We had to really care for ourselves first before we care for others. But what I saw was not really the same as what was agreed. I just challenged this practice because I refer to the document and I said that if this thing happened at the cooperatives, then it was against the core principle because I saw that people ate porridge with just a few – mixed with water lily. And I knew that people were badly treated and it was not really the intention of the Party to mistreat the people and why people were still mistreated. So, I believe that these people were not those who were the honest followers of the Party's policy (31 July, p. 47).

Here, the accused defense lawyer was doing his job by showing that the people's sufferings was the responsibility of local leaders and not that of the top leadership.

Pol Pot and Ieng Sary had been most impressed by the autonomy and self-sufficiency of all tribal villages in Ratanakiri and decided to extend the model to the entire Cambodian territory. They produced everything for everyday life locally from the forest and their *chamkar* (swidden fields), and the entire Cambodian population was to do the same after 17 April 1975. Phi Phuon says, as he had explained earlier, that he saw people eat just clear rice gruel with water lily stems that are not at all nourishing. He wondered why they were ill-treated like this, as this was not Party policy. Were not those responsible for the starvation trying 'to destroy the Party', he wondered?

6 – Conclusion

Although much precious time was wasted during the five and a half days of Phi Phuon's testimony and many repetitive or irrelevant questions were asked, a few essential points were addressed.

The ultimate crime of the KR – the crime that set the regime on a course that ended with the extermination of 25 per cent of its compatriots – was the evacuation of all the towns and the ruralization of the entire population. These murderous decisions, which have no equivalent in the modern world, have given rise to speculation about the KR vision of 'an agrarian utopia'. For me, it was rather the other way round: the KR extended, to rural areas, working conditions that were reminiscent of the first phase of the industrial revolution in Europe, and Great Britain in particular, as described by Friedrich Engels in his 1844 *The Condition of the Working Class in England*.[15] Most farmers had owned their plots; now they were dispossessed. All farmers became proletarians with no control over their work schedules or labour conditions. They became an appendix of a colossal monster, *Angkar*, that tightly grasped the entire territory. All liberties of the normally free-wheeling Cambodian farmers vanished. Terror prevailed.

The prosecutors and defence lawyers of the victims were keen to understand how and why the grand decision to empty the capital had been taken. Well, Phi Phuon tells it all: in an atmosphere of joy and exhilaration, the proposal to immediately evacuate Phnom Penh prompted loud applause after a brief speech by Nuon Chea. No dissenting voice was raised regarding humanitarian consequences, no probing about how the vision would be implemented. Not a single measure of preparation, other than that raw terror and violence would be used. The small group of leaders merely confirmed that they would use the tactic that had proved successful during 1973–1974 – in Kratieh, Oudong, Angtasom, and other places – acknowledging that a year later, in 1975, the guerrilla forces continued to be too small to control any town. All townspeople were understood to be traitors who had refused to join the brave new world of the revolution, and instead had revelled in air-conditioned luxury. They deserved no mercy and they got none.

Finally, Phi Phuon admitted to the Tribunal that he could not fail to notice that in 1977 and 1978, the population in all quarters of the country was living under dire conditions. He raised the issue with the men responsible for implementing the people's communes programme, like Ieng Sary and even Pol Pot. Each time the answer was along the lines of: 'mind your own business'. Under the KR, everyone had to wear blinkers and perform their assigned task,

---

15 See Engels: *The Condition of the Working Class in England*, translated & edited by W. O. Henderson & W. H. Chaloner, Oxford, Basil Blackwell, 1971.

diligently for sure, and also slavishly. Do not look around, and just work hard for *Angkar*; prosperity and happiness can be imagined on the horizon, and present suffering is for the good of the future society. Any kind of suggestion or criticism was restricted to those evening mutual- and self-criticism sessions. This was the only context where such things were to be tackled. And everyone was well aware that if criticism of the regime were expressed in such a session, as in Mao's China, the blow of repression would fall on the person who dared to speak out. Phi Phuon too was in fear.

In the end, Phi Phuon was right to point out the central role of Ta Mok and his thugs in the purges and massacres that spread to the entire territory from 1976. He was quite right almost to lose his usual composure at the Tribunal when he exposed the criminality and responsibility of a persona he vehemently abhorred. But he fails to tell us – or rather was not really aware – that it was not Ta Mok alone who made the fateful decisions to eliminate all perceived 'traitors and enemies' of the revolutionary State. Most of these decisions were taken by a collective leadership at Office 870, with Pol Pot and his alter ego, Nuon Chea, as the leading lights, but also with the continuous presence of Khieu Samphân, who was a kind of *éminence grise* of the regime, while washing his hands of all unspeakable crimes. Phi Phuon proclaimed his great admiration for Khieu Samphân too: 'I respected him. I adored him because it was great to have an intellectual living and working with us in the jungle'.[16] Alas, when it came to Pol Pot, Nuon Chea, Khieu Samphân, Ieng Sary, and Son Sen, Phi Phuon could only see the smiling faces of the men he had served for about three decades – from 1967, when he was barely twenty, until 1996.

---

16 *Extraordinary Chambers in the Courts of Cambodia Trial Chamber – Trial Day 88 – Case No. 002/19-09-2007-ECCC/TC 01/08/2012* p. 98.

– XXII –

Ratanakiri Province under the Iron Rule of the Khmer Rouge, 1968–1978

Ieng Sary said, 'You must kill all the village chiefs who do not come from the people.' The Khmer Lœu answered: 'You said you wanted to create a fair society. So, why do you now want to establish military forces and start a war?' Ieng Sary answered disdainfully: 'You do not know much. We have to struggle. In the future, you will see good things.'
    – interview with Chheang Ngoy

Our base area was in the minority region of Northeast Cambodia. These minorities are quite familiar to me. They were extremely poor and had only breechcloths. They experienced a lack of salt every year. Now, you cannot recognize them as a minority. They are wearing the same clothes and living in the same way as the rest of the people. They have plenty of rice, salt and medicine'
    – Pol Pot to the Yugoslav Press Delegation, 17 March 1978 (Foreign Broadcast Information Service March 1978, H8).

1 – Introduction

*I*n 1959, when the *Sangkum Reastr Niyum*[1] regime of Norodom Sihanouk decided to establish the new province of Ratanakiri ('the Peaks of Precious Stones/Gems'), it was peopled almost exclusively with upland tribal minorities. There were also Lao along the river valleys of the Tonlé Srèpok and the Tonlé Sésan, together with some Vietnamese workers and fishermen on the way to Stung Treng, where the number of Vietnamese settlers was quite significant. However, there were few Khmer people from the lower regions.

---

1   The English equivalent could be: 'The People's Socialist Community' regime: 1955–1970.

This chapter has been elaborated from interviews of surviving inhabitants, almost all in 1994, when the province again became accessible to foreigners. It mainly consists of short vignettes of individuals whose lives have been most characteristic of the lot that befell on them, when the KR leadership grasped hold of the province. They can be divided into three groups; the first ran away from the cruel policies of DK, mainly by escaping to Laos or Vietnam; the second includes those who passively submitted to the strict discipline and total collectivization of the people's communes; and the third chose to join the revolution of their own free will, like Phi Phuon himself.

The background of interviews in Ratanakiri was very different from in lowland Khmer provinces. When arriving anywhere in the lowlands, my two young interpreters and I would go to the provincial authorities and ask them if they knew the places of the ex-KR prisons I was investigating, and if they might know the names of victims or perpetrators – both men and women – who still lived in the area. All I needed was to find people who were old enough to remember their lives during 1968–1978. In 1994 in Ratanakiri, just after the UNTAC mission, there was not yet any long-established local administration and the newly appointed officials, mostly lowlanders who were not present at the time of the DK regime, were not really familiar with the local inhabitants. This was my first difficulty. So, I just went from village to village in the hope of finding witnesses, and I did find many willing to talk. The method was very fruitful and I obtained a lot of useful information. If needed, I was still pepared to use my blanket written permission from Khieu Kanharith, the Minister of Information to investigate Cambodia under the KR.

I know it is the habit among most researchers to anonymize their sources. As for myself, none of what the witnesses told me really concerned their personal lives. Besides, the events described here happened almost half a century ago and many of them might be deceased by now. I was careful not just to note their names and the place and the day of the interview, but also their dates of birth so I could know what age they were during the events they described. This would give more veracity and impact to their declarations. Besides, now we have hundreds – if not thousands – of life stories of the victims of the KR regime and no one believes these should remain anonymous. Many even have been published in Khmer, French and English.

Although I was advised to avoid some places, I was made to feel very welcome at most tribal villages, as these people are mostly friendly with visitors and travellers. My Khmer–French interpreters and I would spend the night in the villages and eat their food. They would kill a chicken and we enjoyed their delicious variety of rice from slash-and-burn paddy, the best I ever ate. I could relax from my backache after sitting for long drives on the back of motorbikes.

The second circumstance was that, more than a quarter of a century ago, when the trend of feminist studies had not yet reached academia, I was not really aware that women could have had a quite different approach to past experiences in their eventful and dramatic lives. If I had not been so, I would have sometimes attempted to push aside the many men who volunteered to be interviewed, and reached out to some individual women who were prepared to talk, and attempted to provide a space where they could open their memories and their hearts to us. However, even if I had managed to single out women ready to testify, we would have been faced with a language problem: no general school system had been established at the time in Ratanakiri and most women would have been illiterate in both their own language and Khmer. Along with Mondolkiri, Ratanakiri was the only province where local traditional languages were at times tolerated under DK. So, it would have been impossible to communicate, as I did not have interpreters into the local languages.

We must not forget too that, in traditional highland societies, women typically are not among the decision-makers; they were responsible mostly for everyday chores like bringing water to the household and cooking the food, and childbearing could often become fatal for them. Many died at childbirth, as there were neither clinics nor trained midwives, while a large percentage of infants did not survive before reaching the age of five. So, morally and physically, women who could have been invaluable witnesses only remained in the background.

2 – New arrivals with Cambodian colonization: Indochinese Communist Party (ICP), Pathet Lao and Vietminh infiltrations[2]

The first Khmers colonizers arrived in 1959, when the new province was detached from Stung Treng Province under the sponsorship of the FARK. For instance, the father of Nhem Vannayouth[3] was a Lon Nol soldier based

---

2   Readers interested in the relationships between the Indochinese Communist Party (ICP), Laos and Ratanakiri can read a most informative article by Martin Rathie, 'Lao links and Khmer Revolution', New Mandala, 2007. See also Martin Rathie, 'The Lao Long of Cambodia', chap. 9 in Goldston (ed.), *Engaging Asia*.

3   Born in 1964, now Sub-Governor of Stung Treng province, interviewed on 23 December 2019. He was therefore just a young adolescent under DK.

in Siempang District where people spoke Lao. He could speak French and read instructions on drug packages. He was captured by the KR during 1970–1971 and taken away for execution like all Lon Nol soldiers. All were shot except him; he pretended to be dead and crawled toward the water. He took refuge with his wife upstream along the Sekong river at a village called Rumkoat, where he lived growing sugarcane and cassava. There was no food problem in that outlying part of DK, close to the Lao border. In fact, at the time, the further you were from the centre of the country, the more food there was. However, his father was arrested again in 1976, and killed. His mother remarried, to a very kind and educated ex-monk – an ideal stepfather. All local Vietnamese survived, except two families that were purged.

All the various tribes practiced swidden agriculture on the rich, basaltic-red soil of the plateau and, like their fellows along the Annamite Range in the ex-colonial Indochinese Federation of Tonkin, Annam, Cochinchina, Laos and Cambodia, knew no borders and freely moved across the hilly territories. French anthropologists had classified them as 'non-Indianised Proto-Indochinese' or 'Montagnards', while Sihanouk simply dubbed them *Khmer Lœu*, or 'Upper Khmers', the better to assimilate them. Among the various ethnicities, we shall mainly mention the Jaraï and the Tampuon, who were closest to the KR, together with a few Brao, Krâchok and Krœung. Although all practised agriculture on slash-and-burn fields temporarily carved inside the forest, they retained many of the traditions of hunter-gatherer societies, which 'tend to be relatively egalitarian, lacking full-time bureaucrats except for hereditary chiefs and having small-scale political organizations at the level of the band or the tribe.'[4] There, 'individuals carried out all types of work. There was no specialisation or division of labour, humans were in touch with their true nature ... There was no 'creation of a surplus.'[5] And Pol Pot loved that camaraderie, which he mistook for 'real' primitive communism, as Marx called it.

Pol Pot and his group (Ieng Sary and Son Sen, and their wives Khieu Ponnary, Ieng Thirith and Yun Yat) completely misunderstood the way of life of tribal people. These groups were well on the way to settling as farmers on defined pieces of land. If the villages looked united – including some with multi-family long houses – it did not mean they were not based on family

---

4   *Guns, Germs and Steel: A Short History of Everybody for the Last 13,000 Years,* Jared Diamond, Vintage, Penguin, 2017, p. 85.

5   Peter Claus and John Marriot, *History: An Introduction to Theory, Method and Practice,* Essex, England: Harlow, 2012, p. 275.

structures; food resources could be shared in case of penury, but this did not mean that people ate collectively; mutual help existed to clear the forest, but the slash-and-burn fields created by a group were divided for individual families. On top of that, vernacular languages, traditional ceremonies, and all customs and mores were swept away once full collectivization was forcibly introduced by the KR. None of the drastic changes in everyday life were welcomed by the vast majority of these minorities, who saw all their centuries-old culture and traditions entirely disappear.

First, thousands ran away to neighbouring Laos or Vietnam, mainly around 1974–1975. From interviews and printed sources, one can reckon there were at least six thousand, perhaps up to a quarter of the province's population. Then, there was a majority that was trapped into the new regime and had to passively submit to it. Finally, a minority joined the ranks of the revolution – usually at a very young age – and those who did not die in combat were among the relatively privileged few of the new regime. During my investigation of the KR prison system in the 1990s across the entire Cambodian territory, I found only one interviewee who regretted the KR regime: he was an adolescent at the time, and an ethnic minority from Ratanakiri.

The big conundrum is: what proportion of Ratanakiri hill tribespeople joined the revolution? Krisna Uk offers one answer: 'At the start of my research, I was interested in knowing who among the people I worked with had actually joined the KR in their revolutionary movement. At the completion of it, I realized that most of them had in one way or another.'[6] This is not surprising, as her fieldwork and selected village of Leu was a Jaraï village in Andoung Meas District. During my own investigation in the area during the 1990s, I was told by my interpreters: 'No need to enter this village. They all joined the revolution and will not speak to you'. But what happened in Krisna Uk's Jaraï village of Leu certainly cannot be extrapolated to the entire province.

On the other hand Ben Kiernan explains that Ratanakiri was a special zone managed by Pol Pot, Ieng Sary and Son Sen, where many young tribal men became the trusted bodyguards and couriers of the leadership; but he gives credence to the quite extravagant estimate by a UNTAC official who claimed in the 1990s that, 'from a plausible estimate, some 50% of the tribal population

---

6   Her PhD thesis on precisely the Jaraï village of Leu in Andoung Meas district, has been published as *Salvage: Cultural Resilience Among the Jorai of Northeast Cambodia,* Cornell University Press, 2016, p. 68.

of Ratanakiri had been killed.'[7] This sweeping statement is based on no serious research at all. If indeed some 50 per cent of those who had joined the revolution had not have survived the tragic years, due to the two civil wars, those who joined the revolution were indeed a minority. Martin Rathie suggests they might be up to a quarter. Personally, I would be more circonspect, as I could never attempt to even give a rough estimate. As to the many who ran away to Laos and Vietnam, Kiernan quotes the PRK figure of 20,000.[8] It is probably impossible to find reliable data concerning the numerical proportion of the Montagnards in the KR revolution, but two points are certain: they were most obedient and fearsome fighters, typically on the front lines of combat; and, to a large extent, their way of life coloured the extraordinary nature of the Cambodian revolution. The forest was the best training camp, if not university, to forge diehard revolutionaries. In April 1975, they might have been a significant percentage of the awe-inspiring young soldiers who entered and overran the cities, an environment that was totally alien to them.

We must not forget that the entire northeast quarter of Cambodia – in particular the plateau that would become Ratanakiri – was conquered by Pathet Lao and Vietminh troops in the course of the First Indochina War (1946–1954). Contemporary anthropologists like Frédéric Bourdier or Krisna Uk tend to ignore or overlook this crucial reality. In his bird's eye view of the history of Ratanakiri, Bourdier skips from the French intervention and delineation of borders in the region together, with the elimination of the Siamese overlords, to the arrival of Sihanouk's administration in 1959.[9] Similarly and curiously, in Krisna Uk's PhD thesis on the Jaraï village of Leu, entitled *Salvage: Cultural Resilience Among the Jorai of Northeast Cambodia*, she completely omits, in her historical summary, any allusion to the time of the First Indochina War. In her 'Historical aide-mémoire', she notes that Vietnamese Communist guerrillas had infiltrated Cambodia during 1964–65, thus ignoring also the post-WW II years.

Similarly, we have Pol Pot's own testimony about the Vietminh presence in Ratanakiri during the First Indochina War. In his *Livre noir (Black Book)*, published in September 1978 in Khmer, French and English versions, we can

---

7   Page 373 of the French edition of *The Pol Pot Regime: Race, Power, and Genocide under the Khmer Rouge, 1975–79*, Gallimard, Paris 1998.

8   Kiernan, ibid., p, 372.

9   The sweeping description of the province under the KR does not always reflect the true reality at the time.

read that 'the Vietminh established its political and military base (c. 1950) near the gem-mining town of Bokéo'.[10] As for myself, when I went for a Christmas trip in 1966 to Ratanakiri on the invitation of my landlord, Colonel Srey Meas,[11] I was surprised to see the rusty remains of military trucks and tanks on the way to Vœunsay. He told me they were the remains of the fierce battle between the Franco-Khmer troops and the invading Vietminh.

On the other hand, Martin Rathie, a historian of the northeast mainly in connection with the nearby Champasak region of Laos, gives a full and well-documented history from the post-WW II years. He explains, with numerous examples, how revolutionary Lao, or Pathet Lao, and the Vietminh closely collaborated to win over the support of a number of local ethnic minorities. The Lao who had settled in all the valleys of Stung Treng and Ratanakiri provinces had more cultural and commercial relations than the Vietnamese coming from Annam. 'The Lao migrants shared a strong belief in the supernatural and quickly acquainted 'neak ta' and 'a r a k' spirit worship with their own 'phi' cults. Thus, the Lao integrated amicably with the upland ethnic communities', he writes. This helps us to understand why, when the *Angkar Lœu* arrived in Ratanakiri, they discovered that Phi Phuon and his peers spoke not just their tribal language, but also Lao: Lao was the language of communication at the time. Rathie adds:

> The Lao Long, the most socially and politically mobile people in the highlands, then carried the seeds of revolution into north-eastern Cambodia. In 1949, revolutionary expansion in north-eastern Cambodia spread through whole village communities, after Viet Minh and Lao Issara activists approached village leaders to join the struggle against the French. The first few villages to be penetrated by revolutionary propaganda teams were populated by Kravet and Brao, ethnic minorities who overlapped the Lao–Cambodian frontier. The teams, consisting of Vietnamese propagandists with Lao and Khmer guides, aimed first to win over three significant villages, namely Siempang, Voeunsai and Lumphat. The first Lao village to be infiltrated was the district centre of Siempang. It was strategically important, being midway between Attapeu and Stung Treng on the Sekong River.[12]

---

10 *Livre noir*, p. 24.

11 Srey Meas later became a general under Lon Nol's Khmer Republic. He, his wife and their four children were massacred at the beginning of the KR regime.

12 Rathie, 'The Lao Long of Cambodia', p. 190.

When, in 1951, the Indochinese Communist Party was disbanded in favour of separate revolutionary parties in Vietnam, Cambodia and Laos, it was mostly ethnic Lao who created the northeastern committee of the Khmer People's Revolutionary Party (KPRP). Later, when Sihanouk began to repress communists after the defection of Sieu Heng, Nuon Chea's uncle by marriage, who returned to civilian life in Battambang, in 1960, 'the surviving members of the KPRP's north-eastern branch (...) based themselves in the *maquis* in the jungles of Bokéo in 1962.' This was not far from the *maquis* that Phi Phuon created in 1963 with a couple of other tribal minorities. Some of these veterans from the First Indochina War against the French, Rathie asserts, came to 'harbour Khmer radicals in the Cambodian wilderness.' Rathie further adds that some children of the Lao group 'served as bodyguards, cooks and messengers' of Saloth Sâr and Ieng Sary. Two daughters 'became favourites' of Ieng Thirith and 'they performed in a small arts troupe for the KR leaders'.

After Pol Pot and his group left the province in late 1970, radicals took charge of the province and repression and purges started, what Rathie rightly calls 'the Cambodian deviation'. This was the time when those who had relocated to Hanoi after the Geneva Accords were coming back to the northeast and Champasak, but 'they had great reservations about the CPK's ideological trajectory'. One Lao Cambodian originating from Voeunsai, Khamphan Thivong, managed to sneak up the Hô Chi Minh Trail with a few Khmer Hanoi friends back to the DRV to warn VWP leaders about the dangerous deviation, but he was not believed. As we know, most returnees were killed by the Pol Pot group. Originally, there were about 1,500 in 1954 who went to the DRV for further 'education' in revolutionary lore. A few had returned shortly afterwards, like Nuon Chea. In 1970, they were in the hundreds. All books on DK speak of the purge of returnees from Hanoi. Most were killed, except Pen Sovann who managed to escape back to Hanoi, later in 1978 being chosen by the Vietnamese as Cambodia's defence minister. Not for long, though; he was not sufficiently docile.

Besides, the promise of liberation from the century-old contempt that lowland Khmers tended to nurse in regard to them, those radical and cruel Vietminh methods differed somewhat from the rest of the country and were, after 1975, to be less radical in Ratanakiri. By and large, it seems that revolutionary Lao used persuasion and comradeship to win new supporters for the cause, while the VC were not averse to using sheer violence and even terror, as Nhiek Tioulong explains in his *Chroniques khmères*. It was clear to him, after being directly involved in the very creation of the province, that the insecurity was caused not by the initiative of the *Khmer Lœu* themselves, but by the massive and lasting VC presence together with their support of the KR. He lists all the main VC sanctuaries from Ratanakiri to Svay Rieng.[13] In the years following World War II, he had become a major creator of the nascent Cambodian national army at the time the French colonialists were leaving the country:

> The classic methods of the Vietminh are well-known: attacks of isolated police stations, arrest of notables, *mekhum* (village chiefs) civil servants and their execution, requisition of crops, livestock and means of transport. Small detachments of Vietnamese, often from the North with black teeth, continually roam around Khmer villages at night, arresting villagers, so-called culprits, that families never find again. The method that inspires more terror among the peasants is to have their own grave dug by the victims themselves and they are then buried alive. The supply of information to the police, coming to visit the villages in the daytime, is punishable by death the following night.
>
> Children are detained to guard against any attempt at flight or desertion. Those are always sanctioned by the death penalty against the family members of the culprits. Vietminh troops are closely supervised by Vietnamese armed with automatic weapons. Subordinates are Cambodians, but distrust of them is methodical. They are only entitled to use old ordinary rifles, while modern weapons are reserved for Vietnamese. The hostage system is the rule.
>
> The supply of arms and equipment of the KR by the Vietminh, the manipulation of the Khmer Lœu from Ratanakiri to sabotage channels of communication in the high region. ...
>
> The Vietminh maintains and supports the Khmer communist rebels and foster troubles on the plateaux among the Khmer Lœu (Moïs) that it compels to commit sabotages of strategic channels of communication and rebel against local authorities.[14]

---

13 In the south, at Koh Thom district, Regiment No. 704; at Svay Rieng district, Regiment No. 709; in Chantrea district, Regiment No. 367; in the Southeast, Svay Teap district, No. 706; at Roméas Hêk district No. 354; at Tbaung Khmum, No. 707; at Mémot district, No. 352 and 353; at Snuol district, No. 350 and 351; at O'Reang; No. 203 and 740; in Ratanakiri, No. 701 and 702. Note from the author.

14 *Chroniques khmères: Cambodge 1863–1969*, chap. XIII, Les Indes savantes, Paris forthcoming 2023. Tioulong was responsible in 1969 for the young and poorly equipped Cambodian army.

On the other hand, Rathie describes in detail how, through the completely porous border between the two countries, militants could travel and even form family links across the two countries. Particularly in the big villages of Siempang on the Sekong, Voeunsai and Ta Veng on the Tonlé San and even Lumphat on the Tonlé Srèpok, cells of the ICP and then, from 1951, and as far as Koh Nhiek in Mondolkiri province. This township was to become the political centre of the province under DK, as Sen Monorom was too close to the Vietnamese border.

Shortly after WW II, French troops, backed up by troops of the nascent Cambodian army sent by Sihanouk, confronted Vietminh invaders in bloody clashes. At the time, the Vietminh and the Pathet Lao managed to persuade some highlanders, like Phi Phuon's father and an uncle, Ta Lav, into believing that revolution would lead to a better future. The Vietminh and their followers had the temerity to wish to impose their presence at the 1954 Geneva Conference, with Keo Moni and Mey Pho[15] – both lowland Khmers, in fact – in order to see the northeast quarter of the country was attributed to the United Issarak Front, and thus to divide Cambodia, just as Laos and Vietnam were to be divided. But, thanks mainly to the absolute determination of Sam Sary,[16] Sihanouk's special representative and a strong supporter of the West in the Cold War, those Khmer Issarak representatives were not even admitted to the negotiating table. Thus, Cambodia preserved its territorial integrity and its independence after the Geneva Agreements.[17] Still, after officially committing themselves to quit Cambodian territory at Geneva, Hanoi kept a secret Vietminh base in the Naga's Tail. In 1960, it decided to resume armed struggle to conquer southern Vietnam. 'Infiltration began in 1961 and increased through 1962 and 1963', according to Pol Pot, in his *Black Book*.[18]

His book covers events from the arrival of the French in 1863 to 1969, when Tioulong retired to Paris, as he anticipated the coming tragedies.

15 Both would fall victim to KR purges of returnees from Hanoi.

16 Sam Sary (1917–1963), Sam Rainsy's father, was a vital aide to Sihanouk in his fight for independence and the creation of the *Sangkum*. But he fell from the prince's graces when he wished to form a loyal opposition to the *Sangkum* regime modeled on the British two-party system, an idea he developed while serving as ambassador to Britain. He beat his maid which brought shame on Cambodia, because he refused to apologize!

17 In a public speech, Sam Sary explained why the Geneva Agreement was only signed on 21 July and not by the 20th which was the latest as promised by French Prime Minister Mendès-France. The speech is preserved in the Cambodian National Library, 1954.

18 *Aggression and annexation: Kampuchea's Condemnation of Vietnam*, by Milton Osborne. Working Paper No. 15, The Research School of Pacific Studies, The Australian National University,

Puy Yung[19] is another witness with a life story similar to Phi Phuon. A Jaraï from Andoung Meas District who had been recruited into the KPRP at the age of 14, in 1956. He followed his father, who had been enrolled in the Khmer Issarak-Vietminh insurrections during the First Indochina War. 'You entered the Party as you entered a religious sect or a monastery: you had to give up all and take up a new name. There were meetings in the forest that lasted ten to fifteen days, or even one or two months. People would learn how to read and write Khmer.' Ta Lav,[20] another Jaraï, was responsible for recruitment.

Muoy Chhœum (មួយ ឈើម),[21] an ethnic Brao trained by the Vietminh during the first Indochina War, received a clear explanation of the origins of the movement later created by Pol Pot and Nuon Chea. He was aware that the ICP had been created in 1930 by Hô Chi Minh in order to oppose French colonialism throughout Indochina. He also knew that the Party was divided into three branches in 1951 and that the Cambodian Party had later become the Workers' Party of Kampuchea. During 1954–1956, he went to Vietnam twice a year to attend secret training sessions that lasted five to ten days. One of even lasted three months. Some Lao were present as well.

Muoy Chhœum noted that Van (Ieng Sary), Pouk (Pol Pot), Kham (Son Sen), Ya (Ney Sarann)[22] Hu Nim, Hou Yuon, and Khieu Samphân were taught communism in France. The last three worked with Sihanouk, 'who won all elections after 1954'. Khieu Samphân was 'a two-headed serpent who worked too long with Sihanouk.' At the time, Muoy Chhœum learnt to organize commandos to harass Sihanouk's troops and to organize a resistance to protect the population. On 7 November 1959, two young men announced that the Vœunsay office wished to see him. He went with them on a boat, but when he arrived, he was handcuffed. He was kept one week in Vœunsay, his

---

Canberra, *A Summary of the Pol Pot Government's Livre Noir (Black Book) with Commentary and Annotations*, 1 August 1979; p. 21.

19 Born in 1942 and interviewed on 14 April 1994.

20 Later, in late 1976, after Ney Sarann's arrest, he was sent to Phnom Penh for interrogation and probable execution, but no trace of him has been found in the S–21 archives of the Tuol Sleng Museum, as his family claims he committed suicide before reaching the dismal institution.

21 Born in 1930, interviewed on 12 January 1994.

22 Muoy Chhœum is misinformed here, as Ney Sarann (1928–1976) never went to France. He was put in charge of the entire Northeast region (*Eisan*) in 1973, but was arrested and executed in September 1976 at S–21, now known as Tuol Sleng, the central political prison managed by Duch.

legs in iron rings (*khnoh*[23]). He was hit and interrogated three times to make him admit that he had been trained in Vietnam. He always said he had seen Khmer-Issarak and Vietminh before, but not since independence. They were not too cruel, they just came to 'educate' the population.

He was then taken to the Stung Treng prison for another week. There were no chains in this large prison, built of concrete by the French and with some fifty prisoners in each room, mostly thieves but about a dozen political prisoners. He was then taken to Stung Meanchey[24] Prison in Phnom Penh. He was again interrogated three times and asked: – 'What are your relations with the Vietminh? – Who is at the head of the Party? – Why did you propagandize against Sihanouk?' He was interrogated in the courthouse, but he had no defence lawyer. A pistol was aimed at him, but he was not afraid. Fortunately, after King Suramarit's death in 1960, all political prisoners were amnestied and he was released.

Back in his village, Muoy Chhœum was called to the forest in 1965. When he met Ieng Sary in 1967, he told him he had been imprisoned by the *Sangkum* regime. He was then appointed commune secretary in Kaol village, Poy commune. In January 1968, he attended a two-week training with Ieng Sary, after which he was placed in charge of propagandizing to frontline adolescents and militia groups (*chhlop*) in each village and each commune.

3 – Colonization by the lowland Khmers

It is not inappropriate to use the word 'colonization' following the creation of the new province of Ratanakiri in 1959. Even the government authorities used the word at the time. The immigration of the lowland Khmers was encouraged, both they and the government considered most of the land to be virgin territory, and Sihanouk wished to rapidly take advantage of the province's rich red basaltic soil. This is why he decided to create a vast rubber plantation of 12,000 hectares, and French experts from the vast Chup Plantation readily agreed to help.[25] At the time of my investigation in 1966, one year before the arrival of

---

23 Iron rings for the legs that slid along an iron bar.

24 Probably Prey Sâr, Phnom Penh's main prison, as this was where other suspects from the northeast were detained. Martin Rathie has an account from a Lao veteran arrested in Siempang in 1961.

25 See my article 'Ratanakiri ou La Montagne au Joyaux', in *Kambuja*, Sihanouk's glossy magazine edited by the ubiquitous Chau Seng, his Head of Cabinet, Phnom Penh, 1966. At the time, the sponsor of the Labansiek plantation at Chup, near Kompong Cham, under the French

Pol Pot, 2,200 hectares had already been planted. The first saplings had been planted in 1961 and the tapping of the trees could have started 7 years later, that is around 1968, exactly when Pol Pot (then Ta Pouk) launched his bloody revolution. This was also when anthropologist Jacqueline Matras-Troubetz-koy[26] was forced to quit the province, probably together with the plantation director Georges Bonzon and the bulk of the plantation management team. Exploitation of the young trees continued under DK, with the rubber being exported to China, as we are told by a witness (see below). The Sihanouk government also planned to have the same surface for family plantations in the area. Land was not really a problem at the time as the population density was very low, as we saw.[27]

However, the new province was placed under the control of the FARK led by the engineering corps which opened up the region with new roads suitable for motor vehicles. This led necessarily to abuse of power on the part of the military that gave rise to resentment on the part of the population. Thus, two Jaraï, Choal Paet[28] and Kusol Paet,[29] the latter a village chief, stated that in *Sangkum* days, the village had enough food, except when government soldiers entered the village, grabbed pigs and chickens, and slept with the girls. When they saw soldiers, the population took fright and ran into the forest. There was resentment, but no rebellion; the first clashes with Sihanouk's army started only during 1968–1969. But, if it had not been for the presence of the KR leadership during 1964–1970, this would *not* have given rise to a well-structured guerrilla movement. The *Khmer Lœu* (KL) used crossbows and arrows, and threw grenades onto passing trucks.

In other villages, we were told that during the *Sangkum*, government soldiers had settled near the border to control it. There was no hostility against them on the part of the inhabitants. They had built barracks and recruited

---

Compagnie du Cambodge, covered 13,500 hectares. It was then the second largest in the world for its size after the Firestone Plantation in Liberia.

26 Matras-Troubetzkoy, J. *Un Village en Forêt. L'essartage chez les Brou du Cambodge*. SELAF, Paris, 1983.

27 Apart from insecurity and incessant feuds in the past couple of centuries, the main reason for the region's low population density was the disastrous lack of modern hygiene and medicine. This caused a high infant death rate before the age of five. We see examples of this in the Rochœm family, not to mention the too-frequent deaths of mothers during childbirth. Anthropologists tend not to mention these sad realities, as often they seem to idealize tribal life.

28 Choal Paet was born in 1934.

29 Interviewed on 14 April 1994, Bokéo district, Kas Chong Nay commune, Lo Khon village.

ethnic minorities. At the time, the soldiers would go through the villages, but did not stop to steal anything. Some civil servants even came to distribute cloth or money. When Sihanouk himself came to Bokéo in 1964 or 1965, the entire population was summoned. Rubber trees were starting to be planted, but the population was not hostile to Sihanouk. People could move from village to village as they pleased. Nor were the KL hostile towards the large Labansiek State Rubber Plantation, near the village of Banlung that was not the provincial capital at the time, but in Lumphat on the Tonlé Srèpok.[30]

We learn also that Sihanouk supplied a lot of local rice to the Vietnamese communist fighters and that the army was involved in the rice trade.[31] One branch of the Hô Chi Minh Trail followed the Tonlé San, and this is how the VC was supplied with rice.[32] Another branch led to Attapeu in Laos, through Ta Veng, without going through Bokéo, and then to Vietnam.

The head[33] of Ka Tieng village in La Ban Muey commune, Lumphat District, told us that his village had been close to the plantation. But, under DK, the village was transferred north of Lumphat, on the right bank of the Srèpok. The rubber plantation started in 1960 and this village took part in its establishment. The local population lived outside the perimeter of the plantation; some houses were dismantled to move outside the perimeter. The French bought the land for 1,000–2,000 riels per hectare. The people did not resent at all the establishment of the plantation and took part in the clearing. The men were paid 20 riels a day (one kilogramme of rice cost five riels at the time) and women 15–18 riels. People practised swidden agriculture and worked in the plantation when they needed money. He described the French director, Georges Bonzon[34] as a kind and tolerant person. If someone needed a vehicle to transport rice, Bonzon would lend one. Soldiers did not steal food from the villages, this former Sihanouk soldier claimed, and, all in all, relations were quite smooth. Those who wished to work for the rubber plantation lived nearby in renovated wooden houses; those who wished to start their own plantation were given free saplings; those who wished to

---

30 See above, I had come to the same conclusion 18 years before, in 1966 for my report. I was accompanied by Ho Tong Peng, the brother of the then Minister of Agriculture Ho Tong Lip.

31 According to Chheang Ngoy, born in 1934 and interviewed on 12 January 1994.

32 According to Hu Ly, born in 1942, interviewed on 7 April 1994

33 Interviewed on 15 April 1994. He prefered to remain anonymous.

34 Georges Bonzon was executed in 1975 by the KR at the state coffee plantation in Pailin.

Figure 15: Part of Labansiek plantation in 1963, the extent of deforestation very clear in this aerial view.

remain free in the forest moved further afield, as space in the rolling hills seemed unlimited.[35]

But this honeymoon of the early days of the plantation did not last. While Matras-Troubetzkoy is mostly silent about the politico-economic context of those locally and nationally pivotal years 1966–1968, she does mention that when she arrived in September 1966, the situation was 'stabilized'. My investigation for *Kambuja* took place in the spring 1966, and we both noted that calm prevailed in and around the vast state plantation. But, contrary to myself, she was also informed that, not unexpectedly, the launching of this vast project met with 'some difficulties' with the local Brao community, who considered the unlimited forested expanses to be their own collective turf. Matras-Troubetzkoy has not a word for the possibility offered to the local tribal groups (Brao and Tampuon) to be involved in this revolutionary development and the hope of a better standard of living. For her, the local inhabitants were just forcibly displaced, with no compensation. Out of necessity, some Brao must have been involved at least in the clearing of the forest and some must have become daily workers, if they did not wish to abandon their village way

---

35 Anthropologist Jacqueline Matras-Troubetzkoy provides addtitional documentation in her lengthy and meticulous *Un Village en forêt: l'Essartage chez les Brou du Cambodge* CNRS, Paris, 1983.

of life and live in the Khmer-style wooden houses offered to workers. At a time of lowland economic prosperity in the 1960s, I doubt the plantation could induce enough workers from the plains to fill all the newly created posts. Even the FARK recruited tribal soldiers.

From 1966 to early 1968 was a period of equipoise for this eastern part of the Ratanakiri plateau and Jacqueline Matras-Troubetzkoy arrived in the province at exactly the right time, mid-September 1966, and left it too on the right date – the end of March 1968. She attributes 'incidents' in early 1968 to the planned extension of the plantation eastwards in Tampuon territory this time, noting in the same breath that public opinion in villages attributed the unrest to 'subversive elements' from Vietnam.

> That was the pretext for an arbitrary military repression that spread havoc among the population and atrocities were committed everywhere. ... Many inhabitants took refuge into the forest and, from there, organized a resistance movement that soon became successful ... [and] Ratanakiri was to become one of the first "liberated zones" of Cambodia.[36]

This broad picture of the security situation includes four actors: the highlanders, the FARK, the VC and the KR; but our anthropologist totally ignores the presence of Pol Pot (Ta Pouk at the time) and his KR crew, together with locally recruited members of his revolutionary army. She ignores too that Pol Pot decided to launch the violent armed revolution precisely in April 1968, admittedly in Andoung Meas District, at the other end of the province, at least some 30 to 40 kilometres from Banlung. But her most important point is that, if the grand plans of the state plantation met with 'some difficulties with the local population' in its early stages (1960–1966), the violent rebellion only started in the spring of 1968, precisely when Pol Pot launched his grand revolution that was to sweep clean the entire territory, wiping out the traditional ways of life of both highland and lowland nationals.

Matras-Troubetzkoy completed the writing of her book in 1975, but an introduction added in March 1981 indicates that, while the mystery of the KR criminal regime had been largely exposed to the horrified world through Hanoi propaganda and the multiple testimonies of refugees, especially those who had flocked to Paris, she was totally ignorant of the fate of her dear Ratanakiri original inhabitants. She speculated that the KR 'have probably not spared the upland minorities any more than the population on the plains – if

---

36 Matras-Troubetzkoy, *Un Village en forêt*, p. 51.

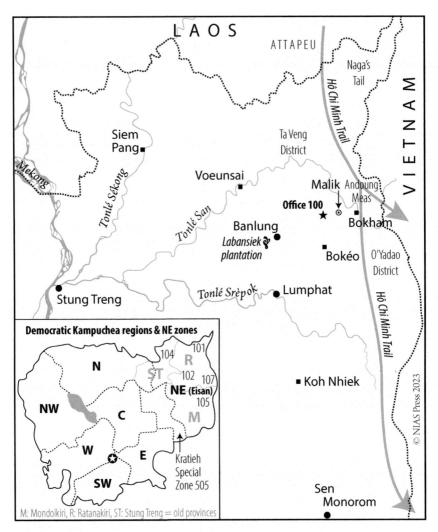

Map 4: Revolution and war in Ratanakiri Province

there are any left at all' (p. 27). Fortunately, these speculations were mostly not grounded in reality; the upland people were less the victims of KR ire than the lowland Khmers.

4 – The Khmer Rouge leadership settles in the province; the beginning of insecurity and the establishment of the totalitarian state, 1967–1970

Some form of opposition started as early as 1964, when the KR started its propaganda in the forest. They developed their theory of political struggle (*torsu noyobay*) and armed attacks against the FARK. Some were lowland Khmers, some Khmers from Vietnam, and some were KL themselves. The VC guerrillas were mixed with Khmers from South Vietnam. Then, a few Khmer revolutionaries arrived and attempted to 'educate' the people. They met the people on their slash-and-burn fields and tried to send them to study in the forest. They chose volunteers and people who were already marginal or had problems with society, or were very poor and hoped for a better future. They were gradually absorbed into the revolutionary groups. Contrary to popular belief, the KR rebellion against the FARK troops was not spontaneous because of land spoliations, but organized by the KR and led by Pol Pot and his group, once they had settled in the province.'

In his revolutionary training, Puy Yung was told that members of all ethnic minorities should learn to read and write Khmer, in order to know the history of the Khmers and to develop solidarity among all groups. They also needed to know the situation of each country in the world. Thus, they needed to be informed about the history of conflicts between peoples, classes and races, so that they knew who were the oppressed peoples and who were the oppressors: the rich oppress the poor. If there had been no oppression, there would have been no revolution. As Puy Yung explains:

> If you want to put an end to wars, you must abolish the poor classes. Long live communism – the shining light of the world! Bong Pouk [Pol Pot] was a very good speaker; what he said was very deep; his policies were excellent: all ethnic groups must collaborate with the Khmers and the Chinese. Thereafter, there would be no classes anymore. His character was very mysterious and secret: when he did something very cruel, no one could guess it. All ethnic groups thought he was a good leader. Everyone followed him like cattle – even teachers and intellectuals.
>
> There were also military trainers, mainly Vietnamese. At the time, Ta Pouk held absolute sway over the Party. He was in contact only with Sino-Khmers around him, there were no Chinese experts. Since 1960, there

was a secret Party organization to oppose capitalism. He went to China with his Sino-Khmer wife. Comrade Pouk had a Chinese private doctor.

When Saloth Sâr arrived in Ratanakiri in 1967, Puy Yung took part in the construction of his secret base, Office (*Munthi*) 100. It was surrounded with trenches and bamboo spikes at the bottom, and mines all around. A number of huts were constructed inside the perimeter: one for resting, a kitchen, and others for meetings. This was the typical base. Ta Pouk's office was made of bamboo and not wooden planks. It was the holy of holies and called 'the secret place'. The entrance was on one side and, diametrically opposed, an emergency exit would enable him to escape. He was surrounded with some thirty bodyguards close by.

Bong Pouk said he could write on a bamboo table. What was important was to attack Sihanouk, Lon Nol and the Americans, and he attacked them with papers, figures, dossiers and books. In actual fact, this was perfectly efficient, as the KR were to triumph not only on the ground in 1975, but their misleading propaganda also spread round the world: they were winning the diplomatic and psychological warfare with international opinion and townspeople alike, and everyone was expecting socialism with a human face. Saloth Sâr had a lot of documentation. Puy Yung had to read two centemetres of documents before being promoted to commandant in the KR army. They described the history of Cambodia in the world, and class conflicts, and instructions about how to conduct a war that would end all those conflicts. This war included three components: the people's war; the guerrilla war where you are lurking in expectation of the enemy; and the strategic war. If we did not put an end to the class struggle, each class oppression would become worse and so conflicts too. In those years, Comrade Pouk had identified the classes, and he identified each ethnic group and its leaders. And he showed that in this class war, Khmers would kill Khmers and Jaraï would kill Jaraï. Puy Yung had become 'a *kamaphibal* trainer of *kamaphibal*', an apparatchik trainer of apparatchiks.

Ta Pouk required a base in the forest, about five kilometres from Bokéo and about 15 kms from the airfield. People were not allowed to see exactly where his base was, but it was quite large, with KL as guards and cordons of soldiers who prohibited anyone from coming near. There were barracks all around – some 1,000 soldiers in all. The base was settled in a very dense forest at Phnom Ban Lay (or Ban Loy) on the border of O'Chum, Bokéo and Andoung Meas districts. One could not see anything and there was not even a generator. Ta Pouk and his group left the area soon after the fall of Sihanouk, when the province was 'liberated' and the Republican forces left Ratanakiri.

There were VC, and PAVN from the North, Centre and South. People had to speak Khmer, Jaraï and Vietnamese. Ta Pouk was always moved about in a hammock. The Bokéo airfield was not operational. Khieu Ponnary was there, with her angular face. Her sister Khieu Thirith gave Khmer lessons. Messengers delivered Ta Pouk's directives to the villages. He was travelling more and more to give ideological trainings here and there, typically with ten to twenty people in his entourage. Village chiefs were told in advance, and they had to supply food. He had five bodyguards close to him, Jaraï, Tampuon and Sino-Khmers. He chose some youths to be his confidants. They had AK-47s, and B-40 rocket launchers. Ta Van (Ieng Sary) was usually with him, together with Kham (Son Sen, aka Khieu after 1970). Ta Pouk was in charge of the Party; Van, first in charge of information and education, and later foreign affairs; Kham (Son Sen), in charge of the army. Ta Pouk always required boiled drinking water and would want lukewarm water to wash. He used mainly the hammock when he was tired or when he had fever, like Van. Tiv Ol[37] taught Khmer to Puy Yung, and he taught very clearly.

The KR started to purge the Khmer Hanoi returning from the DRV – those who had gone to northern Vietnam after the Geneva Conference in 1954 – in the early 1970s after the leadership had left the zone. It is not impossible that up to 300 were assassinated in Ratanakiri.[38] Recommendations were the following:

1 – Be on the lookout and observe from a distance;

2 – Be on the lookout during work;

3 – Be on the lookout according to the *provoatterup* (the autobiography)

People had to rewrite their autobiographies every month. Thus, Ta Pouk's collaborators were constantly under surveillance. If someone behaved suspiciously, Ta Pouk would order him to be executed, or to be arrested and sent

---

37 Tiv Ol (1933–1977), killed at S–21 in 1977, was by profession a teacher of Khmer language and literature at Sisowath High School. He wrote a book to teach the Khmer language to foreigners, which he then used to teach revolutionaries after fleeing into the *maquis* for fear of arrest in 1967.

38 Suong Sikœun was the last to leave Hanoi, where he was a producer for FUNK radio, in 1975. Ieng Sary asked him to incinerate whole crates of autobiographies, so that the identities and memories of those first KR victims would disappear forever. This has proved very important, as much of the history of the Khmer-Hanoi could have thus been lost.

elsewhere. This was the job of special units: *domruet kapir santesokh* (militia to maintain security) and *boh samat phtei knong* (militia to clean (the Party) from the inside). People were not classified as pro-Vietnamese communists or not, but according to a single criterion: either you agree to blindly follow orders from *Angkar*, or you do not. Those 'purifiers' were presented as the *Krosung Mohaptey*, staff of the Ministry of the Interior. During interrogations, the suspect was asked about his father: was he from the police? Was he alive or dead? Did he work for the Khmer-Issarak?[39] You were expected to write pages and pages, along with the names of accomplices or associates, who would then be placed under surveillance from a distance. Saloth Sâr made all decisions, below him there were the district chiefs, and then the commune chiefs. Some used the system to solve personal conflicts. There were secret detention centres, places to learn (*rien*), and places to train (*bompoan*). Real prisons were established with wooden shackles (*khnoh*). Some were found not guilty and released. From 1970, the prison system was developed and became a branch of the army. Victims had their throat slit or were beaten to death, or were shot. Before that, captured Lon Nol soldiers would be interrogated. Atrocities were also committed by Sihanouk's troops before they left the province in 1970.

According to another witness, Phoung Pheav,[40] a *Khmer Lœu* (KL) who ran away from the *maquis* or was tempted to go back his village would be 'criticized' and re-educated. If the case was more serious, they would be taken for *kosang khluon* (to rebuild oneself) very far in the forest, never to come back. More terrifying, the KR exposed tied victims being beaten and tortured in front of others. So, the indigenous people were terrorized by the KR leaders. Indeed, the KL were very scared of the *chhlop* (local militia) and the *santesokh* (security). The main prison of Ratanakiri Province was established in Banlung, the geographical centre of the province. One security chief, the Tampuon Kham Vieng, was very cruel. When the population saw his Land Rover in an area, they knew people would die.[41]

Another witness, Nap Bun Heng[42] arrived in the province in 1963 from the lowlands with his father, who was a mechanic in the FARK. Insecurity

---

39 The Khmer-Issarak were non-communist independentce activists who were mainly affiliated with the Thais.

40 Interviewed in Banlung on 8 January 1994, born in 1960, Krœung, President of the KL Association. Community leader and local judge.

41 Sara Colm makes documents this in *The Highland Minorities and the Khmer Rouge*.

42 Born in 1954, he was cabinet chief of the province at the time of the interview, on 8 January 1994.

started against the authorities in 1967. He was in Lumphat from 1967 to 1970 and 'liberation' forces arrived there just after the fall of Sihanouk. They were a mixture of Vietnamese and KR. This was when the new Republican soldiers regrouped at Bokeo, after many soldiers had been killed at Lumphat airport. There was an ambush on the way and the Republican army had to abandon Banlung in 1970. Nap Bun Heng then lived for two months in Koun Mom District[43] before going back to Labansiek, as his father had been killed in an accident in 1968 and his mother was doing some trading.

During the KR regime, there were many KL among the KR – *kamaphibal* and *yothea*. They were all very cruel because they were very ignorant. They blindly obeyed the Party (*smoh trang Angkar*); the lowland Khmers leaders called them very faithful. Banlung's large prison held hundreds of inmates. The director was Maou Hat. But the majority of 'delinquents' in the eyes of the regime were sent to a very harsh labour camp at O'Kveh, mainly in the case of the families of ex-soldiers or policemen of the Republican regime: 20 per cent died and the rest were released in 1979.

Another witness connected with Banlung prison was Nhiang Bun Him.[44] He first entered the province in 1966, to work at the Labansiek State Rubber Plantation. Nhiang Bun Him remained in the province under DK and was imprisoned at Banlung prison for one month. As early as 1968, the Phnom Penh authorities had started to be confronted with insecurity in the forest. The KL used poisoned crossbows, as they had no rifles at first. This is how the rebellion against the government started. After 18 March 1970, Vietnam-supplied portraits of Sihanouk were distributed and hung up in all houses. The Phnom Penh regime first reacted by dropping pamphlets from aircraft. The Republic could never extend its authority over the province. Most of the KR soldiers were of tribal origin and all the leaders were lowland Khmers, headed by Hu Nim.[45] Hu Nim was based in Office 21, some 30 to 40 km upstream from Lumphat, on the Tonlé Srèpok. His primary role was to do

---

43 Kon Mum district is situated in the western part of Ratanakiri, adjacent to Stung Treng province and along the Tonlé Srèpok.

44 Born in 1947 in Takeo province and living in Ratanakiri since 1966, Nhiang Bun Him oversaw religious affairs at the Sala Khet at the time of the interview, on 10 January 1994.

45 Hu Nim (1932–1977) was one of the so-called 'Three Ghosts' – with Khieu Samphân and Hou Yuon – all Secretaries of State under the *Sangkum*. They left the capital in 1967 to escape government repression. Hu Nim obtained a BA in Law in Paris in 1957 and a doctorate in Phnom Penh in 1966. A Minister of Information and Propaganda under DK, he was to be arrested in 1977 and sent to S–21. His long confession was translated into English and published in *Pol*

political propaganda. He is the one who distributed photographs of Sihanouk everywhere. Hou Yuon[46] was also in the province, at Office 7, near the village of Svay Rieng on the Tonlé San. Koy Thuon arrived later.

During the civil war, Vietnamese troops mixed with the KL and lowland Khmers, always carrying Sihanouk's portraits.[47] By 1973, the Vietnamese had left the territory. Nhiang Bun Him carried messages, always on foot, covering 30–40 km a day from Office 21 to Office 22 and Office 32 in Trapeang Chrey, Koun Mom District. When in Koun Mom District, he would eat and stay with his adoptive mother. He did not meet Hu Nim often, as there were relays between the Offices. He would meet him during meetings. The Office did not consist of houses but were just under the trees in order to remain hidden from planes. The soil had been cleared and swept. He followed a six-month political training session that combined attending seminars with doing manual work like building houses or breaking up stones. There were daily self- and mutual-criticism sessions, and he was continuously warned that he must shed his old-fashioned mentality. His group of 37 men was a mixture of lowland Khmers, KL and Lao.

Nhiang Bun Him was arrested in March 1974 at Trapeang Chrey. He and another person, a Lao, were accused of being *Khmer Sâr*.[48] He did not know such a group existed. He was at Trapeang Chrey at the time, teaching the KL how to grow wet rice.[49] The KL did not like to have to make ploughs to till the plain of the Srèpok valley, near Lumphat. He was arrested at 3:00 pm along with another person, a Lao. Their hands were tied behind their backs as they walked to Banlung, sleeping one night along the way. He had no shoes. He saw three soldiers in front of him, but had no idea how many were behind.

Pot Plans the Future, translated and edited by David Chandler, Ben Kiernan and Chantou Boua. Yale University Press, 1988, pp. 227–317.

46 Hou Yuon (1930–1976), one of the so-called 'ghosts', studied in Paris from 1949 to 1955 and obtained a doctorate in economics. A supporter of establishing 'cooperatives' created by the farmer-cooperators themselves, he objected to *Angkar*'s conception of collectives organized by the regime's centre and to forced ruralization and the abolishment of markets and money. This is why, after the fall of Phnom Penh on 17 April 1975, he was not allowed to join the leadership in the capital and was posted to the B–20 re-education camp in Stung Trang district, Kompong Cham Province, from where he disappeared in 1976.

47 As they did throughout the country at the time.

48 Literally 'White Khmers', *Khmer Sâr* were of right-wing (non-revolutionary) political persuasion. They were anti-Lon Nol fighters trained by the PAVN.

49 The KR sought to abolish the dry *chamkar* (field) rice of the *Khmer Lœu* in favour of the wet (paddy) rice of the lowland Khmers along valleys and *veal* (marshy areas) adjoining the plateau.

Banlung prison was built of timber, with woven slit-bamboo walls. There were three large shacks and three small ones for the guards. Nhiang Bun Him was shut into a small hut with wooden *khnoh* locked by an iron bar and a padlock. The Lao man was in another hut. He was left alone for three days with very little food and no possibility to shower. At night, two 16-year-old guards in a hammock dropped cigarette ashes on him. He was later interrogated, asked about his family origin and standard of education. He never really answered the truth; he said he had come to Trapeang Chrey with other people from Takeo.

After seven days in shackles, he was freed in the daytime to carry water to boil cassava. He could not look around the prison and only used the path between the river and the kitchen, where he prepared food for about 20 people. He heard no noise but was told the place of execution was 100 to 300 metres from the prison. He was released at the end of the month, but he did not know what happened to the Lao man, who remained. They met again in 1979, but have not seen each other since then.

Under the ten years of KR rule, provinces had been abolished and administration proceeded on the basis of large regional divisions, each divided into sectors. The *Eisan* (or Northeast) region included the whole of Ratanakiri Province (sectors 101, 102 and 107), the left bank of Stung Treng Province (sector 104), and the entire Mondolkiri Province (sector 105). Banlung prison was Ratanakiri's main prison, but those *Angkar* viewed as serious offenders were sent on to S–21 in Phnom Penh, the apex of the DK prison network. Toch Vannarith, an ECCC researcher who made lists of S–21 victims, identified some 40 who originated from sectors 101, 102, 104 and 107, most of whom were political commissars or officers in the RAK and lowland Khmers – not indigenous people. The most well-known was Ney Sarann (revolutionary name Ta Ya) who was secretary of the Northeast region when he was arrested in September 1976. Repression and arrests in nearby Mondolkiri (sector 105) seem to have been much more sweeping. We know that virtually all of those were civilian or military officials of the regime, but the Tuol Sleng museum archives organizing system does not enable us to identify those who were from the ethnic minorities. Still, Toch Vannarith managed to identify three Jaraï: យិង, Ying, ភំ Phum and ម៉ាត, Matt. No trace of their confessions or interrogation records have been spotted in the ocean of Tuol Sleng archives that have been digitalized and classified for researchers.

Beyond arrests and executions, two *Angkar* policies antagonized the indigenous people: collectivization, which started to be enforced in 1973, and purges aimed at everyone associated with the Vietnamese. Two of Muoy Chhœum's elder brothers were killed by the KR. One was the secretary of a commune in Ta Veng District. When the people's communes were created, Muoy Chhœum stated that people's communes should never have been created in the first place. But Ieng Sary replied: 'We must do as in China!' Muoy Chhœum pointed out that people did not have enough to eat in the canteens and that food was not tasty enough. Work was too harsh, food insufficient and people complained a lot. Ieng Sary replied: 'It is because of Vietnamese and Lao spies!' Then, Ieng Sary started to massacre the people. He sent messengers to spy on and watch the people in the communes. Those who complained were reported to the leaders. In Ta Mak village, protesters were captured and killed at every hour of the day: after an evening meeting, or even when they went fishing. Many were killed in this way. We were far from the platform of the Indochinese Communist Party when it all began.

This 1967–1970 section can also be illustrated by the testimony of Chheang Ngoy,[50] a Brao who lived in Ta Veng District at the time. The Khmer-Issarak were gentle in comparison to the KR, who were cruel. Sihanouk had arranged to bring a lot of rice to the Vietnamese communist combatants in the region. Chheang Ngoy entered the liberation movement in 1968. His village was a VC military base 20 km from the Vietnamese border and rich with VC military activity. In 1970, the Americans bombed the region massively. Fortunately, everyone was in trenches and only two persons from his village got killed because a bomb fell in their trench. Nonetheless, fear drove Chheng Ngoy further inside the territory, towards O'Kampha.

Chheang Ngoy often met Van (Ieng Sary) when he had settled in the Jaraï villages of Khayuch, Ngong, Hay, Horlœk, Phum, Ta Lav, and Ta Norg, south of Road 19 leading to Vietnam. From 1967, Chheang Ngoy met Pouk, Van, and Kham (Son Sen) at various meetings and training sessions. Van spoke during the visit of a certain Oum Samin, a Khmer Hanoi popular with the tribal people. He was fat, his skin fairer than most, with a very broad forehead. That was the time when the KR leadership was appointing district and commune leaders in Bokéo and Ta Veng districts. They also established militia groups (*kong chhlop*) for every village – a few joined on a voluntary

---

50 Born in 1934, interviewed on 12 January 1994.

basis. Revolutionaries in each village and commune also had to create an assault group.

People asked, 'Why must we struggle against anti-revolutionary Cambodians? Who are they?' The answer was clear: 'They are the civil servants appointed by the government. You must kill them. You must kill all village chiefs who do not come from the people.' The KL wondered: 'You said you wanted to create a fair society. So, why do you now want to establish military forces and start a war?' Ieng Sary answered disdainfully: 'You do not know much. We have to struggle. In the future, you will see good things.'

After that meeting, some participants had no will to launch attacks. That is when the KR started to eliminate tribal people who had avoided working for the revolution. They were said to have betrayed the revolution; hence, they needed to be eliminated. This is also when fortified villages (*phum proyut*) were created: the population was required to dig holes with sharpened bamboo at the bottom, and the villages were surrounded with booby-trapped trenches. KL were instructed to use crossbows and machetes, but not yet rifles.

Chheang Ngoy was appointed chief of Tbong commune in Ta Veng District, on the banks of the Tonlé San. He attended another meeting with Comrades (*Sammit*) Pouk and Van. They developed their propaganda to mobilize the KL. They spoke about solidarity and the need to develop the economy and to fight against enemies. From 1968, the murder of 'enemies' began – one or two per village, 'because they were not honest'. This coincided with an intensification of American bombings, from the border to Vœunsay.

In 1970, his group went to the Vietnamese border to welcome Ta Pouk on his return from a secret visit to Beijing where he had, with Zhou Enlai and Pham Van Dong, the long-time prime minister of North Vietnam, managed to persuade Sihanouk to join the rebellion and be the flag bearer of the revolutionary communist guerrilla movement. Pol Pot's white-haired wife already looked very aged, but she would walk; her younger sister, Ieng Sary's wife, insisted on being transported in a hammock. Their bodyguards were Jaraï and Tampuon because they were very dependable; they did not trust the lowland Khmers. They then crossed the forest north of Bokéo in the direction of Vœunsay, but they did not really know where they were going.[51]

---

51 This might have been the beginning of Pol Pot's 'Long March' to Stung Chinit, his base for most of the civil war, on the border between Kompong Cham and Kompong Thom.

From 1973, all who were accused of having relations with Vietnam were massacred. From 1968 to 1972, five villages escaped to Vietnam, where they hid in the forest for three months. Chheang Ngoy ran away with his family at the end of 1972. In the meantime, three of his children died and he had only one left. In total, 2,000 Brao from west Ta Veng ran away to take refuge in Vietnam. Some stayed in Cambodia and some of these joined the KR army, especially young people; others were executed.

A number of witnesses met Saloth Sâr and Ieng Sary, including Mum Kham Sœun.[52] Sary's physical appearance contrasted sharply with the local population: he stood out with his high stature, his fair complexion and his broad forehead. From July 1969, Mum Kham Sœun, a Tampuon, received four months of medical training near the Vietnamese border. The purpose was to teach how to treat the wounded in the forest. The trainers were Chinese who could speak Khmer or Vietnamese who used interpreters. Half of the eighty trainees were women.

Among the KR leaders, besides Saloth Sâr and his wife Khieu Ponnary, and Ieng Sary whom everyone knew, there was Hu Nim, the de facto propaganda minister. He led revolutionary troops along the Tonlé Srèpok, up from Lumphat, from his base at Office 21. He is the one, for instance, who distributed portraits of Sihanouk that were held aloft everywhere by all combatants, even the Vietnamese. Hou Yuon was also seen in the province. Ieng Sary's wife, Thirith, was in charge of ideological training. 'She spoke very clearly and her political views seemed very apt', explaining the importance of the revolutionary frame of mind, and to honestly focus on work and good discipline as regards *Angkar*. She alluded to the doctrine of Mao Zedong, including the necessity to be as straight as a needle. Combatants needed to brave all difficulties, even if they had nothing to eat and struggled ceaselessly. Mum Kham Sœun became convinced that his village would develop and the standard of living would rise in the future.

But later, after returning to his village, he realized Saloth Sâr monopolized all power and there was a lot of repression. He understood the KR were lying: first they called the Vietnamese very close friends, but later sought to eliminate them. From 1973, collectivization became stricter and the new authorities wanted to kill the local civil servants. Lowland Khmers wanted to teach the KL how to plough the land and grow wet rice; but they failed. They were not

---

52   He was born in 1942 and interviewed at Ta Veng on 13 January 1994.

victims of American bombings, for they were near the border. Mum Kham Sœun therefore escaped to Laos and remained there until 1980.

5– The departure of the top KR leadership and the civil war: 1970–1975 many KL escape

At the time, a general relocation among the indigenous people occurred as people defected from Cambodia and took refuge with their individual tribes in Vietnam or Laos. Martin Rathie details this phenomenon in his ground-breaking 'Lao links and Khmer Revolution':

> The removal of Ney Sarann from North-eastern Cambodia in 1973/74 resulted in a breakdown of local KR support as new lowland cadres, such as Son Sen's brother Nikân, enforced CPK policy more strictly on the indigenous community and overtly criticized the Vietnamese as evil parasites. This resulted in groups of Khmer Lœu and ethnic Lao, led by figures such as Bou Thang (Tampuon), Seuy Keo (Krâchok), Bun Mi (Brao) and Nou Beng (Lao), fleeing to Vietnam and Laos. They later became the new leaders of the People's Republic of Kampuchea (PRK) due to their privileged status with the Vietnamese, which was cultivated during their time in exile. Bou Thang became Defence Minister in the PRK and Seuy Keo his deputy. Nou Beng became the PRK's health minister, but fell from grace after being caught trafficking opium.

Simultaneously, *Angkar* was forcing the relocation of villages on the rich basaltic plateau in an attempt to force the Montagnards to abandon their swidden agriculture in favour of *chamkar* (ploughed fields outside the forest) in closer proximity to the river valleys and the plains, where they could cultivate wet rice. This aroused the anger of the inhabitants, including Muoy Chhœum,[53] who escaped to Vietnam with 30 armed soldiers on 10 March 1975, and remained there from 1975 until 1979. Muoy Chhœum first returned from Vietnam alone in 1979, then brought back his entire family in 1980.

Life was both less dangerous and quieter in Vietnam. The bombings had ceased. The local Jaraï population welcomed them warmly and there was land and food. In 1976, an entire village, some 400 people, managed to cross the dense jungle border. Only four were killed by the KR on the way. It was virtually impossible for single individuals to escape. In all, in Ta Veng District

---

53 See his biography above, pages 238–239, 252.

alone, some 2,000 people took refuge in Vietnam and 4,000 in Laos. In May 1975, Bun Mi (born in 1920), after an exploratory trip to Laos, returned home to convince some 4,000 from about thirty villages to run away to Laos.

However, all was not for the best for the hill tribes over the border in Vietnam. Phor Bupon Nuong,[54] a Jaraï, spent the DK years from 1975 to 1980 in a prison, for he had been a trainer in the *Front Uni de Lutte des Races Opprimées*[55] (FULRO) from 1972 to 1975. After the communist victory in Saigon, he was imprisoned with 200 KL and 800 Vietnamese, and was submitted to propaganda and learning the political theories of Marx and Hô Chi Minh. Some five per cent died in prison.

When the entire region was 'liberated' in 1970 and abandoned by the young Republic in Phnom Penh, solidarity groups were created, and then people's communes in 1973. Most of the population of the province was collected into the plains and the valleys of the Tonlé San and Tonlé Srèpok, where they were formed into collectives arranged in large rectangles. Dwelling huts were lined up in two long, parallel rows that ran hundreds of meters. A rice field could be planted in the centre, but cassava was more common. Rice was 'for the Chinese'. The big commune chief was a Jaraï and his deputy a Tampuon. There were many *chhlop*, up to thirty. Women and children were in good health and mothers had babies. There were lots of very good Chinese pharmaceuticals that protected the population well.

The leaders were not too cruel, for they were fellow tribesmen. But if you complained and said you were hungry or tired, you were killed. Banlung prison was for the military cadres and Party apparatchiks, and there were iron shackles. Ordinary inhabitants were just executed – ten to thirty victims per people's commune. The troops of indigenous or Khmer origin fought against the Republic alongside the Vietnamese until 1973, when the VC fighters were expelled from the province.

According to Tinh Thon,[56] three months after the dismissal of Sihanouk in 1970, Americans transferred a battalion of Republican forces and a fair proportion of the population – 300 to 400 families – from Bokéo District to Vietnam. They were first taken to Pleiku, and then to Phnom Penh by boat through Can Tho. Tinh Thon, who was partner to the journey, stayed one year

---

54 Born in 1945 and interviewed on 10 January 1994 in Bokéo district.

55 Anti-communist movement of Montagnards, supported by the US and active from 1964 to 1992.

56 Tinh Thon was born in 1952 and interviewed on 14 January 1994.

in Phnom Penh, Chak Angrae District, near the Old Stadium. There were a few Jaraï and Tampuon, but mainly Lao and Khmers. Then, they were all taken by coach to Pailin in Battambang province, again under the responsibility of Americans, in early 1971.

More than 300 of the families were settled at the village of O'Lach. Everything was fine, for there were coconuts, mango trees and two coffee plantations. There were no KR at all until 1975, after the fall of Phnom Penh. Then, officer Hul Thon, in charge of Pailin, took the entire population to Thailand. The KR installed loudspeakers on the border and urged the population to return and serve their country. Some came back, including Tinh Thon. Many did not and are now in France or America. Of the 300 families, only about 30 have come back to Bokéo.

After one night in Pailin town, Tinh Thon and the other returnees were displaced to Sala Krau, a commune in Pailin district. Then a voice in a loudspeaker required all army officers to go and welcome Sihanouk. That first purge killed about 170 from the group. Some of the victims were Kola, a Burmese minority from Pailin, dealers of precious stones.[57] But that was still too close to the border and some of Hul Thon and In Tam's[58] troops successfully made incursions, gathered some inhabitants and guided them to Thailand. This is why the KR moved those who remained further inland, to Bavel District in Battambang province, where they stayed throughout the DK regime. They started communal eating in early 1976, but there was not enough food. They all had been categorized as 'new people' or '17th April people' and, as such, were a low priority. To terrorize them, they were forced to witness executions by shooting or slitting stomachs open. The victims had been accused of being Lon Nol soldiers, although they had never been.

Later in the regime, Ta Mœnak, Ta Meang, Ta Ham, and Ta Hep were local *kamaphibal*. In 1978, they were all killed when the *Nirdey*[59] arrived during the dry season (early in the year). They were all taken away in a truck, including Neary Oeun, a female *kamaphibal* who always carried both a pistol and a

---

57 A Kola named Phé, now a French citizen, told me in 2022 that that most managed to run away to Thailand in the early days of the revolutionary regime.

58 In Tam (1916–2006), a founding member of the Democratic Party and an opponent to Sihanouk, was prime minister from May–December 1973. After the fall of the Republic, he started an anti-KR resistance group from Thailand, but soon had to cease all activities, as he lacked the full support of the Thais. They asked him to leave Thailand.

59 The *Nirdey* were KR cadres from the Southwest region under the leadership of Ta Mok. They were notorious for their savagery and their utter loyalty to Pol Pot.

rifle. After that, people were no longer killed, except those accused of having collaborated with the Vietnamese. The people had enough food to eat and could again survive.

There were two resistance groups at the Thai border. One was the White Khmers with Hul Thon and In Tam, the other one was made up of the troops of Sak Sutsakhan.[60] They stole food like cattle and poultry at night to survive, and, when they penetrated into villages, they took away the population. Once, they managed to take the entire village. The KR were afraid of their mortars, but they were too weak to really threaten the KR. When the Vietnamese arrived, the KR ran away. Then, they came back to kill the people when there were no Vietnamese. Tinh Thon went to Battambang and Sisophon with his family where he stayed one year. Later, he returned to Ratanakiri.

Muong Poy,[61] (ម៉ួង ប៉ូយ) a member of the Brao minority born near Vœunsay, joined the 'struggle zone' (*dambon torsu*) in 1968 and was chosen to practise traditional medicine. There was one medic per village, that is, nine men and three women for twelve villages. Unlike most ethnic minorities, he had already benefitted from five years of primary schooling at Vœunsay during the *Sangkum* from 1965 to 1970, while he was a young man, from 20 to 25 years. The KR had required that he identify who, among the older pupils, could become militiamen (*chhlop*). He was also asked to collect information on the movements of Sihanouk's soldiers along the Tonlé San near Vœunsay.

The medical training lasted two months during the rainy season and they were initiated to the knowledge of plants to cure diseases. Trainees were all from ethnic minorities and a few Lao, while the trainers were lowland Khmers. They were taught to make what the Khmers derisively call 'rabbit droppings': concoctions of chopped leaves, roots and rice, formed into small balls. They were effective against fevers or diarrhoea. Families accompanied patients – contrary to what would happen later in the rest of Cambodia. There was also an ideological training to the revolution, as it was necessary to help the people to save the country from capitalist exploitation.

---

60 Sak Sutsakhan (1928–1994) was a career military officer who rose to become minister of defence in 1957, when he was 29 years old. In 1975, he became the Republic's last head of state. He escaped with his family in an army helicopter at 8.30 am on 17 April, flying from the Olympic Stadium to Kompong Thom, then on to Sisophon and, next morning, to Utapao air base in Thailand. His memoirs, *The Khmer Republic at War and the Final Collapse*, were published by the U.S. Army Center of Military History, in 1978.

61 Born in 1945 and interviewed on 8 January 1994 at Banlung, where he was a provincial civil servant.

In 1972, Muong Poy was asked to transport rice for the VC along the Mekong and Tonlé San waterways, a branch of the Hô Chi Minh Trail; this task was abruptly stopped because of a quarrel with the Vietnamese. It was also the time when individual plots were banned and communal meals instituted. Slash-and-burn agriculture was suppressed and flooded rice had to be cultivated, Khmer-style. Food shortages and the lack of rice and salt affected the people, and they began to complain. One day, a man complained to the commune management about eating too much cassava, considered then as food for pigs. Shortly afterwards, a militiaman's arrow struck him in the fields. He died on the spot. *Angkar* sent one of Muong Poy's Brao uncles to Laos to persuade members of his ethnic group to join the revolution. Nobody came back; he was then accused of pushing the residents to flee to Laos, taken to rehabilitation (*rien sot*) and never seen again. Another of his brothers was wounded by an arrow and drowned in the Tonlé San.

In 1974, Vœunsay's elegant, Lao-style wood houses were dismantled and the old planks were used to build three collective long houses: one for men, one for women and one for children up to twelve years. Strict collectivization was imposed earlier than in the rest of the country. In the meantime, everything was done to annihilate the traditional way of life; the past had to be wiped out.

This march towards collectivization in the early 1970s was therefore not at all to the liking of many Montagnards. Thus, a large part of the population of Ta Veng District (Tampuon, Krœung, Brao), in the extreme north of the province, two to three thousand people, he said, decided, in April 1974, to run away to Vietnam with more than two hundred rifles, following a branch of the Hô Chi Minh Trail. The Vietnamese authorities asked them why they did so; they explained that the KR began executing the inhabitants and forcing them into collectives, while food (especially rice and salt) was starting to run out. The Vietnamese therefore created special camps for them, 30 or 40 kilometres from the border, where they had to learn Vietnamese, while practising their traditional farming and putting the children to school. Muong Poy married in Vietnam in 1977. From July 1978, the Vietnamese recruited among them some 400 volunteers to chase the KR in Cambodia. Thus, Muong Poy was able to return to his home country and go as far as Lumphat, Vœunsay and Stung Treng without having to fight, because the Vietnamese troops spearheaded the battle. He served primarily as an interpreter. At this time, the provincial capital was officially transferred from Lumphat to Banlung. But it must be also noted that the KR had moved their local centre of power, including 5,000 men at the Division 801 headquarters in Banlung, before late December 1978, when the Vietnamese soldiers en masse moved throughout Ratanakiri Province and then the entire northeast. Commander So Sarœun[62] had led the region since the arrest of Ney Sarann (alias Ta Ya) in September 1976.[63]

For Puy Yung, the break with the VC certainly took place in 1972. The argument was that when the forces against the Americans had gathered, they had to share the spoils. This was also the moment when the problem of borders arose. It was the time when Ta Pouk started to create problems with the Vietnamese and some Montagnards started to flee to Vietnam. Ta Pouk accused the Vietnamese of trying to attack them to weaken the Cambodian forces. When the Americans bombed Road No. 13 there were always one, two, or three victims. As for the victims among the fighters themselves, Puy Yung estimates that nearly 10 per cent were victims of American bombings: 32 civilians were killed in his commune. The worst case was a bomb dropped by a B-52 which fell directly into a trench, killing everyone there. The rule was one trench per family. An entire family perished.

Puy Yung participated in the Battle of Chenla II along the Phnom Penh – Siemreap Road, No. 6, but returned to Ratanakiri to protect the base and recruit new *kamaphibal* from 1972 to 1975. However, on 25 February 1975, Puy Yung organized the escape to Vietnam of 196 of his village's 254 residents. Families whose children had high positions with Pol Pot could not be notified, and this is why 58 residents were left behind. They fled because, first of all, they now understood that communist regimes killed people, that people were 'swept clean' (*boh sa'at*; purged), as it was said. In addition, the villages on the border were suspicious in the eyes of KR revolutionaries, because they had been influenced by the Vietnamese. Someone noticed that many KR soldiers had gone to the lowlands and there remained only the commune's militia. It was a good time to move. They had prepared for their flight carefully, with their cows and their buffaloes. They also took poultry and pigs on their backs; they had food and equipment. They walked day and night, but they got lost on the way and the trip lasted 13 days. There was no problem at the border

---

62 See Case 002-02 at the Extraordinary Chambers in the Courts of Cambodia (ECCC), Judgment (full).pdf, p. 1460, Sao Sarœun Division 801 Commander was in charge of Ratanakiri after the arrest and elimination of Ney Sarann (alias Ta Ya) and of O'Kanseng Banlung prison.

63 See the judgement of the ECCC, case – 00202, pp. 1452–1529.

and the Jaraï on the other side welcomed them very warmly in the province of Kon Tum.

In Vietnam, Puy Yung was granted Vietnamese citizenship and became a member of the Communist Party of Vietnam. Between 1975 and 1978, as far as he knew, there was no specific plot to overthrow Pol Pot. He was ordered to return to Cambodia after 1979. In 1983, he completed a six-month training course at the Hô Chi Minh School. Puy Yung was deputy governor of O'Yadao District until 1987. After that, he identified Cham roots in his past and converted to Islam, along with his entire village. He became a religious leader, cultivated a long, thin white beard, and changed his name to Puy Dueng Mohammat. He took up residence in Pake Village, Lum Chor Commune, O'Yadao District, along Highway No. 19 to the Vietnamese border.

On balance, a fair proportion of the Ratanakiri population fled the province to escape from the KR's totalitarian grip on society. This was the same, but on a much larger scale, in nearby Mondolkiri (Sector 105) where the revolutionary movement was almost unanimously rejected by the local indigenous people, mainly Bunong. According to my interviews with the local population in the summer of 1994, when I was travelling by elephant from Sen Monorom, the Mondolkiri provincial capital, to Banlung, I estimated that up to 40 per cent of the local population had taken refuge in Vietnam. To avoid losing all its workforce for their grand irrigation plans, the KR leadership transferred most of the population from the 1,000-metre plateau to the plain around Koh Nhiek, some fifty kilometres westwards from the Vietnamese border, where they were ordered to build a new provincial centre. It was complete with a large people's commune, a generator, a production centre for traditional medicines and a textile factory where *kromas* would be woven. Hundreds of victims were executed at the Sector 105 prison, located nearby at Phnom Kraol. A new road was built to join Koh Nhiek directly to Stung Treng on the Mekong, thus making the provincial capital, unlike Sen Monorom, accessible by Chinese trucks in all seasons.[64] According to Rochœm Tveng, Phi Phuon's brother, Puy Yung has moved again to Vietnam.

6 – People's communes in Ratanakiri, 1975–1978

The KR regime in Ratanakiri was, by and large, less deadly than in the rest of the country – some seven to eight per cent instead of the 25 per cent for the

---

64 See also Sara Colm *Khmer Rouge Purges in the Mondul Kiri Highlands*, with Sorya Sim, Documentation Series No. 14, Documentation Center of Cambodia, 2009.

country at large, as Marek Sliwinski demonstrated as early as 1995 and Sara Colm in 1996, a figure that tallies with all of the testimonies I gathered on this subject. If the way of life of the Montagnards was a model for the KR, the reverse is not really true: many Ratanakiri inhabitants suffered from the draconian lifestyle imposed by *Angkar*. The seasoned revolutionary Ney Sarann, alias Ta Ya, was re-appointed to oversee the northeast region. Like Koy Thuon in the North, he was known as a moderate, at least concerning economic policies and relations with the Big Brother, that is, Vietnam. A Vietnamese speaker himself, Ney Sarann was put in charge of border negotiations with the eastern neighbour, in O'Yadao District in particular.[65] Like most KR leaders on the eastern border who were aware of the infinitely superior military might of their brothers-in-arms, he thought negotiations were preferable to confrontations.

We have selected some of the most characteristic experiences, mostly from ethnic minorities, under DK in Ratanakiri. This smaller number of victims is confirmed by the testimony of former KL cadre Lay Bun San.[66] He tells that 24 of his village's 300 inhabitants disappeared and presumably died. This proportion, about eight per cent, is consistent with Sara Colm's estimate. Moreover, while food was somewhat insufficient, the population did not starve as in the rest of the country. Meat was served once or twice a month, which is better than anywhere else, except for big Party celebrations.

Hu Ly[67] (ហ៊ុ លី), the FUNCINPEC[68] representative in the district of Bokéo at the time of the interview, had no sympathy for the revolutionary movement and, moreover, was an 'immigrant': he came from the plains and cast a very different eye on the role of ethnic minorities in the KR revolution. He arrived in Ratanakiri in 1965 in the Sihanoukist army, which he left in 1969 and began to cultivate rice along the Tonlé Srèpok near Lumphat, and married a Tampuon. There was no KR presence, but the VC used the indigenous people as porters and messengers. A branch of the Hô Chi Minh Trail followed the river; rice was supplied to the VC this way. The *Khmer Rumdoh* (Khmer of the Liberation, as they called themselves) were very few at the time. When arrested by the *Sangkum* authorities, the KR were taken to Lumphat Prison and interrogated. The leaders were sent to Phnom Penh and the others were released. KR sol-

---

65 See Phi Phuon's autobiography, p. 88. The border in this district is still not fully settled up to this very day.

66 Interviewed in Banlung on 9 January 2009.

67 Born in 1942 and interviewed on 7 April 1994.

68 National United Front for an Independent, Neutral, Peaceful and Cooperative Cambodia, a Sihanoukist party that was founded in 1981.

diers began moving the population into the forest during 1967–1969, when government soldiers began to regroup in Banlung and Bokeo.

Once the KR controlled the situation, Hu Ly could hide rice and cook it at night. He had two children before 1975 and two after. Some people were arrested and executed after being interrogated. The big prison in Banlung was renamed T–1[69] in 1979 and was used by the Vietnamese. Some twenty kilometres upstream from Lumphat, a large dam was built during 1976–77 at Russey. Most of the KR were tribal men and they were very cruel, having been indoctrinated by *Angkar*. They killed with knives under the throat or in the stomach. Hu Ly`s disdain for both the revolution and the highland peoples is most evident in his claim that the KL entered the revolution because they were completely ignorant and had never been to school.

Heng Bunthan (បេង ប៊ុនថាន) was an ethnic Lao from Vœunsay[70] district who became a messenger at the age of 15–16, going as far as the districts of Bokéo and O'Yadao, along the Vietnamese border. The repression began very early, and some 150 tribal minorities in his district fell victim to the KR. He saw the royal visitors with his own eyes in March 1973, when Sihanouk and his wife Monique arrived from Laos on a branch of the Hô Chi Minh Trail, crossing the border into Siempang District. Blood trickled from Princess Monique's face; she had been scratched by a branch when she put her head out of her vehicle to look at the landscape. Was this when, as she recorded in her travel logbook, she was proud to have given her blood for the revolution? Shortly after this historical visit, the KR expelled not just all PAVN soldiers, but also drove the many Vietnamese civilians in the Tonlé San Valley down to Stung Treng. Those were workers or fishermen, and the event anticipated the banishment of the entire Vietnamese community after 17 April 1975.

Heng Bunthan confirmed that 'solidarity' groups were introduced in 1972, and collective housing and canteens in 1974. This was when those who were *not* considered 'honest' vis-à-vis the revolution disappeared. The KR dismantled the old Lao houses I had seen in Vœunsay in 1965, and used the materials to build new long dwellings, up to 30 or 40 meters and six to seven meters wide. There were two rows of beds with a passage in the middle. The sexes were separated and their relationships became extremely complicated. In case of 'fault', the sanctions were criticism, reform or even death. After

---

69 It was used as a code during the Vietnamese protectorate from 1979 to 1989 to designate prisons. T–3 was the ex-colonial prison in Phnom Penh, now dismantled.

70 Born in 1954 and interviewed on 9 January 1994.

17 April 1975, 'new people' from Stung Treng province arrived in Vœunsay. The largest and oldest houses were dismantled to build the canteens, and individual houses, all exactly the same, four metres by three, were built for the population. All ethnicities were mixed and 50 per cent were hill tribes. Marriages could only take place between couples of the same caste – 'old people' with 'old people' and 'new people' with 'new people'. Heng Bunthan was married in 1976, in a collective marriage ceremony for a dozen couples. From that union he had seven children – five girls and two boys – all alive at the time of interview. He estimates that out of a population of some 10,000 people in Vœunsay District, some 150 could have died, which corresponds to Sara Colm's estimate of a seven per cent extermination rate.[71] From that period, he only keeps most painful memories of separation, hunger, torture and massacre.

Nhiang Bun Him[72] was incorporated into a group of young mobile forces (*kong chalat*) sent to various construction sites. They rebuilt the bridge on the Srèpok on the road from Banlung to Stung Treng. If the work was hard, the food was plentiful. When Ta Van (Ieng Sary) came in 1977 to inaugurate the bridge, he was told about problems with the solidity of the concrete. The construction site manager wanted to execute everyone who had participated in the construction, but Ta Van disagreed and said that only the four building officials in charge should be punished. They were arrested and executed. Then, Ieng Sary led a three-day re-education seminar, explaining that the fundamental cause was Vietnamese spies who wanted to sabotage the construction. The years 1977 and 1978 were very hard and some disappeared.

In the village of Som Kaning in O'Yadao District, along the Vietnamese border, not far from Highway 19, we learn from Sol Yut,[73] a Jaraï born in 1942, that all the villages were relocated along rivers and lakes for flooded rice cultivation, and that swidden rice had to be abolished. Six or seven Jaraï villages had been regrouped to form a people's commune. The other notable development was a purge of Jaraï leaders during 1977–78, at the time of the attacks against Vietnam. Some were taken to Banlung prison and replaced by Tampuon.

The revolution began here in the sixties and, little by little, some Jaraï went as far as Phnom Penh. Before the arrival of the KR leaders, there was

---

71 *The Highland Minorities and the Khmer Rouge in Northeastern Cambodia: 1969–1979*, Documentation Center of Cambodia, Nov. 1995, p. 143.

72 Born in 1947 and interviewed in Banlung on 10 January 1994.

73 Interviewed on 10 April 1994.

no kind of rebellion on the part of the highlanders. The KR leaders came and made their speeches, explaining that this would be the beginning of a new era – communism – in which the KL would be at the top of society. The leaders also formed armed troops along the Vietnamese border, organizing people into different battalions: some in charge of security, others to attack, and finally some to patrol and lead the people's communes. Unlike the people of Ta Veng, no Jaraï escaped to Vietnam. First, it was very difficult to survive in the forest, but also, they would be spotted if they tried to move in daylight, and crossing at night was impossible because, all the way to Svay Rieng, the border had been extensively mined.

The Jaraï chief of the district, called Uncle Lav, was taken to Phnom Penh to be executed.[74] Ta Kham Vieng was a Tampuon chief and the main organizer of the massacres of those who were accused of being Vietnamese traitors. Some joined the KR and never returned after 1979. Some were arrested and never returned. There was a security centre in O'Yadao District; but it was in a house where detainees were temporarily held for a few days before being sent to Banlung. They were tied, but there were no shackles. On the other hand, they did not worry too much about their health, because there was a lot of Chinese medicines and a good hospital in Banlung with Chinese doctors, men and women. There were enough Chinese pharmaceuticals and no need for traditional ones. Chinese doctors even came to visit Sector 107 in O'Yadao.

Some members of ethnic minorities could be sent to Stung Treng Province with their families as military personnel to protect the airport. A certain Yaê[75] was in charge of distributing rice and salt in his people's commune, which numbered exactly 1,005 people. The rice ration worked out to one milk can per person, every second day. Cassava leaves, banana trunks and *kuech* (a wild tuber) were served, but no meat. They picked wild vegetables in the forest. Some died of exhaustion or illness, although there were a lot of Chinese medicines with inscriptions in Chinese. The village of Phum Troap Chas now has about 300 inhabitants. Under DK, there were 1,000 to 1,200, but the population did not receive enough food. Two or three warehouses were filled with rice, but it was carried away. People did not know where it was taken.

---

74 Uncle (*Om* ឪ in Khmer). As shall be seen below (p. 270), Phi Phuon's uncle, Ta Lav, committed suicide, probably in Phnom Penh itself, to avoid being sent to S–21. There are no archives at the Tuol Sleng Museum concerning him.

75 A Jaraï, born in 1939 and interviewed on 10 April 1994.

There was a dam (now demolished; it was planned to rebuild it to produce electricity) and a lake to grow flooded rice.

The people's commune consisted of two rows of houses for one or two families, about 50 houses in each row. Three or four Jaraï villages were amalgamated. There was a large communal kitchen with lots of pots, one for 60 people. Aside from rice (one milk tin for three people), cassava leaves, banana trunks and salt were added – no meat, no fish. There was no school, but they had a hospital where all the pharmaceuticals came from China. There were competent Jaraï nurses; when they gave the Chinese medicine, people were quickly cured.

Working began before dawn and continued until evening, mainly in the rice fields. At night there was a long meeting, two to three hours, to criticize those who were too sluggish at work and to praise the most ardent. Many people were killed, the lazy ones in particular. They were guarded by 10 soldiers, five KL and five Khmers from the plains. The leaders of the commune were Jaraï and they are still alive. After the overthrow of Sihanouk, the people's communes were small, but they grew massively from 1975. The population could not flee because there were soldiers everywhere. Only people near the Tonlé San could flee to Vietnam.

According to Sieu Ang,[76] people listened to revolutionary songs on the radio. The Jaraï language was used, not Khmer. The population managed to produce two crops, one during the rainy season and one in the dry season, three tons each time and therefore six tons a year. The rice surplus was put in boats during the rainy season and left in the warehouse to be transported to who-knows-where.

The KR kept moving the population inland and to Vœunsay. All the chiefs in the collectives, the districts, and Zone 107 were Jaraï. They were well-armed with AK–47s, R–15s and other weapons. There were arrests: a child who stole some cassava would be re-educated during the evening meetings. If he did it again, the father was killed. If there was a third offence, the mother was killed. The chiefs consulted each other about the culprits, who were taken elsewhere and disappeared. About 16 people were executed in Sieu Ang's commune. They were not driven elsewhere, but executed immediately in the forest. If you left your unit to fetch wood or even to relieve yourself, the militia followed you with a gun. When the Vietnamese arrived, the KR made the entire population

---

76   Born in 1956 and interviewed on 11 April 1994.

walk for seven nights to the Tonlé Srèpok, but when they saw Vietnamese soldiers on the banks of the river, all the KR fled, abandoning everybody. Special units guarding the border went into hiding.

Sieu Hang,[77] who carried latex by road to Vietnam, shared some information about the population in the surrounding villages. Many battalion leaders came from these villages. All men had joined the revolution, the army in particular, and few people were left in the villages. By early 1975, the KR had captured the cities of Siemreap, Kompong Thom and Phnom Penh. A large number of KL worked in Phnom Penh. The Jaraï were in charge of transporting weapons from Phnom Penh to the provinces; they were the trusted men of *Angkar*. If you go to these villages, the population will hide all this information. They all took part in many battles. This had been Pol Pot's base area for many years. Ancient revolutionaries like Bou Thang, Héng Samrin, and Chea Sim have been in the revolution since 1954. Bou Thang[78] belongs to the Tampuon clan. These villages fed Ta Pouk, Ieng Sary and others. His own younger sister is still married to a KR military leader who had been responsible for 300 soldiers. Sieu Hang went to Pailin in 1993 to convince her to return to Ratanakiri, but he failed.

Sieu Hang further states that, since the people here are very ignorant, they do not think for themselves, they cannot exercise their free will. You give them orders and they obey. In 1970, the same witness was in Kratieh province. When the VC arrived in 1970, when they invaded all over the country, they started by killing all the officials in the province. All young adults had to either join the army or cultivate rice fields or 'strategic' plants like maize and cassava, which they had to plant on slash-and-burn fields. All rice was produced on paddy flooded with dams and canals. They saw a lot of rice produced, but there were big trucks, Chinese Zils or GMC vehicles, that came to take it away. Irrigated paddy produced two harvests each year; unirrigated land was harvested only once.

Every evening, there was a meeting during which people talked about the difficulties encountered in the work and decided what should be done the next day. Those who were lazy were identified. People were warned twice

---

77 A Jaraï, born in 1950 and interviewed on 12 April 1994.

78 Bou Thang fled to Vietnam during DK. After 1979, he became a politician, serving as Chairman of the Senate Committee of the Interior and Defence (2012–2018). He belonged to the CPP and was elected in 2003 to represent Ratanakiri Province in the National Assembly of Cambodia. He died in 2019.

but, the third time, the slackers were taken to the forest with their hands tied behind their backs, one, two, and three per month. They were told that Ta Ya (Ney Sarann, leader of the Northeast region) had also been arrested; this was announced in a speech delivered by the head of the collective. He was accused of working with the Vietnamese and no one was to do the same thing. Nobody escaped to Vietnam because they did not know the way. Nobody loved life where everything was collectivized, and all had to agree to die in the villages.

Angkar chose marriage partners. If a couple did not get along, they were locked in a house until they got used to each other. The marriages were collective, but no alcohol was consumed and only one chicken was sacrificed. Still, they decorated the houses and sang traditional Jaraï songs and sentimental Khmer songs. For the occasion, they had electricity into the night.

There were three more-educated leaders – an ethnic Lao, a Jaraï and a lowland Khmer – and ten armed militiamen who were ordinary people from the village. They followed and spied on people at work every day. The children collected leaves that were put in a pot with water and everything was chopped up. Older people weaved cloth and watched buffaloes. There was a hospital in the area and enough medicine from China and America. The nurses were local Jaraï. One day, the Chinese came to film the houses and the people. They made a great documentary in which the indigenous people danced and played their traditional music on gongs; they even had them drink alcohol – the only time during the whole regime! – all that, in order to show the film abroad.[79]

After 17 April 1975, total collectivization was established in the people's communes. After the first harvest, at the end of the year and early in 1976, the whole village was moved down from the red soil plateau to the Srèpok valley. All slash-and-burn fields for rice cultivation were abandoned. Instead, flooded rice cultivation was developed thanks to a dam that allowed for two crops per year. No fewer than eight villages were combined: including Phum Tô, Phum Taang Muey, Phum Taang Pi, Phum Katieng, Phum Kom Plang, and Phum Tankap. *Angkar* also brought in 17 April people and Lao from Vœunsay, Phum Phon, and Phum Tiem. In all, thousands of people. All cooking utensils and pots were collectivized. All animals had to be given to the community, including elephants.

Construction of the concrete dam began on 6 February 1977 and was completed on 24 April 1978, using cement that came from the plant in Kam-

---

79   The film is now available at the Bophana audio-visual centre in Phnom Penh.

pot. Thousands upon thousands of people worked to build it, from the entire Sector 102. There were three lock gates; one was made narrower and narrower, as if the KR intended to install a turbine to produce electricity. The whole installation was abandoned during Héng Samrin's PRK regime (1979–1989).

There were enough pharmaceuticals that came from China. Once, Chinese experts came to visit, nine men in a Zil truck, none of them very young, but experienced. They were anthropologists, not doctors, interested in crossbows and arrows and other objects. There were also teachers, as early as 1972, who taught two hours in the morning and supervised the children's manual labour in the afternoon. They taught reading in Khmer and singing revolutionary songs. They sang the *L'Internationale* and the national anthems[80] and this is how the CPK showed the resplendent way to the future. But behind this somewhat idyllic vision of life under DK in the people's communes lay the grim reality of a fierce repression system totally manipulated from Phnom Penh and the central Party leadership. Banlung prison, which has been alluded to through a number of testimonies, is the best example of the totalitarian grip over the province.

7 – Banlung prison

Since the publication of the 2,268-page judgement of the second ECCC[81] trial of Nuon Chea and Khieu Samphân in April 2019 (coded 002-02), we have learned that Banlung prison was one of five prisons selected by the Tribunal for special attention. Some 77 pages concern Banlung prison, then called the O'Kanseng[82] Security Centre. The Tribunal had the means to carry out a much more thorough investigation of the institution than I had attempted a decade earlier. The information corroborates with mine and, not unexpectedly, provides a much fuller description. However, the investigating judges did not attempt to put Banlung prison into the context of the DK prison network; this was beyond their mandate, which was to connect the criminal activities

---

80 In the plural because there were two versions: one before and one after 1975. See Locard, *Pol Pot's Little Red Book*, pp. 38–40.

81 ECCC. The English version of the judgement can be found at www.eccc.gov.kh/en/document/court/case-00202-judgement.

82 I have slightly altered the transliteration into Latin script, as the Royal Academy of Cambodia has not yet produced an official table of transliteration of Khmer into Latin script. The Tribunal transliterates 'Au Kanseng', but the Khmer 'O' means 'stream' and the prison was indeed along the small stream of Banlung in which the inmates of the prison were allowed to bathe every day. The common transliteration of the name of a village situated along a small stream is 'O'.

perpetrated at O'Kanseng with the top leadership in Phnom Penh – and they have done that most convincingly. Nonetheless, providing a broader context will enable us to reassess some of their assertions.

To begin with, the Tribunal found that Banlung prison was created after the arrest of Ney Sarann in late 1976. This cannot be accurate, as I collected evidence it was already operating by March 1974, a year before the fall of Phnom Penh. In regions controlled by the guerrillas, strategic security centres to weed out 'traitors from within' had been established before the fateful 17 April 1975. O'Kanseng could have been one of those. What is certain is that the arrest of Ney Sarann led to a sweeping purge of cadres from the *Eisan* region, most locally, but top leaders met their fate at S–21. One of those could have been Phi Phuon's uncle, Poy Hlœun, alias Ta Lav, who married one of Phi Phuon's aunts, Rochœm Phjing. A Jaraï himself, Ta Lav had gradually climbed all the echelons of the revolutionary ladder to become Ney Sarann's deputy. Not unexpectedly, he too was summoned to a meeting in Phnom Penh, but knowing that this could mean torture and execution, he preferred to commit suicide in the region of Stung Treng on the way or even in Phnom Penh, but witness accounts vary. Later Sao Phœm, the *Bophea* Regional Secretary and longtime associate of Pol Pot, would make the same choice. In late 1978, even the highest cadres were faced with a choice between execution and suicide.[83]

The Tribunal benefitted immensely from its access to DK archives. The judges could see well-grounded evidence in the form of telegrams and notes from personal meetings that directly linked the local O'Kanseng Prison decision-makers to the top leadership, that is Pol Pot, Nuon Chea and Son Sen, the latter two in charge of the entire national prison system, together with Kaing Guek Iev (Duch) at S-21 – not to forget Khieu Samphân, one of the accused. These documents confirm the testimony of my interviewees: O'Kanseng was indeed reserved for DK cadres. Some of these cadres were civilians but most were military, as the province (like in *Sangkum* days) had fallen directly under military control after Ney Sarann's arrest. Division 801 and its three regiments, headquartered in Veunsai and with no less than 5,000 men commanded by So Sarœun, was responsible for controlling the border with Vietnam. It also had been ordered to root out all cadres – above all military – who were accused

---

83 Information collected from his nephew, Rochœm Tveng (born in 1945) on 15 April 2019 in Andoung Meas district, Ratanakiri province. This is why no trace of Ta Lav's confession could be found in the Tuol Sleng (S–21) archives. Suong Sikœun believes the suicide occurred in Phnom Penh itself.

of conspiring with the now-hated Vietnamese to overturn the revolutionary leadership. O'Kanseng also served as a province-level annex to S–21 for the lower grade 'enemies' identified by a special branch of the division, while upper echelons of KR officials were sent directly to S–21. So Sarœun's duty was 'to screen no-good elements' and 'concentrate them in one location' (1457). Hence the creation of the security centre in late 1976 – early 1977, or so the ECCC judgement claims. But the prison must have existed before, as we saw, although it had always been for cadres; ordinary citizens were just put to death in the forest.

The description of the prison tallies with the details I have collected in the mid-90s. What turned out to be a regional prison, specifically meant to deal with suspicious DK cadres, was exceptionally small, especially if we compare it to the northern regional security centre in Siemreap inside the ex-colonial prison, mentioned below by detainee Bun Chan.[84] But, once again, this was not the mission of the Tribunal. O'Kanseng amounted to five or six bamboo huts, four meters wide and six to ten metres long, built on no more than 200–250 square metres (1472) of land situated behind the present Banlung Hospital and along a small stream. Detainees were permitted to bathe in the small stream once a day – a privilege unheard of in other KR detention centre, except for François Bizot at M13[85] (1487) and at Phnom Kraol Security Centre, near Koh Nhiek in Mondolkiri (230ff). There were two meals a day of rice mixed with potatoes and a soup of vegetables collected nearby (1488). Food was insufficient, though, and some detainees could even die of malnutrition, as in all DK prisons (1489). There was some form of medical treatment and some modern medicines were available, as throughout Ratanakiri Province (1490). The interrogation hut was some 30 to 50 metres away from the other constructions. The guards numbered between six and nine, and the number of detainees averaged about 60, escalating up to 100 in 1978, but the prisoners were mostly well below one hundred (1471). This made the institution significantly smaller than most simple district prisons in the lowlands, and shows that the repression in Ratanakiri was on a much smaller scale than in the rest of the country – irrespective of totally undocumented executions in the forest that are reported in this book.

The interrogation procedure began, as throughout DK, by collecting the accused's 'statements' or 'confessions' under duress. These documents were

---

84 See pp. 295–297.
85 Bizot, *The Gate*, Havill, 2004, p. 288.

then passed on to the Commandant of Division 801, who made the final decision. Chhaom Se, the prison warden who testified at the Tribunal, was adamant about that (1469). The prisoner's lot was 'to be resolved' (meaning execution), 'to be lessened', that is to be kept in the prison to do hard labour, or 'to be re-educated', that is, to be sent to a re-education camp – possibly the O'Kveh Camp mentioned by Nap Bun Heng,[86] but not by the ECCC Tribunal. No O'Kanseng detainee was sent to S–21, as the screening was done earlier; the outcomes at O'Kanseng depended on the position in the RAK (or civilian position) of the individual arrested. To the accused, as throughout DK and other communist regimes (and Mao's China in particular), no reasons for the detention were ever given: the victim had to incriminate himself under (actual or threat of) torture (1474). Beatings and electrocution were practised as in all other KR prisons, but the local interrogators were also inventive. For instance, the torturers 'used pliers to squeeze the thighs [of the detainees] until they became unconscious.' (1480). A more insidious form of torture inflicted on some soldiers 'was to give them rice mixed with salt' and then direct them 'to tell the truth to *Angkar*' before being given water (1483). Only once, some twenty prisoners, who were accused of having stolen potatoes, were released (1495). The Tribunal estimates that the total number of deaths at O'Kanseng ran into the hundreds. This, again, indicates that this institution operated on a modest scale compared to most DK prison-execution centres, where the number of victims rose well into the thousands (1499).

To show how much that specific security centre was managed directly from the Party centre, the Tribunal pointed to evidence that a special inter-rogation-torture expert had been dispatched from Phnom Penh in mid-1977 and stayed in Banlung for about three months, 'to uncover communications lines among soldiers implicated in the confessions' (1482). He was a certain Nao (or Nau) who arrived with Keo Sarœun's S–21 confession, with red marks indicating which soldiers should be examined. Implicated soldiers were then forced to confess they were 'counter-revolutionaries collaborating with enemies of the Party' (1483).

A most unusual incident, and most relevant to this study, occurred in mid-June 1977. Some 100 Jaraï were brought by truck at night under armed guard and interned at O'Kanseng. The sheer number, and their being from a single tribal group, gives an historical importance to this event. Who exactly were

---

86 See above, p. 249.

they? Why were they arrested *en masse*? And where did they come from? The Tribunal answers almost all of these questions.

The date can be assessed quite accurately, as the investigative judges found a telegram, dated 15 June 1977, from Vy,[87] who had become the Northeast regional Secretary after the arrest of Ney Sarann. This telegram mentions the capture of exactly 209 Jaraï in Sector 107, along the Vietnamese border. One month elapsed between their capture on the Vietnamese border and the arrival of about half of their number at O'Kanseng. The judgement is silent as to the fate of the other half. Indeed, they were not a gang of soldiers arriving from Vietnam to attack the country, but entire families with wives and children, and carrying a map of Cambodia. They therefore could not have represented the apex of a first Vietnamese invasion that was to take place in late 1978. They had a few rifles, but were not at all equipped to launch an all-out war. We have seen that the Vietnamese government was indeed training some ethnic minorities who had taken refuge from Ratanakiri, but these minorities were not launched as advance troops before the major December 1978 major Vietnamese attack; but they were in the rear-guard, essentially serving as interpreters to the conquering Vietnamese who advanced quickly into DK territory in the final days of 1978. The Tribunal cannot determine if these Jaraï refugees were of Cambodian or of Vietnamese nationality (1504), but it seems obvious to me they must have been of Vietnamese nationality who were totally – and fatally – ignorant of the security situation in Cambodia, like the Khmer Krom from southern Vietnam who were taken to Kaing Ta Chan for execution in Takeo province.

The Tribunal makes another hypothesis: they could have been members of the banned (in Vietnam) FULRO movement or *Front Uni pour la Lutte des races Opprimées*, which acted as supplementary forces, allied to and financed by Americans, during the Second Indochina War. This hypothesis is not impossible, and their act of fleeing indicates that the 209 refugees were opponents to the Vietnamese communist regime, but there is no evidence that they were associated in any way with FULRO. They could have just been a significant group of Jaraï who had taken refuge in Vietnam during the civil war and wished to run away from the discrimination to which the highlanders then were submitted in communist Vietnam. They were ignorant of the real situation

---

87 This was the same Vy, one of the two lowland revolutionary Khmers, who arrived in Ratanakiri in 1964. See pp. 62–64 above, and Philip Short, *Pol Pot*, p. 384.

under DK and fell into the trap: they went from Charybdis into Scylla. And so did a significant number of Khmers, from Kampuchea Krom in the Mekong Delta, when, in Takeo Province much further to the south, they escaped from communist Vietnam only to fall into the trap of Ta Mok's prison in Kaing Ta Chan, where no leniency was shown and all were exterminated. At least in Ratanakiri Sectors 107 and 102, the local KR leaders could have been less cruel and only about half were massacred after being trucked to O'Kanseng. They were marched in lines of 10, tied in ropes, executed and buried in a vast B–52 crater (1506–1507) about one week after their arrival (1509). The Tribunal rightly concludes they were persecuted on political and not racial grounds (1521–5),[88] as they were classified as 'external enemies' (1506).

But what about the second half of the Jaraï group, some 109 individuals? The Tribunal does not address this issue, as it merely looked at the victims of O'Kanseng. However, from the mouth of Rochœm Tveng, Phi Phuon's elder brother, the other half was not spared. All were massacred locally, where they had been arrested.[89] So, as in Takeo province, political refugees from Vietnam, whether they were Khmer Krom or tribal minorities, were butchered indiscriminately by the will of an *Angkar Lœu* whose demented regime was becoming more and more paranoid.

8 – The novel lives of highland revolutionaries

The number of highlanders who were among the troops that conquered Phnom Penh on 17 April 1975 could have been quite significant. Indeed, some *Khmer Lœu* joined the KR because they were poor and felt repressed, and believed the promises of power and prosperity; others and especially very young adolescents, like all the rest of Cambodia, were more or less forcefully conscripted under false pretenses. Moreover, as one witness confessed to me, most of them had never gone to school, they had no critical mind and only knew how to obey blindly. If the KR recruited from all ethnic groups, their propaganda found more resonance among the Jaraï and Tampuon than other minorities. Hence it is unsurprising that command and responsibility func-

---

88 This is obviously an absurd conclusion on the part of the ECCC, as the Jaraï were the darlings of the regime. In this case, they were classified as 'spies' of the hated Vietnamese; therefore, they were all massacred for political reasons as opponents to the radical Khmer revolution.

89 Interview on 15 April 2019 in Andoung Meas district of Ratanakiri, known as Sector 107 under DK.

tions were generally entrusted to Jaraï and Tampuon, while members of other ethnic groups usually became ordinary revolutionaries or local chiefs. Some found themselves collaborating with successive regimes, from Sihanouk's to Héng Samrin and Hun Sèn's.

Here are five examples of Montagnards who joined the revolution of their own accord and who were brought, like Phi Phuon, to become familiar with the much wider world. Among them, it is difficult to classify the tribal people who worked for the technical services, being actually between the civilian and military KR, and the rest of the ordinary population. They had less to fear for their lives, because, fulfilling practical tasks essential for the running of the revolutionary society, they were hardly the targets of purges. We can say that they were the regime's privileged: they had a certain freedom of movement, ate their fill and could organize their work at a more normal pace. Most importantly, they usually never were the victims of purge campaigns.

Kham Phon

Jaraï Kham Phon[90] was one of those and we have some information about the small internal trade that could exist under DK. He was then a truck driver who spent two years in Stung Treng (1976–1977), transporting cassava to Ratanakiri to feed the inhabitants. On the other hand, the paddy loaded in Banlung was always taken to Stung Treng, along with some latex.[91] In Banlung, there was a hospital for sector 102, at Stung Treng one for sector 104. Similarly, at O'Cheik, at the Lumphat junction, flooded rice was transported in ten-ton Chinese ZIL lorries. Timber was not transported. The trucks arrived loaded at Stung Treng and often returned empty to Banlung. This was one-way traffic.

Danh Han

Danh Han[92], a Jaraï, was part of a group of teenage boys and girls who, after the KR took power, were sent to Phnom Penh once they had learnt to read and

---

90   Born in 1952 and interviewed on 10 April 1994.

91   From Stung Treng, we can imagine the paddy was taken by boat to Phnom Penh and then loaded onto trains to Kompong Som. I was told in Kompong Som that one full train of rice (or paddy) arrived weekly at the harbour for export to China, throughout the year, at least in 1977 and 1978. Rice was also transported to Kompong Som by trucks.

92   Born in 1962 and interviewed on 10 April 1994.

write Khmer. Danh Han spent 18 months at Russey Keo Technical School,[93] from early 1977 to June 1978. He became a car mechanic and learned how to drive trucks. There were 1,000 students, all boys. (The girls were in another school near the Chinese Hospital.) There were ten large pots to feed them. They got up at 5 o'clock to do half an hour of gymnastics, then watered the cabbages. They ate rice gruel and worked on car engines until 11 o'clock. After the meal, they could take a nap. Then they planted vegetables or tilled the garden until 13:30 and worked on the engines until 5 pm. Then they had dinner at 17:30. After that, they watered the cabbages again. The food was plentiful: rice, fish, soup, and every day a little meat. To end the day, they had a meeting from 7:00 to 9:00, to talk about their studies and the abominable *Yuon* (Vietnamese) enemy.

The students could be as young as seven years old. Danh Han finished his training when he was 16. About 30 learned to drive trucks and repair engines. But they also learned revolutionary songs during the evening meetings. There were no punishments. If they were sick, they were taken to a hospital that had a small room for two patients: two beds with pillows and a mosquito net.

On the 30th of each month, they were taken to attend a great meeting with thousands of people in a place whose name he did not know. On some of those occasions, he saw Pol Pot, Ieng Sary and others. They asked if everything was fine for them. They spoke for hours about the Super Great Leap Forward and the need to work very hard to improve our socialism and soon reach communism. Kampuchea should not be following the path of the *Yuon*. During the meeting, two or three leaders made speeches. It lasted all morning. The audience was supposed to shout, 'Hurray!' at regular intervals. In the afternoon, there were playlets and revolutionary dances.

One scene could show a criminal who had stolen a box of rice or a little cassava to teach a lesson in morality; another could be about the Vietnamese enemy. Once, Prach Chhuon,[94] the famous blind singer, chanted a story that taught political morality. Today, in the Hun Sèn regime, Prach Chhoun often sings the praise of the Hun Sèn regime on official radio and television.

After his training, Danh Han became a truck driver in Ratanakiri, carrying mainly Chinese weapons from Stung Treng to the Vietnamese border: 60, 85 and R15 shells, and rifles. When the Vietnamese army invaded Cambodia,

---

93 Decades earlier, in 1948, Pol Pot learned carpentry at this technical school.
94 (1936–2018), grand master of *chapey*, a Khmer cord instrument with two to four strings.

they burned his truck and enrolled him in the Vietnamese army unit that operated from the Tonlé Srèpok to Stung Treng. He fled to Kompong Thom province, where the Vietnamese arrested and interrogated him before sending him back to his home village. He became a truck driver again and got married in 1984, and had three children at the time of the interview.

Teng Thiet

Teng Thiet,[95] a Brao, was the head of the La Bang Pi commune, in the village of Katieng, Lumphat District at the time of our interview. He has managed to maintain his status as a local leader under all regimes. He was a *gendarme* under Sihanouk and village chief under DK. What is paradoxical, again with the KR regime, is that while the highlanders represented the very model of the 'old' or 'base' people (*mulethan*), almost all of them were forced to leave the basalt plateau and settle along the two main rivers, the Tonlé San and the Tonlé Srèpok.

At the time of the *Sangkum*, Teng Thiet's village was located not far from Labansiek and took part in setting up the state rubber plantation. The French bought land for 1,000 to 2,000 riels per hectare and paid labourers 20 riels a day; at the time, a kilogram of rice cost five riels. People would work there when they needed money. Director Georges Bonzon was generous and occasionally lent a car to transport rice. Sihanouk soldiers did not steal food in the villages, says this former Sihanouk soldier, and overall the relations were not bad.

The revolutionaries arrived between 1964 and 1968. They were in the forest and came during the day or during the night. They came from either from the plains, Vietnam or Laos, one or two people at a time. They came wearing normal clothes, or loincloths if they were KL. They spoke of social classes, oppression, and American imperialists. The 1969–1970 US bombings did not kill civilians in the village, but did so elsewhere. In Labansiek, those who joined the struggle were often marginal people who were in conflict with society.

But after 1970, they were 'liberated' and everyone entered the revolution. Young people in particular joined the liberation troops. The village chief was arrested and officials of previous regimes were driven into the forest and executed. His brother-in-law and five uncles were executed, including one who was a village chief. The slogan was 'go and study in the forest' where they were killed immediately. Up to twenty were executed. New Brao village chiefs were

---

95   This is an alias, as he wishes to remain anonymous. I have interviewed him too.

selected from among the elders, but not necessarily ex-Khmer Issarak. Teng Thiet then became a group leader and many relatives joined the revolution: twenty to thirty people from his village, including about ten girls. Half of them have since returned. Some were recruited to be messengers, others to learn to sew, and others to cook

The KR moved the village in March 1975 and placed everyone into a people's commune in early 1976, during the dry season. The collective consisted of two long rows of houses, about 300 meters long, incorporating two villages: Phum Katieng 2 and Phum Patang, about 2,000 people divided into four groups (*krom*) of 500. Each meal consisted of one milk tin of rice for three people, plus cassava. There was no meat, or very little; Teng Thiet's father sometimes hunted. But the people were not skinny. There was a large hospital, but few people were sick and Chinese and French pharmaceuticals were plentiful.

The village maintained a small dam two kilometres away, as well as an extensive network of rice fields. Once, five or six Chinese experts came to examine the dam. An older woman came in a small jeep, surrounded by ten to twenty chiefs. The dam took two dry seasons to be built. Many people came from Banlung, Lumphat and Vœunsay – everywhere in Zone 102 – altogether 3,000 people. The cement came from the Kampot cement plant, and also the salt. Lao and lowland Khmers taught the KL how to grow flooded rice. There were three schools in the people's commune. They studied in the morning and manual work was done in the afternoon. Children were taught to read and write Khmer and to sing revolutionary songs, including the *Internationale*.

People got up at 6 o'clock to the sound of a gong, and quietly ate cassava at home. The first meal in the four collective canteens, each with one large pot, was at 11 am. There were 10 cooks per kitchen, plus one man to watch them. He beat the gong and distributed the rice. People could come for food secretly. All the leaders were Brao. The interviewee was a former deputy head of one of the groups. He boasted of having served all the regimes. Some leaders were cruel, some were not. There were also about ten militiamen. People had to write their autobiographies, but no local leaders were arrested, even when Ta Ya and Ta Lav were; these leaders were well known to commune members. There were no purges of local cadres. Among the 25 families considered 'new people', only the family head was arrested and executed. No 'old people' (*mulethan*) were executed after 1975.

A number of villagers joined the KR army, but would return for periods of about ten days, or up to one month. This explains why there were quite a few births, especially in 1977. Nobody tried to escape over the border, especially in 1977 and 1978 when it was well guarded in order to attack Vietnam.

A mandatory nightly meeting for small groups of 10 to 20 people was held every night. While Khmer language was preferred, those who knew only Brao spoke Brao. The propaganda was that one must be responsible for oneself, grow three tons of rice per hectare, 'attack' production, even when the sun was at its zenith. Even at noon it was necessary to plant cassava or sugarcane; rice seedlings should be planted at the end of the afternoon. Dinner was served at 5:00 pm and people could sleep from 9:00 pm. There was no rest day, but a group meeting every 7 days and a big meeting once a month, on the 30th. There were exercises of self-criticism and mutual criticism. It was necessary to denounce those who did not work hard. Many fell asleep. Everyone older than 10 was forced to attend.

Rochœm Tveng

Phi Phuon's elder brother, Rochœm Tveng,[96] was Jaraï tribal commune leader under DK. Rochœm Tveng was two years Phi Phoun's senior, born 29 January 1945. With the same family background, it was natural that he also joined the revolution at a very early age, but he mostly stayed put in his original district, Andoung Meas of Ratanakiri, and did not travel as far and wide as his younger brother. He was born at about the time the revolutionary ideal penetrated through the Vietminh into that northeastern part of the Stung Treng Province that was to become, from 1959, Ratanakiri.

Indeed, he claims that from the age of six, he was taught to write his own Jaraï language in Latin script and some Lao in its original script. The Vietminh claimed the three Indochinese countries of Indochina had been fighting together against ninety years of colonial domination. He heard about the revolution when he was only nine in 1954 and the big 'Samaki' or solidarity between Laos, Vietnam and Cambodia against French imperialism to stand all united until now. They learnt about their national heroes Pô Kambôr,[97] Achar

---

96 Born in 1945 and interviewed in Andoung Meas and Phnom Penh from 2016 to 2020.
97 Pô Kambôr (1820–1867) was a charismatic adventurer who claimed to be a son of Ang Chan (1792–1834). He was in fact a member of the Kuey minority and fought against King Norodom. In 1866, he laid siege at Oudong, the capital. Defeated by the French, he took refuge in Laos (which at that time was controlled by the Siamese and incorporated greater Stung Treng), but reappeared in 1867 in Kompong Thom Province where the population assassinated him.

Sva[98] and Hem Chieu.[99] Achar Hem Chieu was the real patriot – but never a communist – who pointed out that France had betrayed the 1863 Treaty of Protectorate after the loss of all the western and northern territories to the Thais in 1941.

Rochœm Tveng's father served in a revolutionary group with the support of Vietminh agents named Ung Day, Hay Tham and Nay Niam. Ung Day was in village No. 1 in 1954. They were secret agents who remained in Ratanakiri into the late 1950s. At first, they did not want to stay alone after the Geneva Accords, which required all Vietminh to quit Cambodian territory. But a letter from Hô Chi Minh required the three agents to stay in village No. 1 with the indigenous people in Nhang commune. Also, after the Geneva Accords, the Vietnamese installed a permanent revolutionary base with Vietnamese, Lao and Khmer representatives. The base was at the juncture of the three borders, some 30 km from Malik commune.

At the same time, they took thousands of Cambodians to be further educated in Hanoi. The ethnic minorities from the Northeast represented 10 per cent of those taken for re-education. One of his uncles, Romam Yœm, was among them. That was the first stage of the birth of the revolution in Cambodia. Romam Yœm married a Vietnamese girl and died in Hanoi two years later.

Both his father and his grandfather were involved in the revolutionary movement. It was their father who, from 1958, started to cut the Hô Chi Minh Trail through the forest with the help of Jaraï from Ratanakiri and Vietnam after Dien Bien Phu. The Viet agent Ung Day started to open it in 1958–1959. They started to use rifles that came from the Soviet Union, and China and later also through Sihanoukville, with the permission of Sihanouk, as a kind of second Hô Chi Minh Trail to fight the Americans.

Rochœm Tveng entered the revolution in 1962–63, when he was about 17 years old, like others the same age, thinking it was 'beautiful'. This was

---

98 Achar Sava was an ex-slave and an adventurer, and also claimed to be a descendant of King Ang Chan. He caused a rebellion against the king in the early days of Norodom's reign (1860–1904). He was arrested by French authorities and exiled to La Réunion until his death. He and Pô Kambôr were impostors who claimed royal descent in order to grab power for themselves.

99 Achar Hem Chieu (1896–1943), a Buddhist monk and teacher at the Buddhist Institute in Phnom Penh, had been the moving spirit of the first movement for independence in 1942. See Henri Locard's "Achar Hem Chieu, the 'Umbrella Demonstration' of 20th July 1942 and the Vichy regime", *Siksacakr, Journal of the Center for Khmer Studies*, No. 8–9 (2006–2007), pp. 70–81.

before the first lowland Khmer revolutionaries arrived. Ta Vong and Ta Vy were among the first. They came from Phnom Penh and had been educated in Vietnam, and arrived from Kratieh and Mondolkiri. They stayed close to the Vietnamese in a base in the forest. Ta Vy arrived at Lumphat on an elephant; his wife and children joined him later. He settled at Châng commune, Phum No. 1. Unlike his brother Phi Phuon, Tveng remained in his village and, from 1967–68, fought against the Sihanouk army. They had crossbows and mines, and one rifle for 10 people. He first heard about Pol Pot and Ieng Sary during 1965–66.

Tveng's village first experienced ARVN bombs in October 1961, when 12 people were killed, together with animals. They had no elephants. Sihanouk sent his soldiers and took the wounded to Phnom Penh. He also recruited some Jaraïs, Tampuons and Lao to join the *Sangkum* army. At the time, people used local languages and Lao. All these revolutionaries spoke Lao between themselves. Nobody spoke Khmer.

There were hundreds of indigenous soldiers from the time of the Issaraks, with elephants. They had enough food in the forest, with pigs and chickens, fields (*chamkar*) and plantations. They had French guns and AK–47s from the USSR. At the time there were plenty of wild elephants that were killed for food and ivory. When the VC started to come in 1960, the entire Jaraï village was sympathetic to the revolution. Gradually, the Vietnamese soldiers were more and more numerous, from a few hundred to 2,000. His father was cutting paths for them and supplying food. They settled in the forest, but came to the villages at night to make propaganda. Originally no violence was used: everyone was considered as equal, nobody would be rich, nobody would be poor, and no foreigners would take our land.

Sihanouk demonized all opposition to his authority during his quest for absolute power. All opponents became enemies of the state and he had them assassinated by his security services. Both brothers had been encouraged to join the revolutionary movement and were inducted into the Party by their father, whose elder sister Rochœm Phjing (រ៉ូ ជីង) had married Poy Hlœun (ពុយ ហ្លើន), alias Ta Lav, who were the generation of Pol Pot and Ieng Sary, born around 1925–1928. He was a simple Jaraï farmer but closely followed the communist policies of the Indochinese Communist Party inspired by Karl Marx, Mao and Hô Chi Minh. He had two daughters and three sons. One passed away later, at Phnom Malay, after stepping on a mine. The family burnt all family photos in 1979, as they were afraid and mistrustful of the Viet.

The uncle had an enormous influence on the two brothers when they were adolescents, and he gradually climbed up the KR hierarchy to become Ney Sarann's deputy in 1967, while the latter would become the Party secretary in charge of the Northeast region in 1971, after Ieng Sary went to Beijing to control Sihanouk. They (Ta Lav and Ney Sarann) were the secret Office 7 until 1971, when they went to Stung Treng city. Tveng met Ieng Sary and Son Sen.

The Khmer Issarak were in Ratanakiri from 1951 to 1954. This is when Ta Lav entered the revolution to fight against French imperialists. 'We thought French colonization was not good; but after the communists, we know the French were good, as they had abolished slavery', Tveng said. Ta Lav wanted to go to Hanoi after the Geneva Agreement on 21 July 1954, but was not chosen to be among the hundreds selected by the Vietminh for further 'education'. Tveng was just nine years old when the Vietminh left Cambodia after the Geneva Agreements, but he already knew about Issarak revolutionary ideas.

From 1959, the Khmer police and army arrived in Vœunsay District, with Colonel Srey Meas[100] at the head of the military in the area. Bokéo District was created, and some communes: Talao, Bakan, Malik, and Mohear. By and large, there were no problems with the army and they usually paid for the poultry or eggs they took, but some individuals came and snatched chickens. At the time, no civilians came from the plains and there was no land requisition: no rubber plantations at all, nor any plantations of any sort in the eastern part of Bokéo District. Yes, Tveng knew about the 5,000-hectare Labansiek State Rubber Plantation, but this was some 30 km westwards and did not affect them in any way.

From these scattered pieces of information, it becomes obvious that the revolutionaries, a mix of Tampuon, Lao, and VC from over the border and, above all, Jaraï (who joined the revolution in entire villages under Ta Lav's leadership) started the armed revolution in the late 1960s when the first lowland Khmer apparatchiks appeared on the scene. We must also note the involvement of the VC, which shows that the KR leadership's arrival in the far northeast corner of Cambodia was not an initiative of only these leaders, but indeed a clever move suggested by Le Duan,[101] by then the leading VWP luminary, the aging Hô Chi Minh now being semi-retired.

---

100 See above, p. 234.

101 Lê Duân (1907–1986) became first secretary of the Communist Party of Vietnam in 1960, while Hô Chi Minh remained chairman until his death in 1969. He trained Nuon Chea.

Ieng Sary established his base at the foot of the mountains, at Office 105, in the forest near K–5. But Tveng never saw Ieng Sary's base, nor the man or his wife, Ieng Thirith; he was just a low-ranking soldier fighting the Lon Nol troops alongside his father. Son Sen (*Bong* Kham) came with his wife Yun Yat, who was always carried in a hammock by the people whom she made feel inferior, but also afraid. Pol Pot (Ta Pouk) arrived from Vietnam, along the Hô Chi Minh Trail, together with five bodyguards and secretaries.

Before 1970, they were not hit by the American bombings as they hid in the forest. But some 36 people were killed when the bombs fell on a trench. In his revolutionary education he was taught that the French did a lot of bad things and were defeated at Dien Bien Phu. Now it is the Americans. The Vietnamese are very courageous. For years, the indigenous people had been ruled by the Siamese: they were bought and sold as slaves.

As soon as Ney Sarann (Ta Ya) arrived in Ratanakiri, Tveng joined him. Ta Ya had first been posted in Mondolkiri where he married a Lao woman named Vœun and developed close relations with the local people of all ethnicities: Tampuon, Bunong, Kuey, Jaraï, Brao and Lao. The ethnic Lao of Mondolkiri, largely centred on the district of Koh Nhek, also had important networks with Lao in Stung Treng, Lumphat, Voeunsai, Siempang and of course Laos. Ney Sarann was able to tap into these and rapidly develop the revolutionary movement in the northeast. During 1967–1968, Tveng was a soldier. The locals demonstrated against Sihanouk at Bokéo in early 1967 and Vœunsai in October–November because they had not benefitted from the many donations he had received from China, and people were very poor. The first struggle was in Battambang,[102] the second in Andoung Meas. Hô Chi Minh had agreed to return Kampuchea Krom, but the agreement was no longer valid after his death in 1969.[103]

In 1970, Lon Nol's forces stopped fighting against us. The indigenous people drove them to Stung Treng. The highlanders fought Lon Nol to liberate the country. They went to Kompong Cham to liberate Phnom Penh. There were battalions of 300 men, mostly of indigenous people from Ratanakiri that

---

102 Indeed, Nuon Chea had started the revolutionary struggle in Battambang in January.

103 Tveng is mistaken, as that promise was never made; the North Vietnamese had said only that they recognized the colonial borders in exchange for Sihanouk allowing the distribution of Soviet and Chinese weapons through the Cambodian territory.

went to liberate Phnom Penh.[104] One nephew was among them. Just 30 per cent of the soldiers were *Khmer Kandal*. They first liberated Ratanakiri, then Stung Treng, then Kratieh, then Préah Vihear, then Kompong Thom, and then Siemreap. Seventy per cent came from Ratanakiri and Mondolkiri. Tveng was selected for the Chenla II battle along the road between Kompong Cham and Kompong Thom. He did not go: he was scared of dying. After deserting, he lived in the forest for three years before returning to his village.

Tveng knew about Bou Thang. He went to Hanoi in 1954 and came back when Sihanouk was dismissed in March 1970. In 1975, though, he was back in Vietnam. Many ran away to Vietnam. Bou Thang asked for their help; but they were not yet ready to intervene. Bun Mi, a Brao from Ta Veng District, defected to Vietnam with Bou Thang and about 2,000 others from the district.

From 1970, many revolutionaries who had gone away to Hanoi in 1954 returned. Ten-family solidarity groups were established; the harvest was shared and put in storage. There was a hospital in the commune. Tveng was the deputy head of the four villages. 'Solidarity groups' (*krom samaki*) were instituted: at first three to five families worked together, but each family ate by itself. There was no change in rice cultivation. No one ran away to Vietnam; he stayed with his father. In his village he both worked on the security team and cultivated rice. Rifles had been coming along the Hô Chi Minh Trail from the Soviet Union and China since 1963. They were all new weapons from the Soviets. He heard news on FUNK Radio. He thus heard about the fall of Phnom Penh. Everyone continued to work and no refugees from the plains were sent to his village.

Collectivization started in 1973 and, at the same time, Tveng joined the Communist Youth organization and became a provisional Party member. He obtained full membership in February 1975 and became a sub-commune leader (*anakhum*). There never were collective meals in his *sahakor*, which consisted of just one village of about 100 families. They were made to learn Khmer and the heads at meetings spoke Khmer, but everyone spoke Jaraï in everyday life. There was some small-scale irrigation work along the Tonlé San. Along with his uncle Ta Lav, he welcomed Sihanouk when he came to the KR *maquis* in March 1973.

---

104 If this was really the case, highlanders comprised up to 15 per cent of the about 20,000 KR
soldiers that overwhelmed the capital.

At the time, many fled to Vietnam. An entire Brao village within Ta Veng commune escaped in December 1974. Another village, Phum Chaè, in January 1975, and a third from Andoung Meas also went en masse to Vietnam.

Tveng married in 1971 and had 11 children; five are alive today. From 1971 to 1975, he was mainly at home and became a commune medic. He was trained at the K–5 base along with hundreds of others, half men and half women, for the entire *Eisan* region. The regional hospital was at P–5 in O'Chum District. Some specialized in midwifery, and some in surgery. They used tree roots. Trainers came from Vietnam or Cambodia. Some had studied abroad. The trainings lasted between one and three months. The Vietnamese teachers used books in Vietnamese and in French, with drawings and illustrations. He liked to ask people how to make medicines, to stitch a wound, and to comfort people before they died.

After 17 April, he was deputy-chief of a collective consisting of four villages in Andoung Meas district: *phums* Yang (160 people), Kang Yang (also 160 people), Chaè (184), and Khaèt (200); 744 in the whole people's commune. Children remained with their parents, as there was no children's group. There was some form of education: reading and writing and political propaganda. Tveng had a radio from before 1975 and he heard Pol Pot's September 1977 speech. He secretly listened to American radio, and Vietnamese radio broadcasts in Khmer and Lao. But most people did not have a radio, only the top leaders. Information was transmitted by messengers.

On 17 April, there were big ceremonies to celebrate victory day, including three days with a lot of food: a buffalo or a cow, rice, sweets, and traditional gong music. There were celebrations for the anniversary of the creation of the Party. These celebrations emphasized the importance of mutual loyalty and common fealty to *Angkar*.

There was plenty of medicine, but the food was not sufficient. Fortunately, nobody starved and the women had a lot of children. He was the one who chose which young teenagers would be sent to Phnom Penh and even China for education. About ten were selected from each people's commune. During DK, marriages were not forced and the consent of both parties was required; otherwise, they might have committed suicide. Five couples might be married together: a big meal was organized, with clapping and gongs. Unlike in the rest of the country, ceremonies in Ratanakiri did not include a promise to be faithful to *Angkar*. Similarly, funeral ceremonies with gongs were tolerated.

There was one prison in Banlung, but none of his friends were taken there, as it was only for soldiers and apparatchiks; Tveng only heard about the nationwide prison system after 1979. Before, it had been secret and controlled by soldiers. During DK, around 209 Jaraï arrived from Vietnam because they did not want to live in a communist regime. They were Khieu-Ky soldiers with their families. All died.[105] Killings within the commune started too. They were told, 'the wheel of history is turning'. The Party needed to be purified and reliable people would be kept. This is when Ta Ya, Ta Lav, and Chakrei[106] were arrested. At the time, people were not yet arrested in his commune. There were K–51, K–53, and K–54 prisons. K–52 was in Stung Treng. Banlung was the regional prison. There were many corpses when the Vietnamese arrived. At the time, the fighting was very violent. Jaraï who had taken refuge in Vietnam were asked by the Vietnamese government to join them in the fight. They had been trained in Vietnam. The Jaraï were the best fighters.

Ta Ya was arrested in September 1976. His deputy, Ta Lav was about to defect to Vietnam. He went to a secret meeting in Vietnam. In fact, he had gone to secret meetings in Vietnam as early as 1975. That is why people knew he was plotting. He was arrested at the end of 1976. Ta Yung defected to Vietnam in February 1977 and asked Tveng to defect. Bou Thang had defected earlier, in late 1974. Bun Mi, a Brao, was the leader of this defection. He was later killed. Tveng did not want to defect. After the arrest of Ney Sarann (Ta Ya) and in the course of the purge of the *Eisan* leadership that followed, Ta Lav was summoned to Phnom Penh. People say he committed suicide when he was questioned outside S–21. In 2008, Tveng went to Tuol Sleng Museum in search of the confession and photo of his uncle, but found neither, because he had died before entering S–21. There are conflicting testimonies: some say he committed suicide in Stung Treng, others say it was in Phnom Penh.

Tveng's commune leader was a Jaraï who fled to Vietnam in 1979. He admitted that he had killed 36 people. In fact, they were killed by soldiers who were a mix of lowland Khmers and indigenous people. But, during September–October 1978, the commune was dissolved as there was not enough

---

105 Banlung prison is discussed extensively above, pp. 269–274. This is a confirmation that these unfortunate people were just political refugees from Vietnam, running away from repression there.

106 Chan Chakrei, an ex-monk, commanded Division 170 from the Eastern region (*Bophea*) where there was more freedom during the civil war (1970–1975). Chakrei was the first high-ranking official to be sent to S–21, at the end of 1975. He was accused of having plotted a military coup against the leadership and was made to write hundreds of pages of confession before being executed there in 1976.

food, and they reverted to private land ownership. He was given a little more than 2 hectares, enough to produce his own food. A Brao from Ta Veng helped him. The Vietnamese had attacked O'Yadao as early as 1976 and stayed there until 1978. His own village had been three or four kilometres from the border, but, for safety, it was moved further inland. In Sept 1978, there was a massive invasion of PAVN who went as far as Ta Veng, 30–40 km from border.

The invaders were exclusively Vietnamese soldiers, with no Khmers and no minorities. In December 1978, Tveng entered the forest with some 700 other indigenous people, moving in the direction of Vœunsay. They took everything they could, except tools and implements. They carried some rice, but they did not go as far as Preah Vihear province. There was total confusion.

He stayed three months in the forest with a battalion. There was division among the leadership about the Vietnamese. Some wanted to go back and become villagers again. Others went to Thailand and Kao-I-Dang. He led 400 people out of the forest in March 1979. Two hundred defected with him, and the remaining 200 one week later. He went to the Vietnamese leader of battalion 83 at O'Tabok, Ta Veng District, on the banks of the Tonlé San. He had two children then, both girls. He carried one niece in a basket on his back. The Vietnamese pointed guns at them. 'Are there any soldiers?' – 'No, just villagers' – 'Do you have any weapons?'– 'No. All were given to KR who did not want to defect.' When he came out of the forest, a brother-in-law organized a feast for all: they killed a pig, drank alcohol and many thanked him for having saved lives. He had been a good leader. The bad leaders had been killed already. He confessed and was again made commune leader. There were no more people's communes. They were given bags of poor-quality rice. He himself was in charge of radio transmissions from Pol Pot days. He became district deputy-governor at Andoung Meas. The district governor was Roman Yun, a Krâchok.

In Phum Yang, Phum Chay and Phum Ta Nha, it was back to pre-revolutionary life. The community leader was a Jaraï from O'Yadao who had defected to Dak Lak in Vietnam, where he was re-educated for six years. The new community chief had gone to school in Lumphat in the Sihanouk days, and Tveng was his deputy. At first, Tveng refused a leading position since he was 'a bad person' who had worked with Pol Pot. Still, the Vietnamese policy was that those who were leaders should remain leaders and those who were soldiers or local militia should remain so. He had been a good leader. He was trained in Banlung for one month to become a local teacher, but did not like it. Then he was appointed village leader for 14 families.

Figure 16: Rochœm Tveng in his Jaraï loincloth at the funeral of his brother, Phi Phuon, in 2015.

Later, he was imprisoned in Banlung prison for four years, between 12 June 1979 and 13 April 1983. It was under the control of the Vietnamese. He soon served as an interpreter and the Vietnamese appreciated him. When he was released, he took up his post again.

At the time of UNTAC during 1992–93, Tveng became a counsellor and a member of the CPP. He was to control how many political parties there were. FUNCINPEC liked him. Land confiscation became the main issue and some areas were declared state property. Some locals were forced to put their thumb and sign for land concessions. He became a commune leader and a FUNCINPEC member was his deputy. He wanted to keep 500 m² for public buildings, but it was sold. In his commune, 80 per cent were Tampuon, 15 per cent Jaraï, and five per cent Khmer. Each village had one primary school.

New commercial plantations belonged to Khmers from Phnom Penh, Prey Veng and elsewhere. Tveng does not know how much workers were paid, as minority indigenous people do not wish to work there. Today, minorities still comprise some 50 per cent of the population. People have at least 2 hectares per family and up to 30–40 hectares in some cases. Are there indigenous people who moved elsewhere in the country? One of his female cousins married a KR soldier who moved to Thailand and later was repatriated to Phnom Penh. They now have a shop for car parts in Tuol Tompung Market. After the UNTAC period, Tveng was reunited with his younger brother Phi Phuon, who came to visit his parents in Andoung Meas District. All his surviving five children live in houses close to his in Malik commune, in Andoung Meas.

9 – The saga of Bun Chan

Collaboration with DK is strikingly illustrated by the story of Bun Chan[107] (បុន ចាន), a member of the Brao minority from Ta Veng. Born in 1937, he went to work on a coffee plantation in Laos when he was 15. Then he became a servant at a Chinese home in Stung Treng, not wishing to return to his village, where he would face unwanted pressure to get married and settle down. He joined the political resistance at the age of 26, in 1963. There were no lowland Khmers and the chiefs were ethnic minorities: Khun, Bun (head of commune), Yœun and Uon. No one spoke Khmer; Lao was used. Bun Chan carried messages from village to village through the forest. The movement was purely political; nobody had modern weapons, only crossbows.

He moved in dense forests, populated with tigers and elephants, between Ta Veng and the Lao border. He stayed for about three years at a secret base called O'Paya, near the Brao village of Tabok where there were also Lao. He was at the head of a group of ten soldiers. They practiced slash-and-burn agriculture. Immediately after Sihanouk's fall in March 1970, Khmer people from Takeo province, *Bong* Va, *Bong* Peang and *Bong* Hong appeared to help form groups of resistance fighters. They came with rifles: three for a group of

---

107 Born in 1937 and interviewed on 12 January 1994.

ten men and nine in all. He returned to Ta Veng and took all the inhabitants into the forest, so that Lon Nol's soldiers could not attack them. Only the revolutionary leaders remained in the village.

This is when he saw Ta Pouk (Pol Pot), already quite portly and always smiling, and Van (Ieng Sary), with very light skin, a broad face and a wide forehead, but little hair. He talked and laughed a lot with his wife Thirith, and they seemed to be very happy together. He also knew Kham (Son Sen), who was very near-sighted and always wore glasses. Bun Chan helped to carry Kham's wife, Yun Yat. In addition to four porters, a fifth man carried the four supports to rest the hammock during stops. She was very intellectual and learned, and did politics, but did not chat with the people.

In June 1970, all the small groups were regrouped to form Battalion 512, of 100 men from all ethnic minorities: Kravet, Brao and Krœung. Bun Chan was appointed commander. Their goal was to attack and drive Republican troops away from the Tonlé San and Vœunsay. They did it without difficulty since the new Phnom Penh regime had decided, on the advice of the Americans, to abandon the entire northeast, which was too forested to be controlled. The guerrillas went on to Siempang, along the Sekong, then Stung Treng,[108] and then beyond to Preah Vihear Province. They occupied Choam Khsan and the Preah Vihear temple from 1970 to 1974. At the time, some Kuey and Khmers were added to Battalion 512. Bun Chan and his men learned all the forests of this northern region.

On 22 April 1973, Lon Nol soldiers attacked Rovieng, Preah Vihear's provincial capital, and killed the governor of the KR-dominated province. Then, they were pushed back and Bun Chan became the revolutionary army leader for the whole province. Collectivization was organized at this time, now with meals in common, despite the hostility of the population. One of the organizers was murdered, a certain Van, and the murderer managed to escape. The American bombardments made few victims among the combatants, who knew how to take refuge in the forest, but were lethal among the civilian population and domestic animals. KR soldiers ambushed the Lon Nol troops along the Kompong Thom road leading to Preah Vihear (Tbeng Meanchey). They took prisoners, but Bun Chan did not know where they were taken to.[109] Pol

---

108 The People's Army of Vietnam (PAVN) did the job of capturing Stung Treng.

109 It is difficult here to know here if Bun Chan says the whole truth, for, at this time, most war prisoners would have been executed by the KR after interrogation, especially if they were lowland Khmers.

Pot proclaimed that collectivization in Preah Vihear was more advanced than anywhere else in the world and that the province was dominated by ethnic minorities – the Kuey in particular – which was a good thing, he claimed. The population worked a lot and was satisfied with the food.

Bun Chan was at the forefront for witnessing Sihanouk's trip to Cambodia in March 1973, when Sihanouk and Monique drove from Stung Treng to Angkor. He saw Sihanouk on both in and out trips and he was happy to see him again because he had met him in Stung Treng in the 1960s, when the prince came to distribute clothes to the people. The trip lasted two days and two nights, with a stopover at Phnom Tbeng midway. He joined Sihanouk's motorcade in Sroy Thala.[110] There were a lot of cars; the drivers were Vietnamese and Chinese. Far enough ahead was a de-mining vehicle followed by two big Vietnamese vans with radars, a big truck with soldiers, a dark green car with Chinese security personnel, two cars with soldiers and Sihanouk, then many other cars carrying food for the entourage and various materials for local soldiers. On board each of the last three vehicles were Vietnamese with a radio. Sihanouk and Monique were in a large, air-conditioned and well-ventilated car. They did not go out and even slept in the car. In all, there were at least 15 vehicles. Chinese and Vietnamese bodyguards protected the royal couple carefully. I joined the motorcade that only moved at night and remained motionless during the day. Although most of the track was under very tall trees, there was the problem of the dust cloud that would easily have been seen from the air. This is why the caravan moved only at night.

Two nights after crossing the Mekong, the princely couple reached Phnom Kulen. Ieng Sary was with Sihanouk, while Pol Pot and Khieu Samphân were waiting for him there. They also met Hu Nim and Hou Yuon. But the population did not see the prince very much: the inhabitants were kept at least ten metres from the track – a track that had been perfectly flattened the whole way for a quick and safe trip. There were many Chinese advisors and technicians. Once the caravan reached Phnom Kulen, a one-kilometre perimeter around the leaders was established and strictly controlled by the many Vietnamese soldiers present. Bun Chan worked for remote security and did not see any celebrations. He just knows that the visit to the Angkor Wat temple was brief. About 1,000 revolutionary soldiers, mainly *Khmer Lœu*, were protecting the temple area. Lon Nol's soldiers were nearby, on

---

110 Near Thala Barivat, just south of Stung Treng on the left bank of the Mekong River.

the way to Siemreap. Bun Chan saw trenches halfway between the city and Angkor Wat.

Sihanouk and Monique spent five nights in a very comfortable, specially built, stilted pavilion at the foot of Phnom Kulen. Plastic protected the walls and there were comfortable beds and mattresses. At least that's what Bun Chan was told, because he did not see it with his own eyes.

Everything had been carefully planned and timed very accurately. The Vietnamese knew when the American bombers took off and they had devices to tell where they were. No risk could be taken with the lives of Sihanouk and all the *Angkar* leaders. Very few people knew anything before and no more than ten people were aware, all Brao or Kuey. After Sihanouk returned to Hanoi, the route was heavily bombed. But there were no problems during the trip and the effect on the population was spectacular. Many came to join the revolutionaries – the young, the old; it was a national reconciliation. No questions were asked and the district leaders welcomed them. Later in the year, Phnom Penh had broken with the VC revolutionaries and, by the end of the year, they had all gone.

Bun Chan and the capture of Phnom Penh

From 1971 to 1972, there were negotiations between the Americans and the Vietnamese and Lao, but Pol Pot said he wanted nothing but total victory. In early 1975, *Angkar* planned a full victory for the beginning of the year. The forces started to be gathered along all the roads as shown on the maps. The evacuation plan for all cities was drawn up in 1974. It was a necessity; otherwise, it would have been chaos and there would have been a lot of trouble – or so it had been explained to Bun Chan.

Bun Chan was in charge of National Road No. 5.[111] He had to cross the Tonlé Sap from the north and reach the capital through Oudong. Pol Pot predicted that there would be five hundred dead and five thousand injured in the capture of Phnom Penh. In fact, when his troops finally penetrated into Phnom Penh it was almost without a fight. As they progressed on the road to Prek Kdam, they found that the way had already been 'liberated'. On 15 April, RAK Battalion 12 took Pochentong Airport and no plane could take off.

---

111 National Road No. 5 runs from Phnom Penh to Battambang, through Kompong Chhnang and Pursat, on the right or southwest bank of the Tonlé Sap.

On the 16th, the Lon Nol soldiers recaptured the airfield, killing 40 KR and wounding 80. That evening, Battalion 512 was called to move into the area through Pochentong and by day's end they had already reached the monks' hospital, opposite the University of Phnom Penh, and began to arrest fleeing Lon Nol soldiers. They slept on the floors of the university buildings.

In the early morning hours of 17 April, they were welcomed by the population. They followed a Lon Nol army tank with streaming white flags and led by a Republican foot soldier, arriving at the Central Market at 7 o'clock. Battalion 512 stayed in Phnom Penh for five days. Bun Chan did not wish to describe the forced evacuation of the city.

On the eve of the capture of Phnom Penh, In Tam[112] and his troops seized the Preah Vihear Temple. So, on 22 April, Bun Chan's battalion was sent north to take back the temple. During the expedition, one person from his battalion died after treading on a mine, and one was wounded. In Tam's troops fled to Thailand and Bun Chan was back in Phnom Penh by the end of April. On the way back, he still saw many people on the roads. From 5–8 May 1975, there was a big meeting in the main hall of the Institute of Technology of Cambodia (at the time *Institut Khméro-soviétique*) of all the political and military leaders of the new regime. The food was rice with water bindweed, vegetables, cabbage, some meat and fish, and water to drink. The food was quite plentiful. At night they slept in the classrooms of the institute.

Pol Pot dominated the meeting, but Khieu Samphân, Nuon Chea, Ieng Sary and Son Sen were also present. Before entering the amphitheatre, everyone was disarmed and even cigarette lighters were confiscated. The first question raised was the number of victims of the civil war. On a large blackboard the figure of 600,000 dead[113] was written, and 'many wounded'.

---

112 In Tam (1916–2006) started his administrative career as governor of Takeo province and, from 1960 to 1964, was Minister of Interior in the *Sangkum* regime. He later removed his support Sihanouk and was one of the main proponents of his dismissal. He later became president of the National Assembly. He served for seven months as Prime Minister in 1973, but retired from politics to live in Battambang with his family as he disagreed with Lon Nol's undemocratic policies. After, he formed an anti-DK group on the Thai border, but had to abandon it due to lack of support from the Thais and the international community. After taking refuge in France, he received political asylum in the United States in 1976.

113 This must be the origin of the inflated 600,000 figure that is usually given by analysts. For instance, Alexander L. Hinton writes of 'a civil war in which up to 600,000 people died' on p. 15 of *Genocide: An Anthropological Reader*, Blackwell, 2002. This estimate has no scientific basis. The only thorough demographic study of the subject has been that of Marek Sliwinski in *Le Génocide khmer rouge*, l'Harmattan, 1994, which shows that some 240,000 Cambodians

Civilian and military casualties were not distinguished. This figure was the result of discussions between the commanders before the meeting: it was the sum of all estimates from the regions. Only the final number was made public, not the detailed figures.

The big amphitheatre was full. Pol Pot spoke most of the time. He announced that the war had ended and it was a gigantic victory. It was therefore time to develop and rebuild the country, but also to defend it. He spoke the entire first morning, and was often interrupted by applause. He continued in the afternoon, and everyone was calm and silent. The second and third days were devoted mostly to allocating duties and positions to everyone who was present. Division 801, for example, was in charge of Ratanakiri; the *Bophea* or Eastern region was to be under the direction of Sao Phœm; Héng Samrin was placed in charge of the No. 4 battalion.

When the discussion turned to his future role, Bun Chan said that because of his age, he would like to end his military career and return to civilian life. He was asked, 'Where do you want to go?' – 'It's up to *Angkar* to decide.' Pol Pot replied that he should be appointed district chief. He was later named district secretary of the Chey Saen District of Preah Vihear province, known as Sector 103 under DK, a position he held until 1977 and the arrest of Koy Thuon.

The next day, Bun Chan left the capital and returned to Kompong Cham in an American jeep with six passengers. Then he went to Rovieng with the Preah Vihear governor. He did not start his work in the district until January 1976. In the meantime, he stayed at the provincial office. There was no evacuation of Rovieng city since the entire province had been liberated before April 17th. His duty was to organize all six people's communes in his district: one kitchen per commune. There were 13,800 inhabitants in all, just over 2,000 per commune.

People did not have enough to eat: rice porridge and vegetables, rarely meat. Sometimes, Tonlé Sap *prahok* (fermented fish paste) came through Siemreap. The people were thin and their bellies had swelled, but people had to obey the orders from Phnom Penh. All the orders came through the channel of the person in charge of Sector 103. He received coded messages from Phnom Penh by radio. Those had to be deciphered and transcribed. The written dispatches were then sent to the districts by two unarmed messengers on motorcycles. They used people who were literate.

---

were killed during the civil war, of which 17.1 per cent or about 40,000 people – civilian or military – were killed by American bombings.

The population had to dig canals and build small dykes to separate the new rice fields. Frequent trainings in Rovieng taught about how to develop the economy. Outside Rovieng and Siemreap, his district contained no security centres. A separate security team from Phnom Penh came to arrest people, but there were no arrests while he was chief of the district. He had to write his autobiography, which alerted authorities to the fact that his entire family had fled from Ta Veng to Laos.

He was not married, which was a problem when he was sick. So, the sector leader suggested that he should get married. He took a Kuey from Choam Khsant who had relocated to Rovieng and worked as a seamstress. They were married on 18 May 1976. As a member of *Angkar*, he was allowed to have an individual wedding ceremony in the regional office. The question was put to the woman: 'Do you agree to take Bun Chan as a husband?' Similarly, did he agree to take her as his wife? Many officials and locals were invited, an ox was killed and a big banquet was organized.

Arrest

On 5 January 1978, the *Nirdey* (Ta Mok's henchmen in the Southwest region) arrived: Khœum, Rœum and Vorn. All *kamaphibal* in Preah Vihear's 13 districts, as far as Phnom Kulen, were summoned to a meeting in Rovieng. When they arrived, the district chiefs and their deputies, 26 in all, were forced to enter a school. Khœum had organized the meeting. Some *Nirdey* came in and pointed their guns at them while others tied their hands behind their backs. They then were all put in a ZIL truck and taken down the road to Kompong Thom, then to Siemreap where they arrived at about 5 pm. They were put into the old colonial prison and shackled, 15 people per iron bar (*khnoh*). A big room, at least 12 meters long, was packed with prisoners.[114] Only one leg was chained and Bun Chan was allowed to wash once a day. All prisoners in his cell were *kamaphibal*; ordinary people were in other cells. He heard people screaming. They slept on cement; there was no *krâma*, no mat.

They were interrogated one month later, two prisoners at a time. Bun Chan was interrogated in a shed with three people: one asked him questions and

---

114 The ex-colonial prison in the centre of Siemreap city, into which the KR crammed significantly more detainees than it could contain, had become the regional prison for the entire North of Cambodia.

took notes in a school exercise book. The other two were there to hit him. He was asked:

1 – In what year did you join the pro-Vietnamese party?

2 – How did you contact Vietnam: by radio or by messages?

3 – What do you know about Vietnam's plan to invade Cambodia?

Bun Chan replied,

> Why are you accusing me? Pol Pot always had Vietnamese guards in 1970. I participated with him in the liberation of five provinces. I went to his base near the Tonlé San; the Vietnamese guarded him and protected him. When Pol Pot walked with Ieng Sary and his wife, he had about thirty Vietnamese guards. Pol Pot had a big radio, so he could communicate with whomever he wanted. The Vietnamese were then responsible for his safety.

The interrogators were very angry and could not answer that. Bun Chan added that he had made a lot of effort to liberate Phnom Penh and now they have arrested him. He had been interrogated twice in a month and had seen some of his friends taken away for execution, including nine Brao and Krœung. Four or five new detainees arrived in his cell every day. He later learned that the leader of Sector 103 and many soldiers of Battalion 512 had been sent to S–21.

In November 1978, the KR leadership signed an agreement with Thailand that would promote Thai tourism into Cambodia and required the closure of the Siemreap Prison and a facelift for the city and surrounding temples. Bun Chan was taken with some 100 detainees to the Tonlé Sap in a truck. He found his wife and two children, his baby and an adopted daughter. He had trouble when recognizing them because they were so skinny. The boat trip to Phnom Penh lasted two days and they stopped one night near an island. They arrived the next day at 9 am and docked in front of the Royal Palace. They ate in a canteen along the Mekong; rice, twice a day. After a meal, two buses took them to Takhmau High School. About 1,000 people were there, mostly military personnel from the Eastern region.

One hundred were put inside a classroom. They were neither tied nor chained, but the school was surrounded with barbed wire and guards. Bun Chan stayed there for a week and had three meals each day, always a bowl of rice. He could sleep with his wife and children. Then they were taken to a large pagoda, a huge construction called Wat Svay Meas that contained 700 prisoners. The place was twenty-four kilometres south of Phnom Penh at Kompong Kantuot, Phteah La commune, Phteah La Village. They were held overnight and worked during the day, digging a large lake. There were two soldiers to guard ten convicts. They worked very long hours, up to 10 pm. The *kamaphibal* told them that all the prisons were full, so they had to be taken elsewhere. Bun Chan had heard officials discuss the point: 'These, where are we going to put them?' He heard the name of S–21, there was no space anywhere.[115]

In December 1978, they heard gunshots and the sounds were very close on the 30th. At that moment, the KR locked everyone up and ran away. Bun Chan and a few others were strong enough to break the iron bars and take some rice. When the Vietnamese arrived on 9 January and saw the 700 people, they asked who they were and where they came from. They replied that they were prisoners. Everyone was very skinny. The Vietnamese gave them injections, other medicines and food. Bun Chan was named their leader and Lorn was his deputy. There was a woman who could speak Vietnamese very well. She cared for women and everyone could eat rice.

A few days later, the Vietnamese distributed clothes and utensils, and Cambodian soldiers began arriving as the local population gradually returned. They stayed there until June. Bun Chan wanted to return to Preah Vihear immediately, but the Vietnamese forbade people to go to remote provinces as they feared attacks. When Bun Chan reported that he had been chief of the district, the Vietnamese warned him that people could take revenge on him. He replied that he was not worried, as he had been very kind and popular, and had released many prisoners when he was in charge. So, the Vietnamese accompanied him to Rovieng, where a Brao ex-KR was in charge of the districts and the province. The people of Rovieng welcomed him with rice, coconut and eggs.

In July 1979, he left his wife at home and returned to Stung Treng with the Vietnamese. The purpose of the trip was to go to Laos to try to convince Brao refugees to return to Cambodia. He went to Laos with a truck and stayed for a month before returning with more than twenty Brao. He was given an official position in Banlung, but he ate too much dried fish and became ill. He was taken to Vietnam, where he was cured after an extended illness. During

---

115 This may be what he heard, but it is not quite true, as there was plenty of space in S–21 at this time. The leadership in fact was no longer sending inmates and the so-called suspected assassins of Malcolm Caldwell were to be the last detainees at the notorious prison. The repressive DK prison system was about to collapse with Vietnamese advance.

1981–82 the Krœung returned to Cambodia. In 1983, Bun Chan returned to Ratanakiri and was appointed deputy governor of Ta Veng District. He had five daughters, plus one adopted. His wife became a primary school teacher, grade 2, in 1984.

We have here, with Bun Chan's life story, an example of how ex-KR ethnic minorities were integrated into the Héng Samrin regime; Héng Samrin had no choice, as the country was sorely lacking in competent cadres.[116]

When the Vietnamese arrived in Ratanakiri at the end of 1978 and the beginning of 1979, the population had barely had time to see them go by as they hunted down the KR far and wide. Around Lumphat District, the KR collected the entire population and made them walk for seven nights to the Tonlé Srèpok, but when they saw Vietnamese soldiers on the banks of the river, they all fled, abandoning everyone. The special units guarding the border went into hiding. This was the moment when the fugitives escaped, including many Jaraï. The KR fled to the west and, as in the rest of the country, tried to use many civilians as hostages. But they had to abandon their plans shortly before Stung Treng and many, including a number of tribal soldiers, went to Thailand, some never to return. They settled all along the western border, from Samlaut to Pailin, Phnom Malay and Anlong Veng.[117]

10 – In the end, why was DK, which took the indigenous way of life as a model, so lethal?

Ratanakiri was the cradle of the Khmer Rouge revolution. It was there that, for three years, Pol Pot lived in secret bases, indoctrinated the Montagnards, and experimented with and then implemented his very simplistic and ruthless ideology. Only the most ignorant section of the Cambodian population could be impressed by the 'depth' of his thoughts. More importantly, for the first time, Pol Pot and his group tested their methods of identifying the 'enemy' and then eliminating it in the darkness of the dense forests. Many of these methods were borrowed from the Communist Chinese Party (CCP) and Kang Sheng[118] in particular.

---

116 See Ian G. Baird's *Rise of the Brao*, in which Bun Chan is interviewed extensively.
117 For more details, see pp. 192–192, above.
118 Kang Sheng (1898–1975) was in charge of the CCP's internal security apparatus from the 1940s, plus relationships with foreign Maoist parties.

During my investigation, I was always surrounded by a crowd and it was difficult to get biographical information from my interlocutors. I feared that if I had interrupted a spontaneous dialogue to collect names and ages, as I normally would, the interviewees would stop talking and substantive information would be lost. The Tampuon, Brao and Jaraï certainly benefited from special treatment under the revolutionary regime. Not only were some the closest to Pol Pot – as couriers, bodyguards and carriers of goods and weapons, but others were elite troops. They also had the privilege of generally being put into people's communes with their own relatives and friends and not always mixed with 'new people' or Lao. Further, nobody had been relocated to other provinces, unless by their own choice after joining the revolution.

The province of Ratanakiri was indeed special in that all the indicators show that the extermination rate was significantly lower than in the rest of the country. For the KR leaders, the highlanders were role models. Their so-called primitive collectivization, their ignorance of currency, their resistance and ability to survive in the worst circumstances, while constantly moving, and above all their total loyalty and obedience made them model citizens. In a way, *Angkar* wanted to turn the country into a great Ratanakiri and return to what the Revolutionary Organization considered the pre-feudal and pre-capitalist era, annihilating 2,000 years of Khmer history, as Pol Pot himself explained when he 'came out' to the world in his famous 17 September 1977 speech. This was the vision, the KR version, of Rousseau's noble savage and Mao's blank page. This structure enabled a handful of revolutionary leaders to exercise total control over some eight million citizens, with the help of about 50,000 henchmen armed with AK–47 copies donated by their patron country, Mao's China.

We saw that this radical system of forced total collectivization, novel among communist countries, was established in Ratanakiri between 1970 and 1975. Ultimately, the KR cardinal virtue demanded obedience: immediate, absolute, blind subservient. In essence, 'the enemy' was anyone who did not bow to this iron commandment. Some among Ratanakiri's ethnic minorities bowed and *Angkar* called this 'loyalty'. But the vast majority did not, running away or passively kowtowing instead. Only a minority chose to become *Angkar*'s servile and devoted henchmen and, for that choice, became the darlings of the regime.

At the end of the day, is it not paradoxical that the tribes that supposedly served as role models for the society conceived by *Angkar* under the DK were those who, even more that the Khmer themselves, witnessed the disappearance of their culture, to a large extent including their vernacular languages? Although they were among the 'oldest' of the 'old people', most were forced to abandon their ancestral villages and habits, and to live in new ways and in new places in the valleys and the plains.

If solidarity among villagers of tribal origin did prevail in the so-called 'primitive communism' that Pol Pot discovered in Ratanakiri province, when he herded indigenous communities into vast people's communes, he and his Party totally shattered that traditional solidarity and abolished all freedoms. From being poor, they became destitute and from being free, they became slaves, although most were not starved as in the rest of the country. Advanced communism was, for them too, a great leap backward. And let us not forget the fate of those who joined the revolutionary army as teenagers – like Phi Phuon – and then devoted all their adult years to waging war, for more than thirty years. How many survived the three decades of war, 1968–1998?

The KR regime or DK, as it called itself, took such a drastic form and made so many victims, innumerable, that analysts have been puzzled about how to classify this baffling political system. In January 1979, the Vietnamese justified their abrupt and massive invasion by claiming that what they called 'the Pol Pot regime' was a perverted form of red Nazism, and far removed from the 'real and humane' form of communism they represented. This is why they claimed the regime to have been 'genocidal', considering the vast number of victims that had been made during the three years, eight months and twenty days *Angkar* had held sway over Phnom Penh. This 'genocide' was a kind of monstrous hybrid of Nazism, thus giving the revolutionary regime an image far removed from real communism, as we pointed out at the beginning of this study. The leadership – what they called 'the Pol Pot/Ieng Sary clique' – were perverted Maoists who had abused the revolutionary cadres who, in fact, were idealists and good people.

This perspective radically distorts the reality of the revolutionary regime. First, the ruling 'clique' was not Pol Pot/Ieng Sary, but Pol Pot/Nuon Chea,[119]

---

119 Nuon Chea (1926–2019), born in Battambang with a Khmer mother and a Chinese father, left Cambodia in 1942, when the province fell under Thai control, living and studying at Wat Benchamabophit. After completing his secondary education, he studied law at the progressive and modernist University of Thammasat, while having small administrative posts first at the Ministry of Finance and later at the Ministry of Foreign Affairs. In 1949, he renounced a career in the Thai civil service to join his original country and Battambang province, which had been returned to Cambodia by the 1947 Treaty of Washington. This is where he joined the Indochinese Communist Party (ICP), although he had previously joined a secret cell of

the former the regime's charismatic communicator and the latter its brains and main designer of its ideology. Indeed, as Nuon Chea confessed to Thet Sambath: 'I was not Pol Pot's right arm or left arm, we were equals. Pol Pot did not help me and I did not help him. Both served the Party.'[120] This is somewhat cryptic. Was the Party an invisible god above Pol Pot and Nuon Chea? Did the two men introduce a new form of religion that was far removed from reality? When they were masterminding the widespread extermination policies throughout the country, did they believe they were just obeying some superhuman power with a new name – the Party? This ploy had been used by all communist regimes, including Xi Jinping nowadays: leaders claim they do not minister to their inordinate thirst for and enjoyment of totalitarian power, but are the servants of a fiction – the Party – that is the invisible face of revolution. This is just like the absolute kings of yore who claimed they had been selected by God and were just his dutiful servants.

The disastrous combination of these two minds was the original cause of the appalling sufferings of the entire Cambodian people. Beyond being ardent communist ideologues, both were also chauvinists and, above all, totally cut off from reality. They shared the fears of many Cambodians, that their ancient civilization would disappear and their remnants absorbed by more enterprising neighbours – the Thais and the Vietnamese. Both also felt terribly insecure as individuals, convinced as they were that mysterious plotters were about to wrench power from them. Both were besotted with Maoism and its Great Leap Forward and the so-called Cultural Revolution, essentially learnt through Vietminh luminaries, trips to Mao's China and not in Paris – where Nuon Chea never set foot. But already by 1975, their model was being assailed by the hated 'revisionism' and Mao's star was on the wane. Thus, they resolved to take up

---

the Thai Communist Party. But it was in Hanoi, where he stayed from early 1952 until after the 1954 Geneva Conference, that he learnt about the necessity of extreme violence during the revolutionary struggle. From 1955 to 1975, he rose in the Party ranks, learning to escape the ire of Sihanouk's secret services under the alias of a travelling salesman of building materials. While Pol Pot was starting the civil war in Ratanakiri from 1967 to 1970, Nuon Chea was in charge of setting the entire country ablaze, never allowing the authorities to identify him. He became Brother No. 2 in 1962 and, by the time the CPK was in power, 'he was practically in full control of communist policies of the regime and of security in particular – the ultimate authority at S–21. He had no tolerance for weaknesses and liked to dominate others.' This is how the direct S–21 authority, Kaing Guek Iev (alias Duch), described him during his confession to the Tribunal. Much of this has been mentioned already.

120 Gina Chon and Thet Sambath, *Behind the Killing Fields: A Khmer Rouge Leader and One of His Victims*, University of Pennsylvania Press, 2010, p. 135.

the torch, dramatically implementing those policies at breakneck speed and plunging their compatriots into the 'paradise' of total communism *hic et nunc*.

They did not just temporarily close educational institutions to make them battlefields of the class war, as in China; they abolished them altogether. They did not just ruralize millions of townsfolk to be re-educated by the peasantry, they emptied *all* cities and townships. They did not just minimize the use of currency to introduce vouchers in people's communes, they abolished money altogether. They did not just create vast people's communes in key areas of the countryside for the edification of world Maoists, they cast the entire population into labour camps that looked more like penal colonies or concentration camps, where the citizenry was made to labour like convicts and starve to death. The entire population became unpaid slaves – a move Mao had never dared to make. The leadership did not take these extraordinary decisions out of a concerted plan, without discussion and with enthusiasm, but out of absolute necessity: they were far too few to control the millions living in the cities. Hesitation would have been the death blow of the move-ment. So, they rationalized this move, hurried to exterminate all leaders of a potential rebellion in the shape of the elites of past regimes and romanticized the return to the rural self-sufficiency they had witnessed in Ratanakiri and seen in well choreographed tours of the People's Republic of China and North Korea. From there, and with everyone labouring like beasts of burden, the resulting economic growth would surpass all models. The leadership was in a great haste: communist paradise had to be reached before the *Angkar* lost its grip on society. It was a race not just for survival from the hated Vietnamese, but, once again after the Angkor era, to become one of the beacons – if not *the* beacon – of the entire world. Phnom Penh would outshine Moscow and Beijing as the Mecca of communism.

Pol Pot and Nuon Chea believed that even if Mao's dreams of irreversible revolution were not quite about to collapse, his country was at least going down the slippery slope of revisionism. This was, they might have reasoned, because Mao had been too lenient with the 'enemies' of his grand plans. In their eyes, Mao wasted time and resources on his *laogai* and reform camps, and his emphasis on re-education. Cambodia did not have as many resources and could not afford luxuries like re-education. Our duumvirate was more radical and the death penalty needed to be doled out *en masse*: no mercy for the 'traitors'! There was no time for the niceties of Confucian conversions, a sign of hesitation and weakness that was bound to lead to the failure of the revolution.

But the question was: how to identify those enemies? The answer took the form of regular self-criticism / mutual criticism sessions that enabled the people's commune leaders to spot the half-hearted, the dodgers and those who frankly opposed the unprecedented regime – and, naturally, they were many, although most did all they could to disguise their true feelings. It was even risky to remain silent; you had to blurt out platitudes to forestall Angkar's suspicions. The small 'offenders' were ascribed an extra communal task or to perform a heavier assignment during the next day's workload at the collective worksite. Those accused of plotting to sabotage the revolution, would be taken, after nightfall, for 're-education', a litotes for the prison. To the regime, these traitors were trying to ruin Angkar's utopia of prosperity for all. As Wang Chenyi has shown in her 'The Chinese Communist Party's relationship with the Khmer Rouge in the 1970s: an Ideological Victory and a Strategic Failure',[121] the apparatchiks of the Gang of Four used DK as a laboratory experiment to prove that Mao, the aging supreme guide, had indeed been right all along, despite glaring evidence to the contrary. In the last years of Mao's life, only the Gang of Four failed to see that his sweeping policies had failed. Still, they would point to the Cambodian revolution's 'successes' as proof that Mao had been a visionary all along. Contemporary dictators also have been able to extend their own power and destroy their own country thanks to the massive aid of another country, like Bashar al-Assad in Syria, with the aid of Iran and the Russian Federation. Mao proclaimed:

> I have done two things in my life. One is defeating Chiang Kai-shek and driving him to Taiwan, and defeating the Japanese imperialists and driving them out of China; the other is successfully conducting the Great Proletarian Cultural Revolution.[122]

On the other hand, and contrary to the assertions of the invading Vietnamese in 1979, the KR with Thiounn Mumm in charge set out to restart, and create if need be, all sorts of factories and workshops in a country that was to emulate and even surpass China's Great Leap Forward – 'the Super Great Leap Forward' it was called – not just in agriculture, but in industry, too. Marie

---

121 CWIHP Working Paper #88, Dec. 13, 2018.
122 Quoted on p. 3 of Wang, 'The Chinese Communist Party's relationship'.

Alexandrine-Martin in her *Cambodia: A Shattered Society*[123] describes how Phnom Penh, after the 17 April 1975 forced evacuation, soon became an 'industrial centre' when workers and technicians were called back to restart many factories and workshops that were indispensable to the revolutionary goal of total self-sufficiency. In other words, industrialization was also a priority, which turned massive rice production into an absolute necessity, as rice would be bartered for industrial equipment. Weaving factories and small electric power stations dotted the territory as far as Koh Nhiek in Mondolkiri. Among the most important industrial structures, were the Kampot Cement Factory and the Takhmau Rubber Factory just outside Phnom Penh that was making all kinds of tyres, as well as smaller workshops that produced the famous rubber sandals. In the meantime, the railway lines were totally renovated by the Chinese, from Sisophon, near the Thai border, to Kompong Som and a new one was being built directly from Phnom Penh to Kompong Som, following the No. 4 national road made with American aid. The vision seemed to be becoming a reality: paddy was exported to China in exchange for all manner of equipment. The largest industrial project was the total renovation – with Chinese technology – of the Kompong Som oil refinery built by Elf-Aquitaine, a French company, in the late 1960s that had been blown up by a Vietminh commando unit in 1970 and then dismantled during the civil war.

But the most extraordinary of the KR tenets was that, in the Cold War, the secret services of super-powers (the US and the USSR) were working hand in hand for the destruction of the Cambodian revolution. Nuon Chea conceived this balderdash: he explained in his acknowledgment to the Danish Communists:

> It is more widely known that the US will seize power from us in the six months following liberation. The plan involved joint action on the part of the USA, the KGB and Vietnam. There was to be a combined struggle from inside and outside. But we smashed this plan. Immediately after liberation, we evacuated all the cities. The CIA, KGB and Vietnam agents there left for the countryside and were unable to implement the plan. People who had infiltrated the Party could not react immediately, but we discovered them later when they planned to organize *coups d'état*. Their activities were coordinated with aggression from outside. These were not

---

123 University of California Press, 1994. French edition: *Le Mal cambodgien*, Hachette 1989. See also her 'L'industrie dans le Kampuchéa démocratique', *Études rurales*, Paris, 1983, pp. 77–110.

powerful people; their intention was to exploit the opportunity provided by Vietnam's attacks to assassinate our leaders and then announce it to the world. However, when the Vietnamese attacked, our army defeated them and we caught the traitors inside the Party.[124]

Although we say plans have been crushed, we do not mean the enemy has given up. We have to continue to build and defend our Party and our leadership, and to apprehend the people who have infiltrated our Party. We know the current plan involves not only Vietnamese agents, but has something to do with US imperialism and the KGB. All of them! ... Some CIA agents joined up with the Vietnamese in order to come to Kampuchea. Because the US was unable to come into Kampuchea, it had to rely upon Vietnam. The Vietnamese do not discriminate in choosing their agents: they will accept anybody who fights against the Communist Party of Kampuchea (CPK) – even CIA agents![125]

Here, Nuon Chea's delirium – beyond all the top KR apparatus – reaches its climax. With such motivation, it is not impossible that up to 50 per cent of KR political commissars and military personnel could have been purged during the regime's short lifespan. For instance, in Mœung Sonn's Prey Nup District Prison in 1978, most inmates were KR members.[126] Nuon Chea added:

> The leadership apparatus must be defended at any price. If we lose members but retain the leadership, we can continue to win victories. Defending the leadership of the Party is strategic. As long as the leadership is there, the Party will not die. There is no comparison between losing two to three leading cadres and 200–300 members. Rather the latter than the former. Otherwise, the Party had no head and cannot lead the struggle.[127]

Nuon Chea takes the example of Indonesia where, thirteen years after the 1965 massacres of most leaders, the party had not been rebuilt. With such reasoning, one can perfectly understand why hundreds, or even thousands, of innocent victims could be sacrificed in the country's prison network, provided the *Angkar Lœu* was protected. And both Pol Pot and Nuon Chea were

---

124 The Vietnamese army attacked Cambodia in late 1977 and almost reached the town of Takeo. In Mondolkiri, they went as far as Koh Nhiek, some 50 km from the border, and then decided to go back home after 'teaching the KR a lesson'. But the KR did not take the cue and proclaimed they had won a great victory over their powerful neighbour.

125 Nuon Chea, 'Statement of the Communist Party of Kampuchea' pp. 30–31.

126 See Locard, *Prisoner of the Khmer Rouge,* ch. 9.

127 Nuon Chea, 'Statement of the Communist Party of Kampuchea', p. 31.

convinced that there had been endless plots to assassinate them. Possibly, all were imaginary; we have no solid evidence that any were real.

Finally, the ultimate strategy was that all moves should remain absolutely secret, thus demonstrating that transparency is one of the cardinal virtues of democracies:

> Secret work is fundamental in everything we do. We do not use the term "legal" or "illegal"; we use the terms "secret" or "open". Thus, the elections of comrades to leadership positions are secret; the places where the leaders live are secret; we keep secret the hours and places of our meetings, and so on. On the one hand it is a question of principle, while on the other it is a way of protecting us from the infiltration of enemies. As long as there is class struggle and imperialism, secret work will remain fundamental. It is only through secrecy that we will remain the masters of the situation and we will triumph over our enemies who are unable to detect who is who.[128]

By essence, a totalitarian regime must be absolutely opaque. Nuon Chea understood that perfectly and would have had no patience for Gorbachev's 'transparency'. Here, Nuon Chea fully lives up to his reputation, aptly described by Philip Short as 'the opaque master of the underground'. But KR revolutionaries and especially Party members represented only 0.1 per cent of the population, as Philip Short has shown.[129] Any kind of consensus government was unthinkable and only the most brutal terror had to be used. The reason for the expulsion of all urban populations, as well as continual relocations of entire regions thereafter, is that the KR were too few to control. Ruralization, Act I of this tragedy, made possible the spate of disastrous choices that followed, finally throwing the country into the abyss of mass crimes against humanity. This disastrous Act I, unprecedented in modern history, was implemented on the very day the revolution broke out – 17 April 1975. The inhumanity of the KR leaders was revealed in the very way in which the decision was taken: in the secrecy of a meeting of senior leaders in 1974, and then confirmed a few days before the taking of Phnom Penh – with enthusiasm and without discussion – as confirmed by Phi Phuon, the aide-de-camp. There is no need to look for intellectual or ideological explanations for this criminal choice: the KR – apparatchiks civilians and soldiers – were far too few and ignorant of the cities to exert an absolute control over every citizen and to establish a

---

128 Ibid., p. 28.
129 Short, *Pol Pot*.

total collectivization in the capital and even all provincial cities – even for a single night.

The KR were only a small minority, with perhaps only 20,000 soldiers in Phnom Penh and another 20,000 spread throughout the country. Every revolutionary soldier would have had to control 150 to 200 citizens and that was absolutely impossible, even if they were disarmed. The only solution was the immediate expulsion of all along the roads, without any protection. In some twenty-four hours, the entire urban population had become indigents entirely dependent on the goodwill of their new masters, most of whom were without education, and all without the least experience of political and administrative responsibilities. The field was thus free for the explosion of violence and all cruelties – all the more so since many followers of the country's new masters were quite young, often only teenagers, and stood behind rifles as tall as them. This shows that the decision to evacuate is indeed an admission of weakness. Under the veil of organization and rationality, KR policies were just improvised as they went along and they thus brought their country down into a deep precipice.

Our duo, the visible Pol Pot and his shadow, Nuon Chea, invented a new form of totalitarianism: the opacity of the regime was absolute and the decision-makers and masters of all the crimes remained concealed. In 1979, Pol Pot would be designated by the Vietnamese as the great organizer of suffering and massacres; before this, most Cambodians did not even know his name. As for Nuon Chea himself, he managed to remain unknown, even to most analysts of DK, until his death in August 2019. Our duumvirate, always feeling totally insecure and obsessed with the idea of keeping power at all costs, created an original and deadly variant in the constellation of communist regimes. Based on absolute terror and secrecy, their regime was the most totalitarian state ever achieved: civil society had entirely disappeared and the state absorbed all human activities. The totalitarianism of the KR was even more 'total' than both of their two models – China and North Korea. Even in the latter, a small civil society has survived, along with a currency and shopkeepers;[130] not so in DK. Individuals were expected to deposit their own identity at the feet of *Angkar*, a new, invisible Leviathan. The two men became the masters of what George

---

130 See for instance Blaine Harden, *Escape from Camp 14: One Man's Remarkable Odyssey From North Korea In The West*, Pan Books, 2012.

Orwell so aptly calls 'double-think', that is the ability to strongly believe, at one and the same time, in two radically opposite propositions.

Pol Pot sought to project his version of double-think to the world in his historic speech of 27 September 1977, saying first that 98–99 per cent of the population followed the revolution, but, at the same time,

> There also exist such life-and-death contradictions as enemies in the form of various spy rings working for imperialism and international reactionaries, ... constituting only one or two per cent of our population.[131]

The paranoia of the leadership reaches new heights here, affected by both persecution mania and delusions of grandeur: 'If our people could build Angkor Wat, they can do everything. For example, they most creditably achieved the 17 April victory over U.S. imperialism.'[132] And yet, in spite of continuous purges, real or imagined opponents continued to rear their ugly heads.

This collective leadership would have been lost without the massive support of Maoist Chinese in the form of dollars, weapons, all manner of equipment shipped to Kompong Som, and above all manpower in the shape of thousands of Chinese 'experts'. In Syria today, Bachar al-Assad would never have been able to bring about the total ruin of his country without Russian bombings and Iranian paramilitary forces on the ground. Similarly, our *Angkar* would never have been able to wreak havoc upon its own populace without the massive aid from Mao's China, aid that extended over almost three decades: 1962–1991.

Besides, the ethnic minorities of the northeast, along with the Khmers of the periphery, who mainly believed in good and bad spirits that needed to be placated, were in the forefront of devotees who were prompt to comply with insane orders. The devotees' entire lives had been dominated by superstitions and they could easily be duped. They believed they were surrounded by an invisible world and so could easily fall victims to charlatans who exploited their credulity. For them, *Angkar* representatives were the gurus of a new religion that would bring them happiness on earth here and now. In the end, what has been called 'Polpotism' was nothing but a cult; in the name of that creed, devotees were made to carry out the most heinous crimes.

---

131 Foreign Broadcast Information Service, FBIS, 4 Oct. 1977, H 27–28. This could be the percentage of the population inside the prison-extermination centres at any given moment.

132 Ibid., H 26.

In the end, this potentially explosive collaboration between semi-intellectuals from the cities, immersed in Maoist Cultural Revolution lore, who had mesmerized unschooled young men from the periphery of the country – and Ratanakiri highlanders in particular – spread desolation over Cambodia.

11 – The rule of the ignorant

To conclude, although we have collected ample evidence that, to a large extent, Ratanakiri's indigenous communities spearheaded the KR revolution in Cambodia, no one has been able to demonstrate that the KR commissars recruited a higher proportion of young soldiers from tribal minorities than from other peripheral regions in Cambodia. While it is well understood that the majority of the young soldiers who entered Phnom Penh on 17 April 1975 were illiterate and totally ignorant of the capital, mostly coming from deprived family backgrounds, no one has been in a position to prove that the tribal people were over-represented.

The KR leadership romanticized the highlanders' way of life and turned them into role models, or even their idols, as we saw. They proved capable of supplying the wherewithal the leadership needed to survive in the jungle in the late 1960s, but they also proved to be the most battle-worthy. In addition to all the dogmas of Mao's Great Leap Forward and the Cultural Revolution, the indigenous people of Ratanakiri added the exotic return to society that existed at the origin of agriculture without modern implements, when humanity was just coming out of the forest. That total ruralization gave Cambodian totalitarianism its primitive touch, or what Marie-Alexandrine Martin aptly called 'generalizing tribal society to the whole of Cambodia',[133] while those who were supposed to serve as model revolutionaries got little in return. The famine that Phi Phuon occasionally suffered in his youth was extended to the entire society, and most of the time.

Many of the minorities who entered the revolution were doled out death as a reward. It certainly was *not* 50 per cent of the Ratanakiri population that perished under DK; however, much more than 50 per cent of the tribal warriors could well have lost their lives during the three decades of war they served the revolution.[134] Phi Phuon was among the very lucky survivors, as he himself

---

133 *Le Mal cambodgien*, Paris: Hachette, 1989, p. 201.
134 See Phi Phuon's memoirs above, pp. 192–193.

underlines in his memoirs. Still, without the thousands of uncritical and uneducated young men who showed unquestioning and unwavering obedience to the Party in the crucial years that saw the spread of that ruthless revolution, the ensuing tragedies would not have been possible. And Phi Phuon, with his utter devotion while ministering to the needs of the leadership, was one of them.

Epilogue

A Wedding, a Funeral and a Tragedy

1 – A wedding

*U*nder DK, private life was to be subservient to public life, especially for active supporters of the revolution. This is why Phi Phuon's memoirs mention very little of his daily life at Phnom Malay after the collapse of the revolutionary regime.

In the mid-1990s, Phi Phuon retired from his position as vice-governor of his district. This choice provided him with the leisure to recount all the memorable stages of his extraordinary life. This is also why he could attend the

Figure 17: Sâr Patchata and her new husband, Sy Vicheka, the couple's happiness on display.

311

Figure 18: Phi Phuon at the wedding dinner.

lavish wedding ceremony of Pol Pot's daughter, Sâr Patchata. The ceremony was held in Phnom Malay, very close to Phi Phuon's home, and I also had been invited to attend by the bride's stepfather, Tep Khunnal. The wedding was held on 16 March 2014, exactly one year before Phi Phuon's sudden death.

The occasion was singularly elegant and perfectly orchestrated by Tep Khunnal, who had learned during his years in France that, beyond standing for hours at the entrance, as is the habit at weddings in Cambodia, a good host moves among the guests, actively welcoming and introducing them to people who could be of interest. The pink decorations and myriad multi-coloured orchids from nearby Thailand gave a touch of refinement one would never expect in the outer reaches of the Kingdom of Cambodia.

2 – A funeral

At around 7:30 am on 15 April 2015, I received the news of the sudden death of Phi Phuon, aka Cheam, a victim of a cerebral haemorrhage that occurred at 1:30 am on this day, at his home in Phnom Malay, Banteay Meanchey

Province. He was only 68. As he had become a little overweight, his doctor had advised him to exercise, and he would go for long walks every morning.

I heard the news from Suong Sikœun during breakfast. This was quite a shock, for I had spoken to Phi Phuon on the phone late the preceding evening from Battambang, where I was spending the night. Phi Phuon was very much looking forward to travelling with me back to his old village of Malik, in Ratanakiri's Andoung Meas District, and thrilled by the prospect of visiting the beautiful temples of Koh Ker and Preah Vihear on the way. He was also so looking forward to being reunited with his family that he could not sleep and rang me late in the night. Was this what the Khmers call *slap-sabay*: sudden death brought about when you are so overjoyed by a happy event you have been expecting for years that you suddenly die?

This was the sad and abrupt epilogue of Phi Phuon, a critical voice for understanding DK and especially the place of the Ratanakiri ethnic minorities in the revolutionary movement. Our last recordings of his eventful life story had been completed the preceding month, but I had expected not just to go with him to his native village but also to record more memories and sentiments. I was particularly interested in witnessing how he responded to the shock of seeing Ratanakiri's now-destroyed environment. The trip might also have been an opportunity for him to distance himself even more from the extraordinary saga that his life had been. This was not to be.

We could not but ask ourselves why, like most KR officials in the insane days of DK, the Jaraï Phi Phuon never found an opportunity to visit his kinsmen during the dark days of DK and throughout the 1980s. One might suppose that he would not have been allowed to go all the way to the Naga's Tail in Ratanakiri to seek them. 'Familialism' – or too strong an attachment to family ties – was branded as signifying a lack of revolutionary fervour and put one in jeopardy vis-à-vis the Party to which Phi Phuon had belonged since 1972. Finally, in the late 1990s, he had the joy to be informed that both his parents had survived, and the family soon was reunited. He arranged grand Jaraï funeral ceremonies when they died, his mother in 2003 and father in 2011, having six buffaloes immolated. Keep in mind that any form of funeral ceremony had been strictly banned under the revolutionary regime. His grateful kinsfolk reciprocated the lavish ceremonies right in the middle of the Buddhist New Year.

His 71-year-old elder brother, Rochœm Tveng, and about a dozen members of his extended family from Malik village hastened across the country to

Figure 19: Funeral rituals for an ex-official; conical hats on men are never seen at Khmer funerals.

Figure 20: Some half-dozen Jaraï mourners came straight from Ratanakiri with their brass cymbals.

Phnom Malay, arriving at the end of the very same day. They could not miss the two-day funeral ceremony and came prepared with loincloths for men, handwoven sampots for women and a collection of harmonious and soothing ritual gongs. I did not see any Buddhist monks, who typically are present at

Figure 21: Two mourning Jaraï women in their woven sampots.

funerals in Cambodia, and all the ceremonies took place at Phi Phuon's house and not at a wat. Retaining the common habit of all of Ratanakiri's ethnic minorities, he was buried in a coffin, not incinerated. He was placed in his garden and a buffalo was immolated. None of that was Buddhist.

Perhaps the last word will be that of the district governor, whose funeral oration summed up the main stages of Phi Phuon's revolutionary career. From an illiterate adolescent who had never attended school, since there were none in his area, he ended his career as vice-governor of Phnom Malay District. That career began when he and some other youths from his village created a *maquis* in the forest in 1963, four years before Saloth Sâr arrived. He was keen enough to master the Khmer language and its elaborate script. And we can add that if Phi Phuon actively contributed to the destruction of Cambodia in the early 1970s, he certainly contributed significantly to the prosperity of his new district, Phnom Malay, in the 1990s and 2000s. And the local population expressed their gratitude during that touching two-day funeral ceremony.

3 – Funeral ceremony of Phi Phoun's soul, April 2016

I suggested to Rochœm Tveng, Phi Phuon's elder brother, that the second funeral ceremonies of Phi Phuon's 'wandering soul' be held during the Cambodian New Year ceremony, one year after his physical death. But the preceding week was chosen and I could not attend, as I was committed to lecturing at the Royal University of Phnom Penh. Anthropologist Frédéric Bourdier was present, and he kindly agreed to write a brief description of the three-day ceremony:

> The dates selected for the second funeral ceremony of Phi Phuon's 'wandering soul', which would free his spirit forever, were just one year after his demise. April 8, 9 and 10 were chosen. Three days of ceremonies took place in the forested cemetery close to the village Malik, located at the south bank of the Tonlé San, where his clan resides. His elder brother Rochœm Tveng organized the event, contacted the guests and bought three buffaloes for the sacrifices. He acquired some pigs that would also be immolated. At the same time, most guests would bring their personal offerings.
>
> The first day was devoted to the collective preparation of the tomb. The young men of the village put themselves to work with impeccable dexterity (sculpture, graphic design, decoration, and so on). At the same time, both single and married women participated in the planning of the place and prepared food for the workers and the few guests already present. The first libations with rice beer took place in the evening a few meters from the burial place, which now was ready. Once night fell, gongs rang out, alternating with Jaraï music stored on I-pads connected to gigantic speakers. The women sang songs and danced around the burial place. Inside, female relatives took turns expressing the pain of being separated forever from Phi Phuon. The lamentations flew away under the canopy enveloping the cemetery.
>
> A dozen men and women from the Jaraï community of Vietnam had arrived and were staying in Tveng's house. His wife was in charge of the logistics. Most of these Jaraï were relatives from the three highland provinces (Kon Tum, Gia Lai and Dak Lak). On the morning of the second day, the three buffaloes were brought into the cemetery and tied

to the east of the grave. A first animal was sacrificed to apparent general indifference: children continued to play without paying attention to the killing, and adults went here and there, busy with various occupations and conversations in small groups. Only about 15 participants, all close relatives, sat inside the cenotaph and followed the unfolding ceremony with great attention. The leather strap encircling the slaughtered animal was held by the living, who mimed their accompaniment of the spirit of Phi Phuon between the two worlds. While two men cut the animal into pieces, the gongs sounded: the elder brother took the biggest, beating to the rhythm of the others. The twelve men turned around the tomb and the music got carried away. The sun was not yet at its zenith, but the chant gave the impression of joining the highest sunrays announcing a cloudless day. Most of the people present were from the village. Special guests from other communes arrived in the evening. They attended the sacrifice of the remaining buffaloes the next morning, bringing pigs as an offering, or a jar of rice, or a cash donation.

It can be noted that not a single member of Phi Phuon's family from Phnom Malay (Khmer wife, children, grandchildren, etc.) was party to the ceremony, which did not upset the villagers, including the brother, aware that these funerals were about Jaraï community, as much or more so than family, and do not involve the Khmers, even when family-related. Many Jaraï stayed all night on the scene of the festivities; people slept in hammocks, on grass carpets, and sometimes even on the very soil. The important thing was to be there. The atmosphere was joyous: everyone laughed, joked and alternated dry fermented beer with locally distilled rice alcohol. This was a consecration unfolding before our eyes. Rituals of death to reassure the living, as affirmed by the French anthropologist Louis Vincent Thomas, or, more prosaically, the closing ceremony that announced the passage from life on earth to life into an ethereal village where ancestors and non-human entities abide. Phi Phuon was well-departed *ad vitam æternam*; the living, strengthened by the acts accomplished and the homage rendered, had no longer to fear the return of his wandering soul.[1]

4 – Ratanakiri Today

Today lowland Cambodia has turned the page from the destructions of the DK regime in most fields. The same cannot be said of the highlands, where

1 Frédéric Bourdier, Institute for Research and Development (IRD), Phnom Penh, Cambodia.

© Henri Locard.

Figure 22: Rochœm Tveng and the author at Phi Phuon's gravesite

the total ravages caused by practically ten years under the KR, followed by almost fifteen years of Vietnamese communist and military control and occupation, not to speak about unbridled post-UNTAC commercialism since, have given more or less a death blow to the original highland inhabitants. Anglo-American analysts simply call this sort of new regime 'neoliberalism'; in reality, this lawless commercialism[2], largely under the auspices of China, has a free hand in the whole country. If the indigenous people and their descendants do survive as human beings, they certainly do not much survive as traditional highlanders. Only family ceremonies and some beliefs remain, and alas superstitions, perhaps because families continue to be closely knit. They tend to live alongside their immediate relatives, even in the same compound, as the Rochœms do today. Or, at the periphery of the province, as on the right bank of the Tonlé San, towards the Lao border, a few tribal villages have survived. Still, I am not prepared to share the optimism of anthropologists who speak of their 'resilience'. Although the highlanders were the darlings of *Angkar Lœu*, they saw their entire way of life and culture eradicated never really to be revived, or even safeguarded, in any significant way; some arts or crafts remain, and quite a few elegantly woven back baskets can be seen along the

---

2   In French, *le capitalisme sauvage*.

roads. When Pol Pot settled in Ratanakiri, indigenous people were the vast majority. Today, they have been reduced to only 50 per cent of the province's 185,000 inhabitants.[3] As to the remaining artistic, mainly timber, bamboo and straw-roofed tribal cottages, they are now few and far between. The nondescript houses that replaced them have no architectural charm whatsoever.

Phi Phuon's testimony and further evidence on the tragic years in Ratanakiri explain why the KR movement constituted a dramatic acceleration of history, and brutal Khmerization afterwards will make it even more difficult for tribespeople to link up with their past. After the massive immigration from the plains, together with large-scale land spoliation, during the concession boom of the early 2000s, for the benefit of well-connected individuals or companies – foreign and national – the 'irremediable acculturation' is all too obvious for all to see. But this is not a 'Super Great Leap Forward' from primitive communism into the most achieved communist utopia on the planet. Rather, since UNTAC (1992–1993), Ratanakiri has experienced a great leap into the globalized economic world, where the wealthy can freely tap natural resources from plantation crops and mining that blanket the plateau and enjoy the benefits of cheap labour. The forest has totally vanished, except at the periphery in the far north. In this 'neo-liberalism', liberties and liberalities are for the exclusive benefit of the well-connected.

The way of life of the hill tribes and their special relationships with their forested environment is a thing of the past, simply because there is virtually no primary forest left, except remnants in the outer reaches of the mountainous ridges of the Lao border. The elephants in the villages have all gone, the elegantly weaved cottages are virtually nowhere to be seen. The people live in nondescript houses and the poor often wear second-hand clothes from Vietnam. Yes, they survive now as modern human beings with their handphones, motorbikes and even a few cars,[4] but probably not much as Jaraï or whatever their tribal identity might have been. In pre-KR society, they were the proud and free inhabitants of the forest; today, they are among those on the lowest rung of Hun Sèn society, surviving from modest farm plots of at best on average a couple of hectares per household.

---

3   Information from Mr Thol Dina, an official of the Ministry of Land Management, Urban Planning and Construction, who works on land titling, April 2021.

4   One car in the Rochœm Tveng household for 25 individuals covering three generations, while some have a motobike and most a mobile phone.

Phi Phuon did have his five[5] hectares at Phnom Malay before he retired, but he donated these to his four children, who have sold much of this since. One invested the proceeds in establishing a garage, another started a local company that produces drinking water, and a third is in Hun Sèn's army at Anlong Veng, in northern Cambodia. As to the 23 descendants of his elder brother, Rochœm Tveng, and his Jaraï wife, six of their 11 children have survived to this day and all live inside his original compound in Malik commune. Among the eleven grandchildren, two are too young to go to school and two others have completed grade twelve at Andoung Meas Upper Secondary School. Neither has a job or learnt any professional skill. One is married to a local policeman who owns a car. The other studied animal husbandry for two years at Prek Leap Agricultural School. Despite completing her training, she still lives with her parents at Malik, as she has no funding to start a pig farm.

The main issue to be taken into consideration for indigenous communities in Ratanakiri, who still work primarily in agriculture, is how to diversify crops to increase income generation. With limited land but increased population, improved agricultural technology is crucial to producing sufficiently. As has been observed with many indigenous communities, the mode of production is still poor. The present Hun Sèn regime, which has been around for now almost four decades, has been perpetrating what one analyst[6] properly calls an 'ecocide', and the Ratanakiri upland minorities are the first victims of this policy of almost total environmental neglect.

After the KR regime, the Vietnamese started deforestation to cover their expenses from building a hydroelectric power station not far from Banlung. During the 1990s, throughout the country, logs travelled along the rivers or surfaced roads, even some passing Phnom Penh for all to see before continuing to Vietnam, as most logs did. In the meantime, on the Western border, the remaining KR survived by allowing Thai companies to wipe out all the forests near the border, especially around Anlong Veng, Phnom Malay and Pailin. It was only at the beginning of the 2000s that the government tried to control the lawless plundering of the Cambodian forest.

An important Land Law, promulgated on 30 August 2001, classifies land into three main categories: private land, state land and collective land. Col-

---

5   Note that this is half of the usual ten hectares that were distributed at the end of the war. This is proof that Phi Phuon did not take advantage of his administrative position to grow richer.

6   'Ecocide in the shadow of genocide and transitional justice', lecture at The Center for Khmer Studies, 12 March 2021, by Dr Courtney Work, National Chengchi University.

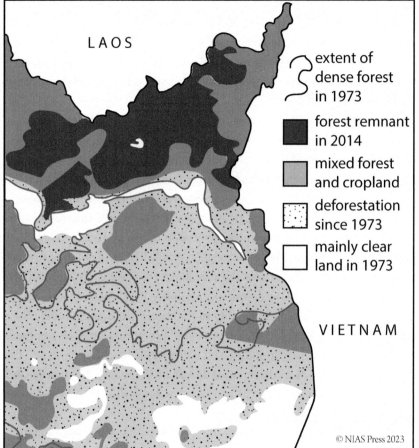

Map 5: Deforestation of Ratanakiri since the 1970s

lective land was specially designated for collective uses, such as monasteries, and by members of indigenous groups that embrace different cultures and identities. The pilot project of collective land title registration started with two indigenous communities in Ratanakiri in the late 2000s. Two indigenous communities named La En located in Teun Commune, Koun Mom District and La En Kren located in O'Chum District were chosen to pilot the collective land titling programme. Both obtained collective land titles in December 2011.[7] However, the process of collective land title registration has been very complicated and few highlanders have had their identity properly registered.

---

7   Information from Thol Dina who contributed to distributing land titles in Ratanakiri.

So, while 114 communities had applied for collective titles, by the end of 2013 only five had been able to complete the process with the financial support of the GTZ (Gdonerman Technical Cooperation). On the other hand, by June 2007, over 943,069 hectares of land in rural Cambodia had been granted to private companies, as economic land concessions for the development of agro-industrial plantations.

Thirty-six of these 59 concessions have been granted to foreign business interests or prominent political and business figures. Economic land concessions continue to impact negatively upon the human rights and livelihoods of communities that depend upon land and forest resources for their survival. Concessions have been granted over forested areas and former forest concessions, contrary to the Forestry Law and forestry regulations. The report raises particular concerns about the impact of economic land and other concessions on indigenous communities, whose rights to collective ownership of land are protected under Cambodian law. The alienation of indigenous land through the granting of concessions is undermining the ability of indigenous communities to register their collective ownership of traditional lands, and enforce their rights to land under the Land Law. Instead of promoting rural development and poverty reduction, economic land concessions have compromised the rights and livelihoods of rural communities in Cambodia. Economic land concessions have continued to be granted over forested areas and indigenous land, in violation of the law.

The establishment of conservation corridors by the Ministry of Environment (MOE) presented a new challenge for Ratanakiri's indigenous communities. In a 2017 sub-decree, the MOE announced the creation of conservation corridors that would include 1.5 million hectares of land in the northeastern provinces (Ratanakiri, Mondolkiri, and Stung Treng). In some cases, the conservation corridors include land that indigenous people have used for years. In some communities, especially those that did not receive collective titles, the corridors cover almost all their land, which made it difficult to proceed with collective land title registration.

But one can even question the very idea of wishing to grant collective land titling to indigenous people, since, in pre-modern highlander groups in Ratanakiri, land was not owned collectively by any specific village, but it was the property of genii that had to be propitiated with elaborate rituals before any part of the primary forest was cut. This was not for collective use, but for temporary ownership by some specific nuclear families. Only the clearing of the trees could be done collectively, with days' work of particular individuals clearly totted up and noted for the arithmetical exchange of services between nuclear families. All communist regimes that have tried to collectivize agricultural land have failed, and what has been happening in Ratanakiri during these last two decades is one more piece of evidence of this.

By and large, the situation of ethnic minorities has not improved much in Ratanakiri since Khmer colonization. Most have lost access to forest products and forest land, as most of the forest has given way to rubber, cashew nut and cassava plantations that blanket the soil. Ironically, it is the same institution that, some three-quarters of a century ago, came from about 1946, early in the First Indochina War for independence, with promises of liberty, equality and affluence, that has grabbed for its own benefit thousands of hectares of rich red soil. I refer to the People's Army of Vietnam, which today owns and controls large chunks of Andoung Meas district, where Phi Phuon and Rochœm Tveng were born. According to a *Cambodia Daily* article from 2012, the PAVN obtained some 40,000 hectares of concessions close to the border. The main one is called Hoang Anh Gia Lai, where mainly rubber has been planted:

> [F]or people living on or near the concessions in Ratanakiri – many of them members of indigenous minorities whose lives revolve around the forests – is quite the opposite to "ostensible benefits", as Mr Hun Sèn argued. Over the years, rights groups and reporters have fielded a litany of abuse complaints against the four concessions: encroaching on communal land, destroying spirit forests and burial grounds, logging outside their boundaries, and illegally exporting luxury-grade timber across the porous border with Vietnam. Chhay Thy, provincial coordinator for rights group ADHOC,[8] who spends much of his time monitoring the province's disappearing forests, said that logging in and around the four concessions peaked in 2012 and 2013, shortly after the PAVN took control of them.[9] There has been also Dam Chanthy (from the Highlanders Association established in 2000), a Tampuon woman involved in upland rights since the 1990s. She was born in Ta Lav, Andoung Meas in 1955.

---

8   The *Association de Défense des Droits de l'Homme au Cambodge* (ADHOC), was founded in December 1991 by Thun Saray.

9   Chhay Thy in *The Cambodia Daily*, 8 April 2015. He was the provincial coordinator of the Cambodian Human Rights and Development Association (ADHOC)

The 2001 land law created community forests precisely for the indigenous minorities, but most of these have failed as dealers have convinced or coerced some nominal owners to put their fingerprint on sales to private companies. They were all too willing to do so, as their priority is now to buy mobile phones, motorbikes and especially cars. Most people are ashamed to identify themselves as indigenous people. North of the Tonlé San, where some forest remains on the hilly slopes up to the Lao border, deforestation is continuing. Little is left of traditional Ratanakiri, except in the outer reaches of the province or so is the conclusion of the UNHCR.

Paradoxically, on the very day I completed a revision of this chapter, the *Phnom Penh Post* published an article precisely on the vast Vietnamese-owned rubber plantations in Cambodia: 'Vietnamese-owned rubber plantations are looking to hire no fewer than 105,000 workers and tappers in particular'.[10] They would be given some $200 a month, which is not regarded as a living wage, according to the UNHCR representative in charge of the northeast.[11] The Jaraï or Tampuon do not even wish to become low-paid daily labourers, and the almost total obliteration of their way of life and culture.

Besides, as in so many other parts of the developing world, Cambodians are now fascinated by cities and Phnom Penh in particular, where jobs in the thriving construction industry are countless. It is likely that both Khmers and indigenous minorities would prefer to avoid working for Vietnamese companies. Cambodians prefer to earn better wages in Thailand or even much higher ones in South Korea. If Vietnamese businessmen fail to revise dramatically the terms of their contracts, they risk seeing their vast plantations in Ratanakiri, Mondolkri and Kratieh standing idle.

Another recent *Phnom Penh Post* article gives the latest details about the vast extension of Vietnamese plantation interests and documents their vast involvement in this highly profitable undertaking – for them. They explain that they are merely responding to the market, specifically China's huge demand for latex. As a result, the Vietnamese are extending their grip over both Cambodia and Laos, thus re-constituting their beloved 'Indochina' of French days, with industry in Vietnam and agriculture in Cambodia and Laos:

> Vietnam Rubber Group JSC's (VRG) natural-rubber processing plants
> in Cambodia have reportedly produced 109,526 tonnes of latex this year,

---

10 *Phnom Penh Post*, 20 March 2020, p. 5.
11 Mr Kim Sambath, interviewed on 4 February 2020.

equivalent to 78.23 per cent of the firm's full-year target, as it strives to meet international demand for the milky white sap, especially from China – the biggest market for Vietnamese rubber.

In a message to the *Post*, VRG's representative office in Cambodia noted that the company, through 16 subsidiaries, has invested in rubber plantations in the Kingdom since 2007, which now cover 74,000 ha out of an allotted area of nearly 90,000 ha across Kratie, Ratanakiri, Kampong Thom, Mondolkiri, Siem Reap, Oddar Meanchey and Preah Vihear provinces. The firm also operates six latex processing plants: four in Kampong Thom and one each in Kratie and Ratanakiri.

VRG says on its website that as external natural-rubber demand outstrips domestic production, Vietnamese companies must invest in plantations in neighbouring countries such as Cambodia and Laos to keep pace, shipping the latex to Vietnam for processing before re-export to other markets, especially China.[12]

Although the highlanders are still some 50 per cent of the Ratanakiri population, they are no longer on the central stage. They are again marginalized, as in the old days of the *Sangkum*, mostly looked down upon by state institutions and mainly protected by a few benevolent foreign NGOs.

---

12 *Phnom Penh Post*, 24 August 2022: 'Vietnam rubber giant's 2022 Cambodia output to pass 140K tonne goal'.

References

Baird, Ian G. *Rise of the Brao: Ethnic Minorities in Northeastern Cambodia During Vietnamese Occupation,* The University of Wisconsin Press, 2020.

Bizot, François, *Le Portail,* La Table Ronde, Paris, 2000. Published in English as *The Gate,* Harvill Press, London, 2004.

Bourdier, Frédéric, *The Mountain of Precious Stones: Essays in Social Anthropology* Phnom Penh: Centre for Khmer Studies, 2006.

———— (ed.) *Development and Dominion: Indigenous Peoples of Cambodia, Vietnam and Laos,* Bangkok: White Lotus, 2009.

————, et al., *From Padi States to Commercial States: Reflections on Identity & the Social Construction Space in the Borderlands of Cambodia, Vietnam and Thailand,* Amsterdam University Press, 2015.

Bouvet, Jean-François, *Havre de Guerre,* Fayard, 2018.

Chandler, David P., *The Tragedy of the Cambodian History: Politics, War and Revolution since 1945.* New Haven and London: Yale University Press, 1991.

————, Benedict Kiernan and Chanthou Boua (eds), *Pol Pot Plans the Future, Confidential Leadership Documents from Democratic Kampuchea, 1976–1977,* Yale University Press, 1988.

Ciorciari, John D. and Anne Heindel, *Hybrid Justice: the Extraordinary Chambers in the Courts of Cambodia,* University of Michigan Press, Ann Arbor, 2014.

Chon, Gina and Thet Sambath, *Behind the Killing Fields: A Khmer Rouge Leader and One of His Victims,* University of Pennsylvania Press, 2010.

Colm, Sara. *The Highland Minorities and the Khmer Rouge, 1969–1979,* Phnom Penh, Documentation Centre of Cambodia, 1996.

———— *Khmer Rouge Purges in the Mondul Kiri Highlands,* with Sorya Sim, Documentation Series No. 14, Documentation Center of Cambodia, 2009.

————. 'The Khmer Rouge's Legacy for Highland Culture and Religion in Northeastern Cambodia, pp. 141–61, in Frédéric Bourdier (ed.) *Development and Dominion: Indigenous Peoples of Cambodia, Vietnam and Laos,* White Lotus, 2009.

China & the Pol Pot Regime, University of Michigan, Routledge, 2013.

Constitution of Democratic Kampuchea, January 1976.

Courtois, Stéphane, *Le Livre noir du communisme : crimes, terreur, répression*, Robert Laffont, Paris 1997, *The Black Book of Communism*, Harvard University Press, 1999.

Criddle, Joan D. and Teeda Butt Mam, *To Destroy You is no Loss: The Odyssey of a Cambodian Family*, Doubleday, 1987

Diamond, Jared, *Guns, Germs & Steel: A Short History of Everybody for the Last 13,000 Years*, Penguin, 2017.

Extraordinary Chambers within the Courts of Cambodia, '[Corrected 1] Transcript of hearing on the substance in Case 002 – Trial Day 84'. www.eccc.gov.kh/ sites/default/files/documents/courtdoc/2015-02-11%2010%3A07/E1_96. 1_TR002_20120725_Final_EN_Pub.pdf.

———, '[Corrected 3] Transcript of hearing on the substance in Case 002 – Trial Day 85'. www.eccc.gov.kh/sites/default/files/documents/courtdoc/2015-02-11 %2010%3A14/E1_97-1.1_TR002_20120726_Final_EN_Pub.pdf.

———, 'Transcript of hearing on the substance in Case 002 – Trial Day 86'. www.eccc. gov.kh/sites/default/files/documents/courtdoc/E1_98.1_TR002_20120730_ Final_EN_Pub.pdf.

———, 'Transcript of hearing on the substance in Case 002 – Trial Day 87'. www.eccc. gov.kh/sites/default/files/documents/courtdoc/E1_99.1_TR002_20120731_ Final_EN_Pub.pdf.

———, 'Transcript of hearing on the substance in Case 002 – Trial Day 88'. www.eccc. gov.kh/sites/default/files/documents/courtdoc/E1_100.1_TR002_20120801_ Final_EN_Pub.pdf.

———, '[Corrected 1] Transcript of hearing on the substance in Case 002 – 02 August 2012'. www.eccc.gov.kh/sites/default/files/documents/courtdoc/2014-12-23%2011%3A47/E1_101.1_TR002_20120802_Final_EN_Pub.pdf.

———, 'Transcript of hearing on the substance in Case 002/02 – 11 February 2015'. www.eccc.gov.kh/sites/default/files/documents/courtdoc/2015-02-24%2013 %3A59/E1_261.1_TR002_20150211_Final_EN_Pub.pdf.

———, Case 002/02, Judgement of Nuon Chea and Khieu Samphân, 16 November 2018. goo.gl/Yfe5S5

Hinton, Alexander L. (ed.), *Genocide: An Anthropological Reader*, Blackwell, 2002.

Hour Chea, *Quatre ans avec les Khmers rouges*, préface de Jean Lacouture, Librairie Tchou, Paris, 2007.

Huff, Barbara and Ted Robert Gurr, 'Toward an empirical theory of genocides and politicides: Identification and measurement of cases since 1945', *International Studies Quarterly* 32:3 (September 1988) 359–71.

Jeldres, Julio, 'A personal reflection on Norodom Sihanouk and Zhou Enlai: An extraordinary friendship on the fringes of the Cold War', *Cross-Currents: East Asian*

History and Culture Review, no. 4 (September 2012). cross-currents.berkeley.edu/ e-journal/issue-4

————, 'Democratic Kampuchea's foreign policy: A leftover from the Chinese cultural revolution', Documentation Center of Cambodia, July 2017.

Kane, Solomon, *Dictionnaire des Khmers rouges*, 2nd edition, Les Indes savantes, 2011.

Karnow, Stanley, *Vietnam: A History*. Penguin Books, 1997.

Khieu Samphân, *Cambodia's Recent History and the Reasons Behind the Decisions I Made*, trans. Reahoo Translation Puy Kea, 2004.

Kiernan, Ben, *The Pol Pot Regime: Race, Power, and Genocide under the Khmer Rouge, 1975–79*, Yale University Press, 1996.

————, *How Pol Pot Came to Power*, Yale University Press, 2004.

Leclère, Adhémard, *Les Proto-Khmers au Cambodge*, écrits de la fin XIXe-début XXe, reproduits par Michel Tranet, Phnom Penh, Atelier d'Impression Khmère, 2002.

Locard, Henri, 'Ratanakiri ou La Montagne au Joyaux', *Kambuja*, Phnom Penh, 1966.

————, 'Hunting KR roots among hill tribes', *Phnom Penh Post*, 20 May 1994.

————, 'Le goulag khmer rouge', *La Question du Totalitarisme; Revue Communisme*, No. 47–48, Paris, 1996, 127–61.

————, 'Réflexions sur le Livre noir du communisme : le cas du Kampuchéa démocratique' *Le Livre noir du communisme en débat, Revue Communisme*, No. 59–60, Paris, 2 000, 45–60.

————, *Le petit livre rouge de Pol Pot*, L'Harmattan, Paris 1996. Revised and enlarged into *Pol Pot's Little Red Book: The Sayings of Angkar*, foreword by David Chandler, Silkworm Books, 2004.

————, with Mœung Sonn, *Prisonner de l'Angkar*, Fayard, Paris, 1993. English edition, *Prisoner of the Khmer Rouge*, Funan, 2007.

————, *Pourquoi les Khmers rouges*, Vendémaire, Paris, 2013.

————, *Pourquoi les Khmers rouges*, 2nd edition, Vendémaire, Paris, 2016.

Long Dany, 'Interview with Rochœm Tun, alias Phi Phuon and Chiem', DC-Cam, 19 December 2010. d. dccam. org/ Archives/ Interviews/ Sample Interviews/ Former_Kh_Rouge/ Phi_Phuon.pdf

Luciolli, Esmeralda. *Le mur de Bambou ou le Cambodge après Pol Pot*, Régine Desforges, Paris 1988.

Martin, Marie-Alexandrine, 'L'industrie dans le Kampuchéa démocratique', Études rurales, Paris 1983.

————, *Cambodia: A Shattered Society*, Berkeley, University of California Press, 1994.

————, *Le Mal cambodgien*, Hachette, 1989.

Matras-Troubetzkoy, Jacqueline, *Un Village en Forêt. L'essartage chez les Brou du Cambodge*. SELAF, 1983.

Muciolli, Esmeralda, *Le mur de bambou: le Cambodge après Pol Pot*, Régine Deforges, Paris, 1988.

Nhiek Tioulong, *Chroniques khmères: Cambodge 1863–1869*, Les Indes savantes, Paris forthcoming 2023.

Nuon Chea 'Statement of the Communist Party of Kampuchea to the Communist Workers' Party of Denmark, July 1978, by Nuon Chea, Deputy Secretary, CPK', *The Journal of Communist Studies* vol. 3, no. 1 (March 1987), 19–36.

Ong Thong Hœung, *J'ai cru aux Khmers rouges*, Buchet/Chastel, 2003.

Osborne, Milton, 'Aggression and annexation: Kampuchea's condemnation of Vietnam', Working Paper No. 15, The Research School of Pacific Studies, The Australian National University, Canberra, 'A Summary of the Pol Pot Government's Livre Noir (Black Book) with Commentary and Annotations', 1 August 1979.

———, *Sihanouk: Prince of Light, Prince of Darkness*, Silkworm Books, 1994

———, *Before Kampuchea*, Orchid Press, 2004.

Ovesen, Jan and Ing-Britt Trankell, 'Foreigners and honorary Khmers: ethnic minorities in Cambodia', pp. 241–69 in C. Duncan (ed.), *Civilizing the Margins: Southeast Asian Government Policies for the Development of Minorities*, Cornell University Press, 2004.

Padwe, Jonathan, 'Cambodia's Highlanders: Land, Livelihoods, and Politics on Indigeneity', in Brickell and Springer (eds), *The Handbook of Contemporary Cambodia*, Routledge, 2016.

Phnom Penh Post, 'Vietnamese-owned rubber plantations are looking to hire no less than 105,000 workers and tappers in particular', 20 March 2020.

Picq, Laurence, *Au-delà du Ciel: cinq ans chez les Khmers rouges*, Barraud, 1984. English edition: *Beyond the Horizon*, St Martins, 1989.

———, *Le Piège khmer rouge*, préface d'Arnaud Vaulerin, Buchet/Chastel, 2013.

Ponchaud François, *L'Impertinent au Cambodge*, Magellan & Cie, 2013

———, *Cambodia: Year Zero*, Henry Holt & Co, 1978.

Rathie, Martin, 'Lao links and the Khmer Revolution', *New Mandala*, 6 November 2007.

———, 'The Lao Long of Cambodia: Ethnic Lao in the Cambodian Revolutions', pp. 190–229 in Desley Goldston (ed.), *Engaging Asia: Essays on Laos and Beyond in Honour of Martin Stuart-Fox*, NIAS Press, 2018.

Sak Sutsakhan, *The Khmer Republic at War and the Final Collapse*, U.S. Army Center of Military History USA, 1978.

Scott, James C., *The Art of Not Being Governed: An Anarchist History of Southeast Asia*, Singapore National University Press, 2009.

Shawcross, William, *Sideshow: Kissinger, Nixon and the Destruction of Cambodia*, The Hogarth Press, 1991.

Short, Philip, *Pol Pot, The History of a Nightmare*, John Murray, 2004.

Sihanouk, Norodom, *Prisonnier des Khmers Rouges*. Hachette, 1986.

Norodom Monineath Sihanouk, *Witness to History: The Journal of Cambodia's Queen Mother*, Documentation Center of Cambodia, 2021.

Sliwinski, Marek, *Le Génocide Khmer rouge: une analyse démographique*, L'Harmattan, 1995.

Slocomb, Margaret, *Colons and Coolies: The Development of Rubber Plantations*, White Lotus, 2007.

Summers, Laura, 'The CPK: Secret Vanguard of Pol Pot's Revolution: A Comment on Nuon Chea's Statement', *Journal of Communist Studies*, vol. 3, no. 1 (March 1987), 5–36.

Suong Sikœun, *Itinéraire d'un intellectuel khmer rouge*, préface by Henri Locard, CERF politique, 2013.

Thet Sambath with Chon, Gina, *Behind the Killing Fields: A Khmer Rouge Leader and One of His Victims*, University of Pennsylvania Press, 2010.

Uk, Krisna, *Salvage: Cultural Resilience among the Jorai of Northeast Cambodia*. Cornell University Press, 2016.

Wang Chenyi, 'The Chinese Communist Party's relationship with the Khmer Rouge in the 1970s: an Ideological Victory and a Strategic Failure', Wilson Center, CWIHP working paper #88,13 December 2018.

White, J., 'Of spirits and services: Health and healing amongst the hill tribes of Ratanakiri Province', Phnom Penh: Health Unlimited, 1995.

Work, Courtney, 'Ecocide in the shadow of genocide and transitional justice', Lecture at The Center for Khmer Studies, National Chengchi University, Taipei, 12 March 2021.

Y Phandara, 'Retour à Phnom Penh : le Cambodge du génocide à la colonisation', Présentation Jean Lacouture, a. m. métaillé, Paris, 1982.

List of interviewees

An anonymous Brao, the head of Ka Tieng village in La Ban Muey commune, Lumphat District, interviewed in April 1994.

Bun Chan, born in 1937, Brao, interviewed in January 1994.

Bun My, born in 1920, Brao, interviewed in January 1994. Not the famous Bun Mi of the FUNSK

Chheang Ngoy, born in 1934, Brao, interviewed January 1994.

Choal Paet, born in 1934, Jaraï, interviewed in April 1994.

Heng Bunthan, born in 1954, Lao from Vœunsay, interviewed January 1994.

Hu Ly, born in 1942, Khmer, interviewed in April 1994.

Kim Sambath, United Nations High Commission for Refugees in Phnom Penh, interviewed 4 February 2020.

Kusol Paet, Jaraï, born in 1934, Jaraï, interviewed in April 1994.

Lay Bun San, Khmer, provincial policeman, interviewed in Banlung in January 1994.

Mum Kham Sœun, born in 1942, Krœung, interviewed in January 1994.

Muoy Chhœum, born in 1930, Brao, interviewed in January 1994.

Muong Poy, born in 1945, Brao, interviewed in January 1994.

Nhem Vannayouth, born in 1964, Khmer, interviewed in December 2019.

Nap Bun Heng, born in 1954, Khmer, head of the provincial Cabinet, interviewed in January 1994.

Nhiang BunThon, born in 1947, Khmer, interviewed at the provincial office in January 1994.

Phi Phuon, born in 1947, Jaraï, interviewed between 2001 and 2015.

Phor Bupon Nuong, a Jaraï, born in 1945, interviewed in January 1994.

Phoung Pheav, born in 1960, Krœung, interviewed in January 1994.

Puy Yung, born in 1942, Jaraï, interviewed in April 1994.

Rochoem Tveng, born in 1945, Jaraï, interviewed in 2016–2022.

Sieu Ang, born in 1950, Jaraï, interviewed in April 1994.

Sol Yut, born in 1942, Jaraï, interviewed in April 1994.

Tinh Thon, born in 1952, Khmer, interviewed in January 1994.

Yaê, born in 1939, Jaraï, interviewed in April 1994.

In all, I interviewed some 50 Khmer Lœu during my Ratanakiri investigations in 1994. I selected the most articulate and informative with the clearest memories.

Index

following Vietnamese invasion
161, 165, 172, 175, 177; ~ and
disintegration of DK 179, 182–
186; ~ flees to Thailand *xv*, 185,
186; ~ rallies to RGC *xv*, 188
hidden role 5, 78, 98, 307; ~ and
identity 20, 307; ~ strategy of
secrecy 78, 306. *See also* secrecy
joins ICP 16, 300; ~ brief training in
Hanoi 86, 235, 282, 301; ~ rises in
Party 301. *See also* Khmer Hanoi;
KPRP; Lê Duân; WPK
in KR core leadership 20, 77, 98,
102; ~ Pol Pot's equal partner 77,
300–301. *See also* Angkar: *Lœu*;
KR: leadership
leads Party outside of NE 77; ~ and
starts rebellion in Battambang *xii*,
77, 283, 301
meetings, seminars and training 74,
102, 106, 111, 115, 119–121, 128,
172, 208, 293
as Number Two 40, 77–78, 301; ~
engineers Saloth Sâr to be Number
One *xi*, 78. *See also* Brother No. 2
paranoia 79, 155, 213, 304–306; ~ and
use of Ta Mok to purge traitors 79.
See also enemies; purges; Ta Mok
personality 77–78, 80, 301; ~ and
secretiveness 78, 306
personally involved in killings 79, 208,
227, 270, 305
Phi Phuon meets 77–78; ~ bodyguard
for 78–80, 107–108, 110; ~
assessment of 77–78, 227
in struggle against Republic 78–80,
101, 107–108, 115
trial at ECCC *xv*, 40, 188, 205, 213,
225; ~ sentenced *xv*, 77, 205, 269;
~ and death in prison 77, 79, 307
urges evacuation of Phnom Penh
115–116, 210, 211, 226; ~ and

directs 118, 207. *See also* evacuation of cities
and Vietnamese 77–78; ~ hostility to
78; ~ negotiations with 110
wife 78, 108, 126, 158; ~ and children
78

obedience. *See* Angkar: loyalty
Oddar Meanchey province 105, 171, 177,
325. *See also* Northern region
Office 7 250, 282. *See also* Hou Yuon;
Ney Sarann; Ta Lav
Office 21 249, 250, 254. *See also* Hu Nim;
Khieu Samphân
Office 24 78, 79, 80, 99. *See also* Hu Nim;
Khieu Samphân; Poc Deuskomar;
Tiv Ol
Office 100 *xii*, 19, 67–68, 70, 71, 72, 86,
91, 94, 95, 120, 197. *See also* Khieu
Ponnary; Pol Pot
Office 102 *xii*, 67, 70, 80, 85, 94, 95. *See
also* Ieng Sary; Ieng Thirith
Office 870 105, 119, 125, 130, 135, 171,
182, 197, 208, 217, 220
on Chinit River 77, 84, 98, 101
decides fate of suspects 217, 227. *See
also* confessions; execution
as leadership HQ 70, 77. *See also*
Communist Party of Kampuchea;
KR: leadership
Phi Phuon and 77, 80, 101, 124, 135,
171, 197, 208, 217, 220
in Phnom Penh 70, 118, 122, 124
see also Dœun; Koy Thuon; Pâng
Office K–5 91, 93, 95, 108, 283, 285. *See
also* Nikân; Pâng
oil refinery. *See* Kompong Som
O'Kanseng Security Centre 260,
270–272. See also Banlung: prison;
security centres